TIMELINE

OF THE

WesternChurch

Books in the Zondervan Charts Series

Charts of Christian Theology and Doctrine
Charts of Cults, Sects, and Religious Movements
Chronological and Background Charts of the Old Testament
Chronological and Background Charts of the New Testament
Chronological and Background Charts of Church History
Chronological and Thematic Charts of Philosophies and Philosophers
Taxonomic Charts of Theology and Biblical Studies
Timeline Charts of the Western Church

TIMELINE

Charts

OF THE

WesternChurch

Susan Lynn Peterson

ZondervanPublishingHouse

. *Grand Rapids, Michigan*

A Division of HarperCollinsPublishers

Timeline Charts of the Western Church
Copyright © 1999 by Susan Lynn Peterson

Requests for information should be addressed to:

🏭 ZondervanPublishingHouse
Grand Rapids, Michigan 49530

Library of Congress Cataloging-in-Publication Data

Peterson, Susan Lynn, 1957-
    Timeline charts of the Western Church / Susan Lynn Peterson.
       p. cm. — (ZondervanCharts)
    Includes bibliographical references and index.
    ISBN 0-310-22353-9 (sc)
    1. Church history Chronology.   I. Title. II. Series.
  BR149.P48 1999
  270'.02'02—dc21
                                        99-15626
                                             CIP

Interior design by Sherri L. Hoffman

Printed in the United States of America

99 00 01 02 03 04 05 06 /❖ ML/ 10 9 8 7 6 5 4 3 2 1

To my parents, Donald and Shirley Johnson

Proverbs 22:6

Contents

Preface

Reading church history is a little like reading somebody else's mail. The stories can be dramatic, thought-provoking, and heartwarming. But the people are often strangers, the plot laced with oblique references and inside jokes. Add to that the ancient Greek names and Latin book titles that many church history writers bandy about as easily as one would speak of one's neighbors over coffee. Reading church history can be confusing and frustrating.

It is my deep conviction, however, that, frustrating or not, church history is a valuable source of nurture in the life of a Christian. It is our roots, our legacy from our brothers and sisters who have lived the Christian life before us. It chronicles their mistakes so that we might learn from them. It chronicles their successes so that we might build on them. It chronicles their faith so that we may be inspired on our own journeys.

Timelines of the Western Church was written for those who wish to delve into the riches of church history but find the details daunting. It is a reference book that allows readers to place the people, events, texts, and ideas of church history into their ecclesiastical and broader historical context. It helps readers get a handle on the details. And it lifts them up out of those details so they can get an overview of the arc of history, of where the church has been, and perhaps even where it might be going.

Susan Lynn Peterson
Tucson, Arizona

9

Acknowledgments

The author's grateful thanks to—

Jon Hart Olson, former dean of the Episcopal Theological School at Claremont—Bloy House, and to the Bloy House students and staff, who gave me the opportunity to road-test the early drafts of the timeline. Joe Erickson, who provided invaluable support in the infancy of the project.

The writers of the CompuServe Writer's Forum, especially the folks in the Research and Craft section. Their moral support and their answers to all sorts of questions—historical, stylistic, business—made the process of writing go much more smoothly. My literary agent, Donald C. Brandenburgh. The folks at KoSho San, especially Kandie Vactor, who helped me keep my coherence, no small thing especially during the editing stage of the process.

Several people who have provided insights into specialized fields. Dr. Lenore Langsdorf, who helped me build a solid foundation for the philosophical areas of the timeline. Dr. Roger Beck for his research and insights into church music. And especially my husband, Dr. Gary Peterson, who has been my closest friend and official-and-unofficial science adviser for twenty years. Without his encouragement and support this project would never have seen completion.

Introduction

T*imeline Charts of the Western Church* has three parts. The first is a detailed, year-by-year summary of the people, events, trends, questions, and texts of Christianity. The second is a series of linear and nonlinear charts that cover specific aspects of church history. The third is a comprehensive index.

The first section is the main timeline. It covers the entire span of church history from 4 B.C.E. to the present and covers events from Protestant denominations as well as the Roman Catholic Church. The format for this section is modeled after Bernard Grun's *Timetables of History,* a best-selling reference work that chronicles the people and events of history from 4500 B.C. to the present.

This first section provides four kinds of information:

Column A— **Theology, doctrine, and beliefs:** What questions and beliefs shaped church life?

Column B— **People and events:** Who were the leaders and organizations who helped mold the life of the church? What did they do, and when did they do it?

Column C— **History of the wider culture:** What was going on in science, politics, the arts, philosophy, technology, world exploration, and the day-to-day lives of people at the time?

Column D— **Texts:** What books, treatises, songs, and letters helped shape the life of the church? Who wrote them? What did they contain? Why are they important?

The second section, the appendices, is a series of one-to-two-page overviews of church history. Each overview is small enough that readers can prop it open in front of them while studying other church history texts. Each gives readers a few benchmark dates to lift them up out of the "trees" and enable them to see the "forest" of church history as a whole.

The third section is a detailed index. Rather than citing page numbers, the index refers the reader to the appropriate date. The letters after each date—for example, the *d* in "1562-d"—refer to the column in which the information is found in the main timeline:

a—theology, doctrine, and beliefs
b—people and events
c—events in the larger society
d—texts

The letters *x, y,* and *z* refer to the appendix charts:

x—overview charts
y—genealogy charts
z—denominational charts

The numbers following the *x, y,* and *z* refer to the number of the chart in the appendix.

The index is designed to be almost as detailed as the timeline itself, detailed enough that in many cases it can be used as a stand-alone reference work. Readers should note, however, that dates in the index are sometimes approximate. If readers check an index date in the main timeline, they may find that it is the beginning or ending date of a period of time, or that it is an approximation (should the actual date that event occurred be unknown).

Timelines of the Western Church

Date	A. Theology, Doctrine, and Beliefs	B. People/Events	C. Wider Culture	D. Texts
−4			Herod the Great, king of Judea and vassal of Rome, dies. His kingdom is divided between his sons. One of them, Herod Antipas, becomes tetrarch of Galilee and Perea (−39). Herod Antipas is the "Herod" most commonly referred to in the New Testament.	
−2		Jesus is born. (possibly as early as 5 B.C.E. or as late as 6 C.E.)		
6			Herod Archelaus, son of Herod the Great, is deposed as ruler of Judea and Samaria. He is replaced by procurators and direct Roman rule. A census is conducted under Syrian legate, P. Sulpicius Quirinius. (cf. Luke 2)	
14			Caesar Augustus dies. Tiberius becomes emperor. (reigns−37)	
26			Pontius Pilate becomes governor of Judea. He is known as a corrupt, cruel, anti-Semitic ruler. (−36)	
27		Jesus is baptized. (the fifteenth year of the reign of Tiberius, possibly as late as 29)		
28		Herod Antipas beheads John the Baptist at the request of his wife Herodias and her daughter Salome. (ca.)		
30		Jesus is crucified. (ca.) The church in Jerusalem is founded.		
34		Saint Stephen is martyred. He was one of the first deacons. His martyrdom is recounted in the Acts of the Apostles. (possibly as late as 36) Paul is directed by the chief priest to suppress Christianity in Damascus. On the Damascus road he encounters a blinding light and the voice of Jesus asking, "Why do you persecute me?" (possibly as late as 37)		
35	Apostolic age (within the lifetime of the apostles) (−65) The problem of the Crucifixion. How could the Messiah have undergone the scandal of being crucified?	Ignatius of Antioch is born.		

Date	A. Theology, Doctrine, and Beliefs	B. People/Events	C. Wider Culture	D. Texts
37			Caligula becomes emperor. He maintains an anti-Jewish policy. Palestine is in turmoil. (–41)	
40		The disciples are first called Christians in the city of Antioch. (possibly as late as 44)		
41			Claudius becomes Roman emperor. (–54) Herod Agrippa becomes the last king of Judea. (–44)	
43			Roman Emperor Claudius I invades Britain.	
44		The apostle James, the son of Zebedee, is beheaded by Herod Agrippa.		
45		The church in Antioch sends famine relief to Jerusalem. (–46)		
47		Paul's first missionary journey. Paul, Barnabas, and Mark leave on a mission to plant churches in Cyprus and Asia Minor. (possibly as early as 46)		
48	Judaism and Christianity. How can people who are not Jewish be Christians? Must non-Jewish Christians keep the Hebrew law? (Petrine vs. Pauline factions at the Council of Jerusalem)	The apostles and elders of the church meet in Jerusalem for the first Christian council. The central issue is whether Gentile Christians need to be circumcised.		
49		Peter and Paul have a falling out over whether Jewish and Gentile Christians should eat together and whether they should follow Jewish dietary laws while doing so.	Jews are expelled from Rome.	
50		Paul's second missionary journey. Paul and Silas leave on a mission to plant churches in Galatia, Troas, Philippi, Salonica, Athens, and Corinth. (–53)		*1 Enoch.* Jewish pseudopigrapha. Its passages on the "Son of Man" may have influenced New Testament writings. It survives only in Ethiopic. (ca.)
51				Paul writes 1 Thessalonians probably from Corinth during his first missionary journey. (50–)
52				Paul writes 1 Corinthians to the church he founded at Corinth. (–56) Paul writes 2 Thessalonians shortly after 1 Thessalonians. (Some scholars suggest 1 Thessalonians is written by a disciple of Paul between 70 and 90.)

Date	A. Theology, Doctrine, and Beliefs	B. People/Events	C. Wider Culture	D. Texts
53		Paul's third missionary journey. Paul begins a mission to Asia Minor, including two and a half years in Ephesus. (–57)		Paul writes the Epistle to the Philippians to the first church he founded. He writes it possibly while in prison in Ephesus, possibly while in prison in Rome. (53–54, or 60)
54			Nero becomes emperor. (–68)	Paul writes 2 Corinthians to the church at Corinth possibly while in Ephesus. (probably before 56) Paul writes the letter to Philemon. (possibly as early as 52 or as late as 62)
55				Paul writes the Epistle to the Galatians. (ca.)
57		Paul ministers in Greece. (–58)		
58		Paul is arrested in Jerusalem for starting a riot. He is imprisoned in Caesarea for two years.		Paul sends the Epistle to the Romans to believers in Rome, possibly from Corinth. (probably written between 55 and 58)
60		Paul appeals to the emperor (Nero), travels to Rome, is imprisoned but is allowed to minister to visitors. (–63) The apostle Andrew, brother of Simon Peter, dies. Traditionally, he is said to have been crucified in Achaia. (ca.)		The Epistle of James is written traditionally by James the brother of Jesus, though this theory of its authorship is not without problems. (almost certainly before 95, possibly as early as 50)
63			Renovation on the temple in Jerusalem, begun around 20 B.C.E., is complete.	
64		Neronian persecution. Christians in Rome are accused of perpetrating Rome's woes, including the great fire. The apostle Peter dies. Traditionally, he is said to have been crucified upside-down in Rome during the Neronian persecutions. (–68)	Rome burns.	
65				The Pastoral Epistles—the Epistles to Timothy and Titus—are written. (Their dating, not to mention their authorship, is a point of substantial controversy. Estimates range from 65 to 110)
66		Linus becomes bishop of Rome.	The first Jewish War begins. It ends with the fall of the temple and the capture of Masada. (–74)	
67		The apostle Paul is martyred. Tradition says he was beheaded in Rome. (possibly as early as 64)		

Date	A. Theology, Doctrine, and Beliefs	B. People/Events	C. Wider Culture	D. Texts
68			Claudius Nero, emperor of the Roman Empire, commits suicide. Qumran and the Essene community that lived there are destroyed.	
69		Ignatius becomes bishop of Antioch. (ca.) Polycarp is born. (ca.)	The Flavian dynasty rules the Roman Empire. (–96)	
70	Early Sub-apostolic period. The period immediately following the apostolic age, it is the time of the "apostolic fathers," the great leaders and writers of the early church. The apostolic fathers are concerned with placing Christianity within (or against) Judaism and with ordering and edifying the young Christian community. Key figures: Clement of Rome, Ignatius, Polycarp. Key texts: Shepherd of Hermas, Epistle of Barnabas, the Didache. (ca.–135)		The first fall of Jerusalem. Titus, head of the Roman Army and later Emperor, puts down the Jewish revolt, razes Jerusalem, and levels the temple.	The gospel of Mark, the earliest of the Synoptic Gospels, is completed. (possibly earlier, during the persecutions under Nero, probably just after the fall of the temple) Disciples of the apostle Paul write Colossians and Ephesians. (possibly as late as 90) Some scholars suggest Colossians is written by Paul around the time of Philemon.
73			The Jewish stronghold of Masada is captured by Roman forces. (–74)	
75	Christian ethics are derived as much from Jewish intertestamental norms as from the teaching of Jesus.	Christians begin to be expelled from Jewish synagogues.		The gospels of Matthew and Luke are finished, completing the Synoptic Gospels. (definitely after Mark, but before 100)
77			Flavius Josephus. *Jewish War.* An account of the first Jewish War and the events leading up to it, written by a Jewish historian. Its purpose it to gain the sympathy of the Roman public. (–78)	
79		Anacletus becomes bishop of Rome.	The eruption of Mount Vesuvius destroys Pompeii. Titus becomes Roman Emperor. (–81)	
80		Christianity is almost entirely an urban religion.	The Colosseum is completed in Rome.	The Letter to the Hebrews is completed. (probably between 80 and 90, though possibly before the destruction of the temple)
81			Domitian becomes Roman emperor. (–96) The imperial cult develops under Roman Emperor Domitian.	
85		Christian antipathy toward Rome grows.	The Roman conquest of Britain is complete. (43–)	Acts of the Apostles is completed. (no earlier than the mid 60s, definitely before 120)

Date	A. Theology, Doctrine, and Beliefs	B. People/Events	C. Wider Culture	D. Texts
90		Domitian persecution. According to *I Clement*, Christians in Rome and Asian Minor are persecuted for refusing to offer incense to the emperor. (–96)		The gospel of John is completed. Tradition says it is written by the apostle John, though some scholars propose John the Presbyter is the author. (probably after 80–90)
91		Clement I becomes bishop of Rome.		
92		Church leadership. Christian communities each begin to be governed by a single leader, though the nature and extent of that leader's authority are still matters of controversy.		
93				Flavius Josephus. *Antiquities of the Jews*. The history of Jews from Creation to the Jewish War, it is highly regarded by the Fathers. 20 vol. (–94)
95	Eucharist. From the Greek word $\varepsilon\dot{\upsilon}\chi\alpha\rho\iota\sigma\tau\acute{\iota}\alpha$ meaning thankfulness or gratitude, the term begins to be used very early in the history of the church to refer to the service of the Lord's Supper. (biblical roots: 1 Cor. 11:23–25 and the Synoptic Gospels)	Roman Emperor Domitian declares Christianity atheistic. Clement of Rome describes the work of deacons and bishops as being the same work as that of the apostles. By the end of the first century, the Eucharist is widely celebrated on Sunday. The practice becomes virtually universal in the second or third century.		Ignatius of Antioch, *Letters of Ignatius*. Seven authentic letters. They show the preeminence of bishops and the desire for martyrdom. (ca.–107) The Book of Revelation is written. (possibly earlier, around 90)
96		The earliest mention of the Sanctus is in the writings of Clement of Rome. It is recited in Greek, not Latin, and its use is not necessarily liturgical. Clement of Rome mentions psalm singing by Christians. He warns them not to sing psalms at pagan festivals. (ca.)	The "Five Good Emperors" (Nerva, Trajan, Hadrian, Antoninus Pius, and Marcus Aurelius) rule the Roman Empire. (–180)	Clement of Rome. *I Clement*. One of the oldest extra-canonical epistles. It is from Clement, bishop of Rome, to the church at Corinth. (–100) Sanctus. "Holy, Holy, Holy." An early hymn of praise. It takes its text from Isaiah 6:3.
97		Saint Timothy, disciple of the apostle Paul, is killed by a mob while opposing a pagan festival.		
98			Trajan becomes emperor.	
100		Saint Clement I, bishop of Rome, is martyred. Evaristus becomes bishop of Rome. Justin Martyr is born as "Justin of Caesarea." The apostle John dies in Ephesus. (ca.)	Jewish leaders at Yavneh firm up the Hebrew canon. (ca.)	*Gospel of Thomas*. Extra-canonical sayings of Jesus. Chester Beatty Papyrus (P46), the earliest extant biblical manuscript, is copied. It contains Pauline Epistles. (possibly as early as the late first century) I Peter is written. (ca.)

Date	A. Theology, Doctrine, and Beliefs	B. People/Events	C. Wider Culture	D. Texts
101	Early Christian rites are rooted in the Jewish liturgy. They include the use of "Amen" and "Alleluia," and the observance of daily prayer hours, especially evening prayer.			
105	Christianity, though emerging as a distinct religion, still lies within the socioeconomic norms of Hellenic Judaism. Catholic. From the Greek *καθολικός* meaning general or universal, in its earliest uses the term describes the church that transcends the local congregation. Only after the Reformation does it come to be applied more exclusively to the Roman Catholic Church.	The term "Catholic" is applied to the church for the first time. (in Ignatius' *Letter to the Smyrnaeans*) Ignatius of Antioch is the first known witness to the church's place in marriage. He suggests the man and woman seek the advice of the bishop before entering into marriage. (ca.)		Jude is written. (ca. possibly as early as 67)
107		Saint Ignatius of Antioch dies, possibly martyred. He was bishop and counselor to the young churches in Asia Minor.		
108				Polycarp. *Epistle to the Philippians.* Quotes various New Testament texts as authoritative. Warns against Judaizing and Docetism. (early second century)
109		Alexander I becomes bishop of Rome.		
110	Old Testament. If Christianity isn't merely a form of Judaism, what do Christians do with the Old Testament?			Earliest plausible date for the Old Roman Creed, a precursor to the Apostles Creed. The Johannine Epistles— 1, 2, & 3 John—are written. (90–) 2 Peter is written. (ca. possibly as early as 67)
115			Jews in Cyrenaica, Egypt, and Cyprus revolt. Many are killed, and the revolt is put down. (–117)	
116		Sixtus I becomes bishop of Rome.		
117			Hadrian becomes Roman emperor.	
120	Bishops of cities on the main imperial route are in communication with each other. The Ignatian model of church polity—a single bishop over each Christian community—gradually becomes normative throughout the second century. Fasting. In the early church fasting usually involves total	According to the *Didache*, baptism is administered both by triple immersion and by affusion. (ca.) The *Didache* mentions regular fasting on Wednesday and Friday. The *Shepherd of Hermas* states the belief that everyone has a guardian angel to guide and protect.		*Shepherd of Hermas.* A series of eschatological/prophetic tracts. (possibly as late as 155) *Didache.* An early manual of church life. (possibly as early as 65 or as late as 150)

Date	A. Theology, Doctrine, and Beliefs	B. People/Events	C. Wider Culture	D. Texts
120 con't.	abstinence from food for a period of time. In later usage, however, it also refers to abstinence from specific foods, most typically meat and dairy. The two most common reasons for fasting are penance for sin and a desire to weaken the physical appetites while strengthening the spirit through prayer.	According to tradition, Pope Sixtus I introduces the Sanctus into the Mass. (ca.)		
125		Telesphorus becomes bishop of Rome.		
126		Saint Sabina, Roman martyr, dies. (ca.)		
128		Pope Telesphorus mandates that the Gloria in Excelsis Deo be said during the Eucharist. (ca.–139)		Gloria in Excelsis Deo. The Latin name for the hymn "Glory be to God on High." The authorship is probably Greek. (before 128)
129			Roman Emperor Hadrian begins to make Jerusalem into a Roman city called Aelia Capitolina. The Roman deities, Jupiter, Juno, and Minerva are worshipped on the Temple Mount. The goddess Aphrodite's temple is erected on the future site of the Holy Sepulchre. (ca.)	
130		Justin Martyr converts. Irenaeus is born.		*Preaching of Peter*. An Alexandrian (?) Christian text that is among the first to engage Greek philosophy to the exclusion of Jewish thought. (ca.) The Pseudo-Clementine literature is written. (–150) *Epistle of Barnabas*. An influential anti-Jewish epistle written by an unknown author. (ca.)
132		After the Bar Kochba revolts, Judaism and Christianity become ever more distinct in terms of ritual and organization.	Second Jewish War (Bar Kochba Revolts). Jews protest, among other things, Emperor Hadrian's decision to make Jerusalem into the Roman city Aelia Capitolina. (–135)	
135	Period of the Ante-Nicene Fathers (patristic period). Christianity becomes a distinct religion during this period. The Ante-Nicene fathers write against Gnostics, Montanists, and Jews. They defend Christianity against accusations of the state and deal with the very real possibilities of persecution and martyrdom. Increasingly, they use Greek philosophical		The second fall of Jerusalem. Persecution of Jews is common throughout the Roman Empire. Jerusalem becomes a pagan city. Jews who enters its gates are executed. The *Diaspora* of the Jews begins.	

Date	A. Theology, Doctrine, and Beliefs	B. People/Events	C. Wider Culture	D. Texts
135 con't.	ideas and methods to build the theology of the new religion. Key figures: Justin Martyr, Tertullian, Theophilus, Irenaeus, Clement of Alexandria, Origen, Cyprian of Rome. (–325)			
138		Hyginus becomes bishop of Rome.		
140		Valentinus, Gnostic theologian, is at the peak of his influence. (–160)		*Gospel of Truth.* An early Gnostic treatise, possibly written by Valentinus. (ca.)
142		Pius I becomes bishop of Rome.		
144		Marcion is excommunicated.		
145	More and more pagans are converting to Christianity without coming through Judaism.			*Old Roman Creed.* Farthest back the Old Roman Creed can be traced textually.
147		Public opinion about Christians grows increasingly negative as Christians refuse to perform imperial cult sacrifice.		
150	Much of the apologetic literature in the early second century is aimed at distinguishing Christianity from Judaism. Increasingly, Christian writers confront the question, What do Christianity and Greek philosophy have to say to each other?	Clement of Alexandria is born. Valentinus, Gnostic theologian, is nearly elected bishop of Rome. (ca.)		*Marcion's canon.* A New Testament canon compiled to Gnostic criteria. It is the first known New Testament canon. Though the text is not extant, it has been reconstructed from the writings of Marcion's critics. (mid second century) *Egerton Papyrus.* One of the oldest papyri containing Christian writing, it contains fragments of a noncanonical account of Christ's life and ministry. (possibly as late as 200)
154	Quartodecimanism. One faction in the paschal controversies, it advocates celebrating Easter on Jewish Passover (14 Nisan), even if it falls on a day other than Sunday.	Polycarp in Rome asserts quatrodecimanism. The pope refuses to make it standard policy. (–155)		
155		Anicetus becomes bishop of Rome. Justin Martyr describes worship in Rome. It includes: Old and New Testament readings, a sermon, an offering of bread and wine, a prayer of the faithful, the kiss of peace, a eucharistic prayer, and communion. Saint Polycarp, bishop of Smyrna, is martyred. He was a proponent of the importance of apostolic tradition. (ca.)		Justin Martyr. *First Apology.* Justin tries to reconcile faith and reason, outlines doctrine, and responds to charges of immorality. (ca.)

Date	A. Theology, Doctrine, and Beliefs	B. People/Events	C. Wider Culture	D. Texts
160	Is Christianity an ascetic religion?	Tertullian, Quintus Septimius Florens, is born. (possibly as early as 155)		Justin Martyr. *Second Apology*. Replies to specific charges against Christians.
164	How can a Christian best stand in the face of persecution and martyrdom?		Plague sweeps through the Roman Empire. (–180)	
165		Shrines to the apostles Peter (the "Red Wall") and Paul are erected in Rome. (ca.) Saint Justin, "Justin Martyr," dies. Christian philosopher and apologist.		
166		Soter becomes bishop of Rome.	"Barbarians" (nomadic tribes who do not speak Latin) invade Italy.	
170	Christianity has the doctrine, literature, liturgy, and organization to be called a distinct religion.		The Egyptian scholar Ptolemy publishes maps of twenty-six countries. Though full of errors, they are the first to use a mathematically accurate form of conic projection. (150–)	
172	Montanist Movement. An apocalyptic, ascetic movement that begins in Phrygia. Key figure: Montanus.	The Montanist movement begins in Phrygia.		
174		Eleutherius becomes bishop of Rome.		
175	What are the philosophical implications of the Incarnation? Irenaeus proposes *recapitulation*: the incarnation of Christ was the summing up of all previous divine revelation.	The earliest references to incense being used in Christian services are from the last quarter of the fourth century.		Hegesippus's lists of apostolic succession. It is the oldest record of the names of the early bishops of Rome.
177		The Martyrs of Lyons die. Among them is Pothinus, bishop of Lyons. Christianity is introduced to Britain. (ca.)		
178		Irenaeus becomes bishop of Lyons.		
180	Gnosticism. A complex religious movement that prompted the young church to consider some crucial questions: How is Truth revealed? How is the Gospel transmitted: orally or in written form? Key figures: Valentinus, Basilides, Marcion (Gnostics); Irenaeus, Tertullian, Hippolytus (anti-Gnostic apologists).	The church in North Africa, according to the *Acts of the Scillitan Martyrs*, is already well-established.		Irenaeus's succession list of bishops of Rome.

Date	A. Theology, Doctrine, and Beliefs	B. People/Events	C. Wider Culture	D. Texts
185	The notions of apostolic succession and biblical authority are emphasized to meet the threat of Gnostic "hidden mysteries." Irenaeus is among the first of the church fathers to develop a doctrine of original sin. He maintains that sin first came into the world with Adam's disobedience.	Origen is born. (ca.)		Irenaeus. *Against Heresies*. A detailed attack on Gnosticism, especially that of Valentinus, it comes to be regarded as a classic formulation of orthodoxy. (ca.)
188	If God is good, how could he have created a world full of evil? (Marcion's question, addressed by Tertullian)	Church fathers (such as Clement in the *Protrepticus*) allow chant, lyra, and kithera in the liturgy, but warn against other instruments, as well as polyphony, chromatic music, and dance.		Clement of Alexandria. *Miscellaneous Studies. An Exhortation to the Greeks (Protrepticus). On Christian Life and Manners.* These three works contain the most thorough synthesis of Christian doctrine and Greek philosophy at the time.
189		Victor I becomes bishop of Rome. He is the first Latin-speaking pope.		
190	The few remaining pockets of Jewish Christianity are thought of as sects rather than the mainstream.	Lectors, readers, deacons and subdeacons, acolytes, exorcists, and doorkeepers are added as "lower orders" of clergy. (late second and early third centuries)		
192		Powerful bishops in Antioch, Alexandria, and Rome try to enforce uniformity of doctrine and practice.		
193			Severan Dynasty begins. (–235)	
194				*Muratorian Canon of Scripture*. The oldest extant list of New Testament writings. The list is somewhat different from the modern one. (late second century)
195	Paschal controversies. Disputes in the early church about the computation of the date of Easter, specifically about whether the Jewish calendar should be used in the computation process.	Paschal controversy flares up. Irenaeus intervenes. (ca.) Sporadic persecution throughout the empire is especially intense in Rome, Alexandria, Antioch, and Corinth. (–212) The threefold hierarchy of bishop, presbyter, and deacon is widespread by the end of the second century.		
197				Tertullian. *Apologeticum* (Apology). Appeals for state toleration of Christianity.
198		Zephyrinus becomes bishop of Rome.		

Date	A. Theology, Doctrine, and Beliefs	B. People/Events	C. Wider Culture	D. Texts
199	Descent into hell. In its most literal sense, it is the belief that Christ, after his death but before his resurrection, visited the souls of the pre-Christian dead to preach and offer salvation. In a less literal sense, it refers to Christ's triumph over evil, or his utter dereliction on the cross. Based on: Mt. 27:52, I Pet. 3:18–20.	One of the earliest evidences that the descent of Christ into hell has become a Christian doctrine is in the *Odes of Solomon*. Catacomb art begins. Catacombs are administered by the church before the third century. They consist of several underground chambers, usually laid out in a grid. Recesses in the walls, one above another, contain the bodies, grouped by family.		*Odes of Solomon.* Forty-two short, lyrical hymns. They are probably composed by a Jewish-Christian community in Syria or Alexandria. Though they show some Gnostic influences, they are early examples of mainstream Christian Eucharistic hymns. (probably collected near the end of the second century, though possibly as early as 100)
200	Creation *ex nihilo*. The doctrine that the universe was brought out of nothing by the will of God. It is almost universally accepted by the end of the second century.	The Montanist movement is officially condemned. (before 200) The term "priest" begins to be used of some Christian ministers. (ca.) Saint Irenaeus, bishop of Lyons, dies (is martyred?). He was the first great systematic theologian. (ca.) Earliest mention of Christianity in Britain. (Tertullian's *Tract Against the Jews*) Cyprian of Carthage is born. Clement of Alexandria reports that Egyptian theologians place the date of Christ's birth on 25 Pachon (May 20) in the twenty-eighth year of Augustus. Tertullian is among the first to mention various Daily Office hours. He notes that vigils, lauds, and vespers are said in Carthage; and that terce, sext, and none are recognized as private prayer hours. (ca.)	Rabbi Judah the Priest codifies the Jewish law in the Mishnah. (ca.) The earliest Mayan temples are built. (ca.)	The process of selection and rejection of canonical New Testament books is nearly complete. (ca.)
202		Clement of Alexandria flees Alexandria. Tertullian speaks of the making the sign of the cross at various times during the day. The sign is made with the finger or thumb on the forehead. (between 197 and 206)		
203		Origen takes Clement's place as head of the Alexandria school. Saint Perpetua and her companions are martyred at Carthage.		*The Diary of Perpetua.* The prison writings of a pregnant woman who insists on being executed as a Christian. It includes a second-person account of her martyrdom.

Date	A. Theology, Doctrine, and Beliefs	B. People/Events	C. Wider Culture	D. Texts
206	How does the possibility of martyrdom affect what and how one believes as a Christian?	Tertullian becomes a Montanist. (ca.) The first explicit mention of infant baptism is in Tertullian's *On Baptism*. He also distinguishes baptism from unction from the laying on of hands in the initiation rite (the first time all three are mentioned together). Baptism involves elaborate preparation involving confession of sin, renunciation of the Devil, fasting, vigil, and anointing.		
210		According to Tertullian, the festival celebrating the death and resurrection of Christ lasts an entire night and is closely associated with baptism. This festival is the precursor of the modern Easter vigil. (ca., before 225)	Attempts at land reform fail. Many farmers become tenants. (early third century)	
215	Infant Baptism. The practice of baptizing the children of Christian parents while they are still infants. Though never universally accepted, it is common, from the third century to modern times.	The custom of saying grace before meals is common by the time of Clement of Alexandria. (before) The earliest evidence of evening prayer is in the *Apostolic Tradition*. It includes a blessing of the light similar to the Jewish ritual. Clement of Alexandria is the first to refer to the fish as a Christian symbol. He recommends Christians have their official seals engraved with either a dove or a fish, symbols of the Holy Spirit and Jesus. (before) Saint Clement of Alexandria dies. Priest and academic. His work in the Alexandria catechetical school gave academic credibility to Christianity. (ca.)		A form of the *Apostles' Creed* similar to the modern creed is contained in *The Apostolic Tradition of Hippolytus*. Hippolytus. *The Apostolic Tradition*. A detailed description of rites and practices in the Roman church. It describes the rite of baptism including a preparatory fast and vigil, confession of sins, renunciation of the Devil, and washing with water. The rite is followed by laying on of hands or anointing with oil. *The Apostolic Tradition* contains the oldest known full text of a Eucharistic prayer. It also contains one of the earliest explicit references to infant baptism. (ca.)
217		Callistus becomes bishop of Rome.		
220	Ember Days. Days of abstinence and fasting, they appear to have been originally associated with harvest, vintage, and planting. Their origin is uncertain but may have had pagan associations.	First recorded observance of Ember Days.	The Goths, a nomadic Germanic tribe from Sweden, invade Asia Minor. The Chinese Han Dynasty falls to Attila the Hun. (206 B.C.E.–)	
222		Urban I becomes bishop of Rome.		

Date	A. Theology, Doctrine, and Beliefs	B. People/Events	C. Wider Culture	D. Texts
225	Monarchian Controversy. Is Christ another mode of God the Father? The first of the Christological controversies. Ransom theory of the atonement. The belief that humanity in sinning comes under the control of Satan. Christ's death buys us back for God. Key figures: Origen, many of the Latin fathers.	Tertullian describes the regular practice of praying privately for the dead. (before) Tertullian, Quintus Septimius Florens dies. (ca.) Deaconesses care for poor and sick women, instruct women, and accompany women on private interviews with male clergy. They also baptize women candidates. The earliest account of their duties dates from the first half of the third century. (ca.)	The codex or bound-leaf style of book becomes popular among Christians. (ca.)	Origen. *On First Principles.* His most systematic and speculative work. It is available only in fragments and bad Latin translation. (between 220 and 230) *Didascalia Apostolorum* (Teaching of the Apostles). An early treatise on church life and order, probably written originally in Syriac. (early third century)
230		Pope Urban I is martyred. Pontian becomes bishop of Rome.		Julius Africanus, Sextus. *Chronographiæ* (History of the World). A history of the world from the Creation to AD 221. He estimates that the Creation took place 5499 years before the birth of Christ. His estimates are subsequently adopted by many of the Eastern churches. (ca. probably written between 200 and 240)
231	Christian asceticism gains favor, in part as a response to potential martyrdom, in part because of Clement and Origen's persuasiveness, and in part because of the uncertainty of the times.	Origen goes to Caesarea to get away from Alexandrian church authorities. He starts a new school there.		
235	Territorial gods and local religions are abandoned as cities fall to the "barbarians." Many pagans become Christians.	Anterus becomes bishop of Rome. The church in Rome speaks mostly Greek, conducts church services in Greek, and writes most of its theology in Greek. (before the mid third century) Christian clergy are executed under Maximinus the Thracian. (–236)	The Roman empire fends off "barbarians," suffers frequent changes of emperor, begins economic collapse, falls into gross disrepair. (–270)	Origen. *Exhortation to Martyrdom.* Written in response to rumors of persecution. (–236)
236		Fabian becomes bishop of Rome. Hippolytus, doctor of the church and voice against Sabellianism, dies.		
238				Gregory Thaumaturgus. *Panegyric to Origen.* Gregory's autobiography, it also includes an account of Origen's teaching methods. (ca.)
240		The earliest known baptistry is in a house-church at Dura-Europos. In it a person can be immersed if they bend over. Prior to this time, baptism was probably carried out in natural water sources. (ca.)		Julius Africanus. *Chronicles.* An apologetic history of Christians and Jews.

Date	A. Theology, Doctrine, and Beliefs	B. People/Events	C. Wider Culture	D. Texts
240 con't.		Julius Africanus, Christian writer and author of *Sextus Chronographiæ*, dies.		
241			The first mention of the Franks is by Roman historians, who record a battle against them.	
243			Plotinus opens a school of philosophy in Rome.	
245		North Africa has ninety bishops and an elaborate disciplinary system. (ca.)		Origen. Hexapla. A parallel edition of various Old Testament Greek translations. (ca.)
248		Cyprian, bishop of Carthage, makes the distinction between baptism and the laying on of hands. The latter rite is probably a precursor of confirmation. (–258)	Goths attack Rome.	Origen. *Against Celsus.* An apologetic work against Celsus, a pagan philosopher who objected to Christianity's supernatural and exclusivist claims. It is issued in eight books. (ca.)
249			Roman Emperor Decius declares all citizens must sacrifice to Roman gods. Those who do not are censured. Some are martyred. (–251)	
250	Bishops are the loci of discipline, charity, and theological speculation. Especially in the west, they are paid exclusively out of tithes. Absolution is the sole prerogative of the clergy. Neoplatonism. Platonism in the third through sixth centuries is much like classical Platonism, but with religious interests. Central is a belief in the One, the ultimate source of all being, unknowable but attainable through contemplation leading to mystical experience. It was an influence in the life and writings of Augustine, and Dionysius the Pseudo-Areopagite. Key figure: Plotinus.	Dionysius of Paris (St. Denys) is sent by Pope Fabian to be a missionary to, and the first bishop of, Paris. (ca.) Pope Fabian makes it obligatory for Christians to receive the Eucharist three times a year—at Christmas, Easter, and Pentecost. (236–) Under Emperor Decius, bishops of Rome, Antioch, and Jerusalem are arrested. Bishops of Carthage and Alexandria go into hiding. Alexander, bishop of Jerusalem, dies in prison. Saint Fabian, bishop of Rome, is martyred. Both mobs and imperial officials begin invading catacombs. Until this time, Christians have been able to meet in catacomb chapels because burial places have been sacrosanct by law. When the catacombs begin to be violated, Christians destroy the old entrances and make new, secret ones. The first known hermit, Paul of Thebes, goes into seclusion and, according to legend, lives as a hermit for over a hundred years. He is known through his biography written by Jerome.	The beginnings of Neoplatonism. Key figure: Plotinus. (ca.) Diophantus, a Greek mathematician, publishes *the Arithmetica*, one of the earliest algebra books.	Gregory Thaumaturgus. *Ekthesis tēs Pisteēs* (Greek: Statement of Faith). Earliest known record of a Marian apparition. (mid-third century) Novatian. *On the Trinity.* A completely orthodox doctrine of the trinity by a man later condemned as a rigorist. Caesarean Creed. The catechetical/baptismal creed of the Caesarean episcopate. It later becomes the basis for the Nicene Creed at the council of Nicea. (ca.)

Date	A. Theology, Doctrine, and Beliefs	B. People/Events	C. Wider Culture	D. Texts
250 con't.		By the middle of the third century, infant baptism has become normative. Manichaeism begins. (ca.)		
251	Novatianist schism. A group in the Western church who refuse concessions to those who have compromised with paganism. Though doctrinally orthodox, Novatianists are excommunicated.	Cornelius becomes bishop of Rome. Antony of Egypt is born. Acolytes are first mentioned. They serve in Rome under the authority of deacons. Their primary duty is service at the altar. Subdeacons are first mentioned. Cyprian notes that the Lord's Prayer is commonly used as a part of the Eucharist. He speaks of it being "the public and common prayer." (ca.) The Novatianist schism begins.		
253		Cornelius, bishop of Rome, boasts 155 clergy and 1500 widows on the church payroll. (ca.) The church in Rome begins to shift from Greek to Latin under Pope Cornelius. (251–) Lucius I becomes bishop of Rome.		
254		Stephen I becomes bishop of Rome. Origen, Alexandrian writer, academic, and theologian, dies.		
255	Rebaptism controversy. Do people who were baptized in heretical sects need to be rebaptized when they embraced orthodoxy? (–257)			
256		Council of Carthage • Is attended by eighty-eight bishops. • Forbids women to baptize.		
257		Sixtus II becomes bishop of Rome. Pope Sixtus II mandates that the Eucharist be celebrated on an altar. (–259) Valerianic Persecution. Christians are no longer allowed to assemble for worship. Their property is confiscated. Cyprian dies. (–260)		

Date	A. Theology, Doctrine, and Beliefs	B. People/Events	C. Wider Culture	D. Texts
258		Edict of Valerian. Christian clergy are rounded up and punished. Christian civil servants are made slaves. Wealthy Christians' property is confiscated. Saint Lawrence is martyred. A deacon in Rome, he was known as the friend of the poor and sick. Saint Cyprian, bishop of Carthage, is martyred. He was known as a writer and a voice of moderation.		
259			Emperor Valerian is killed by Persians.	
260		Dionysius becomes bishop of Rome. The period between the Valerianic and Diocletian persecutions is a time of unprecedented growth and prosperity for the church. (–302)		
264	Paul of Samosata vs. the Council of Antioch. Paul maintains that before Creation the Trinity existed as Father, Wisdom, and Word. The Council of Antioch condemns him as a heretic.	The Council of Antioch • Condemns Paul of Samosata • Suppresses all non-biblical hymns, in part due to the popularity of Paul of Samosata's heretical hymns.		
268	Collegial authority. Also known as collegiality, it is the belief that the bishops of the church when acting together form a body whose nature and authority transcend that of the individuals.	Rome is regarded as the senior bishopric at the Council of Antioch.		*Letter of the Synod of Antioch.* Assumes the collegial authority of bishops over the church catholic.
269		Felix I becomes bishop of Rome.	The Goths are defeated.	
270	Asceticism is present in Christianity before the third and fourth centuries, but only in the rise of monasteries does it find an institutional framework.	Saint Gregory Thaumaturgus dies. An early bishop in Caesarea, he was known as *Thaumaturgus* (the Wonderworker) for his abilities as a channel of divine healing. Antony of Egypt establishes himself in the desert.	Plagues and epidemics spread throughout the Roman Empire. Plotinus, Neoplatonist philosopher and mystic, dies.	
274			Twenty-five foot walls are built around Rome.	
275		Eutychian becomes bishop of Rome. Christianity begins to find its way out of the cities and into rural areas. (ca.)		
280			Constantine is born. (ca.)	

Date	A. Theology, Doctrine, and Beliefs	B. People/Events	C. Wider Culture	D. Texts
283		Gaius becomes bishop of Rome. Clerical celibacy is esteemed, but marriage of clergy is common.		
284			Diocletian becomes Roman Emperor. (–305)	
285			The Roman Empire is divided into four jurisdictions to be ruled by two emperors and two caesars. East and West are ruled separately.	
293			Diocletian reforms. In order to promote stability, Diocletian centers all state power in the emperor as a semi-divine ruler. (–303)	
296		Athanasius is born. (ca.) Marcellinus becomes bishop of Rome.		
298		Christians in the Roman army are forced to resign. (–302)		
300	By the fourth century, private confession of sin to a bishop or presbyter replaces public confession.	Rome has more than forty churches inside the city limits.	Parchment is commonly preferred to papyrus for the making of books.	
303		The Diocletian Persecution. Also known as the Great Persecution, it is the most extensive repression of Christianity to date. Government officials burn churches and Scriptures. They arrest bishops and church leaders (and later laity) and force them to sacrifice to Roman gods. Arrests and executions, especially of civil servants, are widespread. (–305) Saint George, patron saint of England, dies. He was probably a soldier, probably suffered in the persecutions of Maximian or Diocletian. All other stories, including the account of his fight with a dragon, probably date from the Middle Ages, when he was revered especially by crusaders. (306?) The cathedral in Nicomedia is built in full view of the imperial palace.		
304		Saint Agnes is martyred at Rome. She is one of the most famous and widely recognized of the early saints. Saint Alban of Britain is martyred. He is traditionally		

Date	A. Theology, Doctrine, and Beliefs	B. People/Events	C. Wider Culture	D. Texts
304 con't.		considered to be the first British martyr. Saint Vincent of Saragossa is martyred.		
305		Saint Sebastian is martyred. During the Diocletian persecution, Sebastian, a Roman soldier, aided Christians marked for death. As a result, he was ordered to be executed by being shot with arrows then beaten to death. His courage facing the arrows becomes a favorite subject for Renaissance painters. (ca.)	Roman Emperor Diocletian abdicates.	
306	Christ's Nativity. It is the celebration, not only of the birth of Christ, but also of its significance and of the events surrounding it.	Christ's nativity begins to be celebrated on the winter solstice. (early fourth century) Marcellus becomes bishop of Rome. Religious toleration is extended to Rome and North Africa.	Constantine the Great, becomes Caesar in the Western Roman Empire. (–337) Augustus Maximian orders all citizens to sacrifice.	Peter, bishop of Alexandria. *Canons*. It addresses the question: How should those who capitulated during the persecutions be treated?
309		A Spanish council decrees severe discipline for apostasy and adultery. (306?)		
310		Eusebius becomes bishop of Rome.		
311		Miltiades becomes bishop of Rome. Peter, bishop of Alexandria, is martyred.		
312	Donatist Controversy. Donatists claim that the validity of the sacraments depends on the character of the minister. Orthodox Christianity maintains the validity of the sacraments rests solely on the merits of Christ, not on the worthiness of the minister. Center of the controversy: North Africa	The Donatist controversy arises when an "apostate" bishop, one who was believed to have given copies of the Bible to Diocletian's forces for destruction, consecrates another bishop in Carthage. (ca.)	Constantine the Great is victorious in battle at the Milvian bridge and becomes Augustus of the Western Empire. He attributes the victory to his inscribing *XP*, the first two letters of the Greek word for "Christ," on the shields of his troops.	
313		Christian emperors Constantine, Theodosius, and Valentinian III treat heresy as a crime against the state. (–424)	The Edict of Milan gives equal toleration for all religions.	
314	Church dedication. It is a ceremony in which a building is set aside specifically for the worship of God. It later becomes a complex process involving the blessing of the building, its parts, and its fixtures with prayers and holy water.	Council of Arles. Is called by Constantine. Churches from as far away as Britain send bishops. • Considers the Donatist controversy. Silvester I becomes bishop of Rome. Canon law, legislation enacted by an ecclesiastical organization, originates with		Lactantius. *On the Deaths of the Persecutors*. Gruesome details about what happens to those who persecute the church.

Date	A. Theology, Doctrine, and Beliefs	B. People/Events	C. Wider Culture	D. Texts
314 con't.		the regional Council of Ancyra. The dedication of the cathedral at Tyre is the earliest recorded instance of a church building being dedicated.		
315		Cyril of Jerusalem is born. Eusebius of Caesarea makes the distinction between worship of God and appropriate devotion given to angels. (probably between 315 and 340) Hilary of Poitiers is born. (ca.)		
316		The deaths of the "Forty Martyrs," a group of Christian soldiers in Lesser Armenia, is a part of the persecution of Eastern Christians by Roman emperor Licinius. (after 316)		
320	Athanasius vs. Arius. One of the Christological controversies. Is Christ the divine Logos, of the same nature (consubstantial, Gk. ὁμοούσιον) as the Father (Athanasius)? Or is he the first being of a created order (Arius)? (ca. –336, later in Spain)	Constantine builds "old" St. Peter's Basilica on Vatican Hill, the traditional site of Peter's crucifixion. Pachomius founds the first cenobitic (communal) monastery. (ca.)		
321		Constantine adopts a policy of tolerance toward Donatists after trying unsuccessfully to suppress them by force. Sunday becomes the official day of rest for the Roman Empire. Constantine allows unlimited bequests to churches. Churches become increasingly wealthy. Church buildings sprout across the landscape. Ordination starts to be good business.		
322		A picture on a tomb in Rome depicts Christ as Helios. (ca.)		
323		According to Eusebius of Caesarea, the period of preparation before Easter consists of either a two-or-three-day fast or a forty-hour fast. He traces the custom back at least as far as Irenaeus.		Eusebius of Caesarea. *Ecclesiastical History* (final edition). One main source for church history from the age of the apostles. (possibly as late as 325)
324			Constantine reunites the Roman Empire and becomes Roman Emperor.	

Date	A. Theology, Doctrine, and Beliefs	B. People/Events	C. Wider Culture	D. Texts
325	Arius vs. Council of Nicea. How can we say both that there is only one God, and that the Father and Son are both equally God? Arius: Jesus was a created being given the special status "Son of God" by the Father. The council: the Son and Father are coequal and coeternal. One facet of the Christological controversy. Lent. It is a period of solemn spiritual preparation before Easter. Traditionally it has included fasting, penance, and prayer. Consubstantiality. From the Latin word *consubstantialis*, the word is used to describe the relationship between the persons of the Trinity: the three Persons are consubstantial, i.e. of the same being or substance. The Greek (Eastern) counterpart to the term is *homoousion*, which became a central tenet of the Orthodox faith.	Helena, commissioned by Constantine, founds the Church of the Nativity in Bethlehem. (ca.) First Ecumenical Council: The First Council of Nicea. • Declares the consubstantiality of the Father and the Son, i.e. that Christ is one being (*homoousion*) with the Father. • Condemns Arius. • Drafts the Nicene Creed. • Decrees that Easter be celebrated on the first Sunday after the full moon following the vernal equinox. If Easter and Passover falls on the same day, Easter is moved to the following Sunday. Lent becomes a forty-day fast in some parts of Christendom. (some time prior to the Council of Nicea) The custom of giving the Eucharist to the dying is well established. It is considered a *viaticum*, sustenance for a long journey, in much the same way as pagans provided a last meal for the dead.		Codex Vaticanus is copied. The earliest of the great uncials, it contains a Greek text of both the Old and New Testament. It is, however, missing some of the Epistles and Revelation. (ca.)
326	Post-Nicene Fathers. In the period after the Council of Nicea, theologians have three things their predecessors lacked: peace (even partnership) with the government, a widely accepted canon of Scripture, and a distillation of the faith (the Nicene Creed). For the most part, they are not church leaders fighting for the life of their community, but rather deep and precise thinkers hammering out the fine points of Christian doctrine. Key figures: Jerome, Ambrose, Augustine, Athanasius, Basil of Caesarea, Chrysostom. (ca. –460)	Constantine and his mother Helena build the Church of the Holy Sepulchre in Jerusalem. A Roman temple to Aphrodite and a grove to Jupiter and Venus have to be removed to clear the site. It is one of the first building projects in the "era of Christian basilicas." (–335)		
327		The second session of the Council of Nicea is held.		
328		Athanasius becomes bishop of Alexandria. Saint Helena, the mother of Constantine the Great, dies. She founded the Church of the Nativity and the Church of the Holy Sepulchre in Bethlehem and Jerusalem. According to legend, she discovered the True Cross in Palestine.		

Date	A. Theology, Doctrine, and Beliefs	B. People/Events	C. Wider Culture	D. Texts
329		Gregory Nazianzus is born. (ca.) Christian art seldom contains angels before the time of Constantine. At that time, a new angel, one with wings reminiscent of the classic Victory, appears. (fourth century)		
330		Basil the Great is born. (ca.) Gregory of Nyssa is born. (ca.) Martin of Tours is born. (ca.)	Constantine moves the capital of the empire to Byzantium, "the New Rome," which he renames "Constantinople." Pagan rites play no part in the dedication ceremony.	
332		Saint Gregory the Illuminator, Apostle of Armenia, dies.		
333		The Bordeaux Pilgrim begins his journey. The earliest known pilgrim from western Europe to Jerusalem, he also visits Constantinople and ends his journey in Milan.		
335		Council of Tyre. • Athanasius is condemned in part because of his opposition to Arianism, in part because of his over-willingness to use physical violence against the Arians. He is exiled to France. Constantine makes bishops a part of the political structure of the empire by granting them judicial power. (mid fourth century) The Dalmatic, a knee-length tunic, is introduced as the distinctive vestment of deacons during the tenure of Pope Silvester. (314–)	The Roman empire is divided between Constantine's sons.	
336		Arius, originator of the heresy of Arianism, dies. Mark becomes bishop of Rome.		
337		Julius I becomes bishop of Rome.	Constantine I abolishes crucifixion out of respect for the death of Jesus. Constantine the Great, Roman Emperor, is baptized, dies.	
338		New churches, cathedrals, and basilicas spring up across the landscape after Constantine's death.		Eusebius of Caesarea. *Life of Constantine*. It causes some to consider Constantine a saint.
339		Ambrose of Milan is born. The Council of Rome vindicates Athanasius.		

Date	A. Theology, Doctrine, and Beliefs	B. People/Events	C. Wider Culture	D. Texts
340	The West begins to develop a communal, practical monasticism. The East's remains solitary and ascetic. Monasticism grows rapidly throughout the Mediterranean basin. (ca. through the fifth century)	Eusebius of Caesarea dies. (ca.) Ephrem Syrus of Edessa takes over melodies from Bardaisan's docetic hymns, writes orthodox lyrics, and employs them in the fight against heresy. (ca.) Athanasius, during his second exile, visits Rome accompanied by St. Anthony's disciples, the monks Ammon and Isidore. In doing so he introduces monasticism into the West.		
341		Council of Antioch. The first of a series of smaller councils in the fourth century. Their main goal is to tinker with or abandon Nicene theology.		
342		Council of Sardica. Jerome is born. (possibly as early as 330) Saint Nicholas, bishop of Myra and patron saint of children, dies. As "Santa Claus" (an American corruption of the Dutch form of his name), he becomes a mythic figure who brings presents, either on his feast day, December 6, or on Christmas. He is also the patron saint of sailors.		
346		Athanasius is restored as bishop in Alexandria. Pachomius, founder of the first cenobitic monastery, dies. (possibly as late as 361)		
347		The Donatists associate themselves with bands of roving marauders, who use violence to enforce Donatist principles. The state steps in and begins to suppress and exile them. (–361) John Chrysostom is born. (ca.)		
348		Catholic ascendancy in North Africa. Its rural areas become overwhelmingly Christian. (–361) Council of Carthage.		
350	Feast of the Purification of the Blessed Virgin Mary. Also called the Feast of the Presentation of Christ in the Temple and Candlemas, it commemorates the presentation of	Cyril of Jerusalem describes how the *lavabo*, the priest's washing his fingers at the Eucharist, is a symbol of purity of the soul. (ca.) Cyril of Jerusalem reports that the wood of the True Cross	Damaged papyrus volumes in the Pamphilus library in Caesarea are replaced by vellum copies.	Codex Sinaiticus is copied. It is one of the earliest complete manuscripts of the New Testament. (ca.)

Date	A. Theology, Doctrine, and Beliefs	B. People/Events	C. Wider Culture	D. Texts
350 con't.	Jesus in the temple as recorded in Luke 2:21–39.	has been divided up and distributed throughout the world.		
		The Feast of the Purification of the Blessed Virgin Mary begins to be celebrated in Jerusalem.		
		Christianity reaches Geneva. A thriving community grows into a diocese with cathedral in less than fifty years. (ca.)		
		The Sanctus is a part of the Eucharistic liturgy in many Eastern churches and some Western.		
352		Liberius becomes bishop of Rome.		
353		Council of Arles. One of several councils to further the cause of Arianism.		
354		Augustine of Hippo is born. Pelagius is born in Britain.	Germanic people invade Gaul. (–356)	
355		Council of Milan.	In Rome, Latin is used almost exclusively. (ca.)	
356		Saint Antony of Egypt dies. He was the first to organize a community of hermits under a monastic rule. Arians drive Athanasius from his see (Alexandria).		
357	Hagiography. The purpose of these accounts of the lives of the saints is typically inspiration rather than accurate historical rendering. Influenced by not only the Gospels but also by apocryphal writings and by the secular literature of the day, they recount the faith and the sometimes miraculous deeds of saints and martyrs.			Athanasius. *Life of Antony*. Very early hagiography, it is one of the oldest sources for the life of Antony of Egypt.
358		Church music undergoes radical changes. Beginning in monasteries in Antioch, responsorial (alternation between a cantor and the congregation) and antiphonal (alternation between two groups) psalmody are introduced. Ambrose of Milan introduces simpler and more poetic hymns, allowing hymnody to be much more widely used. (mid to late fourth century)		Origen. *Philocalia*. An anthology of the works of Origen compiled by Basil the Great and Gregory Nazianzus. Basil the Great. Monastic Rule ("Rule of St. Basil"). The basis for subsequent Eastern monasticism. (–364)

Date	A. Theology, Doctrine, and Beliefs	B. People/Events	C. Wider Culture	D. Texts
359		Arian influence reaches its peak. "The world groaned and marveled to find itself Arian." —Jerome Early Arian creeds, such as the Fourth Creed of Sirmium, include the statement that Christ descended into hell after his death.	Hillel II commits the Jewish calendar to writing. (ca.)	
360		The first Latin hymns are sung during the tenure of the French prelate St. Hilary. Hilary is credited with having modeled Latin hymns after Ephrem Syrus of Edessa's Greek hymns, which Hilary learned while in exile in Asia Minor. (ca)		
361	Epiphany. It is the feast of the church immediately following the Christmas season (January 6). The name of the feast is from the Greek ἐπιφάνεια, meaning 'manifestation.' Over the years it comes to commemorate the manifestation of Christ to the Gentiles as seen in the story of the Magi and the Christmas star, the manifestation of Christ during his baptism, and the manifestation of the power of God in Jesus' first miracle at Cana.	Athanasius returns to his see. An early reference to Epiphany as an ecclesiastical feast does not differentiate it from the commemoration of Christ's nativity.		
362	Pneumatomachi. They teach that the Holy Spirit proceeds from the Son alone, not from the Father. They are declared heretical in the fourth century. Key figure: Macedonius.	Athanasius is condemned and exiled. The Donatists return from exile. The Pneumatomachi—Macedonius and his followers—are condemned by the local council of Alexandria.	Roman Emperor Julian, "the Apostate," restores paganism.	Basil the Great. *Asceticon.* A collection of questions and answers about the monastic life. With the *Moralia*, it is a part of the Rule of St. Basil. (ca.)
363			Roman Emperor Julian, "the Apostate," dies.	
364			Valens, Roman Emperor of the East, sides with the Arians. (–378)	
365		Athanasius is exiled. Council of Laodicea • Forbids ordination of chorepiscopoi. The chorepiscopoi are bishops with limited authority, usually of a small rural diocese. • Disapproves of metrical hymnody. • Limits singing to canonical cantors. • Establishes a Schola Cantorum.		Tyrannius Rufinus translates Greek patristics into Latin at a time when knowledge of Greek is declining in the West. (–410)

Date	A. Theology, Doctrine, and Beliefs	B. People/Events	C. Wider Culture	D. Texts
366		Damasus I becomes bishop of Rome.		
367		Saint Hilary of Poitiers dies. Bishop, historian, and defender of Western orthodox beliefs.	Roman Emperor Valerian orders witches be hunted down and punished.	Athanasius of Alexandria's *New Testament Canon*. Part of a festal letter circulated within his diocese, it is the first list of New Testament books that matches the list used in modern churches.
370	Cappadocian Fathers: Basil the Great, Gregory Nazianzus, Gregory of Nyssa. They believe the deepest essence of Christianity can't be expressed in Scripture or creed, but must be expressed symbolically.	The Coptic texts of the Nag Hammadi library are assembled. (ca.) The term *archdeacon* first appears as a part of the history of the Donatist schism. An archdeacon is a cleric who is under the immediate authority of the bishop and who carries out primarily administrative duties within a diocese.	Huns invade Europe. (ca. 360–)	Ambrose of Milan. *On the Duties of the Clergy*. A general treatise on ethics, addressed to the clergy. (mid to late fourth century)
372			Books replace scrolls as binding becomes common in Europe. (ca.)	
373	Manichaeism. A system of beliefs and practices that melds Persian Gnosticism with Judeo-Christian beliefs. At its center is a cosmic war between light and darkness, good and evil. Redemption is a cosmic affair. Working toward redemption entails vegetarianism and extreme asceticism. Key figure: Mani. (250–?) All Saint's Day. A feast celebrating the lives and faith of all the saints, both known and unknown. Originally celebrated in May, it later comes to be placed at November 1.	All Saints' Day (called the feast of All Martyrs) is first mentioned in Ephraem Syrus's writings. (before) Augustine of Hippo enters his Manichean years. (–382) Saint Ephrem Syrus of Edessa dies (a.k.a. Ephrem of Syria). An Eastern monk and writer, he laid the foundation for Orthodox Christian liturgical poetry. He also took melodies and meters from heretical chants of his day and adapted them to Orthodox Christianity. Athanasius teaches that Mary remained a virgin even after the birth of Jesus. He is among the first known to have espoused the perpetual virginity of Mary. (before) Saint Athanasius, bishop of Alexandria, foe of Arianism, dies.		
374		Basil the Great speaks of antiphonal and responsorial singing of psalms throughout Eastern Christianity. Catchy melodies are married to orthodox Christian texts to attract and educate especially children and youths.		The Gallican Rite originates in northwestern Europe. It may be a variant of the Roman liturgy or of eastern origins: it contains elements of both traditions. The date of origin is very uncertain, though it possibly dates to the late fourth century when an Eastern bishop ruled the See of Milan.

Date	A. Theology, Doctrine, and Beliefs	B. People/Events	C. Wider Culture	D. Texts
375	The Feast of the Holy Innocents. A commemoration of the children killed by Herod in the time of Jesus' infancy. Canticle. From the Latin word *canticulum*, meaning a 'little song.' It is song or prayer that is not a psalm, but that derives, sometimes very loosely, from passages in the Bible.	The Feast of the Nativity of John the Baptist is fixed on June 24, six months before Christmas. (late fourth century) The Feast of the Holy Innocents is celebrated in Bethlehem. (late fourth century) The assumption of Mary's soul into heaven is first mentioned. (late fourth century) According to the *Apostolic Constitutions*: • the Gloria in Excelsis Deo is used as a canticle of morning prayer. • the Kyrie Eleison begins to be used. • the Nunc Dimittis, also known as the Song of Simeon, is a part of daily prayers.		Gregory of Nyssa. *Great Catechism.* Instruction on the Trinity, redemption, Incarnation, and the sacraments, written for catechists. It is considered to be one of the greatest theological works of the time. (between 371 and 395) *Apostolic Constitutions.* A collection of ecclesiastical law, probably of Syrian origin, having some Arian influence. It is one of the most valuable sources for church life and liturgy of the time. (latter half of the fourth century) Kyrie Eleison. From the Latin phrase for "Lord, have mercy," it is the first line, and hence the common name, for a liturgical prayer. The Nunc Dimittis, also known as the Song of Simeon, is a prayer taken from Luke 2:29–32. The name Nunc Dimittis is Latin for "now dismiss," the first line of the prayer. It is used during the daily office beginning in the fourth century.
378		The Pneumatomachi—Macedonius and his followers—are condemned by Pope Damasus for teaching that the Holy Spirit proceeds from the Son alone, not from the Father. Rome widely observes Jesus' birthday on 25 December. (ca.)		
379		Basil the Great attests to the practice of singing the Phos Hilaron at the start of evening prayer. He calls it "an ancient practice." (before) Saint Basil the Great, bishop of Caesarea, dies. He was a renowned theologian and the author of the Rule that would become foundational for all Eastern monasticism.		Phos Hilaron. From the Greek φῶς ἱλαρόν, meaning joyful or gracious light, it addresses Jesus as the Light of the World. "O gracious Light, pure brightness of the everliving Father in heaven..."
380		Martin of Tours begins his mission to North Gaul.		
381	Macedonius vs. the Council of Constantinople. The Council condemns Macedonius for impugning the divinity of the Holy Spirit. Apollinarius vs. the Council of Constantinople. Apollinarius maintains the divine Logos replaced Christ's	Second Ecumenical Council: The Council of Constantinople. Called by the emperor, it was not attended by the pope, his legates, or any Western bishops. • Affirms the divinity of the Holy Spirit.		Nicene (Niceo-Constantinopolitan) Creed. The creed in its nearly modern form is ratified.

Date	A. Theology, Doctrine, and Beliefs	B. People/Events	C. Wider Culture	D. Texts
381 con't.	human spirit. The council decrees that Christ is completely human and completely divine.	• Condemns Apollinarius, affirming both Christ's divinity and his humanity. • Amends and affirms the Nicene Creed.		
382		Jerome becomes secretary to Pope Damasus I and begins translation of the Latin Vulgate. Under Roman Emperor Theodosius I, heresy is declared to be a capital crime.		
383		Pope Damasus brings antiphonal singing and the Alleluia to Rome. He is credited with having organized the Roman liturgy and chant after the Jerusalem model. (ca.)		*Vetus Itala* (Old Latin Version of the Bible). A translation into Latin based on the Septuagint Old Testament and Greek manuscripts of the New Testament. Augustine of Hippo recognizes it as one of the best translations of the time. It is revised by Jerome and has considerable influence on the Vulgate. (383 is the revision date. Original translation is made before end of the second century.)
384		During the pontificate of Pope Damasus, the term *Apostolic See* is first used to refer to Rome. (before) Saint Damasus I dies. During his pontificate, Latin became the principal liturgical language in Rome. He also commissioned his secretary, Jerome, to revise the Latin biblical text. Siricius becomes bishop of Rome. The paschal candle and a form of blessing like the modern Exultet are first referred to. These practices begin in Rome and spread to Gaul. *Egeria's Travels* • Contains the earliest attestations to an incipient church year including Ascension Day, Whitsunday, Palm Sunday, Nativity, Lent, Holy Week, Easter, and Pentecost. • Contains an early attestations to the full Divine Office (i.e., containing all nine hours). • Is also first to mention the unveiling and adoration of the Cross, which are believed to have originated in Jerusalem somewhat before that time.		*Egeria's Travels* (*Etheria's Peregrinatio*). The autobiographical account of a Spanish nun's pilgrimage to the Holy Land and Constantinople. A valuable primary source for information about fourth century liturgical practices. (ca.) Exultet. Also known as the "Pashal Proclamation," it is a song of praise to God sung by the deacon standing near the paschal candle on Holy Saturday (the Saturday before Easter). Though the form commonly used today did not emerge until the seventh century or later, the song was always one of the church year's finest songs, both poetically and musically.

Date	A. Theology, Doctrine, and Beliefs	B. People/Events	C. Wider Culture	D. Texts
385		Pope Siricius enjoins chastity on priests. Ambrose of Milan introduces the Te Deum into the liturgy in Milan. (ca.)		Te Deum. It is a Latin hymn to God, Father, and Son. Its title derives from the first line, "You are God: we praise you." It is composed, possibly by Niceta, bishop of Remesiana in Dacia. The legends of it having been written by Ambrose and Augustine are probably medieval fabrications. (before)
386	St. John Chrysostom claims that interpretation of the Bible should rest on a consideration of the author, readers, time, intention of the speaker, the occasion, context, place, and manner of writing. (–398)	Ambrose of Milan: "The emperor is indeed within the church, not above the church." Saint Cyril, bishop of Jerusalem, dies. He was a key figure in the Arian dispute. Augustine of Hippo converts to Catholic Christianity.		Ambrose of Milan. *De Sacramentis* (Latin: Concerning the Sacraments). Six Easter addresses to the newly baptized on baptism, confirmation, and the Eucharist. (late fourth century)
387		Saint Monica, mother of Augustine, dies.		
388		Chrysostom lobbies in Antioch for celebrating Christ's birth on 25 December.		
389		Saint Gregory Nazianzus, Cappadocian father and bishop of Constantinople, dies. He was called "the Divine." (ca.)		
390	Chrism. The oil used for Christian ritual, it is usually a mixture of olive oil and balsam. The custom of anointing dates back to Old Testament time. In Christian ritual, the custom is a very old one as well, with more and more custom and formality accruing to it throughout the years. In the West it comes to be practiced mainly during Baptism, confirmation, ordination, and prayers for the sick.	Massacre at Thessalonica. Ambrose, bishop of Milan, excommunicates Emperor Theodosius and brings him to public penance for ordering the massacre. Second Council of Carthage. • Restricts consecration of chrism to bishops. The Ten Commandments play a central role in the teaching of catechumens especially in regions with a large Manichean population, as the Manicheans repudiate the Ten Commandments. (ca.) Pope Siricius is adamant that only Easter and Pentecost are appropriate times for baptism. (ca.)		The Apostles Creed is first known by that name. (ca.) The Canon of the Mass takes on the form used in the modern church.
391			Augustine of Hippo is ordained a priest.	Roman Emperor Theodosius I prohibits pagan worship.
392		Good Friday begins to be observed separately from the festival commemorating the Resurrection. (some time in the fourth century) Prime begins to be said. Compline begins to be said, initially as a repetition of vespers. (before the end of the fourth century)		Jerome. *Gallican Psalter*. A revision of the Latin Psalter based on the text of the Septuagint. It is widely used in Gaul. Into modern times, it is the most common Latin version of the psalms. (ca.)

Date	A. Theology, Doctrine, and Beliefs	B. People/Events	C. Wider Culture	D. Texts
393	Maundy Thursday. The term Maundy comes from the Latin phrase *mandatum novum*, "a new commandment," in John 13:34. Maundy Thursday is a commemoration of Jesus' last night with his disciples before his crucifixion. Held on the Thursday before Easter, its two main foci are Jesus' washing of his disciples' feet and his institution of the Lord's Supper.	The Synod of Hippo. • Publishes the first complete list of canonical New Testament books. • First mentions Maundy Thursday. • Forbids the practice of giving Holy Communion to the dead. • First mentions the Eucharistic fast, which is typically from the midnight before one receives Holy Communion.		Jerome. *Against Jovian*. Jerome extolls asceticism as a Christian norm.
	Eucharistic fast. It is the tradition of refraining from food and drink for a specified period of time before receiving the Lord's Supper. The period of the fast varies throughout the year.			
394		Saint Gregory, bishop of Nyssa and Cappadocian father, dies. He was a philosopher, theologian, rhetorician, the brother of Basil the Great, and one of the chief voices of Nicene orthodoxy. Ninian begins his mission to Scotland. (ca.)		
395		Augustine becomes bishop of Hippo. (ca.)	The Roman Empire is permanently divided into east and west after the death of Theodosius I. Early Byzantine empire (–717)	
397		Saint Martin, bishop of Tours, dies. Proponent of monasticism and former soldier. He is known for giving half his cloak to a beggar. Patron saint of France. (ca.) Saint Ambrose, bishop of Milan, dies. He is best known as a hymnodist and as an opponent of Arianism. One of the original four Doctors of the Church.		Augustine of Hippo. *Confessions*. An autobiographical account of his life/spiritual journey in the form of a confession to God. (ca.) Jerome. *Editio Vulgata* (Latin Vulgate). The Latin translation of the Bible most widely used in the West.
398		John Chrysostom becomes patriarch of Constantinople. The Council of Carthage declares that a cleric can be deprived of his benefice for failing to say the Divine Office regularly.		
399		Anastasius I becomes bishop of Rome.		

Date	A. Theology, Doctrine, and Beliefs	B. People/Events	C. Wider Culture	D. Texts
400	During the fourth and fifth centuries, the time bishops devote to teaching and liturgy decreases as administrative duties increase.	Angels become a prevalent subject in Christian art. (fifth century) The earliest sacristies are built off apses in Syria. They are used as places for keeping vestments and Eucharist vessels. (ca.) Saint Ursula and her companions are martyred by the Huns near Cologne. Most likely her companions include eight to ten young women. A medieval typographical error, however, later expands the number to 11,000 virgin martyrs. (before) The eremitic life, the life of a religious hermit, becomes increasingly common in the West in the fourth century. It is a flourishing and respected lifestyle throughout the fifth and sixth centuries. The Christian symbolism of the fish gradually disappears. For a short time, however, it becomes a symbol of the Eucharist. (after the fourth century) Cassian mentions that the Gloria Patri is used as a closing verse for antiphonal psalms. (ca.)	The rights of tenant farmers are reduced, and many farmers become serfs. (ca.) Roman tax collectors meet such hostility that they need military escort.	*Liturgy of St. Chrysostom.* The liturgy still in use (in modified form) throughout the East. (ca.) Gloria Patri. Latin for "Glory to the Father," it is the first phrase of a prayer of praise to the Trinity. Also known as the Lesser Doxology, it becomes the most common formulaic close for recitation of the Psalms. "Glory to the Father, and to the Son, and to the Holy Spirit. As it was in the beginning, is now, and will be forever. Amen."
401		Innocent I becomes bishop of Rome.		
406		Rufinus notes that the Benedicite is common among Christians throughout the world. (ca.)		Codex Alexandrinus is copied. It is the Greek Bible, written on vellum, probably of Byzantine origin. It also contains the earliest extant Greek text of the Gloria in Excelsis Deo. (early fifth century) Benedicite. Latin for "Bless [the Lord]," it is also known as "A Song of Creation" and as the "Song of the Three Young Men." It is an expanded paraphrase of Psalm 148. Apocryphal accounts of the Israelites in the fiery furnace place the song in the mouths of the young men in the furnace (Daniel 3).
407		Saint John Chrysostom, bishop of Constantinople, dies. He was known as an ascetic and a brilliant preacher. Patron saint of preachers.		

Date	A. Theology, Doctrine, and Beliefs	B. People/Events	C. Wider Culture	D. Texts
410		Popes in the fifth century are capable, and increasingly powerful, administrators. More and more they fill the power vacuum caused by the decline of the empire. Very few people in the West have a working knowledge of Greek. The church takes on Greek-to-Latin translators and scribes to avoid losing practical patristic knowledge.	"The Fall of Rome." Alaric I, king of the Visigoths, sacks and captures Rome. The Roman Empire abandons Britain.	
411		Donatist and Catholic bishops debate, try to settle the Donatist dispute. Donatists lose ground. Pelagius is condemned at Carthage.		
412		The Donatists are condemned.		
414		Donatists are deprived of all civil rights.		
415		John Cassian founds a convent at Marseilles.	Pagans are banned from military office.	
416		The Council of Milevis forbids liturgical formulas not approved by council or appropriate ecclesiastical authority.		
417		Saint Innocent I dies. Pope and proponent of papal supremacy. Zosimus becomes bishop of Rome.		
418	Augustinian thought is largely Platonic. It becomes more extremely so in the controversy with Julian of Eclanum, a capable Aristotelian (ca. 418–430). Because of Augustine's central place in ante-Nicene Christianity, western Christian thought has a decided Platonic tint until the 13th century when Aristotelian thought becomes dominant. Original Sin. Is humanity condemned to eternal damnation because of Adam's sin? Augustine, and eventually most of Western Christianity: yes. Eastern Christianity, Judaism, and (later) Islam: no.	Boniface I becomes bishop of Rome. Council of Carthage. (416–) • Upholds the Augustinian doctrine of original sin • condemns Pelagianism. Roman Emperor Honorius bans Pelagianism. Pelagius, originator of the heresy of Pelagianism, dies.		
419				Palladius. *Lausiac History*. An invaluable historical source, it details the early years of monasticism.

Date	A. Theology, Doctrine, and Beliefs	B. People/Events	C. Wider Culture	D. Texts
420		Augustine of Hippo and Jerome recommend striking the breast during the confession of sin. (early fifth century) Jerome copies manuscripts and recommends the exercise to other monks. His is one of the earliest mentions of monastic copyists. (before) Jerome says that pilgrims come to Jerusalem from every part of the world, even Britain. Saint Jerome, biblical scholar and translator, dies. Also known by his Latin name, Eusebius Hieronymus, he is one of the original four Doctors of the Church. His best known work is the Latin translation of the Bible known as the Vulgate.		
421	Pelagianism vs. Augustinianism. To what degree are human beings free to choose good or evil? Pelagianism: they have freedom to choose. Augustinianism: they are hopeless on their own to resist evil. Pelagianism is condemned in councils throughout the fifth century.	Pelagianism gains a foothold in Britain. (ca.)		
422		Celestine I becomes bishop of Rome.		Augustine of Hippo. *City of God*. A treatise on the special place of Christianity in history, the writing of which was instigated by the Sack of Rome. (416–)
423				The Rule of St. Augustine of Hippo. A monastic rule drawn up by a follower of Augustine, probably during his life, possibly with his input. It contains a list of monastic observances and a reflection on the communal life. (ca.)
425		Pedilavium (washing of the feet) on Maundy Thursday is common, as is capitilavium (washing of the head) on Palm Sunday. (early fifth century) The church in Britain is mostly urban and, because of lack of estate wealth, generally poor.	Alchemy begins to be practiced. (early fifth century) The Palestinian Talmud is compiled. (–475)	
426		John Cassian develops a rule for novice monks.		

Date	A. Theology, Doctrine, and Beliefs	B. People/Events	C. Wider Culture	D. Texts
428			Frankish Merovingian Empire. (–751)	Athanasian Creed. An early Western statement of faith. It deals mainly with the Trinity, Incarnation, and redemption. It also contains anathemas, which are not found in other major early creeds. It is recognized by Lutherans and various other Protestant churches in modern times. (after)
429		The Vandals, a nomadic Germanic tribe, begin an invasion of North Africa. The Vandals are Arian Christians and set out not only to conquer territory but to brings African Catholic Christianity to ruin.		
430		Saint Augustine of Hippo, one of the original four Doctors of the Church, dies. He is among the most influential theologians in Western church history. Saint Ninian, bishop in Galloway, dies. He was the first recorded missionary in Scotland. (ca.)	Vandals attack Hippo, and malaria sweeps the city.	Cyril of Alexandria. *Twelve Anathemas*. A Christological gauntlet, in the form of a letter addressed to the pope, but thrown down before Nestorius. It is approved by the Council of Ephesus, omitted by Chalcedon. Augustine of Hippo. *On Christian Doctrine*. It contains the most complete treatment of the principles of biblical interpretation written to date. (some time between 388 and 430)
431	Cyril vs. Nestorius. Was Mary *Theotokos* or *Christotokos*, i.e., was she the bearer/mother of God or the bearer/mother of Christ? Cyril (and eventually Orthodoxy): *Theotokos*. Nestorius: *Christotokos*. Another of the Christological controversies.	Catholic Christianity is greatly suppressed in North Africa. (mid fifth century) Third Ecumenical Council: The First Council of Ephesus. It was called by Theodosius II, the Eastern emperor • Declares Mary to be *Theotokos*, the mother of the divine person, Jesus, who is the second person of the Trinity. • Defines the Hypostatic Union. • Condemns Nestorius for denying the Hypostatic Union. • Severely curtails Pelagianism. Palladius is consecrated, becoming the first Irish Catholic bishop.		
432		Saint Celestine I dies. Pope and opponent of Pelagianism. Patrick begins his mission to North Ireland. Sixtus III becomes bishop of Rome.		

Date	A. Theology, Doctrine, and Beliefs	B. People/Events	C. Wider Culture	D. Texts
433			Attila the Hun attacks the Roman provinces.	
435	Semipelagianism. The belief that human beings can take the first step toward God, after which God's grace accomplishes their salvation. Key figure: John Cassian.			Vincent of Lérins, "Peregrinus." *Commonitoria.* A semipelagianist work calling into question Augustine of Hippo's doctrine of predestination. It contains the Vincentian Canon, a yardstick for defining orthodoxy: orthodoxy is "what has been believed everywhere, always, and by all."
436			The last Roman troops leave Britain.	
439		Vandals capture Carthage. Catholic Christianity no longer has the political clout it did under the Romans. (–ca. 540)	The Imperial administration in Constantinople begins to use Greek as the official language. Invaders have overrun Western Europe. Travel via the western Mediterranean becomes treacherous due to piracy.	
440		Pope Sixtus III introduces the Sanctus into the Western liturgy. (before) Leo I becomes bishop of Rome.	After the Roman withdrawal, Angles, Saxons, and Jutes—nomadic Germanic tribes from Germany and Denmark—storm England. They bring with them Old English, a Germanic language that is the ancestor of modern English. (early fifth century)	Cyril, patriarch of Alexandria. *Against Julian.* An apology condemning the Emperor Julian, written more than seventy-five years after his death.
444		Saint Cyril, patriarch of Alexandria, dies. He was a supporter of Mary as Theotokos and president of the Council of Ephesus.		
445		The papacy becomes authoritative in the West.		
447			In Ireland the social power of the druids is virtually gone.	
449	*Communicatio idiomatum.* The assertion of the Western church that because of the inseparability of Christ's two natures, attributes of the divine Christ can be predicated on the human, and vice versa. It had its most famous expression in the *Tome* of Leo the Great.	The Council of Ephesus, "the Robber Synod," begins.		Leo's *Tome.* A doctrinal letter from Pope Leo I to the patriarch of Constantinople. It expresses the western view of Christology and asserts the *communicatio idiomatum.* The Council of Chalcedon acclaims it with the famous words "Peter has spoken through Leo."
450		Rhyme begins to be deliberately incorporated into hymns. (fourth century) Vincent of Lérins dies. He was noted for his Vincentian Canon, a formula for determining orthodoxy. (before 450)		Fastidius. *On Preserving Widowhood* and *The Christian Life.* Letters reflecting the British bent toward asceticism. (ca.)

Date	A. Theology, Doctrine, and Beliefs	B. People/Events	C. Wider Culture	D. Texts
451	Monophysitism vs. dyophysitism. How exactly did the human and divine fit together in Christ? Monophysitism (Eutyches): Jesus' divine and human natures combined to create a single nature. Dyophysitism (the Chalcedonian position): Jesus was one person with two natures. Another of the Christological Controversies. Docetism. A point of view within both mainstream Christianity and Gnosticism, it denies that Jesus, as God, could actually suffer. Some docetists believe Jesus' sufferings were simulated in some way. Others believe Judas Iscariot or Simon of Cyrene took his place on the cross. The impassibility of God. An extension of Greek philosophical theology, it maintains that God is without passion. In other words, God's emotions do not change either alone or in reaction to some external stimulus. Such change would fly in the face of immutability, and perfection.	Jerusalem is confirmed as a patriarchate. Fourth Ecumenical Council: The Council of Chalcedon. Convened by Pope Leo I and Emperor Marcian. • Affirms dyophysitism. • Condemns the Byzantine monk Eutyches for Eutychianism, an early version of monophysitism. • Draws up the Definition of Chalcedon. • Officially condemns docetism. • Forbids ordination for money. • Declares Christ's divine nature of to be impassible. His human nature, however, experienced normal human emotions. Anti-Chalcedonian riots take place in Jerusalem and Alexandria. (–452) The monophysite Egyptians (Copts) begin to separate formally from the Chalcedonian Egyptians (Melchites).		Council of Chalcedon. *Definition of Chalcedon.* Contains the first systematic exposition of the doctrine of the Incarnation and the most authoritative definition of the kenosis of Christ.
452	Early Medieval Church. The primary concern of the early medieval church is surviving the invasions. It also standardizes the liturgy and sees the rise of monasticism. (–1054)		Pope Leo I persuades Attila the Hun not to invade Rome.	
453		Nestorius, patriarch of Constantinople, dies in exile. He was the originator of the heresy of Nestorianism. (ca.)		
455			Vandals attack Rome. Pope Leo I persuades Gaiseric, Vandal leader, not to sack the city.	
457		Ibas of Edessa dies. A voice of moderation in the Christological controversies of his time, he and his letter to Maris were condemned by the Second Council of Constantinople.		
459		Saint Simeon Stylite dies while praying atop a sixty-foot pole, where he has lived for most of his adult life. He is the first and best-known of the pillar-hermits. (ca.) Daniel the Stylite inherits Simeon Stylite's cloak and		

Date	A. Theology, Doctrine, and Beliefs	B. People/Events	C. Wider Culture	D. Texts
459 con't.		begins his life as a hermit atop a pillar. His reputation leads many to visit him for prayers and advice. (ca.)		
460		Confirmation begins to emerge as a separate rite from baptism. Baptism is being done more often by priests than bishops. Bishops come in after baptism to do the laying on of hands that used to be a part of the baptismal rite. Saint Patrick, bishop of Ireland, dies. He is credited with bringing Christianity to Ireland.	Mayan culture is at its peak in Mexico. (ca.)	
461		Pope Leo the Great fosters the Roman Rite. He founds a Schola Cantorum in Rome. He popularizes the term *Mass*. He is also reputed to be the first pontiff to institute a Jerusalem-style *annalis cantus*, or cycle of chants for the church year. (440–) Saint Leo I, "Leo the Great," dies. Pope, church administrator, writer, and convener of the Council of Chalcedon. Hilarus becomes bishop of Rome.		Pope Leo the Great. *Sacramentarium*. One of the oldest extant collections of liturgical prayers and chants.
465		Pope Hilarus commissions Victorinus, an astronomer to reform the calendar and fix the date of Easter.		
468		Simplicius becomes bishop of Rome.		
469		The Chalcedonian riots bring confusion and turmoil to the city of Antioch.		
470		Byzantine influences come along the trade route to western Britain. The British church accepts the Alexandrian calculation of Easter, the Byzantine tonsure, and the Eastern view of art and iconography. (fifth century)		
473		A bright and well-educated episcopate is able to have considerable influence over occupying forces, especially in Gaul.	Visigoths take southern Gaul.	
475		Council of Ephesus III. It is an anti-Chalcedonian council.		Socrates Scholasticus. *Church History*. A seven-book non-theological history of the church from 305 to 493.

Date	A. Theology, Doctrine, and Beliefs	B. People/Events	C. Wider Culture	D. Texts
476			"Fall of the Roman Empire." The Roman imperial office becomes vacant after the deposition of Romulus Augustulus, the last puppet western emperor.	
			Beginning of the Early Middle Ages, sometimes called the "Dark Ages." In the absence of Rome's central authority, small feudal states pepper Europe. Invasions pound the continent. Education, trade, and quality of life decline. (ca.–1050)	
			Independent small farmers in Germany, England, and France have to surrender land in exchange for protection from occupying troops. This shift of land is one of the earliest signs of developing feudalism. (after 476)	
480		Benedict of Nursia is born. Boethius is born. Monasticism begins in Celtic Britain.		
481			The reign of Clovis, founder of the Frankish monarchy, begins.	
482		Acacian schism. The East-West split over monophysitism begins. (–519) The chrism used to anoint the newly baptized is commonly consecrated on Maundy Thursday. The custom is mentioned in both the Gregorian and Gelasian Sacramentaries. (fifth century)		Byzantine Emperor Zeno. *Henoticon*. Written by the patriarchs of Alexandria and Constantinople and sponsored by the emperor, it asserts the Nicene Creed and Cyril's *Twelve Anathemas*, but never actually takes a stand on the number of Christ's natures. It is widely accepted in the East; rejected in the West.
483		Felix III becomes bishop of Rome.		
484			Attila the Hun kills the Persian emperor.	
485		The Feast of the Holy Innocents is celebrated in Rome. (end of the fifth century)	The Greek language is uncommon in the West.	
492	Vicar of Christ. A papal title that implies that the pope has inherited responsibility for the whole of Christ's Church, the responsibility given to Peter in Christ's charge to "feed my sheep."	Catechumens and the faithful no longer recite different forms of the church-prayer. (ca.) Gelasius I becomes bishop of Rome. He is the first pope to use the title Vicar of Christ. (–496) The first mention of all four Ember Days. (ca.)		The *Supplication of Pope Gelasius*. The earliest known example of the petition-response style of litany in the West. (–496)

Date	A. Theology, Doctrine, and Beliefs	B. People/Events	C. Wider Culture	D. Texts
493		Saint Daniel the Stylite dies after spending over thirty years of his life atop a pillar.		
496		Saint Gelasius I dies. Pope and renowned writer. He asserted the parity of the papacy with the secular powers and believed the pope had jurisdiction over church councils. Anastasius II becomes bishop of Rome.	Clovis, Frankish king, converts to Catholicism. He is baptized by Remigius, bishop of Reims, on Christmas Day.	
498		Symmachus becomes bishop of Rome.		
500	Apophatic theology. It asserts that because God transcends all human thought and language, all divine attributes that can be thought must be dismissed. The theological enterprise is not description of God but unity with God in a "place" beyond language and understanding. Earliest mention of the term is in the writings of Dionysius the Pseudo-Areopagite. Other key figures: the Gnostics, Gregory of Nyssa.	Most Western monasteries have copying rooms. The earliest authentic reference to the Annunciation of the Blessed Virgin Mary, the Trisagion, and the Feast of the Nativity of the Blessed Virgin Mary is in the Gelasian Sacramentary.	Many large landlords in Europe have their own armies and prisons. Embalming begins to be used in Europe. (ca.)	Dionysius, the Pseudo-Areopagite. *The Divine Names* and *The Mystical Theology*. Two of the earliest works of Christian mysticism. They attempt to blend Neoplatonic thought with Christian doctrine. Gelasian Sacramentary. A collection of celebrant's prayers written/compiled by the nuns of Chelles near Paris. It is the first known Roman Sacramentary to arrange the Feasts in order of the church year. (ca.) Codex Bezae. Probably copied in a Latin-speaking area, it contains a Greek text of the gospels and Acts with a parallel Latin paraphrase. It is the most textually unique of all the uncial manuscripts. (some time between the fourth and sixth centuries) Trisagion. The name is Greek for "three-times holy." It refers to the refrain "Holy God, holy and mighty, holy immortal one, have mercy on us." For centuries a part of Eastern worship, it comes into the West in modern times.
501		In Ireland, the Eve of Easter is celebrated with bonfires of "new fire" kindled with lenses. (sixth century)		
506		It is customary in the sixth century to receive the Eucharist three times a year—at Christmas, Easter, and Pentecost.		
507			Clovis, king of the Franks, defeats Alaric II, king of the Visigoths, at the Battle of Vouillé. In doing so, he gains control over most of Gaul and makes Paris his capital.	

Date	A. Theology, Doctrine, and Beliefs	B. People/Events	C. Wider Culture	D. Texts
511		Catholicism is restored throughout Gaul.	Clovis, founder of the Frankish monarchy, dies.	
514		Hormisdas becomes bishop of Rome. The title "abbess" is first used. The title refers to the female head of a monastic community. The Agnus Dei is introduced to Rome as part of the Gloria in Excelsis in episcopal masses. (before)		Agnus Dei. Latin for "O, Lamb of God," this prayer is based on John 1:29. It is typically sung just before Communion or at the Fraction.
517		The Council of Gerona condemns the practice of baptizing new Christians on Epiphany. Doing so, however, continues to be a regular practice in many places, especially the North African church.		
518		The term "Ecumenical patriarch" is first used. It is a Greek title meaning 'patriarch of the entire inhabited world.' It refers to the Eastern Orthodox archbishop of Constantinople.		
519	Theopaschites. "Those who hold that God suffered." Key figures: John Maxentius and a group of Scythian monks.	John Maxentius and a group of Scythian monks maintain one of the Trinity suffered in the flesh. The notion is rejected by the patriarch of Constantinople but eventually supported by the pope. (–534) The Acacian schism ends.		
520				Boethius. *De Consolatione Philosophiae* (The Consolation of Philosophy). Platonic thought adapted to Christian theology, it is a look at how philosophy leads the soul to God. It is a major source for classical thought, Scholastic philosophy, and English literature. It is translated into Old English under Alfred, king of the West Saxons, in the ninth century. 5 vol. (ca.)
521		Columba is born.		
523		John I becomes bishop of Rome. The Vandals, a Germanic tribe espousing Arian Christianity, gradually become pro-Catholic. (–530)		
524		Boethius, Anicius Manlius Torquatus Severinus, is executed for taking the side of		Boethius. *De Institutione musica* (Latin: Concerning musical education). Boethius

Date	A. Theology, Doctrine, and Beliefs	B. People/Events	C. Wider Culture	D. Texts
524 con't.		an ex-consul charged with treason. Saint Brigid of Ireland dies. Irish nun and one of the patron saints of Ireland. She founded four monasteries, including the monastery of Kildare. (ca.)		plays a key role in the transmission of Greek music theory to the medieval world. His theoretical ideas are applied to the codification of chant. (before)
525		"A.D." is first used by the monk Dionysius Exiguus, who fixes the birth of Christ on December 25 in the year of Rome 753.		
526		Saint John I, pope, dies at Ravenna while imprisoned by Theodoric the Great, king of the Ostrogoths, who controlled Italy. Felix IV becomes bishop of Rome.		
527	Apollinarianism. The beliefs of Apollinarius the Younger, bishop of Laodicea. In many ways orthodox, it does, however, deny Christ had a human mind and soul. Nestorianism. The belief that Jesus possessed not only two natures, but two "persons," one human one divine, united by a single will. Key figure: Nestorius, patriarch of Constantinople.	Byzantine Emperor Justinian promulgates laws against heresies including Nestorianism, Eutychianism, Apollinarianism, Manichaeism, and others. (–529)	Justinian I becomes Byzantine Emperor. During his reign the former Roman Empire, except Gaul and Northern Spain, comes under Byzantine control. (–540) Byzantine empire. (–1453)	
529		Benedict founds the Monte Cassino monastery where he composes his rule to counter monastic abuses of the time. The Second Council of Vaison. A Gallican council. • Declares that when the priest of a parish is ill the deacon should read a sermon written by a priest or bishop. Actual preaching by a deacon is rare and discouraged. • Mandates the liturgical use of the Sanctus and Kyrie during Matins, Vespers, and the Mass. The Council of Orange. • Declares semipelagianism to be heretical. Pelagianism soon disappears. The Empire orders all pagans to become Christians.	The Platonic Academy in Athens closes. Paganism breathes its last breath in the empire.	
530		Boniface II becomes bishop of Rome. Monophysites and Chalcedonians split into two churches with two separate hierarchies.	Persian War begins. (–532)	Dionysius Exiguus's canon law collection. A translation of the canons of the Eastern councils into Latin. It also contains thirty-nine papal decretals, placed on a par

Date	A. Theology, Doctrine, and Beliefs	B. People/Events	C. Wider Culture	D. Texts
530 con't.				with conciliar law. One of the most important early western canonical collection. (early to mid fifth century)
533		John II becomes bishop of Rome. The office of deaconess disappears throughout most of Europe in the sixth century. Saint Remigius, bishop of Reims, dies. He was instrumental in the conversion of the king of the Franks.	The Moors conquer the Vandals and take Carthage. Byzantine Emperor Justinian rebuilds.	
534			Byzantine Emperor Justinian completes his code of law. Attila the Hun brings down the Gupta dynasty in India.	
535		Agapitus becomes bishop of Rome. Catholicism in North Africa is restored to its former authority and privilege.	The Gothic Wars begin.	
536		Silverius becomes bishop of Rome.		
537		The Hagia Sophia (Church of the Holy Wisdom) is dedicated. It is still extant in Constantinople (Istanbul). Vigilius becomes bishop of Rome.	Arthur, king of the Britons, is killed. (ca.)	
538		Gregory of Tours is born.		
540	*Rule of St. Benedict.* A communal, monastic way of life that revolves around the Divine Office. Monks pray, study, and work under the total authority of an abbot chosen by the community. The lifestyle is austere but lacks the extreme asceticism many eastern monastics have practiced.	The term "canonical hours" is first seen in the *Rule of St. Benedict.* Benedict establishes a complete liturgy for matins, lauds, prime, terce, sext, none, vespers, and compline throughout the church year. (ca.) Benedictines begin wearing the scapular, a piece of cloth that hangs from shoulders in front and back. It is a symbol of the yoke of Christ. Gregory the Great is born.		Benedict of Nursia. The Rule of St. Benedict. Administrative and spiritual guidelines for running a communal monastery. It provides structure for prayer, reading, and work and becomes the model for nearly all medieval monasteries. (some time between 529 and 540)
541		Byzantine Emperor Justinian I institutes the Festival of the Purification of the Blessed Virgin Mary (Candlemas), probably as a replacement for the great feast of expiation and purification held in ancient Rome in mid-February.		
542		Monophysitism spreads throughout the Byzantine empire. (–560)	Plagues and earthquakes hit Europe. (–543)	

Date	A. Theology, Doctrine, and Beliefs	B. People/Events	C. Wider Culture	D. Texts
543		Columbanus is born. St. Scholastica, St. Benedict's sister and founder of a convent, dies. (ca.)		
545		Celtic missionaries, including Columba and Columbanus, travel widely throughout the sixth century to win souls, reform abuses, and establish monasteries. Among the monasteries they establish are Derry and Durrow. (mid sixth century)	Slovanic invaders sweep through the Balkan Peninsula. Life becomes semi-nomadic again.	
547		Benedict of Nursia, the "Patriarch of Western Monasticism," dies. He was the author of the Rule of St. Benedict. (between 540 and 550)		
550	By the mid sixth century, Rome, Constantinople, and Carthage are largely Chalcedonian (dyophysite). Alexandria, Jerusalem, and Antioch are largely monophysite.	Bells begin to the used in churches in France. (ca.) Lent begins on Wednesday rather than the first Sunday in Lent. (sixth century) The doctrine of the corporal Assumption of Mary begins to finds its way into orthodox Christianity. (ca.) The Magnificat becomes the canticle most used during vespers. (ca.)	The Babylonian Talmud is completed. Invasions, war expenses, and plagues eat away at the quality of life in the Mediterranean basin. Buildings, including churches, fall into disrepair. Literacy and literature decline. (sixth century)	Johannes Scholasticus. *Synagoge canonum.* One of the oldest collection of Greek canon law. It is organized by subject rather than in chronological order. (ca.)
551				Emperor Justinian. *Confessions of the True Faith.* The last real example of imperial theology.
553	The Second Council of Constantinople decrees that hell is eternal punishment. Before this time, Origen and others taught that hell is purgatorial and temporary.	Fifth Ecumenical Council: The Second Council of Constantinople. • Confirms the Council of Chalcedon, whose authority was contested by some. • Condemns the "Three Chapters"—writings of Theodore of Mopsuestia, Theodoret, and Ibas of Edessa—as Nestorian.	Two Nestorian monks, sent to China by Byzantine Emperor Justinian I, secret mulberry seeds and silkworm eggs into Europe in their walking sticks. Asia's silk monopoly ends.	
556		Pelagius I becomes bishop of Rome.		
561		Saint Brendan founds a monastery in what is now Clonfert, in county Galway, Ireland. John III becomes bishop of Rome. The first Council of Braga condemns suicide. Those who commit suicide are denied a normal Christian burial. The condemnation remains in effect throughout the Middle Ages.		

Date	A. Theology, Doctrine, and Beliefs	B. People/Events	C. Wider Culture	D. Texts
563		Columba founds a monastery on the island of Iona. From there Christianity spreads throughout Scotland. The Second Council of Braga. • Forbids fasting on Christmas Day. • Decrees all hymns must take their texts from Scripture. • Declares the Devil was created good and fell into evil. • Declares the Devil is incapable of creation.		
567		The Second Council of Tours. • Proclaims the sanctity of the "twelve days" from Christmas to Epiphany, and the duty of fasting before Christmas.	Plagues and epidemics hit Italy.	
568			The Lombards invade Italy.	
570			Muhammad is born. (ca.)	
573			The Lombards advance on Rome.	
574		Gregory the Great becomes a monk.		
575	Four great traditions emerge in the sixth century: Antioch, Nestorians in Persian territory; Alexandria, monophysites in the Nile valley; Byzantine orthodoxy in Palestine and Asia Minor; and Western Christianity centered in Rome.	Benedict I becomes bishop of Rome. Gregory of Tours maintains that Mary's body ascended into heaven to be reunited with her soul. (late sixth century)		
578		Saint Brendan the Navigator dies. He was an Irish monk best known for his sea voyages. His travels and adventures become the subject of a popular medieval romance, *The Voyage of Saint Brendan.* (ca.)		
579		Pelagius II becomes bishop of Rome.	The Persian War renews.	
580		The Lombards destroy the monastery at Monte Cassino. The monks flee to Rome and thereby introduce the Benedictine Rule into that city.		
581		The earliest authentic record of the season of Advent states that Advent starts on the feast of St. Martin, November 11. This timing is still observed in the Orthodox church.		
584		The cope, a long semicircular cape, is first mentioned as being as a liturgical vestment. (before)		

Date	A. Theology, Doctrine, and Beliefs	B. People/Events	C. Wider Culture	D. Texts
585		In the late sixth century many of the wealthy begin to see the church as a more stable institution than the civil authority. They place themselves and their resources under the church's care, greatly boosting the church's influence. In Italy, the church is the largest single landowner.		
586		Recared, king of Spain, converts to Catholic Christianity, thus ending the influence of Arianism in his territories. (–601).		
588		David of Wales dies. (some time between 544–601)		
589	Filioque clause. The debate centers on a clause in the Nicene creed. Does the Holy Spirit proceed "from the Father" or "from the Father and Son"? East: "from the Father." West: "from the Father and Son."	The Third Council of Toledo adds the Filioque clause to the Nicene Creed. The Nicene Creed is put into final form.	Floods and plagues devastate Rome. Pope Pelagius II, the city's most powerful leader, dies. The population is halved. Chaos reigns.	
590	Ash Wednesday. The Wednesday six and a half weeks, before Easter, it marks the beginning of Lent. Ashes are placed on the foreheads of church-goers as a symbol of penance and mourning, and as a reminder of mortality.	Gregory I, "Gregory the Great," becomes pope. Gregory the Great introduces Ash Wednesday ashes. (some time during his tenure as pope) Columbanus sets up Celtic-style monasteries in Gaul. He encounters vigorous opposition. The term "canonical hours" comes into popular usage. It refers to the seven formally appointed times for recitation of the Divine Office (Daily Prayer). (ca.)		Isidore, archbishop of Seville. *De Ecclesiasticus Officiis* (Latin: Concerning Ecclesiastical Office). One of the earliest sources for the Mozarabic Rite.
591		Pope Gregory the Great issues detailed directives for the management of church estates.	Persia and Rome establish a treaty. Gregory of Tours. *Historia Francorum*. A history of the Frankish people from the Creation to the year 591. One of the most valuable sources of Merovingian history. (10 volumes)	Pope Gregory the Great. *Liber Regulæ Pastoralis* (Book of Pastoral Care). A directive for the ministry of bishops. Central to the shaping of the medieval papacy. (ca.)
593		Pope Gregory the Great negotiates peace with the Lombards by buying them off with civil and church funds. Pope Gregory the Great teaches that the sins of individuals who have died might be purged in purgatory. He suggests Eucharists be offered for their benefit. His suggestions are more a reflection of popular piety than they are dogma.		Pope Gregory the Great. *Dialogues*. The lives and miracles of Benedict and other Latin saints. A model for medieval hagiography.

Date	A. Theology, Doctrine, and Beliefs	B. People/Events	C. Wider Culture	D. Texts
594		Saint Gregory of Tours dies. He was a Gallic bishop and historian. (ca.)	The plague subsides after wiping out nearly half Europe's population.	
596		Pope Gregory the Great sends Augustine of Canterbury along with forty monks as missionaries to Britain. Augustine was the prior of Gregory's own monastery of St. Andrew. (–597)		
597		Augustine of Canterbury founds a Benedictine monastery in Canterbury. Saint Ethelbert of Kent, Anglo-Saxon king, converts to Christianity, is baptized by Augustine of Canterbury, and directs that episcopal sees be created at Canterbury (his capital), Rochester, and London. Saint Columba, Celtic missionary and abbot of Iona, dies.		
598		According to Pope Gregory the Great, *Christe eleison* begins to be sung as a part of the Kyrie.		
599		The Te Deum becomes a part of the Roman liturgy by the end of the sixth century. Gregorian chant, a specific form of plainsong, begins to take form during the tenure of Pope Gregory the Great. Under his direction, the Schola Cantorum in Rome is reorganized and chant is organized into a *cantus anni circuli nobilis*, a cycle of chants for the entire church year. (590–604)		
600		Pope Gregory the Great mandates that subdeacons no longer wear tunics. (before 604) Pope Gregory the Great standardizes the use of "Alleluia" during the Mass. He directs that it be used throughout the year except between Septuagesima and Easter. (ca.) Advent season begins on the fourth Sunday before Christmas by Pope Gregory the Great's decree. Intinction, or *Intinctio panis*, the dipping of the communion bread into the consecrated wine, becomes common in the early seventh century. The Church of the Holy Sepulchre displays a chalice	The earliest references to King Arthur are in the Welsh poem *Y Gododdin*. (ca.)	Gregorian Sacramentary. A supplementing, editing, and tightening-up of the Western Rite. The modern outline of the Divine Office is completed. (end of the sixth century) The Jesus Prayer ("Lord Jesus Christ, Son of God, have mercy on me"). The earliest attestation dates from the sixth or seventh century.

Date	A. Theology, Doctrine, and Beliefs	B. People/Events	C. Wider Culture	D. Texts
600 con't.		purported to be the actual chalice of Christ. It allegedly contains the sponge that was presented to Jesus on the cross. (sixth and seventh century) A Schola Cantorum (Latin for 'school of singers') is founded in Rome. It trains professional singers to perform parts of the liturgy in the larger churches. Manichaeism has faded into obscurity.		
602		Augustine of Canterbury founds the See of Canterbury.	Persia invades Rome.	
603	Celtic Christianity. Churches in Celtic-speaking regions have traditions that separate them from the medieval Roman church. They have a different way of calculating Easter, a different tonsure, and they find their church leadership in abbots and monasteries rather than in a hierarchy with bishops at the head. In general, Celtic Christianity bears more of a Byzantine influence than the rest of the West.	Augustine of Canterbury orders the Celtic church to submit to the authority and rites of Rome. They refuse.		
604		Saint Gregory, (Gregory the Great, Pope Gregory I), dies. Pope, administrator, writer, patron of monasteries, and founder of the medieval papacy. One of the original four Doctors of the Church. Sabinian becomes bishop of Rome. Bells are first used in churches in Rome. (ca.)		
605		Saint Augustine of Canterbury dies. Missionary to Britain, first archbishop of Canterbury.		
607		Boniface III becomes bishop of Rome. The first St. Paul's Cathedral is built in London. (ca.)		
608		Boniface IV becomes bishop of Rome.	Persian troops cross the Taurus Mountains and invade Asia Minor.	
610	Double Predestination. The doctrine that God not only selects some individuals for salvation, he also specifically selects others for damnation.	The Pantheon in Rome is consecrated as the Church of the Blessed Virgin and All Martyrs. All Saints' Day becomes a church festival. (early in the seventh century) Isidore of Seville is one of the first to use the term "double predestination."		

59

Date	A. Theology, Doctrine, and Beliefs	B. People/Events	C. Wider Culture	D. Texts
612		Columbanus founds the monastery of Bobbio, a Celtic-style monastery in Lombardy, Italy.		
614		Hilda of Whitby is born. Persians destroy the Church of the Holy Sepulchre and remove the True Cross from Jerusalem.		
615		Saint Columbanus, Irish-Celtic missionary to France and founder of the Bobbio monastery, dies. Deusdedit becomes bishop of Rome.		
616		Saint Ethelbert of Kent dies. He was Augustine of Canterbury's patron.		
619		Boniface V becomes bishop of Rome.		
620			Isidore of Seville. *Etymologiae*. An early medieval encyclopedia attempting to compile all secular and religious knowledge. It becomes a standard reference book for students during the Middle Ages. (ca.)	
622			Muhammad's flees from Mecca to Medina (the Hegira). The year 622 becomes the first year of the Muslim calendar.	
625		Honorius I becomes bishop of Rome. Portable thuribles begin to be used. Before this time, incense was burned in stationary vessels. (early seventh century)		
626		The Church of the Holy Sepulchre is rebuilt after being destroyed by the Persians.		
627	Immaculate Conception of the BVM. The belief that God kept Mary, Jesus' mother, free from the stain of original sin from the moment of her conception. The doctrine is an extension of the patristic image of Mary as "the new Eve" (just as Jesus is "the new Adam"). The feast is kept on December 8.	Aidan, bishop of Lindisfarne founds Lindisfarne as a Celtic monastic center/bishopric. The doctrine of the Immaculate Conception of the BVM is first mentioned. (mid seventh century)		
628				Leonine Sacramentary. A private, unofficial collection of miscellaneous liturgical texts. It probably originated outside Rome. (ca.)

Date	A. Theology, Doctrine, and Beliefs	B. People/Events	C. Wider Culture	D. Texts
630	Holy Cross Day, also known as the Exaltation of the Cross. It commemorates the dedication of the Church of the Holy Sepulchre, which was built over the site of the Crucifixion.	Cuthbert is born. (–687) Heraclius recovers the True Cross from the Persians and brings it back to Jerusalem. Holy Cross Day is first celebrated.	Muhammad conquers Mecca, which becomes the spiritual center of Islam.	
632		Saint Edwin, king of Northumbria, dies in battle.	Muhammad, founder and prophet of Islam, dies. Pagans gain a foothold in England.	
633		Council of Toledo. Isidore presides. • Makes the first unambiguous reference to the crosier, the long crook-shaped staff that is the symbol of the bishop's pastoral authority and responsibility. • Allows poetic text to be used in hymns. These texts do not have to be pulled directly from Scripture.		
637			Arab Muslims conquer Jerusalem.	
638			Jews are permitted to return to Jerusalem, which is under Muslim control. Caliph Omar I creates the new Muslim calendar. He makes the Hegira year 1.	
640		Severinus becomes bishop of Rome. John IV becomes bishop of Rome.		
641			Arabs shut down Alexandria's school and destroy the library.	
642		Theodore I becomes bishop of Rome. Saint Oswald, king of Northumbria and martyr, dies. He established Christianity in his country and was killed in battle by a pagan.		
647	Monothelitism vs. dyothelitism. Christ has two nature, but does that mean he also has two wills (dyothelitism)? Or could he only will what his divine nature knew to be right (monothelitism)?	Byzantine Emperor Constans II issues an imperial edict known as "the Typos" forbidding anyone to assert either monothelitism or dyothelitism.	Arabs conquer Tripoli, Cyprus, Armenia, and North Africa. (–670)	
649		The Lateran Synod in Rome. • Condemns the Typos and monothelitism. Martin I becomes bishop of Rome.	The Byzantine navy retakes Alexandria from the Arabs.	

Date	A. Theology, Doctrine, and Beliefs	B. People/Events	C. Wider Culture	D. Texts
650				Stowe Missal. An adaptation of an early Roman Rite. About eighty percent is Roman text, twenty percent Irish embellishment. (ca.)
651		Saint Aidan, bishop of Lindisfarne, dies. He restored Christianity to Northumbria and the midlands of England after the rise of paganism.	The canon of the Koran is formalized twenty years after Muhammad's death. (–652) The Persian empire falls to Arab Muslims.	
654		Emperor Constans II banishes Pope Martin I for defying the Typos. Eugene I becomes bishop of Rome.		
655		Saint Martin I dies in banishment. He is the last pope honored as a martyr.		
657	Double Monasteries. A medieval Celtic practice in which both men and women are part of a single monastic community. The two genders live on the same compound but in separate accommodations. They worship at the same time but in distinct areas of the church. The community is governed by a single superior, often a woman of high social standing. Key figures: Hilda of Whitby, Etheldreda.	Hilda of Whitby founds Whitby monastery, a Celtic-style double monastery in England. Vitalian becomes bishop of Rome.		
658		Willibrord is born.		
664		Synod of Whitby. Officially, the Roman Rite supersedes the Celtic in the Celtic church. In fact, the transition happens gradually throughout the seventh century. Lindisfarne monastery with Cuthbert as prior, accepts Roman Easter and tonsure.		
670		Theodore of Tarsus, archbishop of Canterbury, sets up English dioceses covering all of England. (after 669)	Arabs attack North Africa.	
672		Gregorian chant is further developed during the tenure of Pope Vitalian. It spreads from the papal court to other ecclesiastical uses. Adeodatus II becomes bishop of Rome. Saint Chad, bishop of Lichfield, dies. He was known for his modesty and holy lifestyle.		

Date	A. Theology, Doctrine, and Beliefs	B. People/Events	C. Wider Culture	D. Texts
673		Bede is born. Etheldreda founds a double monastery in Ely. Within ten years, the site has become a place of pilgrimage. The Council of Hertford, the first all-England synod, firms up ecclesiastical reorganization.		
674		Glass is first used in English church windows.		
675		John of Damascus is born. (ca.) Intinctio panis, the dipping of the communion bread into the consecrated wine, is forbidden by the Third Council of Braga.		
676		Donus becomes bishop of Rome.		
678		Agatho becomes bishop of Rome.		
679		Saint Etheldreda dies. She was queen of East Anglia, but left that life to become a nun. She founded and became abbess of the monastery at Ely.		
680		Boniface is born. Saint Hilda dies. She was the founder and abbess of Whitby, a double monastery. Sixth Ecumenical Council: The Third Council of Constantinople. • Condemns monothelitism. • Anathematizes Pope Honorius I posthumously for being a monothelite.		Caedmon writes some of the earliest vernacular hymns in England. (before) Bangor antiphonary. It contains the earliest extant Latin text of the Gloria in Excelsis Deo. It also contains the oldest manuscript of the Te Deum. (–691)
682		Leo II becomes bishop of Rome.		
683		The monastery at Ely, England, becomes a pilgrimage site.		
684		Benedict II becomes bishop of Rome.		
685		John V becomes bishop of Rome.		
686		Conon becomes bishop of Rome.		
687		Saint Cuthbert, Celtic monk and bishop of Lindisfarne, dies. He was one of the most popular saints of the pre-Conquest Anglo-Saxon church. Sergius I becomes bishop of Rome.		

Date	A. Theology, Doctrine, and Beliefs	B. People/Events	C. Wider Culture	D. Texts
690		Saint Theodore of Tarsus, archbishop of Canterbury, dies. He mediated the controversy between Celtic and Roman Rites and was the first archbishop to whom all of England gave allegiance. Willibrord begins his mission to west Frisia.		
691			The Dome of the Rock is completed in Jerusalem.	
692		The Trullan Synod, also known as the Quinsext Council, completes the fifth and sixth ecumenical councils' work. The Mass of the Presanctified is first recorded. Bishops after the Council of Trullo reserve part of the Eucharistic bread on Holy Thursday to be used the next day as a part of the Mass of the Presanctified.		The Codex Amiatinus, the oldest extant copy of the Latin Vulgate, is copied. (ca.)
698		Carthage falls to Islamic armies. Christianity is steadily suppressed during the next four centuries.		*Lindisfarne Gospels.* Illuminated books produced by monks in Northumberland, England. The monks use patterns and mythic creatures of Viking art, which become Irish and Anglo-Saxon motifs. (–721)
700	From the seventh through the twelfth centuries, nearly all Western monasticism is Benedictine. Private Mass. The Eucharist goes from being a communal meal to being a ritual that effects, in and of itself, a spiritual consequence. Solitary priests begin to say Masses that are financially endowed by parishioners, who wish to apply the spiritual benefits of the Mass to specific causes or people.	The monasteries of northern Europe begin to celebrate private Mass. (ca. eighth century) Christian monastic orders adopt the tonsure almost universally. (ca. eighth century) Lay communion in both kinds begins to disappear from the Western church. (eighth century) The stole is first mentioned as being used in Rome. (eighth century) The unveiling and adoration of the Cross is introduced into the Latin liturgy. (seventh or eighth century) Christians begin to wear black instead of white at funeral services. (ca.)	Waterwheel technology spreads throughout Europe. It is used mostly to drive mills.	Saint Adamnan. *Life of Saint Columba.* A biography of the founder of the Iona monastery and missionary to the Picts. It is a major source of information about the early Irish church. (probably between 697 and 700)
701		During the tenure of Pope Sergius I, the Agnus Dei begins to be sung at the fraction. Previously, it has been part of the litany of saints. (687–) John VI becomes bishop of Rome.		

Date	A. Theology, Doctrine, and Beliefs	B. People/Events	C. Wider Culture	D. Texts
704		Saint Adamnan dies. An Irish abbot and scholar, he was noted for his biography of St. Columba.		
705	Annunciation of the Blessed Virgin Mary (March 25). It is the feast commemorating the Angel Gabriel's announcement to Mary that she would give birth to Jesus.	Observance of the Feast of the Annunciation of the BVM has become universal in the West by the beginning of the eighth century. John VII becomes bishop of Rome.		
708		Sisinnius becomes bishop of Rome. Constantine becomes bishop of Rome.	Stirrups are introduced to Europe.	John of Damascus. *Fount of Wisdom*. In three parts: *Philosophy* is mostly Aristotelian; *Heresy* and *On the Orthodox Faith* are comprehensive summaries of the teachings of the Greek fathers. It has considerable influence on later medieval theologians.
711			The Moors invade Spain. Arabs overthrow the Visigoths. (–713)	
714			Charles Martel begins his reign as leader (Mayor of the Palace) of the Franks. (–741)	
715		Gregory II becomes bishop of Rome.		
716			The Arab empire extends from China to Lisbon.	
718		Pope Gregory II sends Saint Boniface as a missionary to Germany including Thuringia, Bavaria, Friesland, Hesse, and Saxony. (ca.)		
725	Iconoclastic controversy. The often-bloody controversy over whether icons are worthy of devotion. The climate in which iconoclasm arises includes anti-material-world heresies and the increasing influence of Islam. Icons' supporters: Empress Irene, Theodorus Studita, John of Damascus, Pope Gregory III, Council of Nicea VII (787), Empress Theodora. Iconoclasts: Emperors Leo III, Constantine V, and Theophilus; Synod of Hieria; General and Emperor Leo V the Armenian. (–842) Icons. They are highly symbolic paintings of Christ, Mary, or the saints usually rendered in tempera paint on wood. Especially in the East they are believed to be windows into spiritual reality and conduits of divine power. As such, they are often venerated—offered kisses, incense, and bows.	Iconoclastic controversies begin. (–842)		Saint Bede the Venerable. *De Temporum Ratione* (On the Reckoning of Time). Introduces the system of dating events from the birth of Christ and brings A.D. and B.C. into popular usage. Apostles' Creed. A form identical to modern creed appears in the writings of St. Pirminius.

Date	A. Theology, Doctrine, and Beliefs	B. People/Events	C. Wider Culture	D. Texts
726		Byzantine Emperor Leo III prohibits image worship.		
730		Germanus, the pro-icon patriarch of Constantinople, is forced by the state to resign. Relations between Constantinople and Rome deteriorate when the Pope Gregory II begins to resist Emperor Leo III's iconoclastic decrees. (–732)		John of Damascus. *Against the Iconoclasts*. (ca.) Saint Bede the Venerable. *The Martyrology of Bede*. One of the earliest calendars of saints days in Anglo-Saxon England. It contains mostly saints recognized by Rome. (ca.)
731		The pope excommunicates Byzantine Emperor Leo III for his prohibition of icons. Saint Gregory II dies. As pope he was known mainly for his defense of icons and his struggle with Byzantine Emperor Leo III. He was also patron of St. Boniface's work in Germany. Gregory III becomes bishop of Rome. Pope Gregory III excommunicates iconoclasts. Bede traces the origin of the word Easter to *Eastre*, the Anglo-Saxon name of a Teutonic goddess of spring and fertility. Her festival included rabbits and colored eggs. The first known church organ is installed.		Saint Bede the Venerable. *Ecclesiastical History of England*. Its attention to detail and carefully selected informants make it one of the most valuable primary sources for the study of early church history in England.
732			Charles Martel, Christian ruler of the Franks, defeats the Moor leader Abd-ar-Rahman, stopping the Arab invasion at Poitiers.	
733			Ravenna, the seat of Byzantine rule, is captured by Lombards.	
735		Saint Bede the Venerable dies. English Benedictine monk and scholar, recorder of English history. Alcuin is born. The state persecutes pro-icon monks in the East. (730s)		
739		Saint Willibrord, archbishop of Utrecht, dies. He was a missionary to Frisia.	Charles Martel, Frankish ruler, responds to Pope Gregory III's request for military defense of Rome. (–740)	
741		Zacharias becomes bishop of Rome. Fulda (Benedictine) monastery is established. It eventually becomes a manuscript transmission and pilgrimage hub. (744?) All Saints Day is set at 1 November.		

Date	A. Theology, Doctrine, and Beliefs	B. People/Events	C. Wider Culture	D. Texts
742			Charlemagne is born. (ca.)	
743		For the first time, the palms carried in procession on Palm Sunday undergo a blessing before being distributed. (ca.)		
745				Bobbio Missal. A Gallican missal. It shows some Gregorian influence but has an ordinary that is virtually identical to the Irish Stowe Missal.
747		Council of Cloveshoe. English churches are required to conform to Roman liturgy and chant.		
749		Saint John of Damascus dies. Monk, theologian and doctor of the church. (754?–760?)		
750	The target of apologetic literature shifts to upholding Christianity in the face of Islamic advances.	The iconoclastic controversy heats up. Many pro-icon monks are martyred. (750s)		St. John Damascene *Discussion between a Saracen and a Christian*. One of the earliest apologetic works written against Islam.
751		Gregorian chant is introduced to France during the reign of King Pepin. Throughout the eighth century, it spreads through England, France, and Germany. (ca.)	Pepin the Short deposes Childeric, the last Merovingian king, and becomes the first Carolingian king of the Franks. The Carolingian empire lasts until 928.	
752		Stephen II becomes bishop of Rome. A mere four days later, he has a stroke and dies. He is, therefore, sometimes omitted from the succession and his successor (Stephen III) is referred to as Stephen II.		
753		The Synod of Hieria is called by Emperor Constantine V. Its decision to mandate the destruction of all icons was easily arrived at as the patriarchs of Antioch, Jerusalem, Alexandria, and the bishop of Rome were not invited to attend. The monastery at Metz becomes the center for Gregorian chant during the tenure of Bishop Chrodegang.		
754		Catholic Christianity has spread throughout Germany, thanks largely to the work of Boniface. Saint Boniface is martyred while bringing the Gospel to the North Frisians. He was an English Benedictine missionary, known as "the Apostle of Germany." (ca.)	Pepin the Short is crowned king of the Franks by Pope Stephen III. Shortly thereafter, he steps in at the pope's "request" to avert a potential Lombard blockade of Rome.	

Date	A. Theology, Doctrine, and Beliefs	B. People/Events	C. Wider Culture	D. Texts
755				Chrodegang, bishop of Metz. The Rule of St. Chrodegang. A quasi-monastic guide to communal life for canons of the cathedral. It does not require vows of poverty but assumes communal life and mandates the Daily Office.
756		In the early Middle Ages, in remote areas of Europe, the only thing close to a reliable way of getting information from one place to another is to send it between bishops and monasteries.		
757		Paul I becomes bishop of Rome.		
766		Alcuin makes York a learning center. (–782)	Carolingian Renaissance. The revival of arts and classical studies under Charlemagne. It is characterized by an architectural boom and by vast numbers of manuscripts copied in Caroline minuscule, the new form of writing. (–early ninth century)	
767		In the West, the earliest controversy concerning the Filioque clause and the double Procession of the Holy Spirit is at the Synod of Gentilly near Paris.		
768		Stephen IV (III) becomes bishop of Rome. The last of the Celtic churches in Britain conform to Roman practices.	Charlemagne, along with his brother Carloman, becomes king of the Franks.	
770				The English scholar Alcuin compiles the first formal catechism manual. (eighth century)
772		Hadrian I becomes bishop of Rome.		
774		The power of archdeacons within a diocese grows. In large dioceses several archdeacons preside in matters of discipline and administration, each over his own archdiaconate (*archidiaconatus rurales*). (after 774)	After various failed attempts at diplomacy and several battles, Charlemagne restores much of the traditional papal land to Pope Hadrian I and crowns himself king of the Lombards.	
778				*Donation of Constantine.* A bogus document in which Emperor Constantine gives full authority over western parts of the empire to Pope

Date	A. Theology, Doctrine, and Beliefs	B. People/Events	C. Wider Culture	D. Texts
778 con't.				Sylvester in exchange for baptism. The implication is that popes have the authority to crown and depose rulers. (first cited)
779		Benedict of Aniane founds Aniane monastery to be a center of French monastic reform.		
780	Carolingian Renaissance and Reforms. Charlemagne founds schools in every monastery and cathedral in France. Though these schools are not known for their theological innovation, they do foster a conservative transmission of medieval liturgy and theology. Charlemagne also bans simony, legislates Sunday as a day of rest, and educates the clergy. Key figures: Charlemagne, Alcuin, Theodulf of Orléans. (late eighth century)	Byzantine Empress dowager Irene, who is regent to the young Emperor Constantine VI, reverses iconoclastic policy. (–797)	Leo IV, iconoclastic Byzantine emperor, dies.	
781		Christianity reaches China. (before)	Alcuin becomes Charlemagne's royal tutor.	
787	Veneration vs. worship. *Latria* ($\lambda\alpha\tau\rho\varepsilon\iota\alpha$) is worship in the strictest and fullest sense. It is properly due only to God. *Dulia* ($\delta o\hat{v}\lambda\varepsilon\iota\alpha$) is the respect or reverence that may be shown to the saints and their relics, and to icons. *Hyperdulia* ($\hat{v}\pi\varepsilon\rho\delta o\upsilon\lambda\varepsilon\iota\alpha$) is a higher level of *dulia*, which is paid only to the Virgin Mary. The distinction between the *dulia* and *latria* plays a part in both Roman and Eastern piety. Relics. They are the bodily remains of a saint after death or an object that had been in contact with the saint during life. From as early as the second century they are valued. In the eighth century, the weight of church authority is thrown behind their veneration.	Seventh Ecumenical Council: The Second Council of Nicea. • Condemns the iconoclasts. • Declares icons worthy of veneration (*dulia*) but not worship (*latria*). • Anathematizes those who reject the veneration of relics. • Declares no church is to be consecrated without the presence of a relic.		Carolingian court theologians. *Libri Carolini* (Latin: Caroline Books). An independent Frankish theology produced by the brain trust Charlemagne has been fostering since taking over Pavia in 774. One central topic is the current iconoclastic controversy.
789		Charlemagne orders the Roman Rite used throughout the empire. For the first time, Western liturgy and church music are fairly standardized.		*Hadrìanum*. The version of the Gregorian Sacramentary sent by Pope Hadrian to Charlemagne. An incomplete text. (ca.)

Date	A. Theology, Doctrine, and Beliefs	B. People/Events	C. Wider Culture	D. Texts
793		Alcuin becomes abbot of St. Martin of Tours, where he founds a school of calligraphy. The school produces beautiful manuscripts in Carolingian minuscule lettering.	Vikings raid the island of Lindisfarne, off the coast of England. Subsequent raids repeatedly pound eastern and southern England. (through the early ninth century)	
795		Leo III becomes bishop of Rome.		
796		The Synod of Frejus in France defends the insertion of the Filioque clause into the Nicene Creed.	Vikings invade Ireland.	
798	Adoptianism. The belief that Jesus was a human being, who at some point in his life was adopted by God as "Son of God." Key adoptianist: Felix of Urgel. Key opponents: Alcuin, Popes Hadrian I and Leo III. Key text: Alcuin's *Contra Felicem*.	Synod of Rome. • Declares adoptianism heretical.		
800	Allegorical interpretation of the Mass. The Eucharist comes to be seen as a sacred drama in which Jesus Christ is the central character. Each vestment, player, movement, and vessel is given an allegorical meaning. Key figures: Alcuin, Amalarius.	Multiplicity of Masses begins. Priests begin to say private masses several times each day. Endowments are established for that purpose. Side altars spring up in the larger churches. (ca.) Charlemagne suppresses the Gallican Rite in favor of the Roman. Though the edict was official, it was less than universally observed. (ca.) Within Charlemagne's realm, the Benedictine order is the only recognized monastic order. (ca.) Amalarius makes the first clear reference to the *amictus* (amice), a linen cloth the priest wears around his neck while celebrating the Eucharist. (the beginning of the ninth century) The maniple, a strip of silk that the celebrant of the Eucharist wears over his left arm, is almost universal in Western Europe. (beginning of the ninth century) A corporal begins to be used (besides the altar linen) under the bread and wine at the Eucharist. (ca.) The Exultet sung during the Easter vigil takes its modern form. (ninth century) The Nicene Creed begins to be said as a part of the Romano-Frankish Mass.	Pope Leo III crowns Charlemagne the first Augustus of the Holy Roman Empire, initially known as the Empire in the West. In return, Leo gains temporal sovereignty in Rome under the suzerainty of the emperor. The coronation marks the beginning of a distinct western European society. Latin has become a language of scholarship and the church. It is a distinct language from the Romance vernaculars.	*Hucusque.* Charlemagne's supplement to the *Hadrianum.* In it he introduces Gallo-Frankish liturgical texts to Rome. It contains masses, prefaces, episcopal blessings, and a preface explaining the deficiencies of the *Hadrianum.* (ca., possibly as early as 794) Alcuin's Missal. Otherwise known as the Romano-Frankish Missal. The *Hucusque* + the *Hadrianum* = Alcuin's Missal. It becomes the basis for the Missale Romanum. Over half of modern Christendom uses liturgical documents descend from this missal. (ca.) *Book of Kells.* A finely illuminated Gospel manuscript, named after the monastery in which is was produced. It is the finest extant manuscript done in an Irish hand. (ca.)

Date	A. Theology, Doctrine, and Beliefs	B. People/Events	C. Wider Culture	D. Texts
804		Alcuin dies. Abbot, liturgist, and Charlemagne's tutor, he was the leader of the Carolingian renaissance.		
806		The Norse sack Iona monastery.		
810		Duns (John) Scotus Erigena is born. (ca.)	Arabs obtain Greek science and philosophy. Arab culture flourishes. (throughout the ninth century)	
813		The Synod of Mainz mandates that priests in the Frankish empire wear stoles, long strips of cloth worn around the neck as a symbol of their clerical office.		
814		The second iconoclastic controversy begins. (–842) Byzantine Emperor Leo V begins to remove icons from the churches. He exiles, imprisons, or executes icons' chief defenders. (–842)	Charlemagne, first emperor of the Holy Roman Empire, dies.	Benedict of Aniane. *Codex regularum monasticarum et canonicarum* (Latin: Book of Monastic and Canonical Rules). A collection of all known monastic rules. (early ninth century) Einhard. *Life of Charlemagne.* A stylistically innovative account of the emperor's life, exploits, and character. (early ninth century)
816		Saint Leo III, pope, dies. He was a builder of churches in Rome and a colleague of Charlemagne. Stephen V (IV) becomes bishop of Rome. English bishops are required to date any acts they write by the era of the Incarnation.		
817		Paschal I becomes bishop of Rome.		
818		Rabamus Maurus records that the alb, a white, long-sleeved, full-length garment, is an essential part of a priest's Eucharistic vestments.		
821		Saint Benedict of Aniane, Benedictine monk and monastic reformer, dies.		
824		Eugene II becomes bishop of Rome.		
825		In the ninth century the Filioque clause is commonly used throughout the Frankish empire and by Western monks at holy sites in the East. The invaders destroy monasteries, libraries, and churches. Christianity barely survives. (early ninth century)		

Date	A. Theology, Doctrine, and Beliefs	B. People/Events	C. Wider Culture	D. Texts
826		Saint Theodore (Theodorus Studita) dies. He was the leader of the pro-icon monks during the second iconoclastic controversy.		
827		Valentine becomes bishop of Rome. Gregory IV becomes bishop of Rome.		
830		Anskar founds the first Christian church in Sweden.		
831				Paschasius Radbertus. *On the Body and Blood of Our Lord.* A doctrinal monograph written for Saxon monks. It maintains that the body and blood of the Eucharist are the same as that born of Mary and are the means by which people are incorporated into the mystical church.
835		Pope Gregory IV orders universal observance of All-Saints' Day. Uncial script, the formal all-capital orthography used for literary works begins to be replaced by minuscule, cursive, script in the copying of biblical manuscripts. (ca.)		
842	Theology of Duns (John) Scotus Erigena. Can the true reality of God be expressed in human language? Duns Scotus Erigena says "no." He maintains that the best language can do is express paradox. The creative tension in the paradox launches us toward the mystery of God. In his own time, Erigena was considered brilliant. Some 400 years later he was condemned.	Theodora, regent for her young son, the emperor, brings icons back to the empire. (–843)		
843			Treaty of Verdun. The Holy Roman Empire is split between Charlemagne's three grandsons.	
844		Sergius II becomes bishop of Rome.		
845			Norse invaders take Paris.	
846			Arabs sack Rome.	
847		Leo IV becomes bishop of Rome.		
848		Alfred the Great is born. The Synod of Mainz condemns Gottschalk, in part for his extreme teaching on predestination. He maintains that		

Date	A. Theology, Doctrine, and Beliefs	B. People/Events	C. Wider Culture	D. Texts
848 con't.		God predestines some for hell, some for blessedness, though he predestines none specifically to sin.		
850	Confirmation begins to be seen as conferring a distinct grace (separate from baptism). The grace given through confirmation is the assistance of the Holy Spirit in resisting evil. Though not officially authorized, this doctrine gains widespread acceptance. (ca.) Feast of the Transfiguration of Christ. It commemorates the vision of the glory of the Lord recounted in Matthew 17:1–13. It is typically celebrated on August 6.	The Feast of the Transfiguration of Christ is first mentioned. Pope Leo IV gives detailed instructions to priests on how to sign the chalice and the Host with the sign of the cross during the Eucharist. He maintains that improper technique makes the gesture invalid. (middle of the ninth century) The custom of sprinkling the congregation with holy water begins. (middle of the ninth century) The earliest record in the Western church of incensing of the altar, celebrant, and people dates to the mid ninth century. (ca.) Polyphony begins to develop in liturgical chant. The earliest form is organum (a single line of chant accompanied by a "harmony" line sung at an unvarying fourth or fifth below the melody line). (mid ninth century through ca. 1250)	The invention of the moldboard plow, harness, and horseshoe increases arable land. (ninth century)	*Admonitio Synodalis* (Latin: Synodal Admonition). Mandates that those who say Mass must wear amice, alb, stole, maniple and chasuble. (ninth century?)
851		Danes sack Canterbury Cathedral.	The crossbow begins to be used in France.	
854		Anskar converts Erik, king of Jutland (Denmark), to Christianity.		
855		Benedict III becomes bishop of Rome. According to a thirteenth century legend, which may have some foundation in reality, a woman named Joan becomes pope. She had been living as a man for some time and had distinguished herself as a scholar before taking the office. (ca.)		
858		Nicholas I becomes bishop of Rome. Photius, patriarch of Constantinople, denies the Procession of Holy Spirit from the Son, and opposes the Filioque clause.		
859			Vikings reach the Mediterranean.	

Date	A. Theology, Doctrine, and Beliefs	B. People/Events	C. Wider Culture	D. Texts
862		Cyril and Methodius are sent as missionaries to the Slavs. Cyril invents the Cyrillic/Glagolitic script to aid in his teaching/celebrating in the vernacular. Saint Swithun dies. He was bishop of Winchester during the earliest of the Viking invasions.		
865		Saint Anskar, "Apostle to the North," dies. He was a missionary to the Scandinavians.		
867		Pope Nicholas I calls Cyril and Methodius to Rome to account for their Slavonic vernacular liturgy. Nicholas dies before they reached Rome, and Pope Hadrian II, his successor, approves the Slavonic liturgy. (ca.) Saint Nicholas I, pope, known as "Nicholas the Great," dies.		
869		Saint Cyril, "Apostle to the Slavs," dies. With his brother Methodius, he was missionary to Monrovia and co-translator of the Slavonic liturgy. Viking invaders martyr Saint Edmund, king of East Anglia, when he refuses to renounce his faith or serve as a puppet ruler. Many monasteries are in ruins. Those still operational are often under lay control and are used as money-makers. (late ninth century) The Eighth Ecumenical Council: The Fourth Council of Constantinople (by Western reckoning) • Formally deposes Photius, patriarch of Constantinople and principal instigator of the ninth-century schism between the Eastern and Western church.		
870		The patriarch of Constantinople declares independence from Rome allegedly because of differences over the Filioque. The Danes destroy the monastery at Ely.		
872		John VIII becomes bishop of Rome.		

Date	A. Theology, Doctrine, and Beliefs	B. People/Events	C. Wider Culture	D. Texts
877		Duns (John) Scotus Erigena dies. Celtic philosopher and theologian.		
878		Many Danes convert to Christianity. Churches and monasteries begin to be rebuilt. (after 878 into the late ninth century) Alfred the Great negotiates a treaty with Guthrum to keep some of England English and Christian.		
879		The pope and the patriarch of Constantinople excommunicate each other.		
880		Works of Bede, Boethius, Gregory, etc., are translated into the West Saxon vernacular by Alfred and his scholars. (late ninth century)		Alfred, king of the West Saxons, translates Boethius *De Consolatione Philosophiae* (Latin: Concerning the Comfort of Philosophy).
882		Marinus I becomes bishop of Rome. Hincmar, archbishop of Reims and practical theologian, considers marriage a sacrament. (before 882)		
884		Hadrian III becomes bishop of Rome. Methodius dies. With his brother Cyril, he was missionary to Monrovia and co-translator of the Slavonic liturgy.		
885		Stephen VI (V) becomes bishop of Rome.		
891		Formosus becomes bishop of Rome.		
896		Boniface VI becomes bishop of Rome. Stephen VII (VI) becomes bishop of Rome.		
897		Romanus becomes bishop of Rome. Theodore II becomes bishop of Rome.		
898		John IX becomes bishop of Rome.		
899		Alfred the Great, king of the West Saxons, dies. He halted the Dane invasion, converted the Danish leader, and rebuilt his country.		

Date	A. Theology, Doctrine, and Beliefs	B. People/Events	C. Wider Culture	D. Texts
900	During the tenth century, society in Western Europe is at its lowest ebb. Invasions continue to drain resources and stifle trade. The only social structure is that of numerous small kingdoms with virtually no communication between them. Travel is dangerous; formal education is sparse; and the population, living hand to mouth, shrinks. Only the monasteries and bishoprics preserve the knowledge of former times. Only they can get messages from one place to another.	Benedict IV becomes bishop of Rome. Monastic garb commonly includes a wide-sleeved robe over a tunic and scapular. Over the robe is a detachable hood called a cowl. (ca.) The episcopal ring becomes a commonly used emblem of the bishop's office. (ca.) Organum, in which sections of the liturgy are sung polyphonically by soloists, begins to develop. (ca.)	Classic Mayan civilization falls. (ca.) Spain begins to drive out the Moors. (ca.) Vikings discover Greenland. (ca.)	
903		Leo V becomes bishop of Rome.		
904		Sergius III becomes bishop of Rome.		
906		When the Saracens invade, the monks of Novalaise carry a library of six thousand manuscripts to Turin. Libraries containing over a thousand books are not uncommon in the larger Western monasteries.		
909		Dunstan is born. The first Cluniac monastic house, the monastery at Cluny, is formed. The Cluniac order is formed as a return to the strict Benedictine Rule.		
911		Anastasius III becomes bishop of Rome.		
913		Lando becomes bishop of Rome.		
914		John X becomes bishop of Rome.		
917			The king of Bulgaria becomes "tsar."	
919			The Saxon or Ottonian house begins its reign in Germany. (–1024)	
922		Saint Oswald, bishop of Worcester and monastic reformer, dies.		
925				*Dialogue of the Three Maries and the Angel.* First known Easter play.
927		The patriarchate of Bulgaria is founded.		
928		Stephen VIII (VII) becomes bishop of Rome. Leo VI becomes bishop of Rome.	End of the Carolingian empire.	

Date	A. Theology, Doctrine, and Beliefs	B. People/Events	C. Wider Culture	D. Texts
929		Saint Wenceslas, duke of Bohemia, is killed by his family for listening to Christian counselors on matters of state. His brother later transfers his relics to Prague where they become a focus of pilgrimage.		
931		John XI becomes bishop of Rome.		
935			Odo of Cluny. *Enchiridion musices.* Develops a method that uses letters to notate musical pitch. The method is a standard throughout the medieval era. (ca.)	
936		Leo VII becomes bishop of Rome.		
939		Stephen IX (VIII) becomes bishop of Rome.		
940		Dunstan, a Benedictine abbot at the time, expands the school and abbey at Glastonbury. The school becomes famous under his administration.		
942		Marinus II becomes bishop of Rome.	Saadia ben Joseph, Babylonian Jewish scholar dies. He was a leading figure in medieval Judaism.	
946		Apapitus II becomes bishop of Rome.		
948		Dunstan earns the title "Patron and Father of the Monks of Medieval England" by almost singlehandedly supervising the post-Viking rebuilding in the mid-to-late tenth century.		
950		Maniples, strips of silk worn over the left arm by Eucharistic ministers, become increasingly ornate, adorned with gold or silver. (ninth century) Miters are worn by bishops in Rome. (mid tenth century) Winchester Cathedral installs an organ with twenty-six bellows and four hundred pipes. (ca.) Olga, ruler of Russia, converts to Christianity.		
954		Alphege is born.		
955		John XII becomes bishop of Rome. Dunstan is banished from England under King Edwy, who doesn't like Dunstan's reproving his conduct.		

Date	A. Theology, Doctrine, and Beliefs	B. People/Events	C. Wider Culture	D. Texts
959		Dunstan becomes archbishop of Canterbury. At the time he is the most influential figure in England. He introduces the Benedictine Rule to reform the monastic system. He fosters education and rebuilds churches. Organs, until this time a secular instrument, begin to appear in the larger churches of England. (tenth century, during the tenure of Dunstan)		
962			Pope John XII crowns the King of Germany, Otto, to be Holy Roman Emperor, thus reinaugurating the Holy Roman Empire.	
963		Leo VIII becomes bishop of Rome.		
964		Benedict V becomes bishop of Rome.		
965		Saint Bruno of Cologne, "Bruno the Great" dies. Monastic reformer, writer, and scholar, he was the brother of Otto I, Holy Roman emperor. John XIII becomes bishop of Rome.		
970		The monastery at Ely, formerly a double monastery, is rebuilt for monks only.		*Regularis Concordia* (Latin: Rule of Concord). A "customary" regulating the life of all English monks. It is based on the Rule of St. Benedict, with adaptations to English life. It is probably the work of Bishop Ethelwold, a leader of the monastic reform movement of the tenth century. (ca.)
973		Benedict VI becomes bishop of Rome.		
974		Benedict VII becomes bishop of Rome.		
975			Arabic arithmetic is brought to Europe. (ca.)	
979		Glass-workers develop a new process for making stained glass. Metallic pigments are fused into the glass, making the painting as durable as the glass itself. It is first used at the Church of St. Denis at Paris. Soon colored picture windows are considered "necessary" in all church buildings.		

Date	A. Theology, Doctrine, and Beliefs	B. People/Events	C. Wider Culture	D. Texts
983		John XIV becomes bishop of Rome. Adalbert became bishop of Prague.		
984		Saint Ethelwold, bishop of Winchester, dies. He was a leader of the monastic reform movement and helped rebuild the English church after the Danish invasions.		
985		John XV becomes bishop of Rome.		
987			France's Capetians begin their rule. (–1328)	
988		Saint Dunstan, archbishop of Canterbury, dies. English statesman and reformer, he was probably the most powerful man in the country during the rebuilding after the Danish invasions. He compiled a coronation rite for King Edgar that survives in part in the modern British rite. He is patron saint of armorers, blacksmiths, goldsmiths, locksmiths, and musicians. Prince Vladimir establishes Christianity as the state religion of Russia. (ca.)		
989		Vladimir, Apostle to the Russians, begins to spread Christianity throughout Kiev and White Russia, often by physical compulsion.		
990			Feudalism becomes a political as well as military institution. "Fief" begins to be used instead of "benefice." A vassal's estate becomes hereditary. (late tenth century)	
993		Earliest official canonization: Pope John XV declares Ulric, bishop of Augsburg, a saint.		
996		Gregory V becomes bishop of Rome.		
997		Saint Adalbert is martyred.		
998	All Souls' Day. It is a memorial, a commemoration of the souls of the faithful departed, celebrated on November 2.	All Souls' Day is first instituted in the monasteries of Cluny, France, as a day for prayers and almsgiving to assist souls in purgatory.		Saint Aelfric. *Lives of the Saints*. An Old English collection of sermons, mostly translated from Latin.
999		Silvester II becomes bishop of Rome. The Conception of Mary is celebrated in several countries. (before the eleventh century)		

Date	A. Theology, Doctrine, and Beliefs	B. People/Events	C. Wider Culture	D. Texts
999 con't.		Minuscule script has replaced uncial script in the copying of biblical manuscripts. (by the end of the tenth century)		
1000		Tunics are used universally by subdeacons. In the eleventh and twelfth centuries manuscript copying becomes a central part of monastic life. Each monastery contains a *scriptorium* where copyists copy and illuminate manuscripts. Intinction or *Intinctio panis*, the dipping of the communion bread into the consecrated wine, becomes common in the early eleventh century. The larger sign of the cross—forehead, chest, shoulders—begins to be used in monasteries. (tenth century)	The abacus is introduced to Europe. Literacy begins to reemerge in Europe. *Beowulf*. A heroic epic poem written in Old English. The date is uncertain, but is probably some time in the eighth century. (oldest extant manuscript) Leif Ericsson discovers North America, calls it "Vineland." The early Middle Ages end, and the high Middle Ages begin. Romanesque architecture. Architecture of western Europe from about 1000 to the rise of the gothic style. It is characterized by separate rectangular bays, round arches, massive stone structure.	The Agnus Dei ("O Lamb of God") takes its modern form: the formula is repeated three times, the first two followed by "have mercy on us" and the third by "grant us peace." (ca.) The Salve Regina ("Hail Holy Queen"), one of the oldest Marian antiphons, is written. (ca.) The dismissal form "Let us bless the Lord/Thanks be to God" (the *Benedicamus Domino*) begins to be used. (ca.)
1003		John XVII becomes bishop of Rome. John XVIII becomes bishop of Rome.		
1004	Feast of the Nativity of the Blessed Virgin (September 8). It commemorates the birth of Mary as recorded in the apocryphal *Book of James*.	The Feast of the Nativity of the BVM becomes universal in the West.		
1009		Islamic soldiers sack the Holy Sepulchre. Sergius IV becomes bishop of Rome. Wulfstan is born.	Danes attack London.	
1012		Saint Alphege, archbishop of Canterbury, dies. He is murdered when he refuses ransom to be paid to his Danish captors. The first systematic persecution of heretics in Germany begins. Benedict VIII becomes bishop of Rome.		
1013			Canute II, Viking leader, completes the Danish conquest of England.	
1014		The Roman church begins the practice of reciting the Nicene Creed during the Mass.	Brian Boru retakes Ireland from the Vikings. Norse rule ends in Ireland.	

Date	A. Theology, Doctrine, and Beliefs	B. People/Events	C. Wider Culture	D. Texts
1016			Canute II, Viking leader, becomes king of England.	
1020		Saint Aelfric dies. English abbot, writer, and grammarian. (ca.)		
1022		Simeon, the New Theologian, dies. He is considered to be the greatest of the Byzantine mystical writers. He emphasized the centrality of Christ, divine light, and the Eucharist. Burning becomes a common penalty for severe heresy. The penalty is typically carried out by the state, not the church.		
1024		John XIX becomes bishop of Rome.	End of the Saxon house in Germany. The Salian house begins its reign. (–1137)	
1025		Norway is converted at the point of a sword. (early eleventh century) Guido D'Arezzo, a Benedictine monk, introduces a four-line system for musical notation, allowing church music to go beyond simple organum—a single line of chant accompanied by a harmony line sung at a unvarying fourth or fifth below the melody line. Notation of more complex polyphony becomes possible. (ca.)		
1027		The Council of Elne establishes the "Truce of God," prohibiting battle on Sunday. Later rulings also prohibit it during Advent and Lent.		
1028		King Olaf II establishes Christianity in Norway.		
1030		The first reliable knowledge of the Feast of the Immaculate Conception is in England.		The two phrases "*Ave Maria*" ("Hail Mary") and "*benedicta tu in mulieribus et benedictus fructus ventris tui*" ("blessed are you among women and blessed is the fruit of your womb.") are recited together as a single prayer. (earliest extant evidence)
1032		Benedict IX becomes bishop of Rome. He is a lay person when elected. He serves from 1032–1044; March through May 1045; and 1047–1048. During the interim periods he (and his family's political dynasty) are out of power but not officially deposed.		

Date	A. Theology, Doctrine, and Beliefs	B. People/Events	C. Wider Culture	D. Texts
1033		Anselm of Canterbury is born.		
1037			Avicenna dies. His Neoplatonic interpretation of Aristotle greatly influenced medieval thought, including that of Thomas Aquinas. His medical writings live for centuries.	
1038		The term *Cristes Maesse*, Old English for "Christmas," first appears.		
1040			Macbeth, chief of the Scottish province of Moray, murders Duncan, king of Scotland, (or possibly kills him in battle) and takes the throne.	
1043		Michael Cerularius, patriarch of Constantinople, closes Latin churches in the city because of the Latins' use of unleavened bread in the Eucharist.		
1045		Silvester III becomes bishop of Rome. Margaret of Scotland is born. Gregory VI becomes bishop of Rome.		
1046		Clement II becomes bishop of Rome.		
1047		Benedict IX returns to power as bishop of Rome.		
1048		Damasus II becomes bishop of Rome.		
1049		Leo IX becomes bishop of Rome. Bishops' wearing miters is referred to specifically in one of Pope Leo IX's bulls.		
1050		The Trisagion ("Holy, Holy, Holy...") is introduced to the Good Friday liturgy as a refrain to be sung during the veneration of the cross. (mid eleventh century) The Roman church claims exclusive jurisdiction over marriage. (eleventh century) The Augustinian Canons (also known as the Black Canons or the Canon Regular) are formed as a group of clerks living communally and within vows of poverty, celibacy, and obedience. (ca.)	Chainmail begins to be used in Europe. (ca.) Astrolabes arrive in Europe. The European obsession with witch-hunting begins. (ca.) The High Middle ages begin during the middle of the eleventh century. Trade, education, and literacy increase. The Roman church becomes a powerful centralized force. (ca.–1350)	The Ave Maria becomes a common popular form of devotion. (mid eleventh century)

Date	A. Theology, Doctrine, and Beliefs	B. People/Events	C. Wider Culture	D. Texts
1054	After the Great Schism, the East and West part theological company. In the East, theology remains a contemplation of the mystery of God. In the West it also becomes an application of Christian principles to practical situations. Medieval Church. The Western church is strong and has a single central authority. Great theologians consolidate prior theology and work out fine points of doctrine. Monastic orders are centers of teaching and scholarship. (–1378)	Cardinal Humbert of Silva Candida, is sent to Constantinople from Rome to deal with the impending East-West schism. He ends up excommunicating the patriarch and his colleagues. The East-West Schism, sometimes called "the Great Schism." It is the end of the last official, long-term unity between the Eastern and Western churches. The ostensive reason is the Filioque clause, though differences of opinion on leavened vs. unleavened Eucharistic bread, as well as a language barrier and long-standing, deep grudges play roles.		
1055		Victor II becomes bishop of Rome.		
1057		Stephen X (IX) becomes bishop of Rome.		
1058		Nicholas II becomes bishop of Rome.		
1059	Investiture Controversy. It is a major church-state dispute over whether lay princes have the authority to install bishops and abbots in their offices. Specifically at issue is whether the prince has the right to bestow the symbols of episcopal authority, the ring and staff. It begins early in the Middle Ages. In England, it settles down with the Concordat of Worms.	The Augustinian Canons receive official approval from the Lateran Synod. The Investiture Controversy becomes a focal point.		
1061		Alexander II becomes bishop of Rome.		
1065		Westminster Abbey is consecrated.		
1066			William of Normandy, "William the Conqueror," defeats the last Saxon king at the Battle of Hastings. He is crowned King William I of England. The House of Normandy begins its reign in England. Middle English Period. After the Norman-French conquest, French becomes the language of government and popular literature. Over the next 400 years, it has a profound effect on the structure and vocabulary of English. (–1485)	
1067		Fire destroys Canterbury Cathedral.		

Date	A. Theology, Doctrine, and Beliefs	B. People/Events	C. Wider Culture	D. Texts
1072		Saint Peter Damian dies. Doctor of the church, bishop, monk, and cardinal.		
1073		Gregory VII becomes pope. Papal power is at its greatest during his pontificate. The title "pope" is reserved exclusively for the bishop of Rome.		
1074		Clerical celibacy is mandated. Married priests are excommunicated.		
1075		The Roman Synod condemns simony (the practice of paying for ordination) and promotes clerical celibacy. Pope Gregory VII forbids all lay investiture. Holy Roman Emperor Henry IV takes vehement exception to this ruling. The pope and emperor exchange a series of depositions and excommunications that last until Gregory's death in 1085.		Pope Gregory VII. *Dictatus Papæ* (Dictates of the Pope). Twenty-seven propositions outlining the spiritual and temporal prerogatives of the papacy at its zenith. It is part of Gregory's attempt to create a theocracy.
1076		Pope Gregory VII confronts Emperor Henry IV. Henry calls for Gregory's resignation. Gregory deposes and bans Henry, and releases his subjects from fealty.		
1077		Gregory VII humiliates Henry IV at Canossa. Henry recants and is reinstated. One of the main volleys in the Investiture Controversy. The first Cluniac house in England is formed.		
1078	Realism. One variant of Scholasticism (the contrary variant being Nominalism). It is built on Plato's theory of Forms. Realism argues that universals or *Forms* are what are truly "real" with particular tangible things being mere shadows of this reality. Key figure: Anselm of Canterbury. Ontological argument for the existence of God. The argument that the *actuality* of God's existence is logically presupposed by the *concept* of God residing in the human mind. Key figure: Anselm of Canterbury.			Anselm of Canterbury. *Proslogion*. Proof of God's existence using the ontological argument. (–1079) Anselm of Canterbury. *Monologion*. Establishes the existence of God from notions of Goodness and Truth. With Anselm's other writings, it lays the foundation for Scholasticism. (–1079)

Date	A. Theology, Doctrine, and Beliefs	B. People/Events	C. Wider Culture	D. Texts
1079	Berengarian controversy. Berengar of Tours asserts the Real Presence of Christ in the Eucharist but denies any material change to the elements. Rome asserts transubstantiation: that there is a change in the elements.	Transubstantiation receives papal authority during the Berengarian controversy. Peter Abelard is born.		
1080	Nominalism. One variant of Scholastic philosophy (the contrary variant being Realism). It maintains that only individual, concrete objects are "real." The universals, forms, and ideas used to classify those particular objects are not imperceptible substances but are rather mere labels or names. Key figures: Roscelin, William of Ockham (ca. late eleventh and twelfth centuries)			
1084	Carthusian order. It is a strict, contemplative order for men. Monks live separately, each in his own cell, spending the days in silence and silent prayer. They join with other members of the order for Mass, the Daily Office, and for meals on feast days. Founder: St. Bruno.	Saint Bruno founds the Carthusians in response to the decadence of his time. He and six companions retreat to a mountain valley north of Grenoble to begin the order.		
1085		Pope Gregory VII prescribes the Ember Days for the entire church. They are set at the Wednesday, Friday, and Saturday after the Feast of Santa Lucia (13 December), after Ash Wednesday, after Whitsunday, and after Exaltation of the Cross (14 September). (before 1085) Saint Gregory VII, pope (also known as Hildebrand), dies. Medieval church reformer. He is best known for his part in the Investiture Controversy, especially his conflict with Emperor Henry IV, which Gregory is thought to have lost. He centralized authority in the papacy and fostered the distinction between the roles of the clergy and those of the laity. The Mozarabic Rite is supplanted by the Roman Rite. The Mozarabic Rite, the traditional Eucharistic form of the Iberian Peninsula, is allowed to remain only in a few of the oldest churches.	Christians seize the Arab citadel of Toledo and begin the reconquest of Spain. Literature, navigational equipment, mathematics come to Christian Europe.	

Date	A. Theology, Doctrine, and Beliefs	B. People/Events	C. Wider Culture	D. Texts
1086		Victor III becomes pope.	*Domesday Book.* A census commissioned by William the Conqueror to assess the taxation potential of his lands. It is a good window on the ruling class of the early Norman period.	
1088		Urban II becomes pope.	The University of Bologna, the first university in the world, is founded.	
1090		The *Micrologus*, an eleventh century Roman Mass book, is one of the earliest texts to describe the practice of omitting the Gloria in Excelsis Deo ("Glory be to God on High") during Advent and Septuagesima (the third Sunday before Lent). (ca.) Bernard of Clairvaux is born.		
1091		Synod of Benevento. The ceremony of placing ashes on the forehead becomes universal. Ash Wednesday is generally observed by both clergy and laity.		
1093		Saint Margaret, queen of Scotland, dies. Church reformer and conscientious mother. Anselm is consecrated archbishop of Canterbury.		
1095	Crusader religion. The beliefs of the common crusader tend to be doctrinally rudimentary. At their center are a powerful, aggressive God and soldier saints like George and Demetrius, whom crusaders sometimes raise to the place of tribal deities.	Saint Wulfstan, bishop of Worcester, dies. He eased the transition between Anglo-Saxon and Anglo-Norman Christianity. Pope Urban II at the Council of Clermont proclaims a remission of all penances for crusaders fighting in the Crusade to liberate Jerusalem. The Crusades begin formally Tuesday, November 27, 1095. First Crusade. It is declared to repulse Turkish pressure on the Eastern empire and to make safe pilgrimage to Jerusalem possible. Crusaders take Jerusalem and Antioch, slaughtering Jews and Muslims in the process. Key figures: Godfrey of Bouillon, Pope Urban II. (–1099)		
1096		The Fiasco of Peter the Hermit. Peter leads a band of mostly unarmed rural "Crusaders" to a Turkish slaughter while he disappears to Constantinople.		

Date	A. Theology, Doctrine, and Beliefs	B. People/Events	C. Wider Culture	D. Texts
1097		The first Crusade arrives in Constantinople.		
1098	Satisfaction theory of the atonement. The belief that sin is an infinitely great offense against God. Only an infinite being, Christ, could offer recompense. The atonement is a debt paid by Christ to God the Father. Key figure: Anselm of Canterbury.	The Cistercian order is founded in the monastery of Citeaux as a stricter, more primitive and ascetic Benedictinism.		Anselm of Canterbury. *Cur Deus homo?* (Why God became Human) A treatise proposing the "satisfaction theory of the atonement." It is one of the most influential theological works ever written.
	Cistercian order. Also known as the white Monks, they follow an extremely strict Benedictine rule. They live in remote communal houses, spend their day in silence, prayer, and labor (usually farming). Their habits, vestments, and Eucharistic vessels are made from simple, inexpensive materials, and they live a life of poverty, both individual and communal. Founder: Robert of Molesme. Key figure: Bernard of Clairvaux.	Hildegard of Bingen is born.		
1099		Crusaders capture Jerusalem.	Chivalry. The mingling of religious and military fervor that is the basis of chivalry begins with the Crusaders. After 1099 the Crusaders maintain a standing army in Jerusalem to prevent recapture of the city. Military orders are formed that vow perpetual warfare against the infidels as their fourth monastic vow.	
		The Order of Fontevrault is founded. Monks and nuns live under a modified Benedictine Rule.		
		In Rome priests may say the Gloria in Excelsis Deo during any mass. Prior to this time, priests only recited it on Easter. Recitation at any other time was the prerogative of the bishop. (end of the eleventh century)		
		Paschal II becomes pope.		
1100		Peter Lombard is born.	Paper is introduced to Europe and begins to be used for manuscripts. (during the twelfth century)	
		Private daily Mass is common.		
		Anselm of Canterbury clashes with King Henry I of England over investiture. Anselm is exiled until 1106.		
		Two corporals are used at the altar: One is placed under the chalice and Host. The other, the precursor of the pall, is folded and used as a cover for the chalice.		
		Baldwin becomes king of Jerusalem and defender of the Holy Sepulchre. (crowned Christmas Day)		
		The surplice becomes a part of the distinctive vestments of the lower clerical orders. (twelfth century)		

Date	A. Theology, Doctrine, and Beliefs	B. People/Events	C. Wider Culture	D. Texts
1101		Saint Bruno the Carthusian dies. German monk, advisor to Pope Urban II, founder of the Carthusian monastic order.		
1104		Lund, Sweden, receives metropolitical rank.		
1105			Solomon ben Isaac, influential Jewish commentator, dies. He was also known as Rashi (from Rabbi Shlomo Itzhaqi). His commentaries on the Bible and Talmud have had a lasting influence on Jewish thought to the present day. Provençal troubadours sing of chivalry and day-to-day life. Theirs is some of the first vernacular, secular musical poetry. (early twelfth century)	
1106	Conceptualism. A compromise between realism and nominalism that proposes that universals exist *in* particular things as properties and *outside* of things as concepts in the mind. Key figure: Peter Abelard.			Peter Abelard. *Sic et Non* (Yes and No). Account of some of the apparently contradictory statements of the Bible and the Fathers. Published to create discussion and clarification, it meets instead with opposition. The work has a profound influence on the Scholastic method. (early twelfth century)
1108				Bernard of Cluny. *De Contemptu Mundi* (Contempt of the World). A three-thousand-line poem on monastic abuses in light of life's transitoriness. It is a source of many hymns. (early twelfth century)
1109		Saint Hugh, abbot of Cluny, dies. He was abbot of the most influential monastery in Europe. Saint Anselm, archbishop of Canterbury, dies. One of the earliest and most important Scholastics, he is known for his ontological argument for the existence of God, and for his satisfaction theory of the Atonement.	The oldest extant paper manuscript in Europe is copied.	
1110			John Cotton. *Musica*. Describes the harmonic system of the medieval period. It is based on four intervals: unison, octave, fourths, and fifths.	

Date	A. Theology, Doctrine, and Beliefs	B. People/Events	C. Wider Culture	D. Texts
1113		The Abbey of St. Victor in Paris is built. It is the house of the Victorines, Canons Regular, who achieve great fame as theologians, poets, and mystics. The Knights of St. John (Hospitallers) are founded to care for pilgrims to Jerusalem.		
1115	Can the existence of God be postulated on the basis of natural reason? Anselm proposed an ontological argument for the existence of God, maintaining "God is that which nothing greater can be thought." Eastern theology is more likely to describe God as that which cannot be thought. Cistercian piety (Bernard of Clairvaux) holds that natural reason detracts from the merit of faith.	Saint Bernard of Clairvaux becomes abbot of the new monastery of Clairvaux. Under his leadership it becomes the most prominent house of the Cistercian order. The Gospel is read on the right, the Epistle on the left, relative to the position of the bishop's cathedra. (during the time of Ivo, bishop of Chartres, ca. 1090–)		
1118		The Order of Knights Templar is formed to protect pilgrims in the Holy Land. Thomas a Becket is born. Gelasius II becomes pope. Baldwin I, king of Jerusalem, dies.		
1119		Callistus II becomes pope.		Charter of Charity (Carta Caritatis). It is the constitution of the Cistercian order, so named to contrast it to the obligatory charters of the Cluniac order. It is thought to be largely the work of Saint Stephen Harding, third abbot of Cîteaux.
1120		The Order of Premonstratensian Canons, an austere Augustinian order, is founded. They are also known as the Norbertines or White Canons.		
1122		The Concordat of Worms settles the Investiture Controversy. The Concordat is between Pope Callistus II and Holy Roman Emperor Henry V. Their compromise: The church elects bishops and bestows the ring and staff. The emperor confers lands and revenues attached to the bishopric and a scepter, a symbol of authority without spiritual connotations.		

Date	A. Theology, Doctrine, and Beliefs	B. People/Events	C. Wider Culture	D. Texts
1123		Ninth Ecumenical Council: The First Lateran Council. • Abolishes lay princes' right to bestow the ring and crosier upon ecclesiastical benefices. • Addresses recovery of the Holy Land. • Decides that a priest who is not married may not marry after ordination.		
1124		Honorius II becomes pope.		
1125		The earliest mention of different colors being used for the different liturgical seasons is by the Augustinian Canons in Jerusalem. (ca.)		
1126		Premonstratensian Canons (Norbertines) receives papal approbation.		
1127		The term "secular clergy" is first used to distinguish clergy attached to a diocese from those attached to monastic orders. (twelfth century)		Bernard of Clairvaux. *De Diligendo Deo* (The Love of God). It is one of the finest works of the Western Christian mystical/contemplative tradition. It speaks of the soul's and God's desire for one another.
1128		The Order of Knights Templars obtains recognition from the church.		
1130		More than ninety monasteries are founded under the auspices of Bernard and the monastery at Clairvaux. (–1145) Innocent II becomes pope. Canterbury Cathedral, rebuilt after a fire, is consecrated.		
1135		Peter the Venerable decrees the Salve Regina be sung processionally on certain feasts. (ca.)	A fraternity of translators is set up in Toledo to translate captured Arabic manuscripts into Latin. Throughout the twelfth century, the main treatises of Aristotle are translated into Latin from Greek and Arabic. The House of Blois begins its reign in England.	
1136				Peter Abelard. *History of My Misfortunes.* In this autobiography, Abelard, a brilliantly creative philosopher-theologian, is brash, arrogant, and more innovative than almost anyone else of his time. He is his own staunchest supporter and his own worst enemy. (ca.)

Date	A. Theology, Doctrine, and Beliefs	B. People/Events	C. Wider Culture	D. Texts
1138			The Hohenstaufen house begins its reign in Germany. (1268)	
1139		Tenth Ecumenical Council: The Second Lateran Council. • Meets to condemn Arnold of Brescia, who maintained that confession should be made to other Christians, not a priest, and that a minister's sinfulness affects the efficacy of sacraments he administers. • Makes clergy marriage illegal and invalid. • Outlaws the use of the crossbow against other Christians.		
1140	Aristotelianism. The rediscovery of Aristotle enables deductive logic to be applied to real-world problems. The field of law— both civil and canon— booms in the twelfth century.	Saint Hugh of Lincoln is born. Several of Peter Abelard's propositions are officially declared invalid. The crusaders renovate the Church of the Holy Sepulchre based on French romanesque cathedral architecture. (–1149)	Gothic Architecture. The last major medieval architectural period, it immediately follows the romanesque. It begins when masons develop the ribbed vault, thin arches of stone running diagonally, transversely, and longitudinally. This vault enables higher, thinner walls to be built. (ca. 1140–end of the sixteenth century)	Gratian, "the Father of the Science of Canon Law." *Decretum* (*Concordance of Discordant Canons*). Based on the principles set down by Ivo of Chartres for interpreting and harmonizing texts, it is a collection of canon law from the early years through the Second Lateran Council. Its publication marks the beginning of the "modern" scientific study of law. (ca. shortly after the revival of Roman law studies at the University of Bologna)
1141			Judah Ha-Levi, Jewish rabbi and influential thinker in Muslim-occupied Spain, dies.	
1142		Peter Abelard dies. He was one of Scholasticism's most innovative theologians/philosophers.		Hugh of St.-Victor. *De sacramentis Christianea fidei* (Latin: Concerning the Sacraments of the Christian Faith). Lists and elaborates on thirty sacraments. (written during his time at St. Victor 1115–)
1143		Celestine II becomes pope.	The Koran is translated into Latin.	
1144		The Abbey Church of St. Denys is finished. Lucius II becomes pope.		
1145		Eugene III becomes pope. Second Crusade. It is prompted by the fall of Edessa. Saladin, the Muslim leader, prevails and captures Jerusalem. Key figures: King Louis VII of France, Conrad III of Germany, preached by Bernard of Clairvaux. (–1149) The construction of reliquaries increases in the twelfth century. They house, among		

Date	A. Theology, Doctrine, and Beliefs	B. People/Events	C. Wider Culture	D. Texts
1145 con't.		other things, relics brought back from the Middle East during the Crusades.		
1147		Hildegard of Bingen builds the convent at Bingen. (–1152)		
1148		Saint Malachy dies. He was the Irish prelate who brought about the use of the Roman liturgy instead of the Celtic.		
1149		The crusaders rebuild and expand the Church of the Holy Sepulchre to include the entire area, including Calvary.		
1150		The *Decree of Gratian* lists forty-one feasts besides the diocesan patronal celebrations. The Benedictine order has over 300 monasteries. The Ave Maria comes into general use. (mid twelfth century) The Gloria in Excelsis Deo becomes a regular part of the Eucharist and is no longer used as a canticle of the morning office. (twelfth century)	A medical faculty, the first known, is established at Bologna University. The paper mill is invented in Spain.	The *Glossa ordinaria*, commonly known as the *Glossa* or the *Gloss*, is the standard commentary on the Bible in the Middle Ages. It is an interlinear gloss, based on Patristic sources, complied by numerous scholars over many years. (complete by the middle of the twelfth century)
1153		Saint Bernard of Clairvaux dies. He was the founder and abbot of the Cistercian monastery at Clairvaux. Immoderately zealous in his love for God, he was one of the most influential abbots, writers, preachers of his day. The Cistercian order has 339 houses. Anastasius IV becomes pope.		
1154	Carmelite order (Order of the Brothers of Our Lady of Mount Carmel). Originally an order of hermits living on Mount Carmel in Palestine, they are later reorganized as an organization of mendicant friars, whose white mantle earns them the name "Whitefriars." Founder: Albert of Vercelli	Hadrian IV becomes pope, the only Englishman to do so. The Carmelite order, an extremely ascetic order, is formed by Berthold in Palestine. (ca.)	The Angevine house (House of Plantagenet) begins its reign in England.	
1155	Sacramentals. Like sacraments, they are means of grace. Unlike sacraments, sacramentals were not instituted by Christ. The concept arises during the twelfth-century effort to determine which sacred signs could be called sacraments.	A large collection of bones is discovered in Cologne. They are immediately (and without substantiating evidence) marked as Ursula and her 11,000 martyred companions. Within a short time they are sent across Europe as holy relics.		Peter Lombard. *Sententiarum Libri Quatuor* ("the Sentences"). These four books on major theological issues draw heavily on the Latin fathers. They are the first to assert seven "sacraments" (as opposed to "sacramentals"). Together they become a standard textbook in the medieval West.

Date	A. Theology, Doctrine, and Beliefs	B. People/Events	C. Wider Culture	D. Texts
1156		Peter the Venerable, abbot of Cluny dies.		
1159	Vicar of Christ. A title used exclusively by popes, it claims the authority over all Christians implied by Jesus' command to "feed my sheep." It supersedes the title "Vicar of St. Peter."	"Vicar of Christ" replaces "Vicar of St. Peter" to describe the pope. (during Hadrian IV's pontificate, 1154–1159) Alexander III becomes pope.		
1160		Peter Lombard, "Master of the Sentences," dies. Beads similar to rosary beads are placed in the tomb of St. Rosalia. They become the first archeological evidence of the rosary. (ca.)		
1162		Thomas à Becket becomes archbishop of Canterbury.		
1163		Anselm of Canterbury is canonized.	Construction on the Cathedral of Notre Dame in Paris is begun.	
1164		The English royal court of Northampton condemns Thomas à Becket for refusing to abide by the Constitutions of Clarendon. He flees to France.		The Constitutions of Clarendon are put forth by Henry II of England. They spell out English ecclesiastical and state jurisdictions but are disputed by Rome and by Thomas à Becket, archbishop of Canterbury.
1167			The existence of Oxford University is first recorded.	
1170		Thomas à Becket returns to England. Thomas à Becket, archbishop of Canterbury, is assassinated by four of King Henry II's knights in Canterbury Cathedral. Dominic is born. Saint Godric, Anglo-Saxon hermit, dies. He was a merchant, perhaps pirate, who adopted an extremely austere eremitic life in penance for his sins. He was thought to have gifts of prophesy and to be able to speak to animals.		
1171	Canonization. The legal process within the Roman church by which a deceased person is declared a saint. It becomes a formalized process in the twelfth century.	Pope Alexander III reserves the right to canonize exclusively for the papacy.	King Henry II of England begins the Norman conquest of Ireland. (–1172)	
1173		Thomas Becket is canonized.		
1174		Bernard of Clairvaux is canonized.	King Henry II of England forces King William the Lion of Scotland to recognize him as overlord.	

Date	A. Theology, Doctrine, and Beliefs	B. People/Events	C. Wider Culture	D. Texts
1175		The Waldenses take shape as a Christian community dedicated to preaching. (ca.)		Anonymous English Cistercian. "Jesu, Dulcis Memoria," the poem excerpted in "Jesus the Very Thought of Thee." (late twelfth century)
		Hugh of Lincoln builds the first English Carthusian monastery.		
		Intinctio panis (intinction), the dipping of the communion bread into the consecrated wine, is forbidden by the Council of Westminster.		Leonin. *Magnus Liber Organi* (Latin: Great Book of Organa). One of the earliest, and most important, extant collections of two-voice organa and early polyphonic Graduals and Alleluias. It is written in Paris. (1163–)
		The use of candles on the altar is first noted. Before this time, they are probably put on the floor behind the altar. (ca.)		
		The elevation of the Host after consecration begins some time in the twelfth century.		
		Robert Grosseteste is born.		
1176		Walter Map compiles the legends of King Arthur into their modern form. Cistercian piety breaths new life into the legend of the Holy Grail.		
1177		The Beguines and Beghards are organized as communal, lay orders without religious vows. (twelfth century, some time before 1177)		
1179	Cathari. A large and influential heresy, of which the Albigenses are a part. It sweeps Europe in the twelfth and thirteenth centuries. Cathari dualistic theology (body/physicality/evil vs. spirit/spirituality/good) leads to rigorous prohibitions against marriage, food from animal sources, belief in the Incarnation, and the Roman Catholic ritual.	Eleventh Ecumenical Council: Third Lateran Council. • Addresses moral abuses of the church. • Condemns the Albigenses and Waldenses. • Proscribes ordination for money. • Regulates the election of popes.		
		For the first time, a church-sponsored military is used against a heretical sect, the Cathari.		
	Waldenses. A diverse heretical group present in western and southern Europe from the twelfth century onward. They rejected Roman clergy, the swearing of oaths, the doctrine of purgatory, and prayers for the dead. They also insisted on their right to preach, despite their lay status.	Saint Hildegard of Bingen dies. A very widespread influence, she corresponded with kings, prelates, saints, and at least one emperor. She is best known for her practical mysticism.		
1180		Most of the Grail romances come into existence in the twelfth and thirteenth century. (–1240)	Moses ben Maimon, "Maimonides" or "Rambam." *Mishneh Torah*. It is one of the most influential codifications of Jewish Law.	

Date	A. Theology, Doctrine, and Beliefs	B. People/Events	C. Wider Culture	D. Texts
1181		Francis of Assisi is born. (or 1182) Lucius III becomes pope.		
1182		Notre Dame Cathedral in Paris is consecrated.	Jews are banished from France. All Latins in Constantinople, including the Norman-born Empress dowager are killed in an anti-Rome uprising.	
1183			The Peace of Constance gives rise to the beginnings of Italian city-states.	
1184		The Synod of Verona charges bishops with the responsibility of searching out heretics and remanding them to the secular authorities.		Pope Lucius III. *Ad Abolendam.* A papal bull charging diocesan bishops with the task of seeking out heresy and, in conjunction with the secular authorities, meting out appropriate punishment. The ineffectiveness of this policy paves the way for the Inquisition.
1185		Urban III becomes pope.		
1187		Saladin's army tears the cross from the Dome of the Rock and plunders churches and convents. Christians are allowed to use the Church of the Holy Sepulchre only if they pay a heavy tribute. Gregory VIII becomes pope. Pope Gregory VIII proclaims the Third Crusade. (October 29) Clement III becomes pope.	Jerusalem is taken by Saladin and his Muslim troops.	
1189		Third Crusade. It is prompted by the capture of Jerusalem by Saladin. The Crusade recovers Acre, but not Jerusalem. A truce between Richard and Saladin makes pilgrimage possible. Key figures: Holy Roman Emperor Frederick I, King Philip II of France, and King Richard I of England. (–1192) Ely cathedral in the Fens of England is finished. Saint Gilbert of Sempringham dies. He was the founder of the Gilbertines, an English order of both men and women built on the *Rule of Saint Benedict.*	Richard I, "Richard the Lionhearted," becomes king of England.	

Date	A. Theology, Doctrine, and Beliefs	B. People/Events	C. Wider Culture	D. Texts
1190	Hospitallers. Also known as Knights Hospitallers, the order has its beginnings caring for the sick of Jerusalem, especially poor pilgrims. Their fourth vow is to serve as serfs to the sick, whom they served as lords.	The Order of German Hospitallers is formed in Acre. It later becomes the Teutonic Order. Church music begins to be written in three and four parts.	Moses ben Maimon. *Guide for the Perplexed*. It is an interpretation of Jewish tradition in light of Aristotle by the foremost Jewish medieval thinker. The University of Paris springs up around several schools associated with the Cathedral of Notre Dame. It becomes one of the greatest intellectual forces in Europe. (ca.)	
1191		Celestine III becomes pope.	Saladin fortifies the walls of Jerusalem to meet the threat of King Richard of England and the third Crusade.	
1194		Chartres Cathedral is begun, marking the beginning of the high gothic period of architecture. A clerestory that is almost as high as the ground-story arcade adds additional height. This cathedral establishes the major divisions of the interior that become standard in all later gothic churches.		
1195		Berthold, founder of the Carmelites, dies.		
1198		Innocent III becomes pope. The Order of German Hospitallers becomes the Teutonic order, a military order under the Templar Rule.		
1199		Malachy is canonized. The custom of ringing a bell at the elevation of the elements in the Eucharist begins. (before the end of the twelfth century)		
1200	Scholasticism. An approach to academic inquiry, its method is dialectical, its foundation Aristotelian (occasionally Platonic), and its aim the harmonization of reason and existing theology. It is the principle method employed by European universities from the late eleventh through the sixteenth century. After the sixteenth century, its use is mainly restricted to some Roman theology. Zenith: 1200–1300. Key figures: Thomas Aquinas, Alexander of Hales, Albertus Magnus, Bonaventure, John Scotus Erigena, Anselm of Canterbury, Peter Abelard, John Duns Scotus, Hugh of Saint Victor.	The Synod of Westminster dictates that the banns of marriage must be announced prior to the marriage ceremony. Saint Hugh of Lincoln, English prelate and Carthusian monk, dies. The Cluniac order becomes recognized as a distinct form of Cistercian monasticism. It stresses the spiritual life, especially the choir office. It, therefore, incorporates less manual labor than Benedictine or Cistercian monasticism. (ca.) In the thirteenth century, England had 40,000 secular clergy and 17,000 monks,	The Jewish Kabbala is developed. (twelfth through thirteenth century)	

Date	A. Theology, Doctrine, and Beliefs	B. People/Events	C. Wider Culture	D. Texts
1200 con't.		canons, and friars, along with 17 dioceses, each divided among two or more archdeacons.		
1201		*Intinctio panis* (intinction), the dipping of the communion bread into the consecrated wine, disappears in the West. (ca.)		
1202	Rosary. The term applies primarily to a sequence of prayers: fifteen decades (sets of ten) of Hail Marys, each preceeded by the Gloria Patri are said. Each decade is accompanied by a meditation on the life of Christ, especially on Mary's role in it. The term has also come to be used to refer to the string of beads used to keep track of the sequence.	The rosary is devised. It is traditionally thought to be invented by Spanish theologian St. Dominic, though this tradition is not backed by proof. (early in the thirteenth century) Fourth Crusade. Originally intended to capture more territory in and around the Holy Land, it is diverted to Constantinople. The Latin Empire of Constantinople is instituted. Key figure: Boniface of Montferrat. (–1204)		
1204		Crusading western armies ravage Constantinople on their way to free the Holy Land from the Turks. The animosity between Eastern and Western Christianity becomes irreparable.	Moses ben Maimon, foremost Jewish medieval thinker, also known as Maimonides or Rambam, dies.	
1206		Dominic founds the first Dominican convent for women.		
1208		Pope Innocent III proclaims a Crusade against the Albigenses. The Crusade eventually eliminates the Abigensian heresy. England is placed under a papal interdict when King John refuses to acknowledge the pope's choice of archbishop of Canterbury. Francis of Assisi denounces wealth.		
1209		King John of England is excommunicated by Pope Innocent III.	Cambridge University is founded.	Albert of Vercelli. Carmelite Rule. Written by the Latin patriarch of Jerusalem, it is one of the most difficult monastic rules of the time, mandating poverty, vegetarianism, and solitude.
1210	The rediscovery of Aristotle leads to a new interest in the relationship between the seen and unseen worlds. In the twelfth and thirteenth century, the natural world begins to be depicted in cathedral art. Transubstantiation is declared *de fide*. The Host is elevated.	The bishop of Paris requires the Host and chalice be elevated immediately after consecration. Pope Innocent III first uses the term "interdict" to describe the almost complete withdrawal of sacraments and	Construction on the Cathedral of Reims is begun, marking the culmination of the high gothic period of cathedral architecture.	Francis of Assisi. *Regula primitiva* (the Rule of St. Francis). A simple monastic rule built mainly on the words of Jesus. It is the founding document for the Franciscans. Pope Innocent III. *Compilatio tertia*. Decretals from the first

Date	A. Theology, Doctrine, and Beliefs	B. People/Events	C. Wider Culture	D. Texts
1210 con't.	The feast of Corpus Christi is inaugurated.	liturgy from a region. (some time between 1198 and 1216) Clergy are forbidden by papal edict from appearing on stage in public. As a result, lay morality plays develop from the liturgy of the Roman Catholic Church.		12 years of Innocent III's reign are compiled at his order for use in courts and law schools. It is the first officially promulgated canon law collection in the West.
1212		Children's Crusade. In response to the diversion of the fourth Crusade, 50,000 French and German children set off to the Holy Land to recapture Jerusalem. Most die before they get across the Alps. Those who reach the Mediterranean are sold into slavery. Fewer than 300 return home. Saint Francis of Assisi receives Clare, a young, well-born nun of Assisi, into the Franciscan fellowship. She later founds the Order of the Poor Ladies (the Poor Clares), and the Second Order of Franciscans.		
1213		King John of England submits to Rome. England and Ireland become papal fiefs.		
1214			Genghis Khan invades China, Persia, and Russia. (–1223)	
1215	Transubstantiation. The doctrine of the Eucharist that says the bread and wine are literally changed into the Body and Blood of Christ. Though the elements appear to be still bread and wine, those appearances are "accidents" (leftovers from their prior state).	Twelfth Ecumenical Council: The Fourth Lateran. It is typically considered to be most important council of the Middle Ages. • Uses the term "transubstantiation" for the first time and declares the doctrine *de fide*. • Decrees each of the faithful must receive the Eucharist at least once each year at Easter. • Establishes the modern system of private penance—confession, absolution, light penance. • Makes the seal of confession canonically binding. • Regulates monastic observance. In general the regulation is based on the Cistercian system. • Declares the doctrine of Creation *ex nihilo* to be dogmatic. • Condemns the Albigenses. • Condemns the Trinitarian errors of Abbot Joachim. • Declares that procession of the Holy Spirit from the Son is dogma.	*Magna Carta*. It asserts that the king must be constrained by law and forms the foundation for constitutional monarchy. King John signs it under duress. The Fourth Lateran Council directs that secular rulers compel Jews to wear yellow badges to distinguish them from Christians. The Dominican order is empowered to preach in Jewish synagogues.	

Date	A. Theology, Doctrine, and Beliefs	B. People/Events	C. Wider Culture	D. Texts
1215 con't.		• Publishes 70 important reformatory decrees. Clare, abbess at Assisi, founds the Poor Clares, a Franciscan order for women.		
1216	Dominican order. Also known as the black friars, they are a preaching order founded by St. Dominic. Rather than engaging in manual labor, they devote their work hours to study, teaching, and preaching. They tend to be rather lax in reciting the divine office and in corporate poverty, but produce some of history's greatest Christian scholars and theologians.	Honorius III becomes pope. Dominic gives the Order of Friars Preachers an official, definitive shape. The new order is commonly known as the Dominicans.		
1217		Fifth Crusade. The last Crusade launched by papal authority, it is aimed against Egypt, the Muslim headquarters. The crusaders have to be evacuated when Cairo floods. (–1221) Giovanni di Fidanza (Bonaventure) is born. The pope sends the Dominicans to Paris to stifle the academic community there.		
1219		Francis of Assisi sends Franciscan friars to Palestine.	The Sultan Malik-el-Mu'az-zam, viceroy at Damascus, destroys the walls of Jerusalem to prevent them being used as protection by the Franks.	
1220		Hugh of Lincoln is canonized, the first Carthusian to be declared a saint. The monks of Cluny are required to recite the Salve Regina daily. A shrine to Thomas à Becket is dedicated at Canterbury Cathedral.		
1221		The Dominicans begin the use of the anthem Salve Regina at compline. (ca.) Saint Dominic, Spanish theologian, dies. He was the founder of the Roman Catholic Order of Friars Preachers, otherwise known as the Dominicans.		
1223				The *Regula primitiva* (the Rule of St. Francis) receives papal approval.

Date	A. Theology, Doctrine, and Beliefs	B. People/Events	C. Wider Culture	D. Texts
1224		Francis of Assisi manifests stigmata. His is the first known case. A Franciscan community settles in Oxford.		
1225		Some Italians' practice of draining money off English benefices they have never seen heightens the animosity of England for Rome. (thirteenth century) Thomas Aquinas is born.		
1226		The first recorded instance of the adoration of the Blessed Sacrament is during Louis VIII's celebration of his victory over the Albigensians. Saint Francis of Assisi, founder of the Franciscans, dies. He becomes the patron saint of ecologists because of his affinity with animals and the natural world.		The Carmelite Rule is approved by Pope Honorius III.
1227	The devotion of the rosary grows with the growth of the Cistercians and Dominicans.	Gregory IX becomes pope.		
1228		Sixth Crusade. Holy Roman Emperor Frederick II takes, and claims jurisdiction over, Jerusalem. (–1229) Francis of Assisi is canonized.		
1229		Lay people are forbidden to read Scripture. The Synod of Toulouse places one clerical and two lay inquisitors in every parish.	Holy Roman Emperor Frederick II is crowned king of Jerusalem. He gains the title through marriage to the daughter of the previous king.	
1230			The Crusades bring leprosy to Europe.	Caesarius of Heisterbach. *On Miracles*. This eight-book work by a Cistercian author reflects the importance of supernatural events to the faith of the time.
1231		Saint Anthony of Padua, Franciscan monk and doctor of the church, dies. The pope lightens the ban on the study of Aristotle. Aristotelian thought begins to permeate university theology departments. The Inquisition begins. Heretics become subject to the death penalty at the hands of the civil authorities. Saint Elizabeth of Hungary dies from exhaustion. She was a sister of the third order of St. Francis and minister to the sick.		Pope Gregory IX. *Excommunicamus*. It marks the beginning of the Inquisition and places inquisitors, mostly Franciscans and Dominicans, under the special jurisdiction of the pope. It also lessens the bishops' responsibility for maintaining orthodoxy and establishes severe penalties for heresy.

Date	A. Theology, Doctrine, and Beliefs	B. People/Events	C. Wider Culture	D. Texts
1233		The Decretals of Pope Gregory IX lists forty-five public feasts and holy days. (ca.) The Order of Servites is founded by wealthy Florentines who abandon their wealth to serve the Virgin Mary. They follow a modified Augustinian Rule.		
1234		Dominic is canonized. Canon law dictates that the chalice and paten used during the Eucharist must be gold or silver. It allows the poorest parishes to use one made of pewter, but forbids brass, copper, wood, and glass. (ca.)		Raymond of Peñafort. *Extravagantes*. An organization of the compilations of canon law commissioned by Pope Gregory IX.
1235		Elizabeth of Hungary is canonized by Pope Gregory IX.		
1237		Extreme unction begins to be distinguished from rites for the healing of the sick. The healing of the sick is much more penitential; whereas, extreme unction involves prayers and invocation of the saints.		The Sarum Rite. Also called the Salisbury Rite, it is the variant of the Roman Rite in use at the Salisbury cathedral. The extant texts include not only a complete collection of the liturgical rites but also a Customary that lends considerable insight into medieval church practices. (before)
1239		Throughout Europe, moderate cases of heresy are met with confiscation of goods and banishment. Severe cases call for burning.		
1240		Saint Edmund of Abingdon dies. He was an English prelate, preacher, teacher, and author of an influential treatise on asceticism.		The Franciscan Breviary. Designed to enable friars to continue to say the Office while on the road, it is the breviary stripped to bare essentials. It becomes the basis for the modern Daily Office. Richard of Chichester "Day by Day" (hymn) (mid thirteenth century)
1241		Celestine IV becomes pope.		Albertus Magnus begins to interpret, mostly by paraphrasing, almost the entire Aristotelian corpus. His intent is to make Greek thought intelligible to the Latin mind. He is the first Christian philosopher to do so.
1243		Innocent IV becomes pope. Pope Innocent IV sanctions Holy Roman Emperor Frederick II's and king of France Louis IX's laws against heretics. Torture becomes part of the heresy trial process, and the guilty are burned at the stake.		

Date	A. Theology, Doctrine, and Beliefs	B. People/Events	C. Wider Culture	D. Texts
1244			Jerusalem falls to the Muslims.	
1245	The Treasury of Merits. The doctrine that the infinite merit of Christ, the merit of the Blessed Virgin Mary (which was undiminished by penalty of sin), and the merit accrued to the suffering of the saints are available to the church. These merits are applicable to the temporal penalty of forgiven sin. The doctrine is explicitly developed by the Scholastics especially Alexander of Hales, Albertus Magnus, Thomas Aquinas. (thirteenth century) Voluntary Poverty. How poor were Jesus and the apostles, and what implications does that have for monastic/mendicant orders that have taken a vow of poverty? (Franciscan Spirituals vs. mainstream monastics)	Albertus Magnus introduces Thomas Aquinas to Aristotelian thought. Thirteenth Ecumenical Council: The First Council of Lyons. • Excommunicates and deposes Holy Roman Emperor Frederick II for trying to make the church a part of the state. • Instigates a new Crusade against the Saracens and Mongols.	Even the most conservative scholars can no longer ignore Aristotle and Arabic philosophers. (mid thirteenth century)	Alexander of Hales, et al. *Summa theologica* (Latin: Complete Theological Commentary). Heavily influenced by Platonism, it is one of the most ambitious works of speculative theology of the time. It is also an important work in the formation of Franciscan theology.
1246			In the twelfth and thirteenth centuries travel becomes easier. Traders and crusaders bring new ideas into Europe from Jewish, Arab, and Eastern science and philosophy.	
1247	Mendicant friars. Monks who are not bound to a monastery and who are not allowed to hold either personal property or property in common.	Simon Stock reorganizes the Carmelites as mendicant friars after the Crusades. (ca.–1265)		
1248		Seventh Crusade. Crusade against Egypt, which is Muslim headquarters. Louis IX is captured at Mansura. (–1254)		
1249		Edmund of Abingdon is canonized.		
1250			The high gothic period in Germany begins. (–1500)	
1252		Pope Innocent IV makes the Inquisition a permanent institution in Italy and sanctions torture as one of its tools. Saint Peter Martyr, Dominican preacher and inquisitor, dies.		
1253		Saint Clare of Assisi dies. She was an Italian nun and founder of the Franciscan Order of the Poor Ladies, commonly called the Poor Clares. Robert Grosseteste, bishop of Lincoln, dies. He struggled against royal and papal	The Sorbonne is founded at the University of Paris.	

Date	A. Theology, Doctrine, and Beliefs	B. People/Events	C. Wider Culture	D. Texts
1253 con't.		infringement on episcopal prerogative. Saint Richard, bishop of Chichester, dies.		
1254		Alexander IV becomes pope.		
1255			French universities make it possible to study philosophy apart from theology.	William Durandus, bishop of Mende. *Symbolism of Churches.* An interpretation of the symbolism of church rites, allegories, and objects, it is written for the more literate parish priest. (mid thirteenth century)
1256		Pope Alexander IV forms the Hermits of St. Augustine under the Augustinian Rule.		
1258		Salisbury cathedral is completed.		
1259	Flagellants. Small, but highly visible, groups of lay people process through towns and cities scourging themselves as penance for the sins of humanity.	A flagellant sect arises in Perugia, in central Italy.		
1260			Franco of Cologne. *Ars cantus mensurabilis.* Proposes a system for rhythmic notation. Musical notation with long and short note values becomes more common throughout the end of the thirteenth century.	
1261		Urban IV becomes pope.		An initiative of Pope Urban IV amends the traditional text of the Ave Maria. *"Benedictus fructus ventris tui,"* ("Blessed is the fruit of your womb") is followed by *"Iesus, Amen."* The prayer ends there.
1263		The Feast of the Visitation of the Blessed Virgin Mary is introduced into the Franciscan order by the General Chapter.		Bonaventure. *Life of Francis.* The official Franciscan biography of Francis of Assisi.
1264	Feast of Corpus Christi. It is a commemoration of the institution of the Lord's Supper celebrated on the Thursday after Trinity Sunday.	Pope Urban IV establishes the Feast of Corpus Christi.		
1265	Thomas Aquinas's *Summa* is very much a product of the time, which sees the enterprise of theology as being accumulation and consolidation of theological tradition.	Clement IV becomes pope. Thomas Aquinas maintains that Christ instituted the sacrament of confirmation. (ca.) Thomas Aquinas pinpoints which echelons of angels may serve as guardian angels. The function is not performed by the higher angels. (ca.)	Dante Alighieri is born.	Thomas Aquinas. *Summa theologica.* It is the greatest summation of medieval theology ever written. To this day, it supplies part of the foundation for Roman Catholic theology. It has three parts: theology proper, anthropology, and Christology/soteriology. (–1274)

Date	A. Theology, Doctrine, and Beliefs	B. People/Events	C. Wider Culture	D. Texts
1265 con't.		Thomas Aquinas devises the classic doctrine of purgatory. He teaches that both punishment (*poena*) and guilt (*culpa*) are purged in purgatory. Johannes Duns Scotus is born. (ca.)		
1266				Jacob of Voragine. *The Golden Legend*. A collection of the lives of the saints and treatises on church festivals intended to foster popular piety. It is of questionable historical accuracy.
1268			Roger Bacon. *Opus Maius* (Major Work). An encyclopedia of grammar, logic, mathematics, physics, experimental research, and moral philosophy, it is written by one of the first Scholastics to take an interest in experimental science. Bacon proposes a new way of doing science based on methods of observation and experimentation. (ca. late 1260s)	
1270		Eighth Crusade. Louis IX dies. The Crusades end with the Muslim forces gradually overrunning Latin territory until 1291.		Mechthild of Magdeburg. *Das fliessende Licht der Gottheit* (German: The Flowing Light of the Divinity). It is an account of the visions of a German Béguine in two volumes. It greatly influences medieval German mysticism. (begun in 1250)
1271		Gregory X becomes pope. Roman Catholic cardinals begin the practice of going into conclave when electing a pope.		
1272		Thomas Aquinas sets up a Dominican school in Naples and works on the *Summa theologica*.		
1274		Saint Bonaventure, "Second Founder of the Franciscan Order," dies. Franciscan theologian, poet, biographer. Saint Thomas Aquinas, "the Angelic Doctor," dies. He is commonly considered the greatest Scholastic theologian. Fourteenth Ecumenical Council: The Second Council of Lyons. It is called by Pope Gregory X. • Temporarily reunites the Eastern and Western churches.		

Date	A. Theology, Doctrine, and Beliefs	B. People/Events	C. Wider Culture	D. Texts
1274 con't.		• Officially adds the Filioque clause to the symbol of Constantinople. • Establishes rules for papal elections. • Defines the doctrine of purgatory. • Condemns metempsychosis (reincarnation).		
1275		Morality plays gain a formalized structure. (late thirteenth or early fourteenth century)	Marco Polo is in China. (–1292) Manuscript copying becomes a secular profession. The universities in Paris have copyists on staff who produce books for the university and for sale. (ca.)	
1276		Innocent V becomes pope, the first Dominican to be elected to the office. Hadrian V becomes pope. John XXI becomes pope.		
1277		The Franciscans condemn Roger Bacon for "suspected novelties" and "dangerous doctrine." Pope John XXI condemns nineteen Thomistic propositions. Nicholas III becomes pope.		
1280		Albertus Magnus, German Scholastic philosopher, Dominican and doctor of the church, dies. He was Thomas Aquinas's teacher and made the Aristotelian corpus accessible to the West.		
1281		Lay people no longer may receive the cup at the Eucharist according to the Synod of Lambeth. Martin IV becomes pope.		
1285		Honorius IV becomes pope. By the end of the thirteenth century, the papacy has become largely corrupt. Cardinals electing popes often do so based on personal or family interests. The popes themselves often partake liberally of papal resources. In the popular imagination is formed a dream of an "angel pope" who will come and cleanse the church of abuses.		
1288		Nicholas IV becomes pope.		
1289		Boniface IX becomes pope.		

Date	A. Theology, Doctrine, and Beliefs	B. People/Events	C. Wider Culture	D. Texts
1290	Scotism. The ideas of John Duns Scotus, one of the most prominent critics of Thomistic philosophy. Scotus gives precedence to the divine will over the divine intellect. He maintains that will rather than intellect creates the laws of nature and morality. Scotism is a middle ground between Realism and Nominalism and has influence in the Roman Catholic Church to modern times. (ca.)		Jews are expelled from England.	
1291		The last crusaders leave the Holy Land with the fall of Acre, the final Latin-held city to be captured by the Muslims. Militarily the Crusades were a failure. Crusaders were unable to hold the Holy Land. Nonmilitary Jews and Muslims were slaughtered. Relations between Eastern and Western Christianity were greatly impaired. However, trade with the East grew. Eastern culture began to have an impact on the stagnant West. The European economy was stimulated.		
1293		Jan van Ruysbroeck is born.		
1294		When the College of Cardinals are unable to elect a successor to Pope Nicholas IV, who had died two years earlier, Peter Celestine, an influential abbot, writes a letter reprimanding them. They elect him pope, and he becomes Pope Celestine V. Pope Celestine V, a completely unworldly man, is exploited by church and secular leaders alike. Miserable and ineffectual as pope, he resigns, becoming the only pope ever to do so. Boniface VIII becomes pope.	Roger Bacon, English Scholastic philosopher and scientist, dies. He was an early proponent of the experimental method.	
1295		Purificators, small pieces of white linen used to clean the chalice after communion, are first used. Henry Suso is born. (ca.)	King Edward I of England summons the "Model Parliament," the forerunner of all future English Parliaments.	*The Harrowing of Hell.* An early English miracle play, it is one of the first of the miracle/mystical plays performed throughout Europe in the thirteenth through sixteenth centuries.
1296				Pope Boniface VIII. *Clericis Laicos* (Latin: Lay Clerks). It declares secular rulers may not tax clergy.

Date	A. Theology, Doctrine, and Beliefs	B. People/Events	C. Wider Culture	D. Texts
1297		The Brethren of the Free Spirit, a class of somewhat pantheistic sects, proclaim themselves to be independent of ecclesiastical authority and beholden only to the Spirit. (thirteenth and fourteenth century) Louis IX is canonized as a part of a deal that allows Philip IV, king of France, and Pope Boniface VIII to glean revenue from each other's people.		
1298		The original four Doctors of the Church are named. They are the Western theologians: Ambrose, Augustine, Jerome, and Gregory the Great.		
1300	By 1300 monastic life has begun to break down. Scholars now have universities to attend. Ascetics have hermitages and no longer need the protection of monasteries. Monasteries are increasingly worldly and have little unique to offer.	The Ave Maria becomes a penitential exercise in part due to the custom of genuflecting or bowing deeply when it is said. (thirteenth century) William of Ockham is born. (ca.) Johann Tauler is born. (ca.) Johannes Duns Scotus is one of the few Scholastics to argue for immaculate conception of the Blessed Virgin Mary. (ca.) Many churches in England have installed wooden benches known as pews. The custom of standing or kneeling exclusively during worship gives way to occasional sitting.	The *ars nova* (Latin for "new art") is developed. It is a musical form incorporating a relatively complex rhythmic structure, notated with the newly developed time signature. For the first time, the Ordinary of the Mass is treated as an integrated whole: musical themes from one part of the mass are echoed in others. Key figure: Guillaume de Machaut. (fourteenth century)	Gertrude the Great. *Legatus divinae pietatis* (Latin: Legate of Divine Piety). A mystical treatise of great literary value, written by one of the first devotees of the Sacred Heart. (ca.) Pope Boniface VIII. *Super Cathedram* (Latin: Upon the Cathedra (Bishop's Chair)). It dictates that only those licensed can preach or hear confessions. It thereby greatly diminishes the influence of the friars. *Messe de tournai* (French: The Mass of Tournai). The first example of a complete setting of the Mass Ordinary (that part of the mass that does not change with the seasons): Kyrie, Gloria, Credo, Sanctus, Agnus Dei. (ca.)
1302				Pope Boniface VIII. *Unam Sanctum* (Latin: One Holy). Declares that the "One holy and apostolic Church" is headed by the pope and that apart from the church there is "neither salvation nor remission of sins." In it the papacy claims unprecedented power for itself. John of Paris. *De Potestate Regia et Papali* (Latin: Concerning the Power of the Royal Court and the Papacy). It maintains the pope can be deposed by council. It is an early foundation of conciliar theory.

Date	A. Theology, Doctrine, and Beliefs	B. People/Events	C. Wider Culture	D. Texts
1303		King Philip IV of France orders French mercenaries to seize Pope Boniface VIII for trial. The charges are exaggerated and largely unimportant as the episode is mostly about Philip and Boniface's struggle for temporal power. Boniface escapes but dies shortly thereafter. Benedict XI becomes pope.		
1304		Pope Benedict XI officially sanctions the Order of Servites. Their principle service and devotion is to the Virgin Mary.		
1305		Clement V becomes pope.		
1306			Jews are expelled from France.	
1307		The Archbishopric of Peking, China, is formed. The French Knights Templar are stripped of property on false charges of heresy.		
1308		Johannes Duns Scotus dies. He was one of the great Scholastics.		
1309		Pope Clement V moves the curia (the papal court) to Avignon beginning the "Babylonian Captivity of the Church." (–1377)		
1310		Franciscans debate the issue of poverty before Pope John XXII. (–1312)	Musical time signatures are developed. (early fourteenth century)	
1311	Fraticelli. An originally derogatory name for the Spiritual Franciscans, who believe that in embracing absolute individual and corporate poverty, they are following the example of both Francis and Jesus.	Fifteenth Ecumenical Council: The Council of Vienne. (–1313) • Examines the errors of the Fraticelli, Knights Templars, Quetists, and the Beghards and Beguines. • Fosters clergy reformation. • Mandates that universities have chairs of oriental languages. An increasing number of scholars become competent in biblical languages.		
1313		Meister Eckhart becomes one of the most famous preachers of his time. (after 1313)	Berthold Schwarz, a German monk, uses gunpowder to propel a projectile. It is the first known use of gunpowder in Europe. (early fourteenth century)	
1314		Pope Clement V condemns indulgences that purport to absolve both guilt of sin and the penalty for sin. (1305–)		

Date	A. Theology, Doctrine, and Beliefs	B. People/Events	C. Wider Culture	D. Texts
1315				Richard Rolle's lyric poetry. They are mystical works written in Middle English extolling the sweetness of communion with God. (early fourteenth century)
1316		John XXII becomes pope.		
1317		Pope John XXII decides against the Franciscan Spirituals and allows the Franciscans corporate ownership. The Spirituals split from the order and formally adopt the name Fraticelli. (–1318) Pope John XXII reformes methods of levying "taxes" on parishes and dioceses. The right ecclesiastical post can now be quite lucrative. Some priests and bishops buy or scheme their way into good (or several) positions. The pope's reforms, however, increase the administrative efficiency of the church and keep the curia financially viable. (–1319)		
1320		John Wycliffe is born.		Dante Alighieri. *Divine Comedy*. A poetic journey through purgatory and hell with a glimpse of heaven. Theology, art, social commentary: it is a masterpiece on all counts. (ca.)
1321			Dante Alighieri, Italian poet, and author of the *Divine Comedy*, dies.	
1323		Thomas Aquinas is canonized.		
1324				Marsilius of Padua. *Defensor pacis* (Latin: Defender of Peace). He argues, based on the example of Christ, that the church should have no state authority. He also maintains that law is inherent in nature.
1325		Pope John XXII bans complex harmony in church music.		
1326	The fourteenth century produces more great mystical literature than perhaps any other. It is the age of Richard Rolles, Juliana of Norwich, and Walter Hilton in England; Meister Eckhart, Johann Tauler, and Henry Suso in Germany; Jan van Ruysbroeck in Flanders; and Jacopone da Todi and Catherine of Siena in Italy.	John "Meister" Eckhart is accused of heresy. He appeals to the pope.		

Date	A. Theology, Doctrine, and Beliefs	B. People/Events	C. Wider Culture	D. Texts
1327		John "Meister" Eckhart, German Dominican mystic, dies. He was one of the most influential mystical theologians of the fourteenth century.		
1328		William of Ockham is excommunicated for maintaining that Pope John XXII's position on Franciscan poverty is heretical. He is forced to flee Avignon.	Sawmills are invented. The French Valois dynasty replaces the Capetians.	Henry Suso. *Little Book of Eternal Wisdom*. A classic of German mysticism, it is a practical guide, not a theoretical treatise. It includes a hundred brief meditations on the Passion. (ca.)
1329		Pope John XXII finds twenty-eight of Meister Eckhart's sentences to be heretical.		
1331		Bernard of Gui dies. He was one of the most famous inquisitors of the time.		
1334		Pope John XXII makes Trinity Sunday a universal celebration. Benedict XII becomes pope. Geert de Groote founds the Brethren of the Common Life in the Netherlands to foster personal spirituality and free top-quality religious education. (mid fourteenth century) Pope Benedict XII institutes substantial reform of abuses in the papacy. (–1342) Most reforms are lost during his successor's term.		
1335			Ockham's razor. If two hypotheses both explain the situation, the simpler of the two is the most desirable. (mid fourteenth century)	
1337			The Hundred Years' War, a series of conflicts between England and France, begins. (–1453) William Merlee of Oxford makes the first scientific attempt to forecast the weather.	
1338			Cannons are first used in warfare.	Pope Benedict XII. *Fidem Catholicam* (Latin: Catholic Faith). A manifesto proclaiming that imperial authority comes directly from God, not the pope.
1340			The earliest extant records of double-entry bookkeeping date to the mid fourteenth century.	

Date	A. Theology, Doctrine, and Beliefs	B. People/Events	C. Wider Culture	D. Texts
1342		Juliana of Norwich is born. (ca.) The general chapter of the Dominican order declares that the doctrine of Thomas Aquinas is sound and universally applicable. Clement VI becomes pope.		
1343				Pope Clement VI. *Unigenitus* (Latin: Only-begotten). Dogmatically asserts the existence of an infinite treasury of merits.
1347		Catherine of Siena is born.		
1348			Black Death. One-third of the European population, at least 25 million people, die of the bubonic plague. (–1350) Ghettoization of Jews begins in Germany.	
1349	The theology/philosophy of William of Ockham signals the beginning of the end for Scholasticism. Reason can do much, but it can't disclose God.	William of Ockham, philosopher and theologian, dies. (ca.) Richard Rolle, hermit and mystic, dies. Saint Bridget of Sweden founds the Roman Catholic Order of Bridgettine Sisters based on a vision in which Christ commanded her to found a new strict religious order dedicated to reforming monastic life. Pope Clement VI calls upon local church authorities to suppress the flagellant bands that have sprung up in response to the Black Death. Their attempts to do so are only marginally successful.		
1350	From 1350 until the Reformation, women play an increasingly large leadership role in the church. Though they still can not be ordained, they can hold leadership roles in religious communities, help shape mystical theology, and are regarded as saints and wise counsel.	The *Gottesfreunde* (Friends of God), a group of mystics in the Rhineland and Switzerland, down-play ecclesiastical life in favor of personal mystical experience with God. (fourteenth century)	The Renaissance begins. It sees the decline of feudalism and the rise of nations. Classical humanism is reborn. The arts, literature, and science begin to flourish. It begins in Italy in the mid fourteenth century and spread from there to the rest of Europe. (ca.–1650) Late Middle Ages begins. The plague changes the demographics of Europe. Education and information, especially in vernacular languages, is more readily available. Exploration expands the boundaries of the known world. The Roman church loses its monopoly. (ca.–1550) Major composers begin to write secular as well as	Jan van Ruysbroeck. *Adornment of the Spiritual Marriage.* A look at three stages in the life of a Christian mystic. (mid fourteenth century)

Date	A. Theology, Doctrine, and Beliefs	B. People/Events	C. Wider Culture	D. Texts
1350 con't.			church music. This secular music is not merely the unharmonized troubadour tunes of the thirteenth century, but is expanded into two- and three-part *chansons* (French for "songs"). In France and Italy, the newest, most innovative music comes from secular sources, not from the church. (ca.) Great Vowel Shift. A change in the pronunciation of English vowels begins. It marks the transition from Middle English to Modern English. It is complete by about 1550.	
1352		Innocent VI becomes pope.		
1354			Strasbourg Cathedral's mechanical clock, one of the earliest in Europe, is installed.	
1361	The Black Death, the Hundred Years' War, the Babylonian Captivity, and the Inquisition all rock Europe at the same time. Western Europe sees all kinds of aberrant behavior by people attempting to gain some kind of sure spiritual footing. This is the period of the flagellants, the Dance of Death performed in cemeteries, the Black Mass to appease the Devil, and regular witch hunts and trials.	Johann Tauler, German Dominican mystic and spiritual director, dies.	The second wave of the Black Death rages through Europe.	
1362		Urban V becomes pope.		
1364		Guillaume de Machaut composes the first known polyphonic setting of the Mass Ordinary. (ca.)		
1365				*The Cloud of Unknowing.* An anonymous mystical guidebook, written to those given to a life of contemplation. The author maintains that only "a sharp dart of love" (i.e. the heart and not the mind) can pierce the "cloud" that hides God from humanity. (late fourteenth century)
1366		Henry Suso, German mystic, dies.		
1367		Pope Urban V and the curia temporarily move back to Rome. Most of the papal bureaucracy remains in Avignon. (–1370)		
1368			The Ming dynasty begins in China.	

Date	A. Theology, Doctrine, and Beliefs	B. People/Events	C. Wider Culture	D. Texts
1370		The Roman Catholic Order of Bridgettine Sisters receives papal confirmation. Pope Urban V returns the papacy to Avignon. Gregory XI becomes pope.		
1372		John Huss is born.		
1373		Saint Bridget of Sweden, dies. Mystic, founder of the Roman Catholic Order of Bridgettine Sisters, patron saint of Sweden. Juliana of Norwich receives her sixteen "showings." Margery Kempe is born.		
1374		John Wycliffe writes several pamphlets upholding the English Parliament's right to limit church power.		
1375		The Exposition of the Blessed Sacrament, in which the consecrated Host is exposed for veneration, first becomes distinct from the Mass. (late fourteenth century)		
1376		Catherine of Siena goes to Avignon to persuade Pope Gregory XI to return to Rome. Pope Gregory XI begins the papal curia's final move from Avignon to Rome. (–1377)		
1377	Dominion as founded in grace. The belief that all authority is conferred directly by the grace of God. A leader forfeits that authority should he commit a mortal sin.	John Wycliffe is called before William Courtenay, bishop of London, to give account of his doctrine of dominion as founded in grace. The interrogation ends when one of Wycliffe's companions begins a brawl with the bishop and his entourage. Pope Gregory XI issues several bulls accusing John Wycliffe of heresy.		John Wycliffe. *On the Church.* Asserts that the papacy is extra-biblical and has no authority to profess any doctrine not explicitly stated in Scripture.
1378	Conciliar theory grows in response to the Great Schism. It is the medieval doctrine that asserts that the general councils of the church have, in some circumstances, more authority than the pope. Late Medieval Church. The cohesion of the Western church begins to break down. The papacy is split. Mystics seek a path to God that is not dependent on church hierarchy. The first signs of the Reformation begin to appear on the horizon. (–1517)	The Great (Papal) Schism. Western Christianity is divided between two or three popes/antipopes. (–1417) Urban VI becomes pope. The Cardinals who elect him do not believe him to be the best candidate, but are under considerable pressure from the Roman authorities and general population. When Pope Urban VI shows signs of mental instability—breaking into violent ranges and threatening to cut back radically on the cardinals'		Ludolf of Saxony. *Life of Christ.* A series of meditations, not a biography, written for edification and moral instruction. It draws heavily on patristic sources. (before 1378, printed in 1474) Wycliffe and others begin an English translation of the Vulgate.

Date	A. Theology, Doctrine, and Beliefs	B. People/Events	C. Wider Culture	D. Texts
1378 con't.		lifestyle—the cardinals retire to Anagni and elect Clement VII, who will later be recognized as an antipope. John Wycliffe is called before Bishop of London Courtenay and Archbishop of Canterbury Simon of Sudbury on the charge of heresy. He is dismissed with only a reprimand because of his influence at court.		
1379		Pope Urban VI's mercenary forces defeat Antipope Clement VII's troops. Clement moves to Avignon. France, Burgundy, Savoy, Naples, and Scotland side with Antipope Clement VII. Most of Germany, the Nordic countries, Hungary and England side with Pope Urban VI. Wycliffe repudiates the doctrine of transubstantiation.		
1380	Lollardry. Originally, and most accurately, it is the teachings of John Wycliffe and his followers. The core of these teachings is personal faith founded on the Bible, which is the sole authority in all religious matters. Lollardry repudiates transubstantiation, clerical celibacy, and indulgences. It is often seen as a foreshadowing of the Reformation in England.	Saint Catherine of Siena dies. Dominican nun (tertiary), mystic, and doctor of the church. She was probably the most influential woman in the church of her time. Thomas à Kempis is born as Thomas Hammerken. (ca.) Wycliffe begins to send out the "Poor Preachers," who preach his religious views across the country. The term "Holy Father" is first used in English to refer to the pope. (ca.)	Flamboyant architecture begins with the French court architect Guy de Dammartin. This late-gothic French style employs lively, flame-like forms in its tracery. (1380s)	
1381			Tyler's Rebellion, often called the Peasants' Revolt. An English uprising over a poll tax imposed to finance a war with France.	
1382		The persecution of the Lollards, John Wycliffe's followers, begins in England. John Wycliffe is expelled from Oxford.		John Wycliffe's earliest translation of the Latin Vulgate Bible into English. Wycliffe was known to have authored commentaries on the Bible, which informed the translation that bears his name. It is uncertain, however, how much of the actual translation he himself did.
1384		John Wycliffe, early reformer, dies.		
1386				Geoffrey Chaucer. *Canterbury Tales*. 17,000 lines in heroic couplets describing pilgrims' visits to the tomb of Thomas à Becket. (ca.)

Date	A. Theology, Doctrine, and Beliefs	B. People/Events	C. Wider Culture	D. Texts
1389	Visitation of Our Lady. The feast commemorates Mary's visit to her Cousin Elizabeth (Luke 1:39–56).	Pope Urban VI dies. Boniface IX becomes pope. The Feast of the Visitation of Our Lady, heretofore a Franciscan celebration, is extended to the entire church.		
1390		Pope Boniface IX offers to allow the schismatic cardinals and Clement VII to retain the purple if they return to Rome and swear allegiance to him.		*Theologia Germanica* (Latin: German Theology). An anonymous mystical treatise. It later influences Martin Luther and German and English pietists. (late fourteenth century)
1391		Antipope Clement VII excommunicates Pope Boniface IX, who returns the favor. Pope Boniface IX declares conciliar attempts to end the schism "sinful." Saint Bridget of Sweden is canonized.		
1392		Sergius, abbot of the Holy Trinity Monastery in Moscow, dies. He later becomes patron saint of Russia.		
1393	Indulgences. According to Catholic doctrine, they are one means by which the church mediates release from punishment for sins. They are based on the treasury of merits, by which the excess merit of Christ and the saints may be applied to sinners who exhibit appropriate penance, usually in acts of charity.	Saint John of Nepomuk dies. Patron saint of Bohemia, confessor to Queen Joanna (the wife of Wenceslas, king of Bohemia and Germany and Holy Roman emperor). He was murdered for resisting the king's attempts to change an abbey into a cathedral, creating a new see for one of the king's cronies. Indulgences begin to be exploited unscrupulously as means of fund raising during the tenure of Pope Boniface IX.		Juliana of Norwich. *Showings.* (*Sixteen Revelations of Divine Love*). A first-person account of sixteen ecstatic visions given to an English anchoress. Chief among the topics are the love of God and the passion of Christ.
1396		Walter Hilton, canon and mystic, dies.		
1398		France withdraws support of the Avignon papacy.		
1399			The House of Lancaster begins its reign in England.	
1400		The Blessed Alvarez symbolically represents Jerusalem's Way of the Cross in a series of small chapels at the Dominican friary of Cordova. In each chapel is painted scenes of the Passion. (before 1420) Naples transfers allegiance from Antipope Clement VII to Pope Boniface IX. This weakens the Avignon	The Aztec Empire arises. (ca.–1519)	

Date	A. Theology, Doctrine, and Beliefs	B. People/Events	C. Wider Culture	D. Texts
1400 con't.		papacy's position considerably. Plainsong sung during the mass intersperses vocal verses with organ verses. (ca.) The Easter vigil service is moved to the morning of Holy Saturday. (before)		
1403		France repledges its support to the Avignon papacy.		
1404		Antipope Benedict XIII offers to meet with Pope Boniface IX to discuss settlement of the Schism, including the possibility of Benedict's abdication. Boniface IX is ill and refuses to meet Benedict as an equal. Pope Boniface IX dies. Innocent VII becomes the third pope during the Great Schism.	Pier Paolo Vergerio. *Concerning Liberal Studies*. The first humanist treatise on education.	
1406		Gregory XII is elected pope for his expressed willingness to restore unity to the church.	Pope Innocent VII reorganizes the University of Rome, adding faculties of medicine, philosophy, logic, rhetoric, and a Chair of Greek.	
1407		Antipope Benedict XIII and Pope Gregory XII pledge to meet to resolve the schism. Due to procrastination and hedging on both sides (mostly Gregory's), the meeting never takes place.		
1408		France withdraws its support for the Avignon papacy, becoming neutral. Papal representatives arrest Antipope Benedict XIII and take him by force into Italy. Benedict escapes and flees to Perpignan (in the south of France, near the Spanish border) making it the seat of his court. Antipope Benedict XIII's cardinals desert him, and with the cardinals in Rome call for a general council to meet in Pisa. Benedict calls his own council in Perpignan. John Huss is barred from his priestly functions in Prague for preaching Wycliffe's doctrine.		
1409		The Council of Pisa meets. Neither Antipope Benedict XIII nor Pope Gregory XII attend. The council deposes both of them and elects Alexander V pope (antipope).		

Date	A. Theology, Doctrine, and Beliefs	B. People/Events	C. Wider Culture	D. Texts
1409 con't.		None of the three is willing to step down. The church has three "popes," beginning the "triple schism." Pope Gregory XII calls his own council in Cividale. It is sparsely attended but manages to excommunicate both Alexander V and Benedict XIII. Antipope Benedict XIII excommunicates Antipope Alexander V and begins to publish polemical tracts defending his papacy.		
1410		John Huss is excommunicated. Riots break out in Prague in his support. Antipope Alexander V marshals military forces and takes Rome from Pope Gregory XII after a lengthy, bloody siege. Antipope Alexander V dies. John XXIII is elected pope (antipope) by the Pisan cardinals.		
1412		Joan of Arc is born. Prague is laid under an interdict for supporting John Huss.		
1413		Sir J. Oldcastle's rising begins. It is a Lollard rebellion against persecution by the English government. (–1414)		
1414		Sixteenth Ecumenical Council: The Council of Constance. Antipope John XXIII convenes it to settle the Great Schism. Only the last sessions (XLII–XLV inclusive) of this council, and the decrees of earlier sessions approved by Martin V are considered ecumenical. (–1418) • Affirms that an Ecumenical council is superior in authority to the pope. • Chooses Cardinal Ottone Colonna to become pope. He takes the name Pope Martin V. • Condemns John Wycliffe, John Huss, and Jerome of Prague.		
1415		John Huss, Bohemian religious reformer, is burned at the stake on July 6, his birthday. One of the earliest church reformers, he predated the Protestant Reformation.	The Battle of Agincourt, a military engagement during the Hundred Years' War, is fought in France. Shakespeare later immortalizes it in his play, *Henry V.*	

Date	A. Theology, Doctrine, and Beliefs	B. People/Events	C. Wider Culture	D. Texts
1415 con't.		The Hussite Wars begin in Bohemia in response to John Huss's execution.		
		The Council of Constance reviews Wycliffe's heresies and orders his body disinterred and burned.		
		The Council of Constance deposes Antipope John XXIII and imprisons him in Germany for perjury, simony, and gross misconduct.		
		Antipope Benedict XIII, anticipating attack, sets up court in a castle in Peñiscola, Spain, calling it "the ark of Noah." Spain, Scotland, and Portugal are his only remaining supporters.		
1416		Jerome of Prague, a follower of Wycliffe's teachings and associate of John Huss, is burned for heresy.		
1417		Juliana of Norwich dies.		
		Pope Gregory XII dies. Martin V becomes pope.		
1418		The Council of Constance revokes all indulgences that purport to absolve both guilt and the penalty for sin.		Thomas a Kempis. *Imitation of Christ*. A manual of devotion in four parts: the spiritual life, inward things, internal consolation, and the communion. (published anonymously)
1419		Antipope John XXIII buys his freedom from prison, goes to Florence and submits to Pope Martin V.		
1420		The first Crusade against the Hussites begins.	Filippo Brunelleschi, a Florentine artist and architect, paints a perspective painting of the baptistry of the Florence Cathedral. The work is a part of his effort to codify the laws of perspective.	
1423		Antipope Benedict XIII dies in Peñiscola. Three of his four cardinals elect Clement VIII to be his successor. The remaining cardinal elects Antipope Benedict XIV, who immediately disappears and is never heard from again.		
1424		The Servites become mendicant friars.		
1425		Joan of Arc hears celestial voices that she believes belong to St. Michael, St. Catherine of Alexandria, and St. Margaret.		

Date	A. Theology, Doctrine, and Beliefs	B. People/Events	C. Wider Culture	D. Texts
1425 con't.		The Cemetery of the Innocents in Paris depicts the Dance of Death in a wall painting. In it Death, pictured as a skeleton, leads people from all walks of life on a dance to the grave. It is among the first of many European graveyards to use the motif.		
1428		Wycliffe's body is disinterred and burned, carrying out the decree of the Council of Constance.		
1429		During the Hundred Years' War, when the English were about to capture Orléans, Joan of Arc convinces the French Dauphin she has a divine mission to save France. Antipope Clement VIII renounces his rank and submits to Pope Martin V.		Jean le Charlier de Gerson, French churchman and Chancellor of Notre Dame. *Propositiones de sensu litterali Scripturae Sacrae* (Latin: Statement Concerning the Literal Meaning of Holy Scripture). A hermeneutic treatise proposing that the literal interpretation is most in keeping with the tradition and the pronouncements of the Church. (before 1429)
1430			Music during the Renaissance is "emancipated" from medieval constraints, including fixed poetic and liturgical forms. A new relationship between music and words arises in which composition of both together is viewed as a simultaneous creative process. Vocal and instrumental virtuosity as well as skill in composition are seen as ends in themselves. Modern terms for harmonic relationships (major, minor, modal) develop at this time. (–1600)	
1431	Conciliar theory vs. indefectibility of the pope. Are popes subject to the authority of church councils or vice versa? Conciliarism. An extreme form of conciliar theory, it is invoked at the Council of Basel. It maintains that councils are *always* the highest authority in the church. It is the last of the reform movements in the Catholic Church before the advent of the Reformation. (peaked in 1431–1449)	Seventeenth Ecumenical Council: The Council of Florence (Basel/Ferrara). Its goal was the pacification of Bohemia and the reform of the church. Because of quarrels with the pope, the council was transferred first to Ferrara (1438), then to Florence (1439). The consequences of this council were largely short-lived. Only part of it is considered ecumenical. (–1439) Eugene IV becomes pope. Saint Joan of Arc is executed after having turned the tide of the Hundred Years' War to France's favor. She was convicted of claiming direct		

Date	A. Theology, Doctrine, and Beliefs	B. People/Events	C. Wider Culture	D. Texts
1431 con't.		responsibility to God apart from the mediation of the church, and of wearing men's clothes. She was burned at the stake on May 30 as a heretic. She later becomes patron saint of France. A unsuccessful Lollard uprising forces the movement underground.		
1433				Margery Kempe. *The Book of Margery Kempe*. Recounts the travels and mystical experiences of a married woman and mother who lived as a ascetic. For the modern reader it raises the question of the relationship between mystical experience and mental illness.
1434			Johann Gutenberg invents movable type. (–1435)	
1436			Filippo Brunelleschi, a Florentine artist and architect, completes the first mathematically designed cathedral dome.	
1438	Unity. The Council of Florence defines "unity" between churches as agreement on matters of faith despite diversity of rites. The definition stands into modern times.	The Council of Florence. • Formally affirms the list of seven sacraments: Eucharist, baptism, confirmation, penance, extreme unction, holy orders, and matrimony. Margery Kempe, author and mystic, dies. (after)	The Incan Empire arises. (–1538) The first mobile artillery is used in warfare. (fifteenth century)	French clergy issue the *Pragmatic Sanction of Bourges*. It asserts France's right to administer its own property and fill its own ecclesiastical offices without Roman intervention.
1439		Council of Florence (Florence session). • Attempts to reconcile the East-West split over the filioque clause. The attempt is unsuccessful. • Defines the doctrine of purgatory. • Condemns metempsychosis (reincarnation). Negotiations between the Eastern and Western church end in acrimony. Eastern bishops leave the council with the statement "Better the turban of the Prophet than the tiara of the pope."		
1440				Nicholas of Cusa *De docta ignorantia* (Latin: Concerning the Learned Ignorant). Maintains that pure truth is unknowable to humanity, that all known truth is incomplete and approximate. God, therefore, cannot be known but only intuited. It sets the groundwork for the height of the Renaissance.

Date	A. Theology, Doctrine, and Beliefs	B. People/Events	C. Wider Culture	D. Texts
1441		The Immaculate Conception of Mary is declared to be a doctrine which is "pious, consonant with Catholic worship, Catholic faith, right reason, and Holy Scripture." It is no longer admissible to preach otherwise.		
1443			Construction of King's College Chapel is begun at Cambridge. It is a masterpiece of the perpendicular style, the English version of late gothic architecture.	
1447		Nicholas V becomes pope.		
1450		Pope Nicholas V founds the Vatican library. The Unitas Fratrum, an organization of Hussites, is formed.		
1452		Girolamo Savonarola is born.	Leonardo da Vinci is born.	
1453		Ottoman Turks turn the Hagia Sophia into a mosque.	The Ottoman Turks capture Constantinople and kill the emperor. The Byzantine Empire falls. The Hundred Years' War ends.	
1455		Callistus III becomes pope.	The houses of Lancaster and York in England fight the dynastic civil wars known as the Wars of the Roses. (–1485)	Johann Gutenberg prints "the Gutenberg Bible," an edition of the Latin Vulgate, using movable type. (some time between 1450 and 1456)
1456		Christians are forbidden social contact with Jews by papal legislation. Joan of Arc is vindicated.		
1457		Pope Callistus III orders universal observance of the Feast of the Transfiguration.		
1458		Pius II becomes pope. The term "Stations" is first used to apply to the Way of the Cross in Jerusalem. Pilgrims begin at Calvary and work their way back to Pilate's house.		
1459		Saint Antoninus, archbishop of Florence, dies. As a Dominican friar he lived a life of poverty despite the temptations of the office. He was renowned both as a theologian and as an administrator. He was also personally involved in charity for victims of the plague and other natural disasters.		

Date	A. Theology, Doctrine, and Beliefs	B. People/Events	C. Wider Culture	D. Texts
1460			The Portuguese import 700 to 800 slaves from Africa to Portugal.	
1461		Pope Pius II canonizes Catherine of Siena.	The House of York begins its reign in England.	
1462			Ivan the Great becomes the first Tsar of Russia. (–1505)	
1464		Paul II becomes pope.		
1465			Music is first printed using the printing press.	
1466			Donatello, Renaissance artist, dies.	
1469		Desiderius Erasmus is born in Rotterdam. (possibly 1466)		
1470			The Portuguese discover the Gold Coast of West Africa. The legend of King Arthur, gleaned from French sources, is rendered in Middle English.	
1471		Sixtus IV becomes pope. Thomas à Kempis, one of the most widely read authors of the Middle Ages, dies.		
1473			Nicolaus Copernicus is born.	
1474			Lunar nautical navigation begins to be used. Guillaume Dufay, French composer, one of the most influential of the fifteenth century, dies.	
1475		Monstrances, the vessels displaying the consecrated Eucharistic Host for veneration, take the modern shape. (late fifteenth century) The Vatican library is first cataloged.	Michelangelo is born.	*Everyman.* An English morality play, an allegory of death and the fate of the soul is written anonymously in the late fifteenth century. It is one of the finest known morality plays.
1476		Pope Sixtus IV issues the first plenary indulgences (in the papal bull *Salvator Noster*). Pope Sixtus IV decrees that the entire Roman Catholic Church adopt the Feast of the Immaculate Conception.		
1478		Ferdinand and Isabella, king and queen of Spain, seek out lapsed converted Jews, beginning the Spanish Inquisition.		
1481		The Spanish inquisitor general Tomás de Torquemada conducts the first *Auto-Da-Fé* (Portuguese for "act of faith") in Seville. It is a public execution of persons condemned by the Inquisition.		

Date	A. Theology, Doctrine, and Beliefs	B. People/Events	C. Wider Culture	D. Texts
1483		Martin Luther is born to a miner and his wife.		
1484		Innocent VIII becomes pope. Ulrich Zwingli is born.		Pope Innocent VIII. *Summis Desiderantes* (Latin: Supreme Desire). The most noteworthy papal bull promulgated as a blow against witchcraft. Innocent appoints regional inquisitors to carry out its provisions.
1485		Hugh Latimer is born.	The House of Tudor begins its reign in England. Sir Thomas Malory. *Morte d'Arthur.* One of the best known renditions of the Arthur legends.	
1489		Thomas Cranmer is born.		
1491		Ignatius Loyola is born. (1495?)		
1492		Alexander VI becomes pope.	The Aztec city of Tenochtitlán has a population of 300,000, making it three times the size of the largest European city. Christopher Columbus makes landfall on islands off North America. Ferdinand and Isabella, king and queen of Spain, conquer the Moors in their country. They order Spanish Jews and Muslims to convert or leave the country.	
1494		William Tyndale is born.	The Medici family is temporarily removed from power and the Florentine Republic is established in Italy. (–1498)	Walter Hilton. *Scale of Perfection.* Though editions were available before this time, Hilton's best known work first becomes available in a printed edition in 1494. It subsequently becomes one of the most popular devotional guides in late fifteenth and sixteenth century England. It describes the renewal of the defaced image of God in humanity. It is concerned with ethics as well as contemplation. (written before 1396.)
1495			Jews are expelled from Portugal.	Earliest extant manuscript containing an Ave Maria identical to the modern version.
1496		Girolamo Savonarola burns "the vanities of Florence." At his urging, Lenten celebrators amass a collection of paintings, books, masks, and mirrors for a public burning. Later that year he is forbidden to preach.	The House of Hapsburg allies with the royal House of Spain.	

Date	A. Theology, Doctrine, and Beliefs	B. People/Events	C. Wider Culture	D. Texts
1497		Girolamo Savonarola is excommunicated. Johannes Ockeghem composes the earliest known polyphonic Requiem Mass. (before) Philipp Melanchthon is born.	John Cabot voyages to North America.	
1498		Girolamo Savonarola is hanged and burned as a heretic. Relics and medals containing his image begin to be circulated throughout Europe.	Vasco da Gama discovers a route to India around the Cape of Good Hope. Leonardo da Vinci finishes the *Last Supper*.	
1499		The Feast of the Holy Name originates. (end of the fifteenth century)	English law lists seven capital offenses: treason (grand and petty), murder, larceny, burglary, rape, and arson.	
1500		Nicholas Ridley is born. Pilgrims walking the Way of the Cross in Jerusalem begin to walk it from Pilate's house to Calvary instead of vice versa. (early part of the sixteenth century) Morality plays reach the height of their popularity (in the fifteenth and sixteenth centuries)	The pencil is invented in England. Michelangelo finishes the *Pieta*. Knighthood is sometimes conferred on civilians as a reward for meritorious service.	The Mozarabic Rite Missal is printed by Francisco Cardinal Ximénez de Cisneros, who preserves the rite by founding the Corpus Christi chapel in the Toledo Cathedral and endowing chaplains to use the rite in it. The rite survives to modern times because of those efforts.
1501		The Roman Catholic Church orders all books opposing the authority of the church be burned.		
1502		The chalice and paten are brought to the altar in a sacculum or lintheum, the precursor of the modern veil. Martin Luther graduates with a B.A. from the University of Erfurt, where he received a traditional Nominalist education.	The University of Wittenberg is founded.	Francisco Cardinal Ximénez de Cisneros prints the Mozarabic Rite Breviary for use in the Corpus Christi chapel in the Toledo Cathedral.
1503		Julius II becomes pope. Pius III becomes pope.	Leonardo da Vinci's *Mona Lisa* is completed.	Jean Chappuis. *Corpus Iuris Canonici* (Latin: Body of Canon Law). It is the *Decretum* of Gratian published with three official and two private collections of decretals. With the decrees of the Council of Trent (1545–63), it is law of the Roman Catholic Church until 1917.
1504			Michelangelo sculpts the *David*.	
1505		Martin Luther receives a M.A. from the University of Erfurt and enrolls in the faculty of law. Martin Luther joins the Augustinian order after a near-death experience in a thunderstorm.		

Date	A. Theology, Doctrine, and Beliefs	B. People/Events	C. Wider Culture	D. Texts
1506	German politics pave the way for Lutheran theology. In Luther's Germany, the working poor increasingly see the church as part of the oppressive ruling class. The growing middle class find they have less and less in common with the old feudal/monarchical air of the church. The princes continue to struggle with Rome over taxes, jurisdiction, and political clout.	Construction on St. Peter's Basilica begins. Johann Tetzel begins selling indulgences in Germany as a part of fund raising campaign to raise money for the rebuilding of St. Peter's Basilica in Rome. Ulrich Zwingli enters the Roman Catholic priesthood. Ulrich Zwingli teaches himself Greek and Hebrew, reads the church fathers, and memorizes the Epistles of Paul. (–1516) Francis Xavier is born.		
1507			The name "America" is first used.	
1508			King Henry VIII of England ascends to the throne and marries Catherine of Aragon.	
1509		John Calvin is born to a middle-class family in Noyon, a village in northern France.	Jews are persecuted in Germany. All Talmuds are ordered destroyed.	Desiderius Erasmus. *In Praise of Folly*. A satire of all elements of society with particular focus on the papacy and the abuses of the church.
1510			Botticelli, Renaissance artist, dies.	
1512		Martin Luther is appointed Professor of Holy Scriptures at the University of Wittenberg. Eighteenth Ecumenical Council: Fifth Lateran Council. Its decrees are mainly disciplinary. (–1517) • Plans a new Crusade against the Turks; but events in Luther's Germany distract the church's attention, and the Crusade never comes together. • Condemns the *Pragmatic Sanction of Bourges*. The elevation of the chalice begins to be given greater importance. The Benedictus qui venit (Mt. 21:9) is no longer sung immediately after the elevation of the Host, but after both elevations have taken place. (early sixteenth century, 1512 in Paris)	Copernicus. *Commentariolus*. Originally a relatively minor manuscript with a small audience, it states the earth and other planets turn around the sun. Almost immediately after publication, it receives papal approbation. Michelangelo finishes Sistine Chapel.	Jacobus Faber. *Sancti Pauli Epistolae* (Latin: Epistles of St. Paul). The earliest rumblings of the Reformation in France, this commentary asserts the doctrine of justification by faith alone.
1513		The dissolution of monasteries in Norway begins. (–1523) John Knox is born. Leo X becomes pope. The first mention of the *Advocatus Diaboli* (Devil's Advocate) is during the canon-	Niccolò Machiavelli. *The Prince*. Proposes self-interest as the foundation for effective rule. Juan Ponce de Leon searches for the fountain of youth in Florida.	

Date	A. Theology, Doctrine, and Beliefs	B. People/Events	C. Wider Culture	D. Texts
1513 con't.		ization of St. Lawrence Justinian under Pope Leo X. (–1521)	Vasco Núñez de Balboa, a Spanish explorer, becomes the first European to discover the Pacific Ocean.	
1514		Pope Leo X canonizes Saint Bruno.		
1515		Teresa of Ávila is born.		
1516	In his study of St. Paul's Epistle to the Romans, Martin Luther discovers that the righteous live by faith, which is a gift of God. This insight eases his personal religious torment and forms the foundation for his later writings and reforming work.	Francis I, king of France, signs the Concordat of Bologne, an agreement with the pope that gives French kings the right to appoint all bishops in their realm.	Ghettoization of Jews begins in Venice.	Desiderius Erasmus. *Novum Instrumentum* (Latin: New Document). The first critical edition of the Greek New Testament, it also contains a parallel Latin text. It becomes the basis for Luther's German translation and, with some revisions, the King James Bible. (second edition: 1519) Thomas More. *Utopia.* Describes an ideal community living under natural law and practicing a natural religion.
1517	The earliest Reformation documents stress return to the doctrinal and organization purity of the early church, especially as reflected in Augustine. Early reformers want not innovation but purification, a purging of medieval doctrinal accretions.	Luther nails his "Ninety-five Theses" to the door of the Schlosskirche (German: Castle Church) in Wittenberg. The Oratory of Divine Love seeks moral reform in the Roman church. Within the Franciscan order, the Observants, those who want a return to strict observance of the Rule, split from the Conventuals. Rome recognizes the Observants as the true Franciscans.	The Turks conquer Egypt and Arabia.	Pope Leo X. *Cum Postquam.* A papal bull outlining the church's doctrine of indulgences. The first formalized doctrine on the subject, it is prompted by Luther's opposition.
1518		Ulrich Zwingli goes to Zurich to become People's Preacher at Grossmünster. Zwingli persuades the Zurich city council to forbid entrance to a Franciscan monk commissioned to sell indulgences in the city.		
1519		Martin Luther and Johann Eck debate at Leipzig. Luther denies the infallibility of the pope and the authority of the General Councils. Ulrich Zwingli preaches expository sermons on the New Testament. The Swiss Reformation begins. Zwingli reads the works of Martin Luther for the first time.	Hernán Cortés conquers Mexico. The Aztec empire falls. (–1521) Leonardo da Vinci dies. Charles I, king of Spain, bribes the electors and becomes Charles V, Holy Roman Emperor. He later also becomes king of Germany.	
1520	Anabaptists. As radical reformers they build their lives on three basic tenets: literal observance of biblical	In the bull *Exsurge Domine* (Latin: Arise, Lord), Pope Leo X gives Martin Luther sixty days to recant. Luther burns	Only 20% of paintings in Europe are nonreligious. Chocolate is brought to Europe.	Martin Luther. *Babylonian Captivity of the Church.* Attacks the denial of the cup to laity, the mass as a

Date	A. Theology, Doctrine, and Beliefs	B. People/Events	C. Wider Culture	D. Texts
1520 con't.	commands, adult baptism, and separation from "the world."	the bull outside the walls of Wittenberg. Cambridge students begin to discuss Martin Luther's ideas. Thomas Münzer begins the Anabaptist movement in Germany. Ulrich Zwingli adopts Luther's doctrines of *sola fide* (by faith alone) and *sola scriptura* (by Scripture alone) to be the heart of his theology. He persuades the Zurich town council to forbid all religious teaching without explicit foundation in Scripture. He also begins to denounce monasticism, purgatory, and relics and to preach predestination and the two (as opposed to seven) sacraments.	Suleiman I, "Suleiman the Magnificent," becomes Sultan of Turkey. During his lifetime, he invades Hungary, Tripoli, Rhodes, Austria. He also destroys the Spanish fleet. (–1566)	sacrifice, and the seven (as opposed to two) sacraments. This work undeniably sets Luther against Rome. Martin Luther. *A Brief Explanation of the Ten Commandments, the Creed, and the Lord's Prayer.* An early Lutheran primer of religion.
1521	Feast of Guardian Angels. This feast acknowledges angels' protection of human bodies and souls. Since the sixteenth century, it has been celebrated separately from the Feast of Saint Michael.	The earliest record of the Feast of Guardian Angels is in Cologne. Pope Leo X excommunicates Martin Luther. Martin Luther is called before the Diet of Worms. He refuses to recant and is put under the ban of the empire. Martin Luther hides at Wartburg castle. (–1522) Ignatius Loyola, a soldier at the time, is seriously wounded during the siege of Pampeluna. He spends a year at Manresa in recovery and meditation, from which he derives *the Spiritual Exercises.* Andreas von Carlstadt is the first Reformer to celebrate the Eucharist in the vernacular. Though it is Christmas Day, he wears no vestments. He also communicates the laity in both kinds.	Hernán Cortés, Spanish explorer, conquers the Aztec city of Tenochtitlán and razes its main temple. The temple stones are used to build a Catholic Church. Emperor Charles V signs the Edict of Worms, an imperial ban on Luther and his followers.	Philip Melanchthon. *Loci Communes* (Latin: Common Places). The first systematic Protestant theology. King Henry VIII of England. *Defense of the Seven Sacraments (Assertio septem sacramentorum).* Directed at Reformation doctrine in general, and at Martin Luther in particular, it asserts the Roman doctrine of the sacraments and wins him the title "Defender of the Faith" from Pope Leo X. Pope Leo X excommunicates Martin Luther in the papal bull *Decet Romanum Pontificem* (3 January). It is the pope's response to Luther's burning a papal bull and several Catholic books.
1522		John Jewel is born. Ulrich Zwingli preaches against fasting. As a result, some of Zwingli's followers in Switzerland publicly eat meat during Lent. They are arrested, tried, and released with only token punishment. The cantonal government of Zurich rules that all customs henceforth will be based on the Word of God. Hadrian VI becomes pope.	Ferdinand Magellan's expedition completes the first around-the-world journey. (Magellan himself was killed in the Philippines in 1521.)	The University of Alcalá publishes the Complutensian Polyglot Bible in Latin, Greek, Hebrew, and Aramaic. It reflects a growing interest in biblical study. Ignatius Loyola. *Spiritual Exercises.* Meditations, rules, and directions for use over four weeks to help the seeker overcome self-will and surrender to God. (Written–1523. Published in 1548.)

Date	A. Theology, Doctrine, and Beliefs	B. People/Events	C. Wider Culture	D. Texts
1522 con't.		John "Oecolampadius" Hussgen wins Basel over to Reformation doctrine.		Martin Luther. *Contra Henricum Regem Anglicum* (Latin: Against Henry, king of England). Luther's response to King Henry VIII of England's *Defense of the Seven Sacraments*. Neither subtle nor tactful, it cost him most of his support in England.
1523	Consubstantiation. The Lutheran doctrine that both the bread and wine, and the Body and Blood of Christ exist whole and unchanged in the Eucharistic elements. Key figure: Martin Luther.	Religious ornament is abolished in Zurich. Zwingli destroys the organ at Grossmünster, knocks out the stained glass windows, whitewashes the walls, puts in plain benches. A wooden table replaces the altar and a simple wooden cup replaces the chalice. Johann von Essen and Heinrich Voss are burned at the stake in Brussels. They are the first martyrs of the Reformation. Clement VII becomes pope.		Martin Luther. *Forma Missae et Communionis* (Latin: Form of the Mass and Communication). The Lutheran view of the Eucharist.
1524		Martin Luther ceases to wear his Augustinian habit.		Johann Walther publishes the *Little Sacred Songbook*, the first Protestant hymnal. Desiderius Erasmus. *De libero arbitrio (On Free Will)*. Emphasizes the importance of human free will. Erasmus enters the Reformation debate and sets himself up against Luther's ideas on the topic.
1525	During the Reformation period, Christianity discovers a new individualism: the individual stands alone before God and may stand opposed to the organized church. Sacramentarianism. The belief that the Body and Blood of Christ are present in the Eucharist *only* in a "sacramental," i.e., metaphorical, sense. The term is coined by Martin Luther and applied primarily to Zwingli and Oecolampadius, though it comes to refer to any doctrine that denies the Real Presence of Christ in the Eucharist.	The Swiss Brethren, an Anabaptist group near Zurich, begins a fellowship distinguished by believer's baptism and a rejection of all infant baptism. Conrad Grebel rebaptizes Georg Blaurock, a former Roman Catholic priest, and several others, marking the beginnings of the Anabaptist movement. The Anabaptists are expelled from Zurich. Jacobus Faber, French humanist, is forced to flee France because of his sympathetic views toward the Reformation. Martin Luther answers Germany's warring peasants, presenting the biblical doctrine of slavery. Martin Luther marries Katharina von Bora.	Peasants' War. 50,000 peasants are killed in an uprising at Frankenhausen, Germany, after Luther encourages the princes to restore order (May 15). Frederick the Wise, Elector of Saxony, dies. John the Steadfast becomes Elector. (–1532) The shotgun is invented.	Martin Luther. *De servo arbitrio (Bondage of the Will)*. Luther answers Erasmus.

Date	A. Theology, Doctrine, and Beliefs	B. People/Events	C. Wider Culture	D. Texts
1525 con't.		At Zwingli's urging, the Zurich town council abolishes the Catholic Mass. Scottish Parliament prohibits the import of Reformation books.		
1526		The "Moravian brothers" (Anabaptists) settle in Moravia.		Martin Luther. *German Mass.* Based on the Latin Mass but without reference to the Mass as sacrifice. William Tyndale. *Tyndale New Testament.* An English translation based on Erasmus' Greek text.
1527	Ubiquitarianism. A Reformation doctrine: If God is omnipresent, and Christ is both human and divine, then Christ's human nature is omnipresent. It is a part of the Lutheran doctrine of the Real Presence of Christ in the Eucharist. Key figures: Martin Luther.	The University of Marburg is founded as the first Protestant university in Europe. Troops of the Holy Roman Empire imprison Pope Clement VII.	The army of Holy Roman Emperor Charles V sacks Rome. "The end of the Renaissance." High Renaissance period begins. It is the age of Michelangelo, Raphael, and Titian. (ca.–1650)	Martin Luther. "A Mighty Fortress is our God." The Schleitheim Confession. The first Anabaptist doctrinal statement.
1528	Zwinglianism. The doctrinal position of the Swiss Reformation centered in Zurich. It was born from Zwingli's expository preaching of Scripture, which was based on a chapter-by-chapter study of the Bible in its original languages. Zwinglianism maintains (1) that Communion is merely a symbolic act with no Real Presence of Christ in the elements; (2) that infant baptism is a natural Christian extension of Old Testament circumcision; (3) that any custom, doctrine, sacrament, etc., not explicitly sanctioned by Scripture should be abolished.	In the 1520s and 1530s, hundreds of Anabaptists are killed by Catholics, Lutherans, and Zwinglians alike. Lower class, and largely lacking in a larger ecclesiastical organization, these Anabaptists are virtually defenseless. Austrian authorities burn Balthasar Hübmaier, Anabaptist leader, as a heretic. After the "Disputation of Berne," John "Oecolampadius" Hussgen secures the Canton of Berne's agreement to support the Reformation. The Reformation begins in Scotland. Patrick Hamilton is burned at the stake for advocating Lutheranism. His death fuels the Reformation in that country. In Switzerland (both Zurich and Geneva), and later in England, the Reformation gains momentum as business people realize a dissociation from the centralized authority of Rome makes good financial sense.	A severe plague strikes England. The first surgery manual is published.	Guillaume Farel. *La Maniere et Fasson.* The first Protestant liturgy in French. F. Kolb and Berchtold Haller. *The Theses of Berne.* The doctrinal statement of the Reformation in Berne. It consists of ten Zwinglian propositions directed against Catholic "abuses."
1529		Marburg Colloquy: Martin Luther and Ulrich Zwingli meet at Marburg in Hesse. They agree doctrinally on most things but differ on the Lord's Supper. John "Oecolampadius" Hussgen defends sacramentarian-	Civil war erupts between the Protestant and Catholic Swiss Cantons.	Martin Luther. *Small Catechism* and *Large Catechism.* Religious education for Protestants. The Small Catechism is for children and the Large for adults. The Capuchin order draws up its own rule, distinguishing

Date	A. Theology, Doctrine, and Beliefs	B. People/Events	C. Wider Culture	D. Texts
1529 con't.		ism, the Zwinglian Eucharistic doctrine, at the Colloquy of Marburg. The term *Protestantism* is first used at the Diet of Speyer, an imperial assembly.		itself from its Franciscan roots.
1530		Diet of Augsburg. Holy Roman Emperor Charles V summons the German Lutheran nobility to Augsburg to account for their "Lutheran" views. They present the emperor with Melanchthon's Augsburg Confession. Roman theologians issue a refutation, and Emperor Charles V declares that the Protestants have been defeated. The Feast of the Holy Name is officially granted to the Franciscans.	Thomas Cardinal Wolsey, Lord Chancellor of England, is arrested on the charge of high treason. He dies in captivity.	Torgau Articles. A summary of the discipline and ceremony of Luther, Melanchthon, Bugenhagen, and Jonas for the Diet of Augsburg. Philipp Melanchthon, et al. Augsburg Confession. A deliberately moderate Lutheran confession of faith. It contains both doctrine and a list of ecclesiastical abuses which demand remedy.
1531		Ulrich Zwingli, Swiss reformer, is killed while serving as a military chaplain at the Battle of Kappel during the Swiss Civil War. The "Forest" (Catholic) Swiss Cantons win the Swiss Civil War. The progress of the Reformation is halted with the country split—half Catholic, half Protestant. Heinrich Bullinger succeeds Ulrich Zwingli as Chief Pastor of Zurich. John "Oecolampadius" Hussgen, the Reformer of Basel, dies. Originally won over by Luther, he established the Zwinglian Reformation in Basel and Berne. An apparition of Mary appears to Juan Diego in Mexico. It is commemorated as "Our Lady of Guadalupe."	Erasmus publishes the "complete" works of Aristotle. The League of Schmalkald is formed. It is a protective alliance of Protestant princes under the leadership of Saxony and Hesse.	Philipp Melanchthon. *Apology of the Augsburg Confession.* Melanchthon's reply to a group of Roman Catholic scholars who critiqued the Augsburg Confession.
1532	In England, early reform was prompted not by doctrinal differences with Rome but by desires to throw off papal authority and to appropriate the resources of the Roman church for England. Decidedly Protestant doctrine did not play a major role until the reign of Edward VI.	Submission of Clergy. In response to royal threats, the English clergy promise to make no new canon without royal license. King Henry VIII becomes supreme in all ecclesiastical affairs. The Religious Peace of Nuremberg grants German Protestants free exercise of religion until further notice.	Frederick the Magnanimous becomes Elector of Saxony. (−1547)	

Date	A. Theology, Doctrine, and Beliefs	B. People/Events	C. Wider Culture	D. Texts
1533		Act of Restraint of Appeals. Ecclesiastical legal appeals from England to Rome are no longer allowed. King Henry VIII becomes England's supreme arbiter of both church and state affairs. King Henry VIII is excommunicated from the Roman Catholic Church. Thomas Cranmer becomes archbishop of Canterbury. John Calvin has what he describes as a "sudden conversion." He leaves his humanistic work on the ethics of Seneca and begins the study that will eventually become the *Institutes*.	Thomas Cranmer annuls King Henry VIII's marriage to Catherine of Aragon. Henry marries Anne Boleyn.	
1534		Ignatius Loyola founds the Society of Jesus (Jesuits). Approximately twenty-four Protestants are burned alive in Paris. (–1535) John Calvin leaves France for Basel. (ca.) Act of Supremacy. King Henry VIII is granted the title "the Only Supreme Head in Earth of the Church of England, Called Anglicana Ecclesia." The Church of England separates from Rome. Paul III becomes pope.	King Henry VIII requires all subjects to sign an Oath of Succession recognizing Elizabeth as the legitimate heir to the throne.	Martin Luther releases the first edition of his German translation of the Bible. Oswald "Myconius" Geisshäusler. The Basel Confession. It is an attempted compromise position between the Lutheran and Zwinglian doctrines of the Eucharist. It earns the distrust of the stricter Zwinglians.
1535		Henry VIII requires subjects to sign the Oath of Succession. The oath ostensibly recognizes Elizabeth's right to the throne, but it also implies Henry's supremacy over the church. Some devout Catholics refuse to acknowledge Henry as head of the church and so refuse to sign the oath. Saint John Fisher, bishop of Rochester; Saint John Houghton, Carthusian prior; Saint Thomas More, Lord Chancellor of England; and three other Carthusian monks and are beheaded for refusing to sign the Oath of Succession. Angela Merici founds the Order of St. Ursula, the first women's teaching order in the Roman Catholic Church.		Coverdale Bible. Mile's Coverdale's first translation. It is an English translation based on the Vulgate, Tyndale's New Testament, and Lutheran texts. Printed in Protestant Europe, it is the first complete, printed English Bible. It forms the basis for Matthew's Bible and the Great Bible.

Date	A. Theology, Doctrine, and Beliefs	B. People/Events	C. Wider Culture	D. Texts
1536		Menno Simons, a former Roman Catholic priest, renounces his connections to the Catholic Church, becomes an Anabaptist, and begins to lead the Anabaptists in Holland. John Knox enters the priesthood. Jacob Hutter dies. He was the leader of the Hutterian Brethren, a communitarian religious sect that originated among the Anabaptists in Moravia. John Calvin becomes Genevan coadjutor. He is twenty-seven years old. Desiderius Erasmus, Renaissance humanist and scholar, dies. Thomas Cromwell spearheads the dissolution of English monasteries (stage one). William Tyndale, Bible translator, is kidnaped from the free city of Antwerp and taken into Catholic Europe. There he is tried for heresy and executed. Pope Paul III establishes a Commission of Cardinals to reform the papal court. King Christian III introduces the Reformation to Denmark.	Henry VIII and Anne Boleyn's marriage is annulled. Anne is beheaded for adultery, which was considered tantamount to treason against her husband the king. Michelangelo adds *the Last Judgement* to the Sistine Chapel. Act of Union of 1536. Wales is incorporated with England.	Wittenberg Concord. Lutherans and Swiss Zwinglians agree over the doctrine of the Eucharist. The agreement soon collapses. John Calvin. *Institutes of the Christian Religion.* One of the most influential books of the Reformation, it is a systematic theology from a Protestant perspective. Its two main sources of authority are the Bible and (a distant second, but far ahead of any other source) Augustine. It is published when Calvin is 26 years old. (final edition 1559) First Helvetic Confession (also known as the Second Confession of Basle). A Lutheran-Zwinglian hybrid, it becomes the doctrinal statement for German-speaking Protestant Switzerland. Thomas Cromwell and Thomas Cranmer. Ten Articles. The first articles of faith issued by the Church of England during the Reformation. It is largely Catholic.
1537		Norway becomes officially Lutheran. Ignatius Loyola and the Society of Jesus receive the oral approval of Pope Paul III.	Denmark conquers Norway. The first music conservatories are established.	Martin Luther. Schmalkaldic Articles. Issued as a statement of Lutheran doctrine, these articles are incorporated into the Book of Concord in 1580. Matthew's Bible. Published under the name of Thomas Matthew, it is actually Tyndale's translation with gaps in the Old Testament filled with excerpts from the Coverdale Bible.
1538		King Henry VIII is excommunicated a second time. John Calvin rejects the Geneva city council's attempts to bring the city into line with the Reformation in Berne. Instead he requires that all Genevans subscribe to *his* confession of faith. He proposes excommunication as a tool for the enforcement of civic law. Along with Guillaume Farel, he is expelled from the city. Thomas Cromwell, English Vicar General and chief		

Date	A. Theology, Doctrine, and Beliefs	B. People/Events	C. Wider Culture	D. Texts
1538 con't.		advisor to Henry VIII, orders that a copy of the (yet to be issued) Great Bible, an English-language Bible be set up in all English churches.		
1539		King Henry VIII and Vicar General Thomas Cromwell dissolve English monasteries (stage two). Hugh Latimer, Henry VIII's royal chaplain, opposes the Six Articles. He is forced to resign, forbidden to preach, and temporarily imprisoned. Though canon law still forbids it, many English clerics have gotten married in an imitation of Lutheran clergy. The Six Articles dictates they separate.	The Religious Truce of Frankfurt grants limited toleration to the Reformation in Germany.	Six Articles. Popularly known as the whip with six strings. It reaffirms Catholic doctrine to prevent the spread of Reformation doctrine and practice in England. Dissent becomes a felony punishable by execution. Great Bible. It is Miles Coverdale's English translation based on the Vulgate, Matthew's Bible, and Lutheran texts. Its literary value far outweighs its scholarship. Its rhythmic expression is preserved in the 1979 *Book of Common Prayer* psalms.
1540		Ignatius Loyola's Society of Jesus (the Jesuits) receives official confirmation from Pope Paul III. Throughout the next fifteen years, they grow to be a dominant force in the Counter-Reformation. (–1555) The Brethren (Anabaptists) in Holland begin to be called Mennonites. (1540s)	Henry VIII marries Anne of Cleves. (January) Henry VIII marries Catherine Howard. (August) Thomas Cromwell, Vicar General and chief advisor to King Henry VIII, is beheaded for treason.	
1541		John Calvin returns to Geneva and institutes a theocratic regime. The Reformed church, backed by secular authority, closely regulates the behavior of Geneva's citizens. (–1564) Francis Xavier sails for India. The "traditional" English text of the Lord's Prayer begins to be used. (during the reign of Henry VIII)		
1542		Largely in response to the Protestant threat, Pope Paul III establishes the "Congregation of the Inquisition," also called the Holy Office, as the final appeal in cases of heresy. They are empowered to discover, try, and judge heretics. John of the Cross is born. Francis Xavier establishes a mission to Portuguese India. The Jesuits arrive in Ulster, but because of Henry VIII's influence, they are unable to stay there safely.		John Calvin. *The Form of Prayer*. The foundational document for subsequent Reformed worship. *Genevan Catechism*. A series of questions and answers about basic Christian doctrine, it becomes of the central documents of Calvinist Geneva. It is published in both French and Latin.

Date	A. Theology, Doctrine, and Beliefs	B. People/Events	C. Wider Culture	D. Texts
1543		The first Protestants are burned to death during the Spanish Inquisition. John Calvin limits congregational singing to monophony, believing polyphony detracts from the impact of the words. He dismisses music in Latin as "Roman" and instrumental music as "Old Testament." (1541–1564)	Nicolaus Copernicus. *De Revolutionibus Orbium Coelestium.* Announces the heliocentric theory to the world and begins the Copernican Revolution. Nicolaus Copernicus dies. Portuguese sailors reach Japan.	Henry VIII releases a revised version of the Sarum Breviary.
1544		John Knox leaves the Roman Catholic priesthood and becomes a private tutor. (ca.) Thomas Cranmer heads the effort to translate the liturgy into English.		The Litany in English. The earliest English liturgy of the Anglican Reformation.
1545	Council of Trent (Roman Catholic). It declares the Old Testament, New Testament, Apocrypha, and unwritten traditions passed through those in the line of the apostles to be authoritative. It also declares the Church to be the only authority allowed to interpret Scripture.	Nineteenth Ecumenical Council: Council of Trent. It lasts eighteen years and spans the administrations of five popes. Its task is two-fold: confrontation of the Protestant Reformation and its effects, and the renovation of discipline and dogma within the Roman church. It issues more dogmatic and reformatory decrees than any other council. Most of the customs, rubrics, and rules for the recitation of the Mass and the Divine Office in place at the time of Vatican I are laid down by the Council of Trent. (–1563) Francis Xavier establishes a mission to Malacca and the Malay Archipelago. Selective and sporadic persecution of Protestants takes place in England. Some are burned at the stake. However, Henry VIII entrusts the education of his son Edward to Protestants. (Mid 1540s)		
1546		Martin Luther, one of the greatest Reformers of his time, dies. Council of Trent—first period. • Declares that in "matters of faith and morals belonging to the building-up of Christian doctrine" the Bible may not be interpreted in a way that contradicts the doctrine held by the Church or the unanimous consent of the Fathers. • Declares that baptism wipes out the stain of original sin.	Earth's magnetic poles are postulated. The League of Schmalkald, Lutheran princes and free states allied with France, goes to war with Holy Roman Emperor Charles V.	Robert Estienne. *Greek New Testament,* "the Stephanus text." Largely a reproduction of one of Erasmus' later editions, it also includes variant readings. (first edition)

Date	A. Theology, Doctrine, and Beliefs	B. People/Events	C. Wider Culture	D. Texts
1547		Pulpits are installed in all English churches. The Council of Trent (session VII) • Declares that Christ instituted all seven sacraments. There is disagreement, however, about when he did so.	King Henry VIII of England dies. King Edward VI ascends. King Edward VI bans freemasonry. Holy Roman Emperor Charles V defeats the Protestant Schmalkaldic League at the Battle of Mühlberg.	
1548	Adiaphorists. A group within German Protestantism that claims confirmation, extreme unction, veneration of saints, and other selected Catholic doctrines are matters not worthy of acrimony. In the interests of peace, they are willing to remain neutral on the peripheral doctrines of Protestantism.	King Edward VI orders all saints' images removed from English churches. Italian refugees in Poland form a Unitarian church that flourishes until the mid-seventeenth century. Philip Neri founds the Confraternity of the Most Holy Trinity, a lay society devoted to aiding convalescents, pilgrims, and the poor.		*The Order of the Communion.* An English supplement to the Latin Mass. With the Litany, it is the precursor to *The Book of Common Prayer.*
1549		Francis Xavier establishes a Jesuit mission in Japan. An ecclesiastical commission, later known as the "Court of High Commission" is established in England to enforce doctrinal and liturgical uniformity.		*Book of Common Prayer,* "the First Prayer Book of Edward VI." A Protestant-Catholic compromise not widely accepted by either side. • Fixes the frequency of Communion at three times per year • No longer orders the mixture of water with communion wine. • Dictates that Christians receive communion at least three times each year. • Omits the confession of sin during morning and evening prayer.
1550		Tables replace altars in England. Julius III becomes pope. Purificators become common. As a result, white wine is increasingly used for Communion. (mid sixteenth century) The Forty Hours' Devotion in its modern form begins to be practiced. (mid sixteenth century) Holy Roman Emperor Charles V suspends Spanish expeditions to the Americas while his theologians and jurists debate whether the native people should be forcibly enslaved and Christianized.	The Modern English (language) period begins.	

Date	A. Theology, Doctrine, and Beliefs	B. People/Events	C. Wider Culture	D. Texts
1551	Propitiatory sacrifice. This doctrine declares that the Eucharistic offering is in itself a sacrifice, one which is an image of the sacrifice of Christ on the cross. As such the Eucharist repairs the sin-damaged relationship between people and God.	Council of Trent—second period. (–1552) • Allows daily Communion. • Reaffirms and elaborates upon the doctrine of transubstantiation. • Declares the Mass to be a propitiatory sacrifice. Saint Francis Xavier, Apostle of the Indies, dies. He was a Spanish missionary and one of the initial group of Jesuits. John Knox becomes chaplain to King Edward VI.		
1552	Black Rubric (the Declaration on Kneeling). A directive in the Anglican *Book of Common Prayer* that calls on the people to kneel to receive the Sacrament. (Kneeling was a Roman medieval custom, by no means universal throughout the West.) According to the Rubric, the purpose of kneeling is to avoid disorder, not to imply adoration of any Real Presence in the Sacrament. Yet Protestants who have begun receiving communion in the pews, protest the Rubric as overly Roman.	Geneva declares Calvin's *Institutes* to be "well and saintly made, and its teaching the holy doctrine of God." The chasuble is no longer used in England. The surplice becomes the only prescribed vestment for Church of England clergy.		*Book of Common Prayer,* "the Second Prayer Book of Edward VI." A truly Protestant book. • First includes the "black rubric" • Adds the Prayer of General Confession at the beginning of matins and evensong in the BCP. • Requires the ringing of a bell at the beginning of all church services.
1553		The Council of Trent decrees that archdeacons no longer have authority in issues of matrimony, excommunication, infidelity of clergy, and criminal misconduct. This decree strengthens the role of the bishop and weakens that of the archdeacon. John Knox flees Scotland as Mary Queen of Scots returns to take the throne. He goes to Geneva where he meets and is influenced by John Calvin. Michael Servetus, a Spanish radical reformer who has denounced predestination and infant baptism, passes through Geneva during his exile from Vienne. He confronts Calvin, is arrested, tried, and burned at the stake.	The violin in its modern form begins to be developed. King Edward VI of England dies. Mary Tudor, Queen of England, ascends.	*Reformatio legum ecclesiasticarum.* (The Reform of the Ecclesiastical Laws). A corpus of largely Calvinist ecclesiastical laws, drawn up by Thomas Cranmer, Peter Martyr, and a council appointed by King Edward VI. The corpus is designed to replace Roman canon law. It is presented to Parliament in 1553, but Edward dies before Parliament can act on it. It is a great influence on the Thirty-nine Articles. Forty-two Articles. An Anglican doctrinal formula drafted by Thomas Cranmer, it is never enforced because of the rise of Mary Tudor to the throne. It does, however, become the basis for the Thirty-nine Articles. Mary Tudor's *Act of Repeal* abolishes the *Book of Common Prayer* in England, replacing it with the traditional Latin Rite.

Date	A. Theology, Doctrine, and Beliefs	B. People/Events	C. Wider Culture	D. Texts
1554		Richard Hooker is born.	Queen Mary of England executes Jane Grey.	
1555	Perpetual Virginity of the Blessed Virgin Mary. It is the doctrine that Mary remained *virgo intacta*, in other words, that God miraculously preserved Mary's virginity even during and after the birth of Jesus. Key figure: Pope Paul IV	Hugh Latimer expresses the reformers' criticism of the Ave Maria, that it is not a prayer but a greeting because it contains no petition. (1535–) Mary Tudor burns Nicholas Ridley and Hugh Latimer, English Protestants and social reformers, for heresy. John Knox returns to Scotland from Geneva. John Calvin shelters English Protestants who flee to Geneva to escape Mary Tudor. The Peace of Augsburg officially recognizes of both Lutheranism and Catholicism in the German Empire. It states that *Cuius regio, eius religio*: the doctrinal preference of the sovereign dictates that of the region. Marcellus II becomes pope. Paul IV becomes pope. He maintains doctrinal conservatism while battling immorality and abuse within the church. His agenda sets the tone of the Counter-Reformation. Pope Paul IV declares Mary remained a perpetual virgin.		
1556		Saint Ignatius Loyola, founder of the Jesuits, dies. Thomas Cranmer, archbishop of Canterbury, is executed by Mary Tudor. He is best known for writing much of the first *Book of Common Prayer*. Lancelot Andrewes is born.	The European influenza epidemic begins. Charles V abdicates as both head of the Holy Roman Empire and Spain. Pope Paul IV establishes a ghetto for Jews in Rome.	
1557				*Index librorum prohibitorum* (The Index of Prohibited Books). A list of books Roman Catholics are forbidden to read or possess, it is first issued during the papacy of Pope Paul IV. The penalty for reading the books is excommunication. (revised 1559) The fourth edition of Robert Estienne's *Greek New Testament* introduces the verse divisions that become the standard way to cite location of biblical text.

Date	A. Theology, Doctrine, and Beliefs	B. People/Events	C. Wider Culture	D. Texts
1558			Queen Elizabeth I of England ascends to the throne.	
1559	Elizabethan Settlement. Queen Elizabeth I's structuring of the Church of England to include both Catholic and Protestant elements. Because of this compromise, Anglicanism is sometimes referred to as the *via media,* the middle way. Key theologians: John Jewel, Richard Hooker. Virtualism. The belief that though no actual change occurs in the nature of the bread and wine in the Eucharist, those who receive those elements receive the power or virtue of the body and blood. Key figures: John Calvin and Calvinists. Puritanism. The beliefs of English Calvinists, who hold that the Reformation of the Elizabethan Settlement is inadequate. They wish to "purify" the Church of England of nonscriptural (largely medieval and Roman) accretions, bringing it in line with the Genevan model. (–1660)	The Act of Uniformity requires uniformity of worship in England. Dissenters are fined. The Act of Supremacy restores, in a revised form, the Act passed during Henry's reign and repealed during Mary's reign. The Church of England reimposes the use of the chasuble. A separatist group, later know as "Puritans," arise in England. (–1660) Pius IV becomes pope. The French Protestant church adopts Calvinism at the Synod of Paris. John Calvin founds the Genevan Academy to train theologians from all over Europe.		*Book of Common Prayer,* "the Elizabethan Prayer Book." It makes minor changes on the 1552 book to minimize offense to Roman Catholic sympathizers. It adds the Ornaments Rubric and eliminates the Black Rubric. Puritans hate it; Elizabeth doesn't care so long as they use it. Ornaments Rubric. A directive inserted in the 1559 *Book of Common Prayer* mandating that vestments and liturgical vessels used in the Church of England conform to guidelines of Parliament in the second year of the reign of Edward VI. What those guidelines are is a matter of dispute. Gallican Confession. Drafted by Calvin, it is a distillation of Calvinist central doctrines. It is adopted at the First National Synod of Protestants in Paris.
1560	Huguenots. Protestants in France. From 1539, they are organized along a Calvinist model.	The name Huguenot is first applied to French Calvinists. (ca.) The Reformed Church in Scotland is founded as a Presbyterian church. Carlos Borromeo, archbishop of Milan, begins the Catholic "model" reform. The traditional work of preparing annotated editions of the church fathers declines as scholars suspiciously eye the increasing power of the Inquisition. Philipp Melanchthon, one of the greatest minds of the Lutheran Reformation, dies.	Queen Elizabeth I sends military aid to Protestants in Scotland.	John Knox. *First Book of Discipline.* A plan for ordering the new Scottish Reformed church, based on the Genevan model. *Geneva Bible.* An English translation of the Bible prepared by English Puritans during their exile in Geneva under Mary Tudor. It is the most influential Calvinist Bible until the King James Version. The Scots Confession. The first confession of faith adopted by the Scottish Reformed church.
1561		French Catholic bishops and Protestant ministers attend the Colloquy of Poissy in France. Though they find dogmatic agreement impossible, the conference lays the groundwork for eventual official recognition of the Huguenots.	Fire badly damages St. Paul's Cathedral in London.	John Calvin's *Institutes of the Christian Religion* is translated into English. Belgic Confession. A classic Reformed statement of faith.

Date	A. Theology, Doctrine, and Beliefs	B. People/Events	C. Wider Culture	D. Texts
1562	More than any other facet of the Reformation, the progress of the Calvinist movement is tied to several armed struggles—the Wars of Religion, the Thirty Years War, and the Netherlands' revolt against Spain. Doctrine of Concomitance. The belief that both the Body and Blood of Christ are present in each of the consecrated species of communion. The cup, therefore may be withheld from the laity as nothing is truly withheld by doing so. The doctrine is developed in the 12th century or earlier. It is formally asserted at the Council of Trent.	The Edict of 1562 gives official recognition to the French Protestants. The War of Religion, a conflict between Roman Catholics and Huguenots, begins in France (1562–1594). Queen Elizabeth I sends military aid to Protestants in France. Council of Trent—third period. (–1563) • Reaffirms concomitance. • Decrees that music must be uplifting to the faithful, and that the words must be sung intelligibly. The Mass, however, is still sung in Latin. Teresa of Ávila founds the Convent of St. Joseph at Ávila, the first community of Discalced Carmelite nuns.	In England, the Statute of Elizabeth makes witchcraft a serious crime, as serious as murder, whether or not it is used to the injury of others.	John Jewel. *Apologia Ecclesiae Anglicanae* (Latin: Apology for the Anglican Church). The nature of the Church of England in comparison and contrast to the Roman Catholic Church. Teresa of Ávila. *Life*. The spiritual autobiography of one of Christianity's most respected mystics. Thirty-nine Articles. The final version of Anglican doctrine accepted during the reign of Elizabeth I. It places the Anglican church in contrast to both Roman Catholicism and Reformed churches. John Knox. *Book of Common Order*. The Scottish (Reformed) service book is approved by the General Assembly of the Scottish church for use in public worship.
1563		The Council of Trent (session 25) • Directs that "the holy bodies of holy martyrs... are to be venerated by the faithful, for through these [bodies] many benefits are bestowed by God on men." • Makes the novitiate obligatory for all candidates wishing to take the vows of a Roman Catholic religious order. • Proscribes ordination for money • Declares that "purgatory exists, and that the souls detained therein are helped by the suffrages of the faithful, but especially by the acceptable sacrifice of the altar." The Council of Trent ends. A group of English separatists are first called Puritans for their desire to rid the Church of England of papist trappings.	Plague kills 20,000 in London.	John Foxe. *Christian Martyrs of the World* ("Foxe's Book of Martyrs"). Compiled by a Puritan based on manuscript and eye-witness testimony, it is an account of martyrdom during both the early Christian period and the Reformation. Heidelberg Catechism. A classic Reformed statement of faith, it seeks to harmonize Lutheran, Calvinist, and Zwinglian theologies. It comes to be used by modern Reformed churches in the U.S.
1564		John Calvin, French Reformer and leader of the theocratic Reformed government of Geneva, dies. Theodore Beza succeeds Calvin as the head of the Calvinist movement centered in Geneva. Philip Neri founds the Congregation of the Oratory, a community of secular priests and clerics. (–1575)	Michelangelo dies. Galileo is born.	Pope Pius IV promulgates a revised *Index of Prohibited Books*. Pope Pius IV's bull *Benedictus Deus* confirms the decrees of the Council of Trent.

Date	A. Theology, Doctrine, and Beliefs	B. People/Events	C. Wider Culture	D. Texts
1565		The first American Roman Catholic parish is founded by secular priests in St. Augustine, Florida. Guillaume Farel, Protestant Reformer, dies. He worked along side Calvin in Geneva and established the Reformation in the Canton of Vaud.		Teresa of Ávila. *The Way of Perfection.* Her spiritual autobiography. (some time after 1565)
1566		Pius V becomes pope.	Dutch Revolt. King Philip II of Spain tries to suppress Protestantism in the Netherlands. Spain is defeated, but the Catholic south and Protestant north continue to war.	Heinrich Bullinger. *Second Helvetic Confession.* A confession/ theological treatise, based mostly on Calvinism, with some Zwinglian thought mixed in. Both groups widely accept it. *The Roman Catechism* (also called the *Catechism of Pius V*). Based on the work of the Council of Trent, it is the first official catechism of the Roman Catholic Church. It is not a textbook, but a doctrinal for pastors and teachers.
1567		Pope Pius V cancels all indulgences involving fees or other financial transactions. The title "cardinal" is no longer applied to influential clergy, but solely to counselors of the pope.	Two million American Indians die of typhoid.	
1568	Discalced. From the Latin word for "unshod," the term describes those monastic orders who take Matthew 10:10 literally and refuse to wear shoes. Modern discalced orders usually wear sandals.	John of The Cross founds the first Discalced Carmelite monastery. The Jesuits are welcomed in Japan. The Breviary of Pope Pius V makes obligatory the reciting the Salve Regina after compline from Trinity to Advent. Thomas Aquinas is made doctor of the church. The Eastern doctors of the church are named: Saints Athanasius, Basil, John Chrysostom, and Gregory of Nazianzus.	The Mercator projection is developed.	The Latin (Roman Catholic) Breviary, also called the Breviary of Pope Pius V, is revised after the Council of Trent. Bishops' Bible. A revision of the Great Bible, it is the officially sanctioned Bible of the Church of England until the translation of the King James Version.
1569		Miles Coverdale, translator of the Coverdale Bible, dies.		
1570		Queen Elizabeth I is excommunicated. The act marks the final separation between England and Rome. The *Ritus Sevandus*, the customs and ceremonies of the Mass printed in the front of the Tridentine Missal, requires a bell be rung during the Mass at the elevation of the consecrated Host and at the Sanctus.	Andrea Palladio. *The Four Books of Architecture.* Illustrations and plans for Palladio's Italian villas, which are Roman-influenced High Renaissance designs augmented by his own direct, extensive study of Roman architecture. Palladio influences Inigo Jones in England and Thomas Jefferson in Virginia.	*Missale Romanum* (also called the "Tridentine Missal" or the "Missal of Pius V"). An attempt to clear away medieval accretions and return to the missal of Gregory the Great, it is based on Alcuin's texts. It becomes the foundation for most modern missals.

Date	A. Theology, Doctrine, and Beliefs	B. People/Events	C. Wider Culture	D. Texts
1570 con't.			Japan opens its ports to foreign ships. Abraham Ortelius. *Orbis Terrarum*. The first modern atlas, produced by a Flemish mapmaker.	
1571		John Jewel, Anglican bishop and champion of the Anglican *via media* (Latin: middle way), dies. Jesuit missionaries begin work in Mexico. John Donne is born.		
1572		John Knox, Scottish reformer, dies. St. Bartholomew's Day Massacre. It is the bloodiest episode in the French Wars of Religion. Catherine de Médicis, the French Queen Mother, persuades King Charles IX to kill Huguenot leaders. Claude Goudimel, Flemish Huguenot composer, dies in the St. Bartholomew's Day Massacre. He is best known for his psalms settings. Saint Pius V, Grand Inquisitor and pope, dies. He brought the Roman Catholic Church through the Counter-Reformation by enforcing the decrees of the Council of Trent. Gregory XIII becomes pope.	The Peace of Constantinople ends Turkish attacks on Europe.	
1573		Franciscans first come to America. Pope Gregory XII allows the Feast of the Rosary to be celebrated by those churches who have an altar specifically dedicated to the Holy Rosary. William Laud is born. Spain adopts the policy that all future expeditions to the Americas should "pacify" the native people rather than "conquer" them. All conversions to Christianity should be peaceful.		
1575		Calvinism supplants Lutheranism among the Dutch. (late sixteenth century) Heinrich Bullinger, Swiss Reformer, dies.		
1576		Calced Carmelites imprison John of the Cross for his attempts at monastic reform. In prison he begins his writing. (–1577)		

Date	A. Theology, Doctrine, and Beliefs	B. People/Events	C. Wider Culture	D. Texts
1577				Jakob Andreae, Martin Chemnitz, and other theologians. Formula of Concord. One of the last of the classical Lutheran statements of faith, its intent is to bring together various factions within Lutheranism.
				Teresa of Ávila. *The Interior Castle.* Teresa's description of the contemplative life.
1578		Saint Charles Borromeo founds the Oblates of Saint Ambrose.		
		The Shroud of Turin first arrives in Turin.		
1579		Calced and Discalced Carmelites (new and primitive) separate. Key figures: John of the Cross and Teresa of Ávila		John of the Cross. *Noche Obscura del Alma* (The Dark Night of the Soul). A classic of mystical literature. It describes how the soul comes to transcend sense-bound devotion by a course parallel to Christ's crucifixion and glory.
				Robert Stapleton *Principiorum fidei doctrinalium demonstratio* (Latin: Demonstration of the Doctrinal Principles of the Faith). After a spate of name-calling and recriminations (from both sides), this work is among the first reasonable Catholic apologies against Protestantism.
1580		Jesuits establish a mission in England.		The Book of Concord (*Konkordienbuch*). A collection of documents that form the confessional foundation of Lutheranism. It includes: The Nicene and Athanasian Creeds, the Augsburg Confession, the Schmalkaldic Articles, and Luther's Large and Small Catechisms.
		Lutheran princes and cities adopt the Book of Concord.		
1581		Pope Gregory XIII tries without success to reconcile Catholicism and Russian Orthodoxy.	The United Provinces of the Netherlands declare Protestant loyalties and political independence from Spain. The southern provinces (Belgium) remain loyal to Catholicism and Spain.	James VI of Scotland signs the Second Confession of Faith.
		Saint Edmund Campion is executed for treason. One of the "Forty English Martyrs," he is the best known of the English Jesuits who were martyred during the reign of Queen Elizabeth I.		Edmund Campion. *Decem Rationes* (*Ten Reasons*). This attack on the Church of England by an English Jesuit is distributed at Oxford commencement. It is a cause of Campion's arrest and execution.
		Theodore Beza presents the Codex Bezae to Cambridge University.		

Date	A. Theology, Doctrine, and Beliefs	B. People/Events	C. Wider Culture	D. Texts
1582		Jesuit Matteo Ricci founds a mission in China. Saint Teresa of Ávila dies. She was a Spanish mystic, author, and founder of the religious order of Discalced Carmelites. Robert Browne argues against the Church of England saying it is so corrupt that true Christians must separate from it and form their own autonomous churches. His followers are among the first Congregationalists.	Pope Gregory XIII adjusts the Julian calendar (45 BC) to make the vernal equinox occur on March 21, as it had in AD 325 (during the first Council of Nicea). The reform adds additional leap years and eliminates difficulties in fixing the date of Easter.	The Rheims Testament. The New Testament of the Douay-Rheims Bible is released. Teresa of Ávila. *The Foundations*. The origins of the Discalced Carmelites. (1573–)
1584		Saint Charles Borromeo dies. An Italian prelate and Roman Catholic reformer, he oversaw the deliberations at the Council of Trent.	Walter Raleigh annexes Virginia. Ivan "the Terrible," tsar of Russia, dies.	*Roman Martyrology*. The first official list of people the Roman church considers worthy of veneration as martyrs. It replaces several smaller, local lists.
1585	Feast of the Presentation of the Blessed Virgin Mary (November 21). It commemorates the presentation of Mary in the Temple when she was three years old. The account is contained in the Apocryphal *Book of James*.	The Jesuits are expelled from England. Sixtus V becomes pope. Queen Elizabeth I sends military aid to Protestants in the Netherlands. Persecution of Catholics in England becomes vigorous. (–1591) The Feast of the Presentation of the Blessed Virgin Mary becomes universal.		
1586		Pope Sixtus V sets the number of cardinals at seventy. England passes its first laws mandating an imprimatur on books printed in that country.		
1587		Pope Sixtus V establishes the Sacred Congregation of Rites to deal with the process of beatification and canonization and to enforce the dictates of the Council of Trent.	Queen Elizabeth I executes Mary Queen of Scots.	John Knox. *History of the Reformation in Scotland*. Knox's most influential work. It is immediately suppressed in England. (published posthumously)
1588		The Inquisition is reinstated. The Vatican library building is completed. It was designed by Domenico Fontana.	England defeats the Spanish Armada.	
1589		The Russian Orthodox Church establishes its own patriarchate. In doing so it becomes independent from Constantinople.	The knitting machine is invented. Henry IV, a Huguenot, becomes king of France. The House of Bourbon replaces the House of Valois in France.	
1590		Urban VII becomes pope. Gregory XIV becomes pope.		

Date	A. Theology, Doctrine, and Beliefs	B. People/Events	C. Wider Culture	D. Texts
1591		Saint John of the Cross dies. He was a Spanish mystic and the founder of the first Discalced Carmelite monastery. Innocent IX becomes pope. Saint Aloysius Gonzaga, Italian Jesuit priest, dies while caring for victims of the plague. He is the patron saint of Christian youth.	Shakespeare writes his first play.	
1592		Nicholas Ferrar is born. Clement VIII becomes pope. Trinity College, Dublin, is founded as an Irish center of Anglicanism.	Plague sweeps through London.	
1593		Sweden adopts the Augsburg Confession and becomes officially Lutheran. George Herbert is born. Parliament passes acts against Puritans and Catholics in England. King Henry IV of France converts to Roman Catholicism in an attempt to end religious wars.		Pierre Charron. *Les Trois Vérités* (French: Three Truths). A French theological treatise and Roman Catholic apologetic work. It is a precursor for deism.
1594		Francis of Sales becomes a missionary to the Calvinists.	Giovanni Pierluigi da Palestrina, Italian composer, dies. His work brought Franco-Flemish composition techniques to the service of the Counter-Reformation.	Richard Hooker. *Laws of Ecclesiastical Polity.* A philosophical and logical foundation for the Anglicanism of the Elizabethan Settlement. Though broad in scope, it addresses specific questions regarding the episcopacy, natural law and the source of revelation, and the nature of the Eucharist.
1595	Sabbatarianism. The belief that Sunday should be a day for abstaining from all activity. It is most firmly held by Puritans, who spread its influence throughout England and the American colonies. It is revived during the First Great Awakening. (–1677)	Saint Philip Neri dies. Italian priest and mystic, called the Apostle of Rome. He began the Congregation of the Oratory, a community of secular priests and clerics.		Lambeth Articles. An English Calvinist theological document, compiled by committee in Lambeth. It captures the supralapsarian (extreme predestination) beliefs of many Puritans at the time.
1596			The thermometer is invented. Rene Descartes is born.	The Latin (Roman Catholic) Pontifical is revised after the Council of Trent. It contains the prayers and ceremonies performed by bishops.
1597		The Martyrs of Japan die. Christianity in Japan goes underground. Saint Peter Canisius, German Jesuit theologian, dies. He was a leader of the Counter-Reformation and the first German to join the Jesuit order.		Thomas Morley. *A Plaine and Easie Introduction.* The earliest source of Anglican chant, it is a formula for singing harmonized psalms and canticles as a part of the liturgy of the Church of England. Anglican Chant is further developed in the seventeenth century.

Date	A. Theology, Doctrine, and Beliefs	B. People/Events	C. Wider Culture	D. Texts
1598	Molinism. A doctrine of grace proposed by a Jesuit theologian. It maintains that efficacious grace and sufficient grace are not intrinsically different from one another (the Thomistic doctrine). They are, rather, only apparently (accidentally) and situationally different. Key figure: Luis de Molina.	King Henry IV of France's Edict of Nantes ends the French Wars of Religion and gives Huguenots freedom of religion. Pope Clement VIII calls the *Congregatio de Auxiliis* (Latin: Congregation of Help) to resolve the fighting between the Thomists and the Molinists (Dominicans and Jesuits). (–1607)		
1599				James I of Scotland. *Basilikon Doron* (Greek: *Βασιλικὸν Δῶρον* —A Royal Gift). On kingly duties and the divine right of kings.
1600		Giordano Bruno is burned at the stake for speculating on the theological and philosophical implications of Copernicus's theories. He becomes known as a martyr to science though he is also an apostate Dominican and leans toward pantheism. Richard Hooker, one of Anglicanism's most preeminent theologians, dies. His work helped establish Anglicanism as the *via media*, the middle way between Catholicism and Protestantism. Devotion to the precious blood begins in the seventeenth century. The use of the confessional "box" becomes common. (before) Roman Catholics are persecuted in Sweden.	The baroque period in European music and art produces highly energetic, emotional forms. In church architecture and painting, it is linked closely, though not exclusively, to the Counter-Reformation. Key figures: Bernini, Rubens, Rembrandt, Handel, Bach. (ca.–1750) A charter is granted to the English East India Company. It is a major political and economic force in India for nearly 200 years. William Shakespeare. *Hamlet*.	
1602			The Dutch East India Company is founded.	
1603		English Puritans present the Millenary Petition to King James I on his way to the Hampton Court Conference. It asks that they be relieved of duty to Anglican rites and ceremonies.	The Act of King James VI of Scotland makes witchcraft a capital crime. Elizabeth I, queen of England dies. King James VI of Scotland ascends to the throne of England, becoming James I, king of England and Scotland. The Scottish and English crowns are united under his rule, and the Stuart dynasty begins its tenure in England.	
1604		The Hampton Court Conference is held. In attendance are both English bishops and Puritans. The only thing they	*Seconda Prattica* (Second Practice). A style of music composition associated with the baroque era. It subordi-	*Book of Common Prayer*, the Hampton Court Conference Revision. Based on the Conference's decisions, its largest

Date	A. Theology, Doctrine, and Beliefs	B. People/Events	C. Wider Culture	D. Texts
1604 con't.		agree on is that a new translation of the Bible should be made. King James I of England authorizes a new English translation of the Bible. Scholars begin the seven year process of translating the Authorized Version of the Bible. Excommunication becomes more overt in the Anglican *Book of Common Prayer*. It is imposed increasingly often.	nates counterpoint and rhythm to the text. It supersedes the "first practice" in which melody, harmony, and rhythm govern the choice of words. (seventeenth century)	change is the addition of the second half of the catechism. *Code of Canons.* Canon law of the Church of England. It presupposes that the *Corpus Iuris Canonici* is in effect except where contradicted by English statute or custom.
1605		The Gunpowder Plot is foiled. It is the attempt by a fringe element to blow up the fully occupied English Houses of Parliament in the hopes that the Roman Catholic Church would step in and take over the country. Leo XI becomes pope. Paul V becomes pope. Christmas trees are first mentioned. They are used in Strasburg.	William Shakespeare presents *King Lear* and *Macbeth*. Francis Bacon. *Advancement of Learning.* A treatise on reason and scientific investigation, it calls for a new scientific method based on generalization from careful observation and experiment. Bacon is the first to formulate rules of inductive inference.	
1606		Pope Gregory VII is canonized.	Willem Janszoon discovers Australia. Rembrandt is born.	
1607		The Church of England comes to the Americas with the founding of the Jamestown Colony.	Jamestown Colony is founded. It is the first European settlement on the continent.	
1608		Philipp Nicolai, German hymn writer, dies.	The first permanent French outpost in the Americas is established in Quebec. The telescope is invented.	Francis of Sales. *Introduction to the Devout Life.* Among the most popular works of Christian spirituality at the time. (ca.)
1609	Baptist churches. The hallmarks of these churches are believers' baptism by immersion and local church government. Early Baptists are influenced by Mennonites and Anabaptists. Baptists distinguish them as being separate from both Catholics and Protestants. Founder: John Smythe.	The first modern Baptist church is formed by English Separatist, John Smythe, who is in exile in Amsterdam at the time.	The Bank of Amsterdam is founded Samuel de Champlain establishes the French colony of Quebec.	The Douay-Rheims Bible. It is the English translation of the Bible most used by Roman Catholics during the next three centuries. Published in two quarto volumes. (–1610)
1610		Charles Borromeo is canonized. Francis of Sales founds the Order of the Visitation of Our Lady specifically for persons whose physical disabilities keep them from entering other orders.		

Date	A. Theology, Doctrine, and Beliefs	B. People/Events	C. Wider Culture	D. Texts
1611			Peter Paul Rubens paints his *Descent from the Cross*.	The Authorized Version of the Bible, "the King James Version." A translation revision done by fifty scholars at the behest of King James I of England. It is based on the Bishops' Bible in consultation with all other available English translations and the extant Greek and Hebrew manuscripts. It is unexceeded in its combination of literary beauty and scholarship.
1612	Calvinism vs. Arminianism. The two central issues in the dispute are whether salvation can be lost because of post-conversion sin, and whether the Fall has impaired humanities ability to know and choose God.	Pope Paul V approves the Congregation of the Oratory. It is a congregation of secular priests living in community without vows, dedicated to evangelism through preaching and prayer. The last recorded burning of a heretic in England takes place. Thomas Helwys founds the first Baptist church in England. These Baptists, who call themselves "General Baptists" are Arminian.		
1614		Christianity is banned in Japan as a part of an overall isolationism that lasts over two centuries. (–1854)	John Napier discovers logarithms.	
1615	The Divine Right of Kings. The doctrine that a monarch who comes to the throne through legitimate success is granted authority by divine sanction. During the Stuart dynasty of England, most Anglican divines proclaim the doctrine unquestioningly.	A census of the Society of Jesus counts 13,112 Jesuits.	Miguel de Cervantes' *Don Quixote* is completed.	
1616			William Shakespeare dies.	
1617		Saint Rose of Lima dies. A Peruvian Roman Catholic nun of the third order of Dominicans, she was the first native-born South American saint. Vincent de Paul founds the first Confraternity of Charity, an organization of wealthy women ministering to the sick and poor in Châtillon-les-Dombes, near Lyon. Pope Paul V decrees that no one may teach publicly that Mary was conceived in original sin.		

Date	A. Theology, Doctrine, and Beliefs	B. People/Events	C. Wider Culture	D. Texts
1618	The Five Points of Calvinism. (1) Unconditional election, (2) Limited Atonement, (3) Total depravity of humanity, (4) Irresistibility of grace, and (5) Perseverance of the Saints. They are affirmed in the Canons of the Synod of Dort.	The Synod of Dort, a Dutch Reformed assembly, convenes to deal with the Arminian controversy. They approve the "Five Points of Calvinism." The Jesuits are expelled from Bohemia, Moravia, and Silesia. King James I of England allows recreation on Sunday while continuing to disallow work and commerce. His judgement causes considerable controversy.	The Thirty Years' War begins. It is a series of European conflicts fought mainly in Germany. Originally it was a struggle between German Protestants and Catholics, but it expanded to include other issues and most of the countries of western Europe. (–1648) Johannes Kepler publishes his three laws of planetary motion: (1) Planets orbit in ellipses. (2) Planets move faster when closer to the sun. (3) The time a planet takes to orbit the sun is proportional to its distance from the sun. (1609–)	
1619	Irresistible grace. A Calvinist and Jansenist doctrine that states that grace is the means by which God frees the human will from its bondage to sin. The will, in its bound state, is helpless to choose grace, and so, therefore, grace must be irresistible and given only to those predestined by God for salvation. Key figures: John Calvin, Cornelius Otto Jansen, and Pope Innocent X (who condemns it).		The first black slaves arrive in North America at Jamestown, Virginia, brought by English privateers. They enter a kind of indentured servitude that is common among not only black Africans but also American Indians and whites.	Canons of the Synod of Dort. The classic Reformed statement of faith, it contrasts Calvinism to Arminianism and details the "Five Points of Calvinism."
1620		The Mayflower lands at Plymouth Rock. Plymouth colony is founded by Puritan Separatists called "Pilgrims."		
1621		Gregory XV becomes pope, the first Jesuit to occupy the office.		
1622		Pope Gregory XV canonizes Philip Neri, Ignatius Loyola, Teresa of Ávila, and Francis Xavier. Saint Francis of Sales dies. A French Roman Catholic prelate and writer, he is remembered for his unusual belief that it is possible to lead a pious and saintly life without joining a monastic order.	King James I of England dissolves Parliament.	
1623		Urban VIII becomes pope.	Patent law is developed in England. William Byrd, the single most important English composer of the Elizabethan era, dies. Blaise Pascal is born. Peter Minuit buys Manhattan Island from the Algonquins and establishes New Amsterdam (later New York).	

Date	A. Theology, Doctrine, and Beliefs	B. People/Events	C. Wider Culture	D. Texts
1624		George Fox is born. Jakob Boehme dies. German Lutheran theosophical writer and mystic. His writing had great influence on the German Romantics and the Cambridge Platonists. The first American *blue laws*, laws that forbid work on Sunday, are passed in Virginia.		Edward Herbert. *De Veritate* (Latin: Concerning Truth). Herbert's best known work, it attacks empiricism and lays the foundation for his later work on ideas common to all religions. Together they are the earliest rumblings of English deism. John Donne. "A Hymn to God the Father"
1625	Caroline Divines. English Theologians/writers of the seventeenth century (roughly during the reigns of Kings Charles I and II). They believe that the reformation of the Anglican church entails the recovery of the purity of the premedieval church. Key figures: Lancelot Andrewes, John Cosin, Thomas Fuller, Jeremy Taylor, Nicholas Ferrar, and others.	Lutherans settle in New Amsterdam (later named New York City). They are of Dutch, German, and Scandinavian background. Saint Jean de Brébeuf arrives in Canada. A French Jesuit missionary to the Huron in Québec, he arrived with the French explorer Samuel de Champlain. Vincent de Paul founds the Congregation of the Mission, also called the Lazarists. They are a congregation of diocesan priests living from a common fund, dedicated to the education of the clergy and ministry in rural dioceses.	King Charles I of England ascends to the throne.	
1626		The Jesuit mission to the Hurons begins. (–1649) Lancelot Andrewes, Anglican preacher and a translator of the King James Version of the Bible, dies. Nicholas Ferrar founds Little Gidding, an Anglican monastic community for families. (–1646)	Francis Bacon, English philosopher and champion of the inductive method, dies.	The Codex Alexandrinus (A), one of the earliest of the uncial manuscripts of the Greek New Testament, comes to England as a gift from the patriarch of Constantinople. (ca.)
1628		The first Dutch Reformed church organization in America is established in New Amsterdam (later "New York City") by the Reverend Jonas Michaëlius.		
1629		The Edict of Restitution restores a large amount of German land to the Roman church.	King Charles I dissolves the English Parliament.	
1630	Receptionism. A doctrine of the Eucharist propounded mainly by the sixteenth and seventeenth century Anglican divines, it holds that though the elements of the Eucharist remain unchanged, the communicant, in the act of reception, receives with them the actual Body and Blood of Christ. Most proponents of Receptionism are intention-	Pope Urban VIII decrees that the title "Eminence" may only be used to refer to cardinals. The Massachusetts Bay Colony is established by English Puritans, who run it as a Calvinist theocracy. Samuel Skelton establishes the first Congregational church in America.	The "Great Migration" of immigrants from Europe to America begins. Before it is over, over 65 million Europeans will have moved to North or South America. America's Thanksgiving Day begins to be celebrated annually.	

Date	A. Theology, Doctrine, and Beliefs	B. People/Events	C. Wider Culture	D. Texts
1630 con't.	ally vague as to the actual mechanics of how it "works." (The term "Receptionism" is not used until the nineteenth century.)			
1631		Under Pope Urban VIII, the *Advocatus Diaboli* (Devil's Advocate) becomes an essential part of any beatification or canonization. John Donne, English metaphysical poet and divine, dies. The Jesuits are expelled from Germany.		
1632			John Locke is born.	
1633	Cambridge Platonists. They are a group of philosophical divines who hold a very British combination of Cartesian and neo-Platonic thought. They seek a middle way between High Anglicanism and Puritanism. Key figures: B. Whichcote, N. Culverwel, Ralph Cudworth, and Henry More (flor. 1633–1688) Particular Baptists. Their roots are in English Puritanism, their beliefs Calvinist, their polity congregational. Their name comes from the belief that only particular individuals chosen by God are destined to be saved. Later in America they become known as Regular Baptists. Key figure: Samuel Eaton. Key document: London Confession.	George Herbert, poet, writer, Anglican priest, dies. A group of London Separatists led by Henry Jacob begin to practice believers' baptism by immersion. They are Calvinists and call themselves "Particular Baptists."	The Inquisition forces Galileo Galilei to abjure Copernican theories.	Abraham Elzevir. *Greek New Testament.* Elzevir is the first to coin the name Textus Receptus for a class of Greek New Testaments dating back to Erasmus, Estienne, Beza, and the Complutensian Polyglot. The text of the Textus Receptus is largely Byzantine. It forms the basis for nearly all vernacular translations of the New Testament until the mid-nineteenth century.
1634		Modern canonization requirements are instituted by Pope Urban VIII in two constitutions. The right of canonization and beatification is reserved to the papacy. Local bishops no longer have that authority. (1625 and 1634) Jesuits from the English missions arrive in Maryland to minister to the Catholics of that colony and to convert the local Indians. Archbishop William Laud declares that altars in Anglican churches be returned to the east wall, and altar rails be restored. He removes the pulpit from its central focus and in doing so incurs the hostility of the Puritans. The Oberammergau Passion Play is performed for the first time.	The Catholic colony of Maryland is founded.	

Date	A. Theology, Doctrine, and Beliefs	B. People/Events	C. Wider Culture	D. Texts
1635	Congregationalism. A form of church polity that recognizes no church structure as being more authoritative than the autonomous local congregation. It rests on the doctrine of the priesthood of all believers.	Phillipp Jakob Spener is born.	The French Academy is founded to establish standardized grammar and usage for French.	John Cotton. *True Constitution of a Particular Visible Church.* One of the earliest descriptions of congregationalist life and polity, written by a leader of the Massachusetts Bay Colony. (ca.)
1636		Massachusetts Bay Colony Congregationalists found Harvard College.		
1637		King Charles I of England and Archbishop of Canterbury William Laud attempt to impose the Anglican liturgy on Scotland. This act leads to rioting by Presbyterian Scots. Nicholas Ferrar, Anglican deacon, dies. Thomas Ken is born.	Rene Descartes. *Discourse on Method.* Cartesianism. A rationalist system, it is one of the foundational schools of modern philosophy. Its most revolutionary aspect is the "Cartesian turn," in which René Descartes argues for the existence of both the perceived world and God based on the existence of a thinking self ("*Cogito ergo sum*" (Latin: I think; therefore, I am)).	
1638		Swedish immigrants found New Sweden, an early Lutheran settlement in what is now Delaware.	Torture is abolished in England. Galileo Galilei. *Discourses Concerning Two New Sciences.* It reviews and refines Galileo's earlier studies of motion and ushers in a new scientific age by applying mathematics to the formulation of scientific laws. In doing so, it creates the foundation for the science of mechanics: For the first time, science begins seeing the universe in mechanical terms.	
1639		Saint Martin de Porres, Peruvian Dominican friar, dies. Roger Williams founds the first Baptist church in America.		
1640	Presbyterianism. A form of church government in which the church is governed by elected lay elders (presbyters, Gk. πρεσβύτεροι), who minister beside pastors, teachers, and deacons. Theologically, they Reformed. Historically, they trace their roots to Calvin's Geneva and the Reformed church in Scotland.	English colonists on Long Island, New York, and in New England form the first Presbyterian churches in America. (1640s) The Jesuits have more than 500 colleges throughout Europe. William Laud, archbishop of Canterbury, proposes the "Etcetera Oath," which requires much of England's leadership to swear to the divine right of kings. The proposal, which marks the beginning of the end of Laud's career, is met with derision and is eventually suspended by the king.	The English Revolution, also called the Puritan Revolution, begins. (–1660) The "Long Parliament," the English Parliament that sits throughout the Puritan revolution and the interregnum, convenes. (–1660) Peter Paul Rubens dies. His rich and sensuous handling of color make him one of the greatest painters of the baroque era.	The *Bay Psalm Book* is printed. The first book printed in America, it is a rhymed and metered version of the psalms for use in Puritan worship services. (1636–)

Date	A. Theology, Doctrine, and Beliefs	B. People/Events	C. Wider Culture	D. Texts
1641		English Parliament orders the removal of altar rails in Anglican churches. The Court of High Commissions, England's judicial body for doctrinal and liturgical uniformity, is abolished. (1640–)	Rationalism. In contrast to empiricism, rationalism maintains that faculties of the mind exists apart from experience. It maintains that certain innate ideas can be discovered apart from sense data. Key figures: Baruch Spinoza, Rene Descartes, and Gottfried Wilhelm Leibniz. Rene Descartes. *Meditations*.	
1642		Pope Urban VIII (in *Universa per orbem* (Latin: Through the whole world)) reduces the number of feast days to thirty-six feasts and eighty-five days free from labor. He also limits bishops' rights to establish new Holy Days. Saint Isaac Jogues and the North American Martyrs are killed by the Iroquois while working as Jesuit missionaries in Ontario, Quebec, and New York.	Civil war breaks out in England between the Royalists and the Parliamentarians. (–1651) Galileo Galilei dies. Blaise Pascal invents the first mechanical adding machine. Isaac Newton is born.	
1643		Solemn League and Covenant. An agreement between the English and Scottish Parliaments. Its goal is uniformity of the church in the two countries and the eradication of all Roman Catholic influence. It is also a mutual defense treaty. The Feast of the Holy Name is extended to the Carthusians.	Claudio Monteverdi dies. He was one of the greatest early baroque composers.	
1644		Innocent X becomes pope. Christmas is forbidden by Act of Parliament in England. Commerce is conducted as usual, fasting is enjoined, plum puddings are condemned as heathen.	The Ming Dynasty in China ends. The Manchus come to power.	The London Confession. The Calvinist doctrinal statement of the Particular Baptists. A century later it forms the basis for the Philadelphia Confession.
1645		William Laud, archbishop of Canterbury, is executed allegedly for "popery" and political subversion. More likely, however, his death was a result of his imposing high Anglican liturgy and the divine right of kings on a population with strong Puritan and republican sympathies.		Westminster Assembly. *The Directory of Public Worship*. It is a Presbyterian replacement for the *Book of Common Prayer*. Any English or Scottish church refusing to use the *Directory* receives stiff penalties. Later, when the *Book of Common Prayer* is restored in England, the *Directory of Public Worship* continues to be used in Calvinist Scotland.
1646			Oliver Cromwell defeats the English Royalists.	

Date	A. Theology, Doctrine, and Beliefs	B. People/Events	C. Wider Culture	D. Texts
1647	Covenant Theology (also known as Federal Theology). This common facet of Reformed theology sees the relation between God and humanity as a covenant or agreement. Key document: Westminster Confession of Faith.	George Fox, an English lay preacher begins to preach the doctrine of "Christ within." Though he has no intention of beginning a separate denomination, he and like-minded Christians join together and eventually call themselves the Society of Friends. They are more commonly known as the Quakers.	Margaret Brent is the first American woman to claim the right to vote. She is unsuccessful.	The Westminster Confession, an English Puritan doctrinal statement, is ratified. Its purpose is to provide a Presbyterian statement of doctrine and church order for the British Isles. It supersedes the Scots Confession. Assembly of Divines at Westminster. The *Larger and Shorter Catechisms*. With the Westminster Confession of Faith, they become the standard catechism in Presbyterian churches throughout Great Britain and the U.S. (1645–)
1648	Devotion to the Immaculate Heart of Mary. It is the homage paid both to the physical heart of Mary and to her interior life. It consists of devotion to her love of God, her maternal love for Jesus, and her compassion for those on earth for whom she intercedes.	The Peace of Westphalia establishes the principle: *Cujus regio illius et religio*; the lord of the land shall also be lord of religion. The feast in honor of the Immaculate Heart of Mary is first celebrated in France largely due to the efforts of St. Jean Eudes to propagate it. An English ordinance makes the denial of the Trinity an offense punishable by death.	The Thirty Years' War (1618–) ends with the Peace of Westphalia. France is strengthened, Germany and Spain weakened. Only three-eighths of Germany's population survives. The Holy Roman Emperor becomes a mere figurehead. War, famine, and plague have halved the population of Germany since 1618. The French Civil War begins. (–1652)	Lancelot Andrewes. *Preces Privatae* (Latin: Prayers in Private). A collection of devotions accumulated for his private use, it is published only after his death.
1649		The Presbyterian church becomes the state church of England. Saint Jean de Brébeuf, French Jesuit, is martyred while serving as a missionary to the Huron in Québec, Canada. The Maryland Assembly passes an Act of Toleration providing freedom of religion for all Trinitarians.	King Charles I of England is beheaded by the Parliamentarians. The Commonwealth, English Republican rule, is established.	*A Platform of Church Discipline* (also known as the *Cambridge Platform*). The definitive statement of the essential principles and polity of New England Congregationalism. (1648–)
1650		The Latin term *hermeneutica* begins to be used, though the concept of systematic biblical interpretation dates back at least to the fourth century. (mid seventeenth century)	The nonindigenous population of North America is 107,000. Tea comes to England. René Descartes, French philosopher, mathematician, and "Father of Modern Philosophy," dies. As the plantation system in the southern American colonies grows, so does the number of Africans imported as slaves. The end of the High Renaissance. (ca.)	Jeremy Taylor. *The Rule and Exercise of Holy Living* and *The Rule and Exercise of Holy Dying*. The products of both a finely honed literary sense and a deep and unquestioning faith, they are characteristic expressions of the piety of the time.

Date	A. Theology, Doctrine, and Beliefs	B. People/Events	C. Wider Culture	D. Texts
1651		By the end of the mid seventeenth century, Quakers have spread throughout England.	Thomas Hobbes. *Leviathan.* Set in the context of great social change and the rise of the new science of mechanics, it lays the foundations of modern scientific sociology by seeing human beings as governed by the same physical principles that govern the material world. It fosters the split between English philosophy and Scholasticism. England's Navigation Act is enacted. It is designed to ensure that trade wealth from England's colonies finds its way to England rather than to its enemies, especially the Dutch. It becomes one of the causes of the American Revolution.	
1652		John Cotton, Puritan theologian and leader of the Massachusetts Bay Colony, dies.	Giovanni Lorenzo Bernini. *Ecstasy of Saint Teresa* (sculpture) Rhode Island is the first American colony to outlaw slavery.	George Herbert. *A Priest in the Temple; or the Country Parson.* Herbert expresses the ideal for English clergy: duty, piety, and devotion to God and ministry. (published posthumously)
1653		The doctrine of irresistible grace (*gratia irrestibilis*) is declared to be heretical by Pope Innocent X. The first Seventh-day Baptist congregation begins holding Saturday services.	Oliver Cromwell becomes Lord Protector of England.	
1654			Rembrandt paints *Jan Six.*	James Ussher. *Annals of the World.* The work in which Ussher establishes the date of Creation as 4004 B.C.E. This date subsequently becomes widely accepted, even included in the margins of many editions of the King James Version of the Bible. (first edition)
1655		Alexander VII becomes pope.	Oliver Cromwell, Lord Protector of England dissolves parliament. Oliver Cromwell readmits Jews to England.	
1658			Oliver Cromwell dies. His son resigns from power, and the Puritan government of England ends.	Savoy Declaration. A statement of Congregationalist doctrine and polity. The doctrine owes much to the Westminster Confession, but the polity repudiates any authority higher than the individual Christian.
1660		The episcopacy is restored in England. Altar rails are again installed in Anglican churches.	King Charles II returns to England. The first scientific society is founded.	

Date	A. Theology, Doctrine, and Beliefs	B. People/Events	C. Wider Culture	D. Texts
1660 con't.		Saint Vincent de Paul dies. He was a French priest and the founder of the Congregation of the Mission, called the Vincentians or the Order of the Lazarists. Quakers begin to immigrate to the American colonies.	Feudal tenures are abolished by statute in England. Neoclassicism in literature is the stylistic trend between the English Restoration (1660) and the Romantic period (nineteenth century). It strives to imitate the literary conventions of classical Greek and Latin writing.	
1661		The Savoy Conference in England is convened by royal warrant to discuss the *Book of Common Prayer*. It decides that ministers not ordained by bishops must be reordained. Though it is attended by both Anglican bishops and English Presbyterian leaders, its declarations and changes to the prayer book are largely unacceptable to the Presbyterians. Excommunication begins to taper off in the Church of England, becoming ever rarer over the next two centuries. John Eliot translates the Bible into Algonquin. His is the first American Bible translation.	Charles II is crowned king of England. England's return to monarchical rule is typically referred to as "the Restoration." King Louis XIV, one of France's longest-reigning and most powerful kings, comes to power. He begins to build Versailles.	Pope Alexander VII promulgates the *Sollicitudo omnium Ecclesiarum* (Latin: Care for All of the Churches), which defines the doctrine of the Immaculate Conception of Mary and forbids further discussion on the topic.
1662	Halfway covenant. It is a Congregational membership standard under which the church may baptize the child of a baptized but unregenerate person.	John Biddle founds the first Unitarian congregation in England. The Feast of the Visitation of Our Lady becomes a black-letter day (lesser saints day) in the Church of England. The 1662 Act of Uniformity requires all Church of England services to use the 1662 *Book of Common Prayer*. All ministers not ordained by a bishop are deprived. The Licensing of the Press Act prohibits the printing or import of anti-Christian books into England. The imprimatur is also not granted to politically seditious books or books that could subvert the discipline of the Church of England.	Blaise Pascal, French philosopher, theologian, and scientist, dies. He invented the mathematical theory of probability and the adding machine, and did pioneering work on barometric pressure. A devout Jansenist, he was also known for his mystical theology.	*Book of Common Prayer* (the Savoy Conference Revision). About 600 changes are made, mostly minor details. The revision includes a modified "black rubric" and specifies the Authorized Version of the Bible be used for the Epistle and Gospel readings.
1664		English Conventicle Act of 1664. Forbids worship meetings other than Church of England. Worship groups of five people or more must use the *Book of Common Prayer*. Pope Alexander VII recognizes two separate "observances" within the Cistercian order: the common and the strict. The "strict observance" Cistercians abstain from meat and are dedicated to a stricter separation from the world.		

Date	A. Theology, Doctrine, and Beliefs	B. People/Events	C. Wider Culture	D. Texts
1665		Five-Mile Act. Dictates that non-Church-of-England clergy must promise not to teach against church or state, or, alternatively, they must stay five miles outside town. Francis of Sales is canonized.	The Great Plague in London kills 75,000 people. Rembrandt paints *The Return of the Prodigal Son*.	
1666		Philipp Jakob Spener begins work at the parish in Frankfurt where he becomes the leader of pietism in German Lutheranism. London's St. Paul's Cathedral is completely destroyed in the Great Fire.	The Great Fire of London.	
1667		Mexico City cathedral is finished. Jeremy Taylor, bishop and writer, dies. Clement IX becomes pope. The Basilica of Saint Peter is completed in Vatican city.	Maryland and Virginia pass laws that Christians can be enslaved. Slaves are baptized, some at their own request, some at their owners' insistence. Hand grenades are invented.	John Milton. *Paradise Lost*. A blank-verse epic written to "justify the ways of God to man." It details the story of Lucifer's rebellion and the fall of Adam and Eve.
1669			Rembrandt (Rembrandt Harmenszoon van Rijn), the greatest of the Dutch painters, dies.	
1670	Devotion to the Sacred Heart of Jesus. It is the veneration of the purity of Jesus' life, of his love for humanity, and of his physical heart, which was pierced on the cross. Key figure: Margaret Mary Alacoque	The Feast of the Sacred Heart is celebrated for the first time at the Grand Seminary of Rennes. Clement X becomes pope. Pope Clement X makes the Feast of Guardian Angels universal.	Jews are expelled from Vienna.	
1671		Rose of Lima is canonized by Pope Clement X. She is the first native-born South American saint. Margaret Mary Alacoque enters the convent at Paray-le-Monial after recovering from paralysis and attributing that recovery to the Virgin Mary. While in the convent, she has numerous visions of the bleeding and compassionate heart of Christ.		
1672		Organized ecclesiastical nonconformity is legalized in England. Heinrich Schütz, German composer, dies. He is considered the greatest religious composer of the seventeenth century.	The banking industry is born. Goldsmiths keep the gold of private citizens for safekeeping. They loan out part of this reserve against promissory notes for both the principal and the interest. (ca.)	

Date	A. Theology, Doctrine, and Beliefs	B. People/Events	C. Wider Culture	D. Texts
1673		Margaret Mary Alacoque's "great apparition" of the Sacred Heart of Jesus sends her on a mission to propagate the new devotion. The Test Act mandates the Oaths of Supremacy and Allegiance and the reception of communion in the Church of England for all civil and military officers.		
1674		Isaac Watts, English hymn writer, dies. He was the author of "When I Survey the Wondrous Cross" and "O God Our Help in Ages Past." John Milton dies. Puritan writer and the last great poet of the English Renaissance.	The Anglo-Dutch Wars end with the division of colonies between England and Holland. Holland gets the East Indies; England gets America. (1652–)	
1675	Pietism. Emphasizes conversion, individual spiritual responsibility, practical holiness, and a relationship with God that entails emotional involvement. It arises as a response to the increasing worldliness of organized religion, both Catholic and established Protestant. The established church has become more about worship than piety, more about enjoyment than service. (–present.)	Quakers purchase land and settle in New Jersey. Sir Christopher Wren begins Saint Paul's Cathedral in the English baroque style. In this and other churches built after the great fire, Wren introduces the single square-tower belfry with tall steeple. Since his time, this steeple has become the hallmark of English and American church architecture.	King Philip's War. Philip (an American Indian), leads the Wampanoag tribe and other warriors against Puritan settlers. Several thousand die. The war ends hopes of a widespread peace between the American natives and the immigrants. (–1676) Four-part singing becomes popular. (late seventeenth century)	Phillipp Jakob Spener. *Pia Desideria* (Latin: Holy Desire). A German Protestant book calling for a practical, biblical, laity-centered Christianity. It is the first programmatic statement of pietism. Baruch (Benedict de) Spinoza. *Ethics.* Claims God is the substance that makes up both matter and mind: a Rationalist, mystical pantheism.
1676		Innocent XI becomes pope.	Bacon's Rebellion. Virginia farmers fight against the colonial authorities. Former indentured servants led by Nathaniel Bacon maintain the governor is not protecting them from Indian raids. The farmers form an army to retaliate against raiding tribes.	
1677		The English Ecclesiastical Jurisdiction Act abolishes the death penalty for heresy.	The microscope is invented.	
1678				John Bunyan. *Pilgrim's Progress.* An allegory of the Christian life, it is one of the most widely read English books. Robert Barclay. *An Apology for the True Christian Divinity, as the Same Is Held Forth and Preached by the People Called in Scorn Quakers.* The authoritative Quaker systematic theology.

Date	A. Theology, Doctrine, and Beliefs	B. People/Events	C. Wider Culture	D. Texts
1679			Thomas Hobbes, English philosopher, dies.	
1680	In the late seventeenth century, cutting-edge thinkers begin to disassociate religious uniformity and national solidarity.		Giovanni Lorenzo Bernini, one of Rome's most famous baroque architects and sculptors, dies.	
1681		Eusebio Francisco Kino, a Jesuit missionary, lands in Mexico and begins to establish missions to the Pima Indians. William Penn receives a charter for the colony of Pennsylvania.		
1682	Gallicanism. A mix of theology and politics supporting French Catholic independence from Rome. Key figures: J. B. Bossuet, King Louis XIV. Key document: *Declaration of the Clergy of France.* Higher Criticism. The study of the sources and literary methods used by authors of biblical texts.			William Penn. *No Cross, No Crown.* It is the definitive work on early Quaker ethics. Richard Simon. *Critical History of the Old Testament.* The scientific method is applied to biblical studies, foreshadowing the coming of higher criticism. *Declaration of the Clergy of France,* called "the Four Articles." It is the first systematic presentation of Gallicanism. It states: (1) Kings aren't subject to ecclesiastical authority in temporal matters. (2) The decrees of the Council of Constance are authoritative. (3) Papal authority is limited by canons and constitutions in the Gallican church. (4) The authority of the pope is reformable and subject to the judgement of the Church as a whole. In general, it puts severe limits on papal primacy.
1683	Holy experiment. The charter of William Penn's Pennsylvania colony provides for freedom of religion for any theist who is willing to live in peace. Citizens aren't compelled to attend religious services, but only Christians may hold civil office.	Mennonites from the line of Dutch Anabaptist Menno Simons land in America to join William Penn's "Holy Experiment." Francis Makemie, Scottish Presbyterian minister and "the Father of American Presbyterianism" comes to the American colonies Roger Williams, Anglican priest and founder of Rhode Island, dies.	Isaac Newton explains the earth's tides.	
1684		Approximately 7000 Quakers have settled in Pennsylvania.	Gottfried Wilhelm von Leibniz publishes the fundamental principles of infinitesimal calculus. His method was discovered in 1675, after Sir Isaac Newton's, but	

Date	A. Theology, Doctrine, and Beliefs	B. People/Events	C. Wider Culture	D. Texts
1684 con't.			published before Newton's work was. Leibniz's method of notation becomes universal. The Massachusetts Bay Colony charter is revoked, and Massachusetts becomes a royal colony.	
1685		The Edict of Nantes is revoked under King Louis XIV of France, spurring Protestant migration to America.	George Frideric Handel is born. Domenico Scarlatti is born. King James II of England ascends to the throne. Johann Sebastian Bach is born.	
1686		William Law is born.		
1687		King James II of England calls for freedom of conscience in matters of religion. Anglicans fear a return to Roman Catholicism and demand the "Glorious Revolution."	Isaac Newton. *Philosophiae Naturalis Principia Mathematica* ([Latin: Mathematical Principles of Natural Philosophy] commonly known as "the Principia"). Newton establishes a scientific paradigm that allows nature to be represented in mathematical terms.	
1688		The Religious Society of Friends (Quakers) protest slavery in the American colonies.	The Glorious Revolution (also known as the Bloodless Revolution). In England, Roman Catholic King James II is dethroned and Dutch Reformed William of Orange and his wife, Mary, come to power. (–1689)	
1689		Alexander VIII becomes pope. The English Toleration Act of 1689 grants freedom of religion to Separatist Protestant groups who are willing to sign Oaths of Allegiance and Supremacy as well as a modified version of the Thirty-nine Articles.	England and Holland band together in a coalition war against Louis XIV's France. (–1713) The French and Indian Wars begin. It is a struggle between Britain and France. Both sides had Indian allies in their battles for North American influence and territory. (–1763) Peter I, "Peter the Great," becomes Tsar of Russia. He modernizes and increases the political and military power of his country.	
1690		Papal nepotism is outlawed. The Scottish church is legally established as Presbyterian. Saint Margaret Mary Alacoque, French nun, dies. She was an early devotee of the Sacred Heart.	John Locke. *Essay Concerning Human Understanding*. The theoretical foundation and framework for empiricism. It shifted the course of modern philosophy away from ontology toward epistemology. Empiricism. Maintains that all knowledge is based on experience, that no thought is possible apart from sense data or learned patterns of thinking. It	

Date	A. Theology, Doctrine, and Beliefs	B. People/Events	C. Wider Culture	D. Texts
1690 con't.			contrasts itself to rationalism. Key figures: John Locke and David Hume Ole Römer calculates the speed of light.	
1691		Innocent XII becomes pope. George Fox, British founder of the Quakers, dies.		
1692		The Salem witchcraft trials are held in Massachusetts. Three hundred men and women are accused. Twenty people are executed. Joseph Butler is born.	Dudley North proposes the law of supply and demand, part of early economic theory.	
1694			Anglicans found William and Mary College.	
1695	Deism. A belief system arising out of the Enlightenment. At its core is the belief in a reasonable God who created a reasonable universe. Though God is personally distant, humanity can know God by rational analysis of the universe.	The Licensing of the Press Act expires. British books no longer must bear an imprimatur.	Henry Purcell, one of England's greatest composers, dies.	John Toland. *Christianity Not Mysterious.* It turns up the heat under the deist debate by maintaining that Christianity is not dogmatic and supernatural but reasonable and natural. John Locke. *The Reasonableness of Christianity as Delivered in the Scriptures.* It approaches the Bible as a whole, not as a collection of independent verses. In doing so it presents a new, scholarly approach to biblical hermeneutics.
1697	Quietism. A form of mysticism that emphasizes a meditative, passive inner life that brings one in touch with the Spirit of God. The term is used both of the Roman Catholic teaching of Miguel de Molinos and the beliefs of Quakers, who hold to a more moderate mysticism than Molinos.	Miguel de Molinos, Spanish Quietist, dies. He was known for his abilities as a confessor and spiritual director. His mystical teachings had great influence on the pietists.		
1698		The Society for Promoting Christian Knowledge (S.P.C.K.) is formed to spread charity schools, Bibles, and religious tracts throughout England and Wales.		
1700		Clement XI becomes pope. Armand Jean de Rancé restores the original practices of seclusion, silence, manual labor, and vegetarianism to his Cistercian monastery at La Trappe, France. Followers of his strict observance becomes known as the Order of Cistercians of the Strict Observance or the Trappists. (before 1700)	Europe's literacy rate is 30–40%. By the end of the seventeenth century, Latin is used in Europe only as the mode of communication in international academic contacts and in Roman Catholic official documents and liturgy. Reformed churches use exclusively vernacular liturgy.	Thomas Ken. "The Doxology." This song, "Praise God from whom all blessings flow...," referred to in Protestant circles as "the Doxology," is usually sung to the tune "Old One Hundredth." (ca.)

Date	A. Theology, Doctrine, and Beliefs	B. People/Events	C. Wider Culture	D. Texts
1700 con't.		The Amish split from the Swiss Brethren. The Amish observe the Lord's Supper more frequently, wear only "plain" clothes, and shun those who have been excommunicated. (ca.)	Much of the instruction, even in universities, is conducted in the vernacular. The European obsession with witch-hunting ends. (ca.)	
1701		Thomas Bray forms the Society for the Propagation of the Gospel (SPG), an Anglican society. It fosters the spread of the Anglican church into British colonies.	Yale College is founded by conservative Congregationalists. War of Spanish Succession begins. It is fought between the Grand Alliance—consisting originally of England, the Netherlands, Denmark, Austria, and Portugal—and a coalition of France, Spain, and a number of small Italian and German principalities. (–1714)	*Acta Sanctorum Ordinis Sancti Benedicti* (Latin: Acts of the Saints of the Order of Saint Benedict). A hagiography of the lives of Benedictine saints.
1702			Queen Anne of England ascends to the throne. Queen Anne's War begins. It is one phase of the French and Indian Wars. (–1713)	
1703		John Wesley is born. Jonathan Edwards is born. Justus Falckner is the first Lutheran pastor ordained in America.	Gottfried Wilhelm Leibniz. *New Essays Concerning Human Understanding*. This work, by one of the greatest minds of the seventeenth century, has great influence on eighteenth century German philosophers, including Immanuel Kant.	
1704		Jacques Bénigne Bossuet, French preacher and apologist for Catholicism, dies.	Johann Sebastian Bach writes his first cantata. His cantatas were written to be a part of the Lutheran liturgy. John Locke, English philosopher and political theorist, dies.	
1705	Latitudinarianism. Largely the descendants of the Cambridge Platonists, these Arminian rationalists are reasonable, sincere, moral, and very British. As such, they distrust ecstatic and individualistic religion. Latitudinarianism is a dominant religious force in Britain during the Georgian Age. Key figures: Joseph Glanville, Simon Patrick, Thomas Tenison, and John Tillotson. (1714–1830)	Phillipp Jakob Spener, Father of Pietism, dies. The Camisards, also known as the French Prophets, begin a guerilla revolt against the French crown. They are known for ecstatic prayer and prophesy, and for ruthless fighting for their cause. (–1709)	Insurance companies begin using actuarial tables.	
1706		Francis Makemie organizes the first American presbytery.		

Date	A. Theology, Doctrine, and Beliefs	B. People/Events	C. Wider Culture	D. Texts
1707		Charles Wesley is born.	Scotland becomes part of the United Kingdom of Great Britain. It maintains its own legal system and church polity, but is represented in and governed by British Parliament.	Isaac Watts. *Hymns and Spiritual Songs.* Though Watts is a nonconformist and his songs are not widely accepted in the Church of England during his lifetime, some hymns in this hymnal eventually become British and American favorites. Watts marks the trend away from settings of literal psalm translations toward hymnody that expresses the thoughts and feelings of the singer. Songs contained in this hymnal are: "When I Survey the Wondrous Cross," "O, God, our Help in Ages Past," and "Joy to the World."
1708		Pope Clement XI extends the Feast of the Immaculate Conception of the Blessed Virgin Mary to the universal church and makes it a Feast of Obligation.		*Saybrook Platform.* A statement of Congregationalist discipline. It establishes a consociation of lay and ordained leaders to resolve disputes among Connecticut Congregationalists. It is not universally accepted.
1709		Thousands of German Reformed people leave the high taxes and dynastic wars of their homeland for London. From there, most of them travel to America.	The pianoforte is invented.	
1710		Christopher Wren finishes St. Paul's Cathedral in London.	George Berkeley. *Principles of Human Knowledge.* The foundational work of Subjective Idealism Subjective Idealism. Develops the notion of *esse est percipi,* that to exist means to be perceived or to be capable of perception. According to Subjective Idealism there is no material reality, only ideas. Key figure: George Berkeley.	
1711		Thomas Ken, bishop of Bath, dies.	David Hume is born.	
1712		Pope Pius V is canonized.	Thomas Newcomen invents the steam engine.	
1713			The Peace of Utrecht gives England trading rights in Spanish-held American territory and marks the beginning of the British Empire.	
1714		Schism Act. Only Church of England communicants may teach in schools. (repealed 1718)	The House of Hanover begins its reign in England. (–1837)	

Date	A. Theology, Doctrine, and Beliefs	B. People/Events	C. Wider Culture	D. Texts
1715		George Whitefield is born.	Rococo Architecture. Characterized by delicacy, lightness, and elaborate ornamentation, it begins with the reign of King Louis XV of France and disappears completely with the French Revolution in 1789.	
1716		The first American Presbyterian synod is formed. Pope Clement XI makes the Feast of the Rosary universal. Christian religious education is banned in China.	Gottfried Wilhelm von Leibniz, German rationalistic philosopher and mathematician, dies.	
1717			George Frideric Handel. *Water Music.* The first inoculation against smallpox is developed. The first modern Mason Grand Lodge is founded in England.	
1718		The Schism Act is repealed in England. Teachers need no longer be Church of England communicants. William Penn, Quaker statesman and founder of Pennsylvania, dies.	Gabriel Fahrenheit invents the mercury thermometer and devises the fahrenheit temperature scale.	
1720	Subscription Controversy. Presbyterians dispute whether they should require that ministers subscribe to a written doctrinal confession. One faction focuses on the fallibility of human documents, the other on the need for doctrinal purity. (eighteenth century)	Pope Clement XI makes St. Anselm of Canterbury a doctor of the church.	The classical period in music begins. It seeks a less rigid structure than baroque compositions with more emotional flexibility within each piece. The climax of this period is the Viennese classical school. Key figures: Joseph Haydn, Wolfgang Amadeus Mozart, and Ludwig van Beethoven. (ca.–1805) New efficient farming methods make it possible for farmers to "cash crop." (ca.)	
1721		Innocent XIII becomes pope. Pope Innocent XIII extends the Feast of the Holy Name to the Church as a whole.	J. S. Bach writes the *Brandenburg Concertos.*	
1722		Nikolaus Ludwig Graf von Zinzendorf organizes groups of Brethren (who later evolve into the Moravian church) in his home. He introduces a pietistic tone to the organization. Pope Innocent XIII makes St. Isidore a doctor of the church.	The last regular execution of someone accused of witchcraft takes place at Doruoch.	
1724		Benedict XIII becomes pope.	Longman's Publishing House is founded. Immanuel Kant is born.	

Date	A. Theology, Doctrine, and Beliefs	B. People/Events	C. Wider Culture	D. Texts
1725		John Philip Boehm forms the first congregations of the Reformed Church in the U.S. (RCUS). Most of the congregants are German immigrants.		
1726	First Great Awakening. It is a wave of evangelistic revivals that sweep through the American colonies, peaking in 1740–1742. The hallmark is the need for New Birth or being "born again." The revivals are built on a pessimistic estimation of humanity's chances for holiness apart from God. Key figures: Jonathan Edwards and George Whitfield.	Pope Benedict XIII canonizes Aloysius Gonzaga and John of the Cross. The "beginning" of the First Great Awakening takes place among the Dutch Reformed Churches in New Jersey.	Jonathan Swift publishes *Gulliver's Travels*. Sir Isaac Newton, the most renowned modern mathematician and natural philosopher, dies.	
1727	Voluntaryism (also known as volunteerism). The belief that individuals should have the right to choose their own religious associations without coercion from religious or state institutions. It grew in American culture as a result of the First Great Awakening.	The Ursuline convent is established in French New Orleans as the first regular religious community for women in America.		
1728	Teleological argument for the existence of God. The argument that the Creation embodies design and purpose and, therefore, points to the existence of a purposeful Creator.	Cotton Mather, American Protestant apologist and founder of Yale College, dies.		William Law. *A Serious Call to a Devout and Holy Life*. It calls the Christian to a temperate and ascetical life. Based on the writings of Thomas à Kempis, Jan van Ruysbroeck, and other mystical writers, it exhorts the reader to glorify God in all aspects of life. It is one of the best-known post-Reformation spiritual classics.
1729	Methodism. Originally a pietistic, holiness offshoot of the Anglican church, its evangelistic nature and dynamic organization allowed it to develop into one of the most influential denominations on the American frontier. The polity of the various Methodist offshoots range from episcopal to congregational. Doctrinal emphases also vary. Virtually all Methodist churches, however, share a stong emphasis on ethical behavior and nurture of individual Christians. Key figures: John and Charles Wesley, Francis Asbury.	Pope Benedict XIII makes St. Peter Chrysologus a doctor of the church. Johann Sebastian Bach. *St. Matthew's Passion*. Pope Benedict XIII canonizes John of Nepomuk. John Wesley begins to attend Oxford. There he joins a group of other serious Christians called the Holy Club. They are the first to use the name "Methodists."		Adopting Act. The Presbyterian church in colonial America adopts the Westminster Confession and Catechism. Subscription is required of all ministers.
1730		Thomas Bray dies. He oversaw the work of the Anglican church in America and advocated prison reform in England. Clement XII becomes pope.	The first Mason lodge in the United States is founded in Pennsylvania.	Matthew Tindal. *Christianity as Old as Creation*. In it Tindal maintains that natural religion and reason form the basis for moral law. It eventually becomes the "bible" of deism.

Date	A. Theology, Doctrine, and Beliefs	B. People/Events	C. Wider Culture	D. Texts
1732		St. Alphonsus Liguori founds the Missionary Congregation of Liguorians Redemptorists to spread Christianity among the poor. The Moravians (Renewed Moravian Church) begin missionary work, which takes them to the West Indies, Greenland, Tasmania, South Africa, and elsewhere.	Benjamin Franklin begins publishing *Poor Richard's Almanack*. (–1757)	
1735		The Log College is founded as a school for training colonial American Presbyterian ministers. Its tendencies were toward revivalistic and pietistic Christianity. (1726–)		
1736		John and Charles Wesley, Church of England missionaries, arrive in the colony of Georgia. Their mission is not very successful, prompting them to return to England within two years.	"India rubber" comes to England. English witchcraft laws are formally repealed.	Joseph Butler. *Analogy of Religion, Natural and Revealed*. Written by a British apologist in the Enlightenment tradition, it is a tightly argued demonstration of the harmony between the order in nature and that of revealed religion. Though not specifically addressed to the deists, the deistic debate is obviously its context.
1737		Saint Vincent de Paul is canonized.		
1738	Old Side Presbyterianism. These Scottish and Scotch-Irish clergy oppose the pietism and religious enthusiasm of the Log College graduates. They call for enforcement of the Adopting Act and the requirement that Log College graduates submit their credentials to the synod for approval before they can be ordained. Key figures: Francis Alison and John Ewing. New Side Presbyterianism. Presbyterian ministers whose beliefs showed the influence of Congregationalism and continental pietism. Intellectual center: the Log College. Key figures: William Tennent.	John Wesley's conversion occurs at a Moravian meeting in London. He describes it as not only *believing* that Christ is his salvation but coming to *feel* it and *trust* it.	Johann Sebastian Bach. *Mass in B Minor*. A musical setting of the mass in the style of a cantata, it is too Catholic for Bach's Lutheran church and too long for an ordinary Catholic service. It is, however, a passionate reflection of Bach's personal faith and a landmark of the baroque era.	
1739		John Wesley begins to form Methodist societies within the Anglican church to provide guidance for the converts drawn to the church by his evangelistic efforts.		Charles Wesley. *Hymns and Sacred Poems*. His first collection of hymns, it is part of the 5,000 hymns he wrote during his lifetime.
1740	Old Lights. During the Great Awakening it is the conservative faction that believes religious enthusiasm is both a mental aberration and divisive to the cohesiveness of	The First Great Awakening "peaks." (–1742) Benedict XIV becomes pope. The Jesuits have more than 650 colleges and 200 semi-	David Hume. *Treatise of Human Nature*. Maintains that human beings have no innate ideas apart from sense experience, that even cause-effect is learned. It brings	

Date	A. Theology, Doctrine, and Beliefs	B. People/Events	C. Wider Culture	D. Texts
1740 con't.	the church. Center: New England, especially Boston; Cambridge College. Key figure: Charles Chauncey New Lights. The supporters of George Whitefield and the revivalism of the Great Awakening. They maintain that emotion and reason both are necessary in the human response to God. Key figure: Jonathan Edwards.	naries and houses of study throughout Europe. Moravian immigrants to American celebrate Christmas with a visit from Santa Claus.	empiricism into skepticism and becomes one of the most important works of British empiricism. (3 volumes, 1730–) King George's War. It is a part of the French and Indian Wars. (–1748)	
1741		George Frideric Handel writes the *Messiah*.	Vitus Bering discovers Alaska. Antonio Vivaldi, Roman Catholic priest and late-baroque composer, dies.	Jonathan Edwards delivers the sermon *Sinners in the Hands of an Angry God*.
1742		Henry Melchior Muhlenberg, German Lutheran missionary, comes to America.		Philadelphia Confession of Faith. The confessional statement of the Philadelphia Baptist Association, it is a Baptist modification of the Westminster Confession. In subsequent years it becomes one of the most influential statements of Baptist belief.
1743	Separate Baptists. They are the Calvinist, revivalist Baptists of the First Great Awakening. Their unpaid, untrained clergy includes many women preachers.	The first identifiable Separate Baptist church splits from Regular Baptists. Lutheran Pastor Peter Nicholas Sommer is the first colonial minister to baptize American Indians.		Thomas Prince. *The Christian History*. It is the first religious magazine in America. (–1745)
1744		The first conference of Methodist workers is held.	The first recorded cricket match is played. "God Save the Queen" is first published.	
1746		Absalom Jones is born. Princeton University is founded by New Light Presbyterians as the College of New Jersey.	The Battle of Culloden Moor. British troops defeat Scottish Jacobite rebels. The Jacobites, led by Prince Charles Edward Stuart, a pretender to the British throne, seek to overthrow the Protestant regime set in place by the Glorious Revolution.	
1747		William White is born.		
1748	Syncretism. A Roman Catholic doctrine of grace, it is the belief that prayer is the way the grace necessary for the performance of the difficult works of salvation is obtained. "Who prays will secure his eternal salvation; who does not pray will be lost." Key figures: the Paris Sorbonne.	Henry Melchior Muhlenberg founds the Pennsylvania Ministerium, the first Lutheran synod in North America. Pietists form a majority of the Lutheran clergy in America. Francis Xavier is declared patron saint of the Orient.	David Hume. *An Enquiry Concerning Human Understanding*. A key work of British empiricism. It greatly influenced Kant's work. Charles Louis de Secondat, Baron de la Brede et Montesquieu. *The Spirit of Laws*. An examination of government, including the theory of separation of powers upon which the U.S. constitution is built.	David Hume. *Essay on Miracles*. It dismisses accounts of miracles asserting that the the possibility of deceit or misinterpretation outweigh the possibility of something unprecedented and contrary to natural law actually occurring.

Date	A. Theology, Doctrine, and Beliefs	B. People/Events	C. Wider Culture	D. Texts
1749			The first systematic sign language for the deaf is invented.	
1750	New Divinity Theology. Within Congregationalism it is an interpretation of Calvinism that allows for the possibility of sinners repenting. It is a response to the revivalism of the time. Key figures: Jonathan Edwards. (–1850)		Hasidim, a pietistic branch of Judaism, is established in Poland by Israel ben Eliezer, who becomes known as the Ba'al Shem Tov (Master of the Good Name). (ca.) Johann Sebastian Bach dies. Enlightenment. Also known as the Age of Reason. It is a time of great faith in the powers of reason, observation, and experiment. Two of its most important pillars are Empiricist philosophy and Newtonian physics. (peaks in the mid eighteenth century)	
1751			Carolus Linnaeus invents the modern system of botanical classification. (ca.)	
1752		The Gregorian calendar is adopted in Great Britain and Ireland. Easter is celebrated on the same day throughout Western Christianity. Joseph Butler, Anglican bishop of Durham, apologist and theologian, dies.		
1753	Equiproblemism. A principle in casuistry. In a moral decision, when arguments on both sides are equally probable, the laxer course may be followed. Key figure: Saint Alphonsus Liguori		Jews may be naturalized in England.	
1754		Pope Benedict XIV makes St. Leo I a doctor of the church.	Columbia University is founded by Anglicans (with a distinct Presbyterian minority). Dartmouth College is founded. Americans enter the French and Indian War. (–1763) The first woman doctor begins to practice medicine in Germany.	
1755				John Wesley issues the first "paragraph Bible" version of the New Testament, in which the text is divided into paragraphs rather than the standard verses.
1756			Wolfgang Amadeus Mozart is born.	

Date	A. Theology, Doctrine, and Beliefs	B. People/Events	C. Wider Culture	D. Texts
1757			The sextant is invented. It supersedes the astrolabe.	
			Robert Clive, Baron Clive of Plassey, and his British troops defeat the army of Indian leader Siraj-ud-Dawlah. The victory brings India under British power.	
1758		Jonathan Edwards, Congregational minister and leader of the First Great Awakening, dies.	The first American Indian reservation is established.	
		Clement XIII becomes pope.		
		The organizational breach between Old Side and New Side Presbyterianism is healed.		
1759		The Jesuits are expelled from Brazil and from Portugal.	George Frideric Handel dies.	
		William Wilberforce is born.	Voltaire (François-Marie Arouet). *Candide.* A skeptic's satire of Gottfried Wilhelm Leibniz's "best of all possible worlds."	
1760		Churches in America are no longer supported by state revenue.		
		The earliest American societies of the Methodist Church are formed in New York City, Philadelphia, and near Pipe Creek, Maryland. (throughout the 1760s)		
1761		William Law, Anglican priest and spiritual writer, dies.		
		William Carey is born.		
1762			Jean Jacques Rousseau. *The Social Contract.* Rousseau maintains that governance resides with the people, who delegate it to a sovereign with the understanding that it can be withdrawn if necessary. His work helped form the ideological background of the French Revolution	
1764		Brown University is founded as a Baptist institution dedicated to religious freedom.	Cesare Beccaria. *On Crimes and Punishments.* A short treatise that fosters efforts to abolish the death penalty in Europe.	
1765		The Feast of the Sacred Heart becomes a liturgical feast.		
		Robert Raikes founds Sunday Schools in England, leading to the Sunday School Movement. (ca.)		

Date	A. Theology, Doctrine, and Beliefs	B. People/Events	C. Wider Culture	D. Texts
1766	Wesleyan Tradition. The teaching of John Wesley that God's work among believers is in two stages: justification and sanctification. It lives on today in Holiness and Pentecostal churches, Methodist and African Methodist Episcopal Churches, and in the Wesleyan Church proper.		Rutgers University is founded as Queens College by the Dutch Reformed Church.	
1767		Jesuit missionaries are expelled from Mexico and Spanish South America.	Joseph Priestly. *The History and Present State of Electricity*. European society is fascinated with electricity and electricity toys.	
1768		Greek Orthodoxy comes to America when Greek pioneers found the colony of New Smyrna south of St. Augustine, Florida. Friedrich Daniel Ernst Schleiermacher is born.	Wolfgang Amadeus Mozart writes his first opera.	
1769		John Wesley sends the first Methodist missionaries to America. Clement XIV becomes pope.	Napoleon Bonaparte is born.	
1770		George Whitefield, Anglican preaching deacon and Methodist evangelist, dies. He was an important voice of the first Great Awakening. Mother Ann Lee sets up the first Shaker colonies. Voltaire: "If God did not exist, it would be necessary to invent him."	The spinning jenny is patented. Ludwig von Beethoven is born. "Boston Massacre." British soldiers kill five American colonists. Georg W. F. Hegel is born.	William Billings. *The New England Psalm Singer*. Compiled by one of the New England "tunesmiths," it introduces a distinctly American form of church music, the fuguing tune, which is a four-part piece that begins like a hymn and ends like a round.
1771		Francis Asbury is commissioned as a Methodist missionary.	Denis Diderot. *Encyclopédie*. The most advanced scientific, philosophic, and artistic thought of the Enlightenment is presented in seventeen volumes of text and eleven volumes of engravings. Contributors include some of the best known thinkers of the day. (1751–)	
1772		Francis Asbury begins the practice of reaching the American frontier through Methodist circuit riders. These itinerant pastors preach and tend churches on the farthest reaches of the frontier. They both benefit from and fuel the conversions of the Second Great Awakening. (through the mid nineteenth century)		

Date	A. Theology, Doctrine, and Beliefs	B. People/Events	C. Wider Culture	D. Texts
1773		The first conference of Methodist preachers in the American colonies is held in Philadelphia. The preachers agree to follow Wesley's leadership. They also agree that their people will receive the sacraments at their local Anglican parish church. Pope Clement XIV suppresses the Jesuits. The order survives in Russia where the empress is an admirer of Jesuit education.	Boston Tea Party. A group of American colonists dumps imported British tea into Boston harbor to protest the tea tax and other British import policy.	
1774		Mother Ann Lee leads a group of Shakers (the United Society of Believers in Christ's Second Appearing) from England to New York. For the first time, this communal Millenarian society begins to prosper.	Hypnosis is first used. The first American Continental Congress is formed.	
1775	Textual Criticism. Necessitated by the inaccuracy of human manuscript copyists, it is the study of variant readings in biblical manuscripts. Its purpose is reconstruction of the history of the text and, ultimately, reconstruction of the text in its original form.	Pius VI becomes pope. During the American Revolutionary War, prayers for the British monarch are removed from Episcopal services. Some clergy, mostly northern, close the churches rather than remove the prayers.	The American Revolutionary War begins. (–1783) James Watt begins manufacturing steam engines.	Johann Jakob Griesbach. *Greek New Testament.* It is the first edition based on Greek codices. It marks the beginning of textual criticism.
1776		Quakers may no longer hold slaves. About 85% of American colonists are Reformed. The State of Virginia drafts a constitution that is the first to mandate religious freedom.	Adam Smith. *Wealth of Nations.* David Hume, Empiricist philosopher, dies. Black workers imported from Africa are no longer indentured servants but slaves in the strictest sense of the word. (by the time of the American Revolution) The American Declaration of Independence is written. Thomas Paine. *Common Sense.* A series of pamphlets that spurred the American desire for independence.	
1777			Vermont becomes the first state to outlaw slavery.	
1778	Universalism. The teaching that all of humanity will eventually be saved. In America it develops in small towns along the Atlantic coast in the late eighteenth and early nineteenth century. Key figures: John Murray, Hosea Ballou, Elhanan Winchester.	The General Society of Universalists is formed. The first biblical manuscript discovered in modern times is a papyrus manuscript found in Egypt.	France intervenes in the American Revolutionary War on the side of the Americans. James Cook discovers Hawaii.	
1779			Spain enters the American Revolutionary War on the side of the Americans.	

Date	A. Theology, Doctrine, and Beliefs	B. People/Events	C. Wider Culture	D. Texts
1780	Free Will Baptists. These Arminian Baptists reject the Calvinist predestination of the Regular Baptists. Key figure: Benjamin Randall.	Benjamin Randall breaks with the Regular Baptists to form the first Free Will Baptist church in New England. Holy Roman Emperor Joseph II reforms both church and state to bring them in line with Enlightenment principles. He grants religious toleration to Protestants and reorganizes the Roman Catholic Church. In particular, he simplifies the Catholic liturgy, closes many monasteries, and limits the power of the pope in Austria. (–1790)	The modern piano is invented. Holy Roman Emperor Joseph II ends discriminatory laws against Jews, frees the serfs, and promulgates a new law code. (–1790)	
1781		The Lord's Day Observance Act revives Sabbatarianism in England. It prohibits recreation and monetary transactions on Sunday.	Immanuel Kant. *Critique of Pure Reason*. Combines the empiricist notion that all knowledge has its source in experience with the rationalist belief in deduction as the source of knowledge. A gearing system is invented that allows an entire factory to run off a single engine. The Articles of Confederation, the first United States Constitution, is written.	
1782	Clapham Sect. An influential, but loosely knit, group of Anglican evangelicals who believe in Christianity made practical by social action. Key figures: Henry Venn, William Wilberforce, Zachary Macaulay, Granville Sharp, and others. (ca.)			William White. *The Case of the Episcopal Church Considered*. It proposes an Episcopal church that is Anglican in doctrine, democratic in polity, and organizationally separate from the state. It is a dominant influence in shaping the polity of the Protestant Episcopal Church in the United States.
1783			England and America sign a definitive treaty of peace. The Revolutionary War ends. Joseph Michel and Jacques Étienne Montgolfier invent the hot air balloon and become the first people ever to fly.	
1784		The Christmas Conference of preachers is held in Baltimore. The Methodist Episcopal Church in the U.S. becomes a distinct body from the English Methodist structure. Francis Asbury and Thomas Coke are made bishops and become leaders of the new church. Samuel Seabury is consecrated bishop by nonjuring bishops of Scotland, becoming the first bishop of Connecticut and the first bishop of the Protestant Episcopal Church in the U.S.	The locomotive is patented.	John Wesley releases the *Deed of Declaration*, rules and regulations for the guidance of Methodist societies.

Date	A. Theology, Doctrine, and Beliefs	B. People/Events	C. Wider Culture	D. Texts
1785		The first Episcopal Church General Convention is held. Delegates petition the archbishop of Canterbury to obtain parliamentary permission to consecrate American bishops.	In the Treaty of Hopwell, the U.S. government agrees to respect Cherokee territory and sovereignty. The treaty is broken with the 1830 Indian Removal Act.	The Methodist Episcopal Church publishes its first *Discipline*.
1786		Legislation in the British Parliament allows the consecration of American bishops without their taking the Oath of Allegiance. The Methodist Missionary Society is formed.		
1787		Saint Alphonsus Liguori dies. Italian prelate and theologian, founder of Missionary Congregation of Liguorians. The Episcopal Church in the U.S. obtains English parliamentary permission to have bishops consecrated. Bishops of the Church of England consecrate Samuel Provoost the first Episcopal bishop of New York, and William White the first bishop of Pennsylvania. The Religious Society of Friends (Quakers) have no member who is a slave owner. The first Anglican colonial bishop (of Nova Scotia) is consecrated. His jurisdiction is British North America. Richard Allen founds the first African Methodist Episcopal congregation after being turned away by a Methodist church.	Wolfgang Amadeus Mozart. *Don Giovanni*. The Constitution of the United States begins to be ratified. Delaware becomes the first state to be admitted to the United States.	
1788		Alexander Campbell is born in County Antrim, Ireland. Charles Wesley, song writer for the infant Methodist church, dies. The Presbyterian General Assembly is formed. Though it builds on Scottish systems, it forms a Presbyterian church that is uniquely American. Ultimate power lies with the presbyteries. A modified Westminster Confession and Larger Catechism are adopted.	The U.S. constitution goes into effect. Immanuel Kant. *Critique of Practical Reason*. Edward Gibbon. *History of the Decline and Fall of the Roman Empire*. (6 volumes)	
1789		Gallicanism is no longer taught in French seminaries and universities. The second session of the Episcopal church's first General Convention is held in Philadelphia. The Episcopal	The fall of the Bastille begins the French Revolution. (−1799) George Washington becomes the first U.S. President. In the Northwest Ordinance, the U.S. government promises	The first American revision of *the Book of Common Prayer* begins to be used by the Episcopal church.

Date	A. Theology, Doctrine, and Beliefs	B. People/Events	C. Wider Culture	D. Texts
1789 con't.		church is formed as an independent denomination. It does not intend to depart "in any essential point of doctrine, discipline, or worship" from the Church of England. The Methodist Book Concern is formed. It is the first church publishing house in the U.S.	that "Indian lands will never be taken without their consent."	
1790		The United States gets its first Roman Catholic bishop, John Carroll, who is appointed to the See in Baltimore. The Society of St. Sulpice arrives in America. Their mission is the training of future Catholic priests.	Mutineers from the H.M.S. *Bounty* settle on Pitcairn Island. French Jews are granted citizenship. (–1791)	
1791		John Wesley, founder of Methodism, dies. Georgetown College is founded as the first Roman Catholic college in the U.S.	Wolfgang Amadeus Mozart dies. The United States Bill of Rights goes into effect. William Wilberforce's anti-slavery motion is passed in the British Parliament.	
1792		Charles Grandison Finney is born. James O'Kelly, a Methodist circuit rider, and a group of people calling themselves merely "Christians" separate from the Methodist Episcopal Church over the authority of the bishop. They are one of the earliest churches of the Restoration Movement. The Dutch Reformed Church in America, which later becomes the Reformed Church in America, becomes an organizationally distinct body. The Baptist Missionary Society is formed by an association of Particular Baptists who have been inspired by William Carey's pleas and his motto "Expect great things from God and attempt great things for God." It is the first of a number of Protestant missions founded around the turn of the century. John Keble is born. The Pennsylvania Ministerium (Lutheran) grants voting rights to the laity.	Denmark abolishes the slave trade. It is the first European country to do so. Beginning of the First Republic in France.	
1793	Philosophy of Religion. The investigation of the full spectrum of religious belief and experience, using the tools of philosophical inquiry. (late	William Carey begins his mission to India. The German Reformed Church in the United States of America breaks its organiza-	The French "Reign of Terror" begins. (–1794) The cotton gin is invented.	

Date	A. Theology, Doctrine, and Beliefs	B. People/Events	C. Wider Culture	D. Texts
1793 con't.	eighteenth century until the present)	tional ties with Europe. Though a confessional church, practically it tends to be very pietistic.		
1794		Friedrich Daniel Ernst Schleiermacher leaves the Moravian church to becomes a Reformed minister.		William Paley. *A View of the Evidences of Christianity.* A compilation of arguments for the existence of God and for Christianity, it is one of the first written works to set down the "watchmaker" argument for the existence of God. Thomas Paine. *Age of Reason.* A deistic treatise by an influential American Revolutionary War leader. It is commonly denounced as atheistic and costs Paine most of his old friends. (issued in three parts: 1794–1807)
1795			Joseph Haydn completes the *London Symphonies.*	
1796		The New York Missionary Society is founded, marking the beginning of an interdenominational push to bring the spiritual and moral benefits of Christianity to the American frontier. William Augustus Muhlenberg is born.		
1797		The first Lutheran seminary in America, Hartwick Seminary is founded in New York as a training institute for missionaries.	John Adams becomes U.S. President.	
1798		The Church Missionary Society is formed as the foreign missionary arm of the Church of England.	Samuel Taylor Coleridge. *The Rime of the Ancient Mariner.*	
1799		Teresa Lalor and others of her order found the first Catholic women's school, the Georgetown Visitation Academy, in America.	The Rosetta stone is found, and Egyptian hieroglyphs are deciphered. France comes under the domination of Napoleon Bonaparte. The French Revolution ends. The Napoleonic Wars, a series of wars between France and several other European nations, begin. (–1815) Joseph Haydn. *The Creation.*	Friedrich Ernst Daniel Schleiermacher. *On Religion: Speeches to Its Cultured Despisers.* His audience is the educated classes. He defines religion not as dogma or revelation but as a universal human intuition about the existence of the infinite within the finite.
1800	Before the nineteenth century, religion in America was largely imported from Europe. In the nineteenth century, however, the Second Great Awakening, the debate over slavery, unprecedented multi-	The Church of the United Brethren is founded. James McGready holds the first frontier camp meeting in Kentucky. Lyman Beecher brings revival to Yale College. (ca.)	The battery is invented. English law lists more than 200 capital crimes. Children between seven and twelve years old make up one-third of the work force in	Reginald Heber. "Holy, Holy, Holy, Lord God Almighty." (ca.)

Date	A. Theology, Doctrine, and Beliefs	B. People/Events	C. Wider Culture	D. Texts
1800 con't.	culturalism, and increasing sectarianism give American Christianity a distinct, indigenous tint.	Edward Pusey is born. Pius VII becomes pope. William Billings, American composer of sacred music, dies.	U.S. factories. (early part of the nineteenth century) The Act of Union unites England and Ireland. Irish Parliament is abolished. Ireland is represented in the British Parliament. (–1801)	
1801		The Plan of Union unites Connecticut Congregationalists and Presbyterians in the task of evangelizing the American frontier. Member congregations may choose a minister of either denomination. Abner Jones and Elias Smith lead a group of Christians out of the Baptist church. They oppose the doctrine of predestination and the use of the name "Baptist." Their "Bible-only" emphasis places them within the Restoration Movement. John Henry Newman is born. Second Great Awakening begins at the Cane Ridge Revival The General Convention of the Episcopal Church in the U.S. meets. It approves a modified version of the Thirty-nine Articles of Religion The General Conference of Seventh-day Baptists is organized.	Thomas Jefferson becomes President of the United States. The first fossil remains of an extinct animal are discovered.	
1802		The legal standing of the Huguenot church in France is established.	Atomic theory is introduced to chemistry.	
1803		Jacob Albright, a Lutheran farmer and tilemaker in eastern Pennsylvania, officially organizes the Evangelical Association (which takes that name in 1816). The Evangelical Lutheran Synod and Ministerium of North Carolina is formed.	The steam-powered boat is invented. Louisiana Purchase. The United States purchases 828,000 square miles between the Mississippi River and the Rocky Mountains from France.	
1804	Second Great Awakening. Is conversion a punctiliar event accompanied by manifestations of the outpouring of the Holy Spirit? Revivalists: "yes." New England Theology, Catholicism, High Church Anglicanism: "no."	Absalom Jones is ordained to the Episcopal priesthood. He is the first African American ordained in the United States by a hierarchical church. The British and Foreign Bible Society is formed. It is the forerunner of hundreds of American and English Bible societies. Presbyterian minister Barton W. Stone and several of his	The Lewis and Clark expedition begins. (–1806) Immanuel Kant, German philosopher and founder of modern critical philosophy, dies. Napoleon is proclaimed emperor of France. The first Empire in France begins.	

Date	A. Theology, Doctrine, and Beliefs	B. People/Events	C. Wider Culture	D. Texts
1804 con't.		followers break all denominational ties and begin calling themselves merely "Christians." A part of the Restoration Movement, they oppose presbyteries as unscriptural.		
1805		The Dominicans begin their mission to the Kentucky frontier. Frederick Denison Maurice is born.	Emperor Napoleon crowns himself with the crown of the Lombard kings in the Milan Cathedral.	
1806		The "haystack prayer meeting" is held. It is a founding event of the American foreign missions movement.	Francis II, the last Holy Roman Emperor, dissolves the empire because he fears Napoleon I will annex the imperial title.	
1807			The British government bans slave trading. Georg W. F. Hegel. *Phenomenology of Mind.* Hegelian Idealism. Understands history as absolute reality unfolding dialectically in a process of self-development that follows a specific pattern: thesis, antithesis, synthesis.	John Henry Hobart. *An Apology for Apostolic Order.* An attempt to combine "evangelical faith and apostolic order," it fuels the High vs. Low Church debate.
1808		Andover Seminary is founded. It leans toward New Divinity theology. Approximately 130 Bible Societies are founded in the United States. Their purpose is to dispense Bibles. (–1816) Fire partially destroys the Church of the Holy Sepulchre. The tomb is enclosed in the modern marble covering. The last *auto-da-fé* (Portuguese for "act of faith") takes place. It is the public execution of persons condemned by the Inquisition. More than 340,000 persons suffered the *auto-da-fé*. Of these, 32,000 were burned. The Methodist Episcopal Church drafts a constitution.	Johann Wolfgang von Goethe. *Faust.* Slave import is outlawed in the United States. However, a quarter of a million slaves are illegally imported over the next fifty years. Ludwig von Beethoven. *Fifth Symphony.*	
1809	Restoration Movement. Also called Primitivism. It is a prominent sentiment in much of American Christianity, propelled by the desire to return to New Testament Christianity and to purge Christian organizations of the accretions of subsequent history and tradition. Key organizations: the Churches of Christ, Disciples of Christ, the Christian Churches, and many Pentecostal churches.	Thomas and Alexander Campbell found the Christian Association of Washington, the first Disciples of Christ church, on the principle "Where the Bible speaks, we speak; where it is silent, we are silent." They are part of the Restoration Movement.	James Madison becomes President of the United States. Washington Irving. *Rip van Winkle* Braille is invented. Joseph Haydn dies.	

Date	A. Theology, Doctrine, and Beliefs	B. People/Events	C. Wider Culture	D. Texts
1810	Romantic Movement. A mood in Western intellectual history, it is a reaction to the cool intellectualism of the Enlightenment. It values feeling, intuition, inspiration, history, and exoticism. The movement leads to twentieth-century liberalism. Key figures: Johann Wolfgang von Goethe, R. W. Emerson, Friedrich Schleiermacher, and many others.	The Church of the Holy Sepulchre is rebuilt after being destroyed by fire.	Food canning technology makes feeding a large army possible. Napoleon's zenith. Simón Bolívar wins Venezuelan independence. Romantic period of music. Introduces a new spirit of novelty and a bending of classical formulas and outlines. Values expression and inspiration. Key figures: Franz Schubert, Carl Maria von Weber, Hector Berlioz, Franz Liszt, Robert Schumann, Johannes Brahms, Richard Strauss, Giacomo Puccini, Richard Wagner, Felix Mendelssohn, Anton Bruckner, Peter Ilich Tchaikovsky, Nicolò Paganini, and Gustav Mahler. (through the end of the nineteenth century)	
1811	Baptismal Exclusivism. The belief that baptism administered by invalid ministers is also invalid. The belief is held by some in the Restoration Movements and by Landmark Baptists, who term baptism by non-Baptists "alien immersion." (early nineteenth century to the present)	Robert Raikes, founder of the Sunday School Movement, dies. Abner Jones and Elias Smith's Christian church unite with James O'Kelly's "Christians" to form the Christian Connection.		
1812	Princeton Theology. A traditional Reformed confessionalism, it prides itself on being the keeper of unaltered Calvinism. Key figures: Archibald Alexander, Charles Hodge, Achibald Hodge, Benjamin B. Warfield, and J. Gresham Machen. (–1921)	Princeton Seminary is founded. Henry Martyn, Anglican priest and translator of the Bible into Hindi and Persian, dies. Adoniram Judson, Congregational/Baptist missionary to Burma, leaves America for South Asia.	The War of 1812 begins. The United States declares war on Britain over maritime rights. (–1815) "The Star-Spangled Banner" is written.	
1813		Excommunicated persons in England are no longer subject to civil disabilities. Søren Kierkegaard is born.		
1814	Open Communion. The practice in Baptist churches of allowing all believers to partake of the Lord's Supper, regardless of whether they have been baptized. It becomes increasingly common in the nineteenth century, but is opposed by "Strict Baptists."	The first Anglican bishop from India is ordained. Pope Pius VII restores the Jesuits after 41 years of official suppression (in *Solicitudo Omnium Ecclesiarum* (Latin: Care for All Churches)). Baptist congregations and sects reach the height of their proliferation. (–1830)	The House of Bourbon is restored in France.	

Date	A. Theology, Doctrine, and Beliefs	B. People/Events	C. Wider Culture	D. Texts
1815		The term "Unitarianism" begins to be commonly used.	Napoleon Bonaparte abdicates after the Battle of Waterloo. The first Reformed Jewish synagogue is opened in Berlin.	
1816		The American Bible Society is founded. Several African Methodist Episcopal Churches are organized into a denomination. Richard Allen becomes their first bishop.	The stethoscope is invented. Jane Austen. *Emma*. Regular transatlantic service between New York and Liverpool, England, begins.	
1817	Neo-Lutheranism. A reaction to Lutheran rationalism and a proposed union of all Protestant denominations, it calls for a return to the centrality of the Scriptures and to historic Lutheran doctrines. Key figures: Claus Harms, Ernst Wilhelm Hengstenberg, and Adolf von Harless		James Monroe becomes President of the United States.	
1818	New Haven Theology. Sometimes called Taylorism. It combines rationalism with the revivalist feeling in the air. Though rooted in Calvinism, it emphasizes rational choice in both sin and regeneration. Key figures: Nathaniel Taylor, Chauncey A. Goodrich, and Eleazar T. Fitch. Key institution: Yale. (–1840s).	John Mason Neale is born. Absalom Jones, the first African-American Episcopal priest, dies. James Lloyd Breck is born.	Karl Marx is born.	Joseph Mohr and Franz Xavier Gruber. "Stille Nacht Heilige Nacht" ("Silent Night").
1819		General Theological Seminary is founded as a High-Church Episcopal seminary. William Ellery Channing, a Congregational minister, forms a Unitarian congregation.	Sir Walter Scott. *Ivanhoe*. The Independent Order of Odd Fellows is introduced to the United States. Arthur Schopenhauer. *The World as Will and Idea*. Schopenhauer rejects Hegel's notions of reason and progress in favor of an atheistic and pessimistic philosophy. He maintains that only through art and philosophical renunciation can humanity escape the unrealistic desire for happiness.	
1820		Lyman Beecher tries to protect New England from the revivalist enthusiasm of the Second Great Awakening calling for moderation. (ca.) The Jesuits are expelled from Rome and from Russia. The General Synod of the Evangelical Lutheran Church in the United States of America is founded. It brings together most of the Lutheran synods in the country (except the New York Ministerium).	United States immigration records begin to be kept. Immigration is mostly from western and northern Europe. (–1890) Missouri Compromise. Missouri is admitted to the United States as a slave state, but the Louisiana Purchase north of 36°30' N is free territory.	

Date	A. Theology, Doctrine, and Beliefs	B. People/Events	C. Wider Culture	D. Texts
1821		Charles G. Finney is converted. Saint Elizabeth Ann Bayley Seton dies. She was the founder of the American Sisters of Charity, a group of Catholic sisters organized according the Rule of Vincent de Paul, devoted to the well-being of the poor and the education of children.	Napoleon Bonaparte dies. Mexico gains independence.	
1822				Lowell Mason. *The Boston Handel and Haydn Society Collection of Church Music.* A collection of church music by the composer of more than twelve hundred hymns. Friedrich Ernst Daniel Schleiermacher. *The Christian Faith.* The essence of Schleiermacher's theology. It focuses on finite human beings' feeling of absolute dependence on the Infinite God. For Schleiermacher, religion is not dogma or revelation but universal human intuition about the existence of the infinite within the finite. An important work for modern Lutheran theology.
1823		Leo XII becomes pope.	Monroe Doctrine. The United States declares it will protect independent Latin American countries from European recolonization.	
1824		The Theological Seminary of Virginia is founded as an Evangelical Episcopal seminary. The American Sunday School Union is founded.	Ludwig van Beethoven. *Missa Solemnis.* A classical setting of the Mass. Beethoven regarded it as his greatest work.	
1825	Unitarianism. Christianity without belief in the Trinity, it denies the divinity of Jesus but maintains that Christianity is a divinely inspired, unique historical phenomenon. Center: Boston, especially among the intellectual and social elite. Period of greatest influence: early nineteenth century. Key figure: William Ellery Channing.	The American Unitarian Association is formed. The American Tract Society is formed as the first national tract-distribution society in America.	The Erie Canal is opened. John Quincy Adams becomes President of the United States. The middle of the eighteenth century sees an unprecedented number of colleges and universities founded. Many of them are launched in young frontier cities and fueled by the revivalist energy of the Second Great Awakening.	
1826		The American Temperance Society is formed to promote abstinence from alcohol. Churches are its main source of members.	Andre Marie Ampere. *Electrodynamics.* American Independence Day (July 4) becomes a national holiday. Carl Maria von Weber. *Oberon.* It helps establish Romantic opera, especially in Germany.	

Date	A. Theology, Doctrine, and Beliefs	B. People/Events	C. Wider Culture	D. Texts
1827	The Watchmen of the East. A group of mostly clerics, revivalists, and scholars, they oppose both Charles Finney's "new measures" and the overall emotionalism of the Second Great Awakening. Key figure: Asahel Nettleton. New Measures. They are the revivalist techniques most commonly associated with Charles G. Finney, though similar techniques date back to the Cane Ridge revival. They justify the use of direct public pressure to secure "convictions" in revival meetings.	Charles Grandison Finney holds revivals in the United States. The New Lebanon Conferences discuss revival etiquette, women as revivalists, and cooperation between itinerant evangelists and local congregations.	London purifies the public water supply. Ludwig van Beethoven dies.	John Keble. *The Church Year*. Poems for holy days and Sundays, it is a source for many hymns.
1828		The Corporation Act is repealed in England. Catholics and nonconformists may hold public office. The British Test Act is repealed. The reception of communion in the Church of England is no longer mandated for all civil and military officers. Pope Leo XII makes St. Peter Damian a doctor of the church. Liberal Quakers in America split from the Orthodox. The liberals focus on "the Christ within," the Orthodox on traditional doctrines as expressed in creedal formulas.	Webster's Dictionary is published. Franz Schubert dies. He was famous for his *lieder*, a Romantic music form in which music portrays the mood and content of poems.	
1829	Perfectionism. Sparked by the optimism of the Second Great Awakening, perfectionism teaches that a second work of the Holy Spirit (after conversion) creates complete happiness and holiness in the believer. It is influenced by, and influences, Methodism and the Holiness Movement. In modern times it survives in Pentecostal churches.	Pius VIII becomes pope. The first Roman Catholic Provincial Council in the United States is established. Between 1829 and 1860, the number of Episcopalians grows 500% largely due to concentrated missionary efforts.	Andrew Jackson becomes President of the United States. Frédéric François Chopin makes his debut. The typewriter is invented.	
1830	Mormonism. Originally an American Christian offshoot, it becomes a major world religion of more than eight million members. Founded by Joseph Smith, known as "the Prophet," it recognizes four scriptures: the Bible, the *Book of Mormon*, the *Doctrine and Covenants*, and the *Pearl of Great Price*. In addition to more traditional Christian doctrines, it believes in the Trinity as three physically separate individuals united in	The Congregationalist Plan of Union begins to break down. "Our Lady of the Miraculous Medal" appears in Paris. Pope Pius VIII makes St. Bernard a doctor of the church. The Millerites are organized. They spread the message of Christ's imminent Second Coming. John Henry Hobart, influential Episcopal bishop, dies.	Nuclei in plant cells are discovered. Simon Bolivar dies. Reformed missionary Samuel A. Worcester sues the State of Georgia to sustain Cherokee sovereignty over their lands in Georgia. The Supreme Court of the United States rules that Georgia does not have the right to move them. The Indian Removal Act goes into effect during Andrew Jackson's presidency. It moves	The *Book of Mormon* is published.

Date	A. Theology, Doctrine, and Beliefs	B. People/Events	C. Wider Culture	D. Texts
1830 con't.	purpose; the prenatal existence of human souls; and the human potential for godhood in future aeons. Antimission Movement. A Calvinist Baptist response to large missionary organizations. Pretribulationism. The eschatological doctrine that Christ will snatch away the saints before the beginning of the Great Tribulation. After the Tribulation he will return with his saints to rule the earth. Key figure: John Nelson Darby.	Joseph Smith founds the Mormon church. Missionary and Primitive Baptists split over the Antimission Movement. At issue is predestination and the autonomy of local congregations.	entire tribes from their homelands and forces resettlement beyond the Mississippi river. Positivism. It discounts theology, metaphysics and any other speculative thought and asserts that only the observed data of sense experience and the thought processes of logic and mathematics are valid components of the philosophical enterprise. Key figures: Auguste Comte. Key concepts survive today in logical empiricism. The House of Orleans begins its rule in France. The first railroad is built between Liverpool and Manchester England.	
1831	Old School Presbyterianism. These Presbyterian traditionalists oppose interdenominational missions, interdenominational social-aid societies, the religious enthusiasm of the Second Great Awakening, and overall doctrinal shallowness. They stand for the Westminster Confession and Presbyterian polity. Intellectual center: Princeton Seminary. Key figures: Archibald Alexander, Charles Hodge. New School Presbyterianism. Part of the revivalism of the nineteenth century, New School Presbyterians are interested in moral reform rather than strict adherence to the Westminster Catechism. This branch of Presbyterianism exists as a separate denomination in the mid nineteenth century. Central figures: Lyman Beecher, Albert Barnes.	William Lloyd Garrison is wanted by Georgia officials for his antislavery work. Basing his argument on Christian principles, he calls for the freeing of slaves in his speeches and in the *Liberator*. The state of Georgia offers a $5000 reward for his arrest. Old School Presbyterians try Albert Barnes, George Duffield, and Lyman Beecher (New School Presbyterians) for heresy. They are not convicted. (–1836) James DeKoven is born. Gregory XVI becomes pope. The "Christians" and the "Disciples of Christ" agree to join together with a formal handshake.	The Nat Turner rebellion breaks out. It is a rebellion of slaves in Virginia. Georg W. F. Hegel, German Idealist philosopher, dies.	Karl Lachmann. *Greek New Testament*. Lachmann completely sets aside the Textus Receptus and constructs a critical New Testament from what he considers to be the most reliable manuscripts. *The Lutheran Observer*. It is the predecessor of *The Lutheran*, the communication vehicle of the Lutheran Church.
1832		William Lloyd Garrison helps organize the New England Anti-Slavery Society.	Archaeological time is divided into the Stone Age, Bronze Age, and Iron Age. The Great Reform Bill of 1832 gives the vote to British middle-class men.	
1833	Oxford Movement (known as Tractarianism in its earliest stages). A High-Church Anglican movement, it defends apostolic succession, monasticism, an elevated place of Mary and the saints, and the Church of England as a divine institution. Central figures: John Keble, John Henry	Socially aware evangelicals found Oberlin College. It is the first coeducational college in the United States. The Theological Institute of Connecticut (Hartford Seminary) is founded as a reaction against the revivalists of the Second Great Awakening.	The British Empire abolishes slavery. The Orient Express opens rail service between Paris and Istanbul.	John Keble. *National Apostasy* (sermon). It is commonly regarded as the inception of the Oxford Movement. *Tracts for the Times*. The communication vehicle for the Oxford Movement. Most of the tracts are written by John

Date	A. Theology, Doctrine, and Beliefs	B. People/Events	C. Wider Culture	D. Texts
1833 con't.	Newman, and Edward Pusey. (ca.–1845) The early to mid nineteenth century witnesses increasing urbanization, industrialization, and the breakdown of extended families. For the first time, it becomes possible for people to turn away from the religion of their forebears.	William Wilberforce, Christian reformer in the British House of Commons, dies. He is best known for his unwavering fight against slavery. Frederic Ozanam founds the Society of St. Vincent de Paul, a Roman Catholic lay organization. Their mission is aid and advocacy for the poor. The Greek Orthodox Church becomes independent from Constantinople. The Universalist Church of America is formed.		Keble and John Henry Newman. (–1841). *The New Hampshire Confession of Faith.* A moderate Baptist creed in the Reformed tradition, it is accepted by the Southern Baptists and the General Association of Regular Baptists.
1834	Millenarianism. It is the belief in a thousand-year period of divine order on earth. Some Millenarians believe the Second Coming of Christ precedes the Millennium, others that the Millennium ushers in Christ's return.	Millenarians predict the imminent Second Coming of Christ. Friedrich Daniel Ernst Schleiermacher, German Protestant theologian, dies. Spain suppresses the Inquisition. William Carey dies. He was a Baptist missionary and Bible translator in India.	The American Anti-Slavery Society is formed under Charles Finney's auspices. Within four years, it has a quarter of a million members.	
1835	The Sunday School Movement in America. Sunday schools are started throughout the country. They become one of the largest sources of prospective church members. Redaction Criticism. (German: *Redaktionsgeschichte*). An approach to the study of biblical text, it analyzes similarities in existing texts to postulate the genealogy of those texts and what preexisting sources they were compiled from.	Phillips Brooks is born. Karl Lachmann defends the Marcan Hypothesis: the Gospel of Mark was the earliest and most basic of the gospels, and was a source for the other Synoptic Gospels.	Texas revolts against Mexican rule. P. T. Barnum begins traveling with a company of carnival attractions.	David Friedrich Strauss. *Life of Jesus.* An application of "myth theory" to the Gospels. It denies all miracles and other supernatural events.
1836	Transcendentalism. It is an American literary and philosophical movement influenced by deism and Romanticism. Transcendentalism opposes both institutional religious ritualism and strict Puritan mores and Calvinist orthodoxy. Among its central themes are quasi-religious meditations on the union of human beings and nature, and the appreciation of intuition over logic. Central figures: Ralph Waldo Emerson, Margaret Fuller, Henry David Thoreau. (ca.–1860)	William White, "Father of the American Episcopal Church," dies. The Transcendental Club in Boston is founded, beginning American transcendentalism. Charles Simeon, leader of the Anglican evangelical revival, dies. Australia's first Anglican bishop is consecrated. Union Theological Seminary is founded in New York by New School Presbyterians.	The McGuffey Readers are published. (–1857) Ralph Waldo Emerson. "Nature" (essay). A major work of the American transcendentalist movement. Mexican troops attack the Alamo. John Stuart Mill. *Utilitarianism.* Mill develops and refines the empiricist and utilitarian traditions. Texas gains independence from Mexico. (April 21) The Marriage Act of 1836 establishes civil marriages in England.	Thomas P. Hunt. *The Book of Wealth: in Which it Is Proved from the Bible That it Is the Duty of Every Man to Become Rich.*

Date	A. Theology, Doctrine, and Beliefs	B. People/Events	C. Wider Culture	D. Texts
1837		The Presbyterian church splits over slavery (etc.). The Reformed Church in America accepts the Westminster Catechism.	Martin Van Buren becomes President of the United States. Queen Victoria of England ascends to the throne. The House of Saxe-Coburg and Gotha, later known as the House of Windsor, begins its reign in England. (–present) Samuel F. B. Morse invents the telegraph and Morse code. Georg W. F. Hegel. *Philosophy of History*.	Auburn Declaration. A New School Presbyterian statement of faith, its purpose is defending New School belief against Old School accusations of heresy. The result is a moderate, but orthodox, Calvinism
1838	Branch theory of the church. The notion that though various Christian offshoots may be out of communion with each other, they still may be considered part of the "one holy catholic and apostolic church" if they maintain apostolic succession. The roots of the theory lie in the Oxford Movement. (–present)	Joseph Smith, Mormon leader, flees to Missouri. William Reed Huntington is born.	Grimm's Law is developed. It is a part of the rise of historical linguistics. Charles Dickens. *Oliver Twist*. The Cherokee Indians' "trail of tears" leads from Georgia to Oklahoma.	
1839		Alphonsus Liguori is canonized. German Saxon immigrants in Missouri under the leadership of C. F. W. Walther join with Wilhelm Loehe's Bavarian followers to form the German Evangelical Lutheran Synod of Missouri, Ohio, and Other States, the precursor of the Lutheran Church—Missouri Synod. (–1847)	The Opium Wars between Great Britain and China begin when the Chinese government tries to stop the illegal import of opium by British merchants. (–1843, 1856–1860) Photography is invented.	
1840	Revivalism. It emphasizes religious enthusiasm and intensity, conversion of the unregenerate, and emotional and spiritual renewal of the saved. Its main tools are prayer meetings and evangelistic crusades. Revivalist meetings are extremely successful in bringing people into Protestant churches in the nineteenth century. (Revivalism dates from the First Great Awakening to the late twentieth century, peaking during the mid nineteenth century.)	Anglo-Catholicism peaks in United States (–1850s). The 1840s and 1850s see the peak of tension between evangelical and High Church Episcopalians in the United States. Several bishops are tried; some become Roman Catholics. Christmas trees are introduced into France and England.	Blackface minstrel shows. White, four-man troupes perform African-American style music on banjo, tambourine, bone castanets, and fiddle. (ca.–Civil War) Nicolò Paganini, Italian Romantic composer and violinist, dies. He revolutionized violin technique. The first wave of Asian immigrants from China, Korea, Japan, and India arrives in the United States.	
1841	The rise of Roman Catholic Romanticism and piety. Catholic evangelists encourage personal piety centered on the cult of saints, the rosary, and other personal devotions. They also seek to		James Fenimore Cooper. *Leatherstocking Tales.* (five volumes published 1823–) American universities begin to grant degrees to women.	Constantin Tischendorf publishes the first of his critical editions of the Greek New Testament. It is based in part on the previously obscure Greek texts he discovered during his travels to libraries

Date	A. Theology, Doctrine, and Beliefs	B. People/Events	C. Wider Culture	D. Texts
1841 con't.	strengthen individuals' sacramental lives and connection to the church. For the most part, the movement fell in the wake of liberalism. (1840s)		William Henry Harrison becomes President of the United States. John Tyler becomes President of the United States. The first wagon train travels west across the United States	throughout Europe and the Near East.
1842	Tübingen School. A group of largely German theologians apply Hegelian dialectic to the tensions between the Petrine and Pauline factions in early Christianity. Key figure: Ferdinand Christian Baur.	The University of Notre Dame is founded. The Episcopal church tries to establish a monastic community for men at Nashota, Wisconsin. The community fails as an order but survives as the Nashota House seminary.	The first surgery using ether is performed. The Ashburton Treaty (between Great Britain and the United States) provides for American and British patrols along the African coast to enforce the prohibition of the slave trade. The first orchestra in the United States, the New York Philharmonic Society, is founded.	
1843		Wesleyan Methodists split from the Methodist Episcopal Church over the refusal of the MEC to embrace immediate abolition. Sojourner Truth begins an itinerant ministry lecturing on abolition in a style couched in biblical metaphors. The Millerites predict the end of the world on October 22, 1844.		Henry George Liddell and Robert Scott. *Greek-English Lexicon.* (first edition)
1844		Joseph Smith, leader of the Mormons, is murdered. The Methodist Episcopal Church clashes over slavery at its General Conference. Bishop James O. Andrew is suspended from his office so long as he keeps the slaves he acquired through marriage. The church splits into the Methodist Episcopal Church and the Methodist Episcopal church, South. George Williams forms the Young Men's Christian Association (YMCA) to give young men a Christian alternative to the temptations of urban life. The Millerites' date for the Second Coming comes and goes.	Karl Marx and Friedrich Engels meet in Paris to discuss the theoretical underpinning of the revolution. Dialectical materialism. An ideological component of Marxism, it is based on the Hegelian dialectic but makes social institutions the driving force of the dialectic rather than physical nature of individual mind. Key figures: Karl Marx and Friedrich Engels. Historical materialism. An ideological component of Marxism and communism, it is the theory that culture is driven by economic relations and that social evolution can come only through class conflict and periodic revolutions. Key figures: Karl Marx and Friedrich Engels The first public telegram is sent from Washington to Baltimore.	Constantin Tischendorf discovers Codex Sinaiticus, a fourth century Greek manuscript of the New Testament, at the monastery of St. Catherine of Sinai. It is one of the chief variants of the Alexandrian or Neutral text. (–1859) Codex Vaticanus, previously secreted behind Vatican library doors, is published.

Date	A. Theology, Doctrine, and Beliefs	B. People/Events	C. Wider Culture	D. Texts
1845	Manifest Destiny. The belief that United States expansionism is part of a divine plan. (–1890s).	John Henry Newman becomes a Roman Catholic. Baptist churches in the United States split into the Southern Baptist and the Northern (American) Baptists. Central is the issue of slave-holding southern missionaries. The Methodist Episcopal Church, South adopts the Plan of Separation and formally splits from the Methodist Episcopal Church. J. A. A. Grabau founds the Synod of the Lutheran Church Emigrated from Prussia, better known as the Buffalo Synod. Caspar René Gregory devises a cataloging system for uncial biblical manuscripts.	Edgar Allan Poe. "The Raven." (poem) James Knox Polk becomes President of the United States. Texas' annexation by the United States begins the Mexican war. (December 29) The rules of modern baseball are invented. (ca.)	Phoebe Palmer. *The Way of Holiness.* It popularizes the notion that Pentecostal Spirit baptism, which is available to all believers, is the route to holiness. It paves the way for the Pentecostal and charismatic movements.
1846	Christian Existentialism. It begins with human experience, not mere intellectual reasoning, as the basis for the search for truth. Key figure: Søren Kierkegaard. Key concept: the "leap of faith."	The Evangelical Alliance is formed to oppose Roman Catholicism. It begins in England and spreads to United States and western Europe. Pius IX becomes pope. Elling Eielsen founds the Hauge's Norwegian Evangelical Synod in America.	The steel moldboard plow is invented, revolutionizes farming. Existentialism. Stresses human beings' role in the shaping of their own lives. Focuses on individual existence and choice. Key figures: Jean Paul Sartre, Friedrich Nietzsche. It influences the theology of Søren Kierkegaard, Karl Barth, Reinhold Niebuhr, and Paul Tillich. (–present) The Mexican War begins between the United States and Mexico. (–1848)	Søren Kierkegaard. *Fear and Trembling.* Focusing on Abraham's willingness to sacrifice his son Isaac, it asserts that to avoid ultimate despair, human beings must make a similar "leap of faith" into a religious life that cannot always be understood in ethical or logical terms. His work has found much more acceptance in twentieth century theology than it did among philosophers and theologians of his own time.
1847	Christian Socialism. It is a movement, initially within the Church of England, that sees social policy and Christian principles as inseparable. It does educational and relief work and pushes for social reform. Not all Christian Socialists are, however, politically socialist. Central figures: John Malcolm Forbes Ludlow (founder), Charles Kingsley, Frederick Denison Maurice. (mid nineteenth century)	The Lutheran Church—Missouri Synod is formed (originally as the German Evangelical Lutheran Synod of Missouri, Ohio and other States). It is a German immigrant church based on the Book of Concord. Brigham Young leads a group of Mormons to Salt Lake. Pope Pius IX makes Joseph Valerga the Latin patriarch. The pope proclaims the title is no longer a mere formality and orders the new patriarch to take up his residence in Jerusalem, where he finds 4,200 Catholics.	Michigan becomes the first state to abolish the death penalty. Felix Mendelssohn, German Romantic composer, dies. The Irish potato famine begins. (–1848)	
1848	Landmark Baptist Movement. It asserts the unbroken succession of Baptist churches from New Testament times to the present, thereby fostering Baptist exclusivity. The movement is influential in the	Wesleyan Methodists found Wheaton College, originally named Illinois Institute, as an independent, evangelical liberal arts college. John Humphrey Noyes founds the Oneida Commu-	Friedrich Engels and Karl Marx. *The Communist Manifesto.* The Treaty of Guadalupe Hidalgo is made between the United States and Mexico. It fixes the Rio Grande as the	

Date	A. Theology, Doctrine, and Beliefs	B. People/Events	C. Wider Culture	D. Texts
1848 con't.	southern states of the United States in the nineteenth century. Prominent figure: James R. Graves. Mercersburg vs. "Old Reformed" controversy. It is the controversy over revivalism and sectarianism in the German Reformed church. The Mercersburg group focuses on catechism, liturgy, unity of the church, and "true revival" from within. Members of the "Old Reformed" group like their German sectarian identities, maintain the centrality of preaching over liturgy, and cultivate revivalism. Centers: Mercersburg Seminary and the "Old Reformed" Ursinus College.	nity, one of the nineteenth century communal experiments.	southern boundary of Texas. It also grants land in territory now forming the states of Arizona, California, Colorado, New Mexico, Nevada, Utah, and Wyoming to the United States. The Second Republic in France begins.	
1849	Liberalism (also known as modernism). It seeks to preserve Christianity by adapting it to the intellectual and social climate of the time (which includes evolutionary theory, biblical criticism, psychology, sociology, Kantian philosophy, etc.). It emphasizes God in history, Christian experience, goodness of humanity, and ethics.	Pope Pius IX declares every first Sunday of July be dedicated to the Most Precious Blood. General C. G. Gordon proposes a site for Calvary and the "Garden Tomb" that is different from the traditional site. The new site becomes known as "Gordon's Calvary."	Zachary Taylor becomes President of the United States. The California gold rush begins. Henry David Thoreau. "Civil Disobedience." (essay) Great Britain repeals the Navigation Acts. Frédéric François Chopin, Polish Romantic composer and pianist, dies.	Horace Bushnell. *God in Christ.* Asserts that all religious language is poetic, not literal. It contains some of the earliest American liberal theology. Archbishop Kenrick's revision of the Douay Bible becomes common in the United States. (–1959)
1850	The mid nineteenth century sees a new emphasis on history including Hegel's *Philosophy of History*, historical linguistics, archeological "ages," and Darwin's evolutionary theory. Christianity sees Anglo-Catholicism's emphasis on apostolic succession and historic rites, the Landmark Baptist Movement, and higher criticism's focus on historical context of texts. Broad Church Episcopalianism calls for acceptance of modern thought and social trends. (mid nineteenth century)	Deism's influence peaks and begins to wane. (1850s) The Roman Catholic Church has more people in the United States than any other church. The culture these Catholics live in, however, is largely Protestant. The Wisconsin Evangelical Lutheran Synod, a conservative Lutheran denomination, is formed by German Reformed and Lutheran immigrants to America. The Lutheran church ordains its first American deaconess.	Millard Fillmore becomes President of the United States. Elizabeth Barrett Browning. *Sonnets from the Portuguese.* During the latter half of the nineteenth century, the number and influence of fraternal orders increases dramatically. Nathaniel Hawthorne. *The Scarlet Letter.* Realism. It values the faithful imitation of real life in art and literature. Realism is the dominant position in literature and criticism in the second half of the nineteenth century. Key figures: Stephen Crane, Mark Twain, Henry James,	Honoré de Balzac and Gustave Flaubert.
1851		Pope Pius IX makes St. Hilary of Poitiers a doctor of the church.	Herman Melville. *Moby Dick.*	
1852		The first Swedish Baptist congregation is formed in the United States. It is the roots of what will later become the Baptist General Conference.	Harriet Elizabeth Beecher Stowe. *Uncle Tom's Cabin.* The Second Empire in France begins.	

Date	A. Theology, Doctrine, and Beliefs	B. People/Events	C. Wider Culture	D. Texts
1853		Women are first ordained officially in the Congregational Church in the United States. Initially their ordination is recognized only by their local churches.	Franklin Pierce becomes President of the United States. Commodore Matthew Perry negotiates a treaty to open Japan to United States ships, opening a long-closed door to Western contact and trade. (–1854) Several American states adopt a ten-hour workday for children under 12 years of age. The Gadsden Purchase. The United States purchases 45,000 acres in what becomes the American southwest from Mexico. The Crimean War begins. Britain, France, Turkey and Sardinia ally to stop Russia's push to the Mediterranean Sea. (–1856)	
1854		George Anthony Denison is prosecuted in English civil court for teaching the Real Presence of Christ in the Eucharist. Frederick Denison Maurice establishes the Working Men's College.	Cholera is linked to polluted water. Henry David Thoreau. *Walden, or Life in the Woods.* An account of Thoreau's attempt to live in harmony with nature, it is a major work of the American transcendentalist movement. Alfred, Lord Tennyson. "Charge of the Light Brigade." It commemorates the chief engagement of the Crimean War. Stephen Collins Foster. "I Dream of Jeanie with the Light Brown Hair."	Pope Pius IX. *Constitution Ineffabilis Deus* (papal bull). Pronounces and defines Immaculate Conception of the Blessed Virgin Mary.
1855		The Office and Mass of the Most Pure Heart of Mary is approved, though not made universal. Vincent de Paul is named patron saint of works of charity. Søren Kierkegaard, religious Danish philosopher, dies.	Henry Wadsworth Longfellow. "The Song of Hiawatha." Its aim is to portray indigenous American themes as a suitable topic for serious literature. Frederick Douglass. *My Bondage and My Freedom.* Walt Whitman. *Leaves of Grass.*	
1856		Pope Pius IX extends the feast of the Devotion to the Sacred Heart of Jesus to the universal church.	Sigmund Freud is born.	
1857	Prayer Meeting Revival. A lay movement led by businessmen and others, it is fueled by noontime prayer and testimony meetings. (–1858)	Prayer meetings held during the midweek become common as a result of the "prayer meeting revival." (–1858)	James Buchanan becomes President of the United States. Dred Scott Decision. This United States Supreme Court decision declares that an African Negro cannot be a citizen of any state and, therefore, has no judicial	

Date	A. Theology, Doctrine, and Beliefs	B. People/Events	C. Wider Culture	D. Texts
1857 con't.			recourse. It also maintains that Congress has no power to keep slavery out of any United States territory. Karl Marx. *Grundrisse.* Gustave Flaubert. *Madame Bovary.* The *Atlantic Monthly* is founded.	
1858		The Congregation of the Missionary Society of St. Paul the Apostle (Paulists) is founded to provide a reasonable evangelism. The Virgin Mary ("Our Lady of Lourdes") appears to Bernadette in a vision at Lourdes. Nathaniel William Taylor, theologian, dies.	Henry Gray. *Anatomy of the Human Body.* (first edition)	*Psalms and Hymns.* One of the earliest Baptist hymn books. William E. Smith. *The Higher Christian Life.* An important work in the Holiness Movement.
1859	Higher Christian Life Movement. It emphasizes sanctification and the pursuit of holiness through the Holy Spirit. (late nineteenth century) Keswick Movement. A personal holiness movement that spreads throughout the United States and England in the late nineteenth and early twentieth centuries, it emphasizes a "second blessing" after salvation that enables a believer to rise above the tendency to sin. Center: Keswick, England. Key figures: William E. Boardman, Hannah Whitall, Robert Pearsall Smith.	Constantin Tischendorf discovers Codex Sinaiticus and presents it to the Tsar of Russia. Some Churches of Christ begin to use instruments to accompany singing at worship services. Others site the lack of biblical precedent for instruments and label the innovators "apostates." Channing Moore Williams enters Japan, the first Anglican missionary to work there.	Charles Darwin. *Origin of the Species.* John Stuart Mill. *On Liberty.* Daniel Decatur. "Dixie."	
1860		The General Conference Mennonite Church is founded. The Free Methodists split from the Methodist Episcopal Church over the refusal of the MEC to embrace immediate abolition. The name "Seventh-day Adventists" begins to be used. D.L. Moody quits a job in sales to become a full-time Christian worker.	The first American transcontinental telegraph line is completed. Impressionism (art). An initially French movement in painting, it rejects the classical subjects and formalism of the established French school. It seeks, rather to explore the effects of natural light on landscapes, street scenes, and everyday figures. It marks the beginning of the modern period in art. Key figures: Edgar Degas, Claude Monet, Camille Pissarro, and Pierre Auguste Renoir.	
1861		The Women's Union Missionary Society is founded. The first of many organizations that make up the Women's Missionary Movement, it is	Abraham Lincoln becomes President of the United States. The American Civil War begins. (–1865)	*Hymns Ancient and Modern.* A product of the Oxford Movement to encourage congregational singing. It is the first Anglican hymnal to

Date	A. Theology, Doctrine, and Beliefs	B. People/Events	C. Wider Culture	D. Texts
1861 con't.		formed to send single women overseas to evangelize women. The American Northern and Southern Presbyterian Churches split over religious enthusiasm and over slavery. The Protestant Episcopal Church and the Protestant Episcopal Church in the Confederate States of America split from each other.		include hymns for both the liturgical cycle and for personal devotion.
1862		Charles Henry Brent is born.	The Homestead Act grants free land to settlers. The Land Grant Act funds agricultural education and eventually the state university system. The machine gun is invented.	
1863	Seventh-day Adventists. An off-shoot of the eighteenth century Millerites, Adventists are distinctive in their belief that Christ began an "investigative judgment" upon his arrival in the heavenly sanctuary in 1884. Also central to Adventist faith is the belief in the imminent personal return of Christ to earth and the practice of keeping Saturday as the Sabbath. Adventists on the whole are very conscientious about health and education, founding schools and hospitals to further their cause. Many are vegetarians. Key figure: Ellen White.	Lyman Beecher, minister and reformer, dies. The Seventh-day Adventist Church is formed in the United States. The General Synod of the Evangelical Lutheran Church in the confederate States of American is formed. President Abraham Lincoln names the last Thursday in November "Thanksgiving Day," a nationwide celebration.	John Stuart Mill. *Utilitarianism.* President Lincoln issues the Emancipation Proclamation. In Baghdad, Bahaullah proclaims himself a divine leader through whom God is manifest, beginning the Bahai faith. The International Committee of the Red Cross is founded. Swiss philanthropist Jean Henri Dunant and five other Swiss citizens call an international conference in Geneva to form relief societies for victims of war and disaster. The conference is attended by delegates from 16 nations.	
1864		A small group of New Orleans Greek merchants builds the first Greek Orthodox church in America.	Leo Tolstoy. *War and Peace.* Jules Verne. *Journey to the Center of the Earth.* Pasteurization is invented. Pragmatism. It is the inheritor of both the empiricist tradition of grounding knowledge on experience and the inductive procedures of experimental science. It maintains that there is no truth apart from human experience and that a theory is true if it "works." It becomes a dominant system of thought in early twentieth century America. Key figures: Charles Sanders Peirce, John Dewey, and William James.	Pope Pius IX. *Syllabus of Errors.* A compendium of "the principle errors of our time." John Henry Newman. *Apologia Pro Vita Sua* (Latin: Apology for His Own Life). Newman's most famous work, it is a theological autobiography, including his reasons for changing from the Anglican to the Roman Catholic Church.

Date	A. Theology, Doctrine, and Beliefs	B. People/Events	C. Wider Culture	D. Texts
1865	Holiness Movement. The Holiness Movement is the institutionalization of perfectionism, the belief that the Holy Spirit's second, post-conversion work in a believer's life enables that believer to live a holy life. Key institutions: Oberlin College, the National Holiness Association, Keswick Conventions, Salvation Army. Faith Missions. These mission organizations believe that God will provide for the needs of their missionaries. Neither the organizations nor the missionaries, therefore, specifically solicit financial support.	The Overseas Missionary Fellowship is founded under the name "China Inland Mission" by James Hudson Taylor. The first faith mission, it begins the Faith Mission Movement. Numerous Holiness churches arise during the period between the Civil War and World War I. The Community of St. Mary, the first Episcopal religious order for women, is formed in New York. Richard Benson founds Cowley Fathers (the Society of St. John the Evangelist), the first official Anglican monastic order. The Salvation Army is founded by William Booth, a Holiness evangelist, in the slums of London. Its two-fold mission is the salvation of souls and relief of human suffering. Chalices made of glass, wood, copper, or brass may not be consecrated by a bishop or used in the Roman Catholic Eucharist. The Protestant Episcopal Church and the Protestant Episcopal Church in the Confederate States of America are reunited.	Lewis Carroll. *Alice in Wonderland.* Abraham Lincoln is assassinated. Andrew Johnson becomes President of the United States. "In God We Trust" is first seen on United States coins. The Thirteenth Amendment to the United States Constitution abolishes slavery. The American Civil War ends. (1861–) Between the American Civil War and World War I, American cities become multiracial, multicultural, and increasingly crowded due to the northward movement of slaves and the immigration of Europeans.	Edward Pusey. "The Church of England a Portion of Christ's one Holy Catholic Church and a Means of Restoring Visible Unity" (a letter to J. Keble). It considers the barriers between the Church of England and the Roman Catholic Church and maintains the biggest ones are ritualistic, not doctrinal.
1866		John Mason Neale, hymnodist, dies. Lay readers may conduct nonsacramental services in the Church of England. John Keble, leader of the Oxford Movement, dies.	The Ku Klux Klan is formed. The first trans-Atlantic cable is laid.	James Hilton. *The Mystery of Pain.* It challenges traditional notions of the impassibility of God that date back to the Council of Chalcedon and before.
1867		The first Lambeth Conference, an assembly of bishops of the Anglican Communion, is held. Subsequent conferences are held approximately every ten years. The Dutch Reformed Church in America drops the "Dutch" from its name to become the Reformed Church in America.	The British North America Act creates the Dominion of Canada.	
1868			The Benevolent Protective Order of Elks is founded.	
1869	The Dogma of Papal Infallibility. The belief that the pope, when speaking *ex cathedra*, i.e. in his official capacity as pope, speaks irreformable truth. In these circumstance, he possesses a divine assistance that enables him to	Thomas Huxley coins the term "agnostic." The National Liberal League is founded to combat government alliances with Christianity, especially a Christian preamble to the Constitution.	Ulysses S. Grant becomes President of the United States. The Knights of Labor is founded as the first national labor union. The United States transcontinental railway is completed.	Those who read books specifically prohibited by the office of the pope face excommunication.

Date	A. Theology, Doctrine, and Beliefs	B. People/Events	C. Wider Culture	D. Texts
1869 con't.	teach divinely revealed doctrine on matters of faith and morals. Key document: *Pastor Aeternus*.	Twentieth Ecumenical Council: Vatican I. (–1870) • Decrees the pope is infallible when speaking *ex cathedra*. • Passes several canons relating to the Faith. • Limits the pope's temporal authority. No longer does the papacy rule a large part of central Italy. The Anglican church is disestablished (is no longer the state church) in Ireland.	Hector Berlioz, Romantic composer, dies. The Suez Canal is opened.	
1870	Dispensationalism. An American conservative Christian approach toward hermaneutics. It maintains that history is divided into time periods (dispensations), and that God's revelation grows progressively through the ages. Key figure: John Nelson Darby. (1870–present) Universal Jurisdiction of the Pope. It is the belief that there is one universal catholic church on earth, and that the pope is the head of that church. According to this doctrine, the pope is the head bishop of all bishops, and authority flows down the church hierarchy from that head.	The Old Catholic Church is founded. It refuses to accept the Vatican I doctrines of infallibility and universal jurisdiction of the pope. The Jehovah's Witnesses are formed as the Watch Tower Bible and Tract Society of Pennsylvania. Protestant activists begin a campaign against birth control. Jackson Kemper, the first Episcopal missionary bishop in the United States, dies. He was assigned to Missouri and Indiana, but oversaw the establishment of Episcopal parishes throughout the American frontier. The Russian Orthodox Church establishes its first diocese in the United States. The General Conference of the Methodist Episcopal Church, South, votes to transfer all its African-American members to a new church, the Colored Methodist Episcopal Church (whose name is later changed to the Christian Methodist Episcopal Church). The Holiness Movement begins to have a significant impact on conservative Christianity. (1870s)	Colleges and universities become available to women, blacks, and the middle and working classes after the Civil War. Franco-Prussian War. France versus German states under the leadership of Prussia. (–1871) Jewish ghettos are abolished in Italy.	Albrecht Ritschl. *The Christian Doctrine of Justification and Reconciliation*. Ritschl maintains metaphysics and philosophy hinder faith and theology. He sees the Bible as a product of a community's consciousness. His work is an important influence on modern German theology. (–1874) William Reed Huntington. *The Church Idea*. A call for church unity, it is the basis for the Chicago-Lambeth Quadrilateral and the twentieth-century ecumenical movement. *Pastor Aeternus* (Latin: Eternal Shepard). The constitution of the first Vatican Council that defines the doctrines of the primacy and infallibility of the pope.
1871	Ultramontanism. A movement within Roman Catholicism that focuses on the pope as the infallible central authority of the church.	Pope Pius IX makes St. Alphonsus Liguori a doctor of the church. John Coleridge Patteson, bishop of Melanesia, is martyred.	Chicago's great fire destroys 2,000 acres. The Third Republic in France begins.	*Programme Catholique* (French: Catholic Program). An expression of French-Canadian, Ultramontane ideals.
1872		Jerry McAuley founds the Helping Hand for Men Mission, later named the Water Street Mission, in New York. It is one of the first of the large rescue missions of the late		

Date	A. Theology, Doctrine, and Beliefs	B. People/Events	C. Wider Culture	D. Texts
1872 con't.		nineteenth and early twentieth centuries. A branch house of the English Society of St. John the Evangelist, the first regular Episcopal monastic house for men, is formed in Boston. Frederick Denison Maurice, Christian Socialist, dies.		
1873	Ritualism. An Anglican/Episcopal church approach to liturgy that embraces the traditional practices of the Roman Catholic Church. Its central focus is the Eucharist. Its theological underpinning is that of the Tractarians and the Oxford Movement.	The Reformed Episcopal Church breaks from the Protestant Episcopal Church in the United States over ritualism and willingness to extend full fellowship to non-Episcopal Protestants. D. L. Moody conducts large and successful evangelistic meetings in the eastern United States and England. In doing so he becomes the best-known evangelist of his time. (–1893)		*Ordo Poenitentiae* (Latin: Order of Penance). Encourages face-to-face dialog between the penitent and confessor in the Roman Catholic Church.
1874	Speaking in tongues. It takes two forms: In the first, people miraculously speak a language that they haven't learned (*xenolalia*). In the second, they speak a collection of speech sounds that don't comprise any natural language (*glossolalia*). Both are considered manifestations of the Holy Spirit.	James DeKoven pleads at the Episcopal Church General Convention for the Anglo-Catholic ritual. The Roman Catholic Sacred Congregation of the Holy Office decides that a chalice is no longer consecrated if it is used for any profane purpose, for example as an ordinary drinking cup. Jakob Hutter establishes the Hutterites, a communal utopian colony in the American Northwest. It is one of many such utopian experiments throughout the United States and Europe in the nineteenth century. The Seventh-day Adventist Church sends out its first missionary. The "Gift People" begin speaking in tongues, marking the first recorded occurrence of the phenomenon in America. John Bachman, "Patriarch of Southern Lutheranism," dies. He organized Lutheran synods, a college and a seminary in the American South.		
1875	Christian Science. An indigenous American religion based on the dualism between matter and spirit. Matter, and so physical illness, is considered to be an evil illusion. Spirit is truly real, and can generate	Charles Grandison Finney, revivalist, dies.	The United States Congress begins to restrict immigration of undesirables, especially criminals. Mark Twain. *Tom Sawyer*.	Hannah Whitall Smith. *The Christian's Secret of a Happy Life*. An important work in the Holiness Movement. Mary Baker Eddy publishes the first edition of *Science and Health*. It later becomes

Date	A. Theology, Doctrine, and Beliefs	B. People/Events	C. Wider Culture	D. Texts
1875 con't.	spontaneously healing. Key figure: Mary Baker Eddy.			*Science and Health with Key to the Scriptures.* Its publication marks the beginnings of Christian Science.
1876		James Lloyd Breck, Episcopal missionary, dies.	Battle of the Little Big Horn. George A. Custer and 264 troops are killed in the Sioux Indian War. The telephone is invented. In a 42-page booklet, Melvil Dewey describes the Dewey Decimal library classification scheme.	
1877		William Augustus Muhlenberg dies. He espoused "Catholic Evangelicalism" in the Episcopal church and introduced a number of ceremonial innovations into the Episcopal worship service. The Pacific Garden Mission is founded in Chicago. It becomes one of the country's best known rescue missions and a model for many other missions. Its *Unshackled* radio program does much to promote urban ministry. Pope Pius IX makes St. Francis of Sales a doctor of the church.	Rutherford B. Hayes becomes President of the United States. The phonograph is invented.	
1878	Heresy trials are conducted within many Protestant denominations and seminaries in reaction to liberalism's rise in influence. (–1906)	Leo XIII becomes pope. George Augustus Selwyn, missionary bishop of New Zealand, dies. The First American Bible and Prophetic Conference is held in New York. It is the first of several conferences to focus on the premillennial and immanent return of Christ. These conferences bolster the premillenial dispensationalist position and fuel the fundamentalist movement.	Thomas A. Edison founds Edison Electric Light Co.	
1879		James DeKoven, American Anglo-Catholic, dies. Saint Bernadette dies. As a teen she saw a vision of Mary at Lourdes. As a young woman she was an unwaveringly committed nun. "Our Lady of Knock," an apparition of Mary, appears in Knock, Ireland. The national body of the Swedish Baptist General Conference is formed.	H. J. Ibsen. *A Doll's House.* The first laboratory of experimental psychology is founded in Leipzig, Germany. Albert Einstein is born.	Robert Young. *Analytical Concordance to the Bible.* (first edition) Pope Leo XIII. *Aeterni Patris* (papal encyclical (Latin: Eternal Father)). In it Leo commends the church to the study of philosophy, especially the works of Thomas Aquinas.

Date	A. Theology, Doctrine, and Beliefs	B. People/Events	C. Wider Culture	D. Texts
1880	Evangelical liberalism. Also called new theology or progressive orthodoxy, it is traditional Protestant thought but with a modern expression. (–1930)	The Society of Biblical Literature is formed. It provides a forum for the newer critical views of Scripture. Holiness denominations and organizations shoot off and split for reasons of both doctrine and polity. (–1910) Frances Xavier Cabrini founds the Order of the Missionary Sisters of the Sacred Heart.	Auguste Rodin. *Thinker.* Modern American football is invented. Fyodor Mikhaylovich Dostoyevsky. *The Brothers Karamazov.*	
1881		The Presbyterian church debates (occasionally fights over) the new biblical criticism. The Ecumenical Methodist Conference is held to coordinate worldwide Methodism. Pope Leo XIII canonizes Cyril and Methodius. The Church of God (Anderson, Indiana) is formed by a Holiness group believing in instantaneous, entire sanctification.	James Abram Garfield becomes President of the United States. Chester A. Arthur becomes President of the United States. Henry James. *The Portrait of a Lady.* Portrays the conflict between European and American values.	Brooke Foss Westcott and Fenton John Anthony Hort. *New Testament in the Original Greek.* A strongly Alexandrian, critical edition of the New Testament.
1882		Edward Pusey, Tractarian, dies. The Knights of Columbus is formed as a fraternal and beneficent society of Catholic men. The International Bible Reading Association is formed to encourage individual Bible study.	Composers, notably Richard Wagner, develop chromaticism, the use of tones that do not belong to the musical scale on which the composition is based. By the turn of the century, lavish use of chromaticism leads to twelve-tone composition and a breakdown of the major-minor key system.	
1883		The Newman movement begins to provide religious education and leadership for Catholic students on non-Catholic campuses. (–present) Pope Leo XIII makes St. Cyril of Alexandria, St. Cyril of Jerusalem, and St. John Damascene doctors of the church.	Mark Twain. *The Adventures of Huckleberry Finn.* Karl Marx dies. Richard Wagner, German composer of Romantic opera, dies. His work marks the peak of Romanticism in opera.	Friedrich Nietzsche. *Thus Spoke Zarathustra.* Nietzsche introduces the concept of a superman who can transcend the rote morality of Christianity, who is motivated by a "will to power" and by creativity. He also supports the assertion that "God is dead."
1884	Settlement House Movement. In England and the United States, university and seminary students are recruited to live in the poorest neighborhoods and work at social reform. (peaked in 1910)	A conference of Scandinavian free churches in Boone, Iowa, marks the earliest American roots of the Evangelical Free Church of America. Pope Leo XIII prescribes that the Salve Regina be recited after every low Mass. The tribunal of the Holy Office of the Roman Catholic Church decrees that no Catholic Church can consider the willful termination of a pregnancy lawful. The first settlement house is established in London.	Workingmen in Great Britain are given the vote by Act of Parliament.	*The Christian Century* (magazine). It is founded by the Disciples of Christ under the name *Christian Oracle.* It eventually becomes a nondenominational reflection of the thought of liberal Protestantism. The *Missale Romanum* is revised under Pope Leo XIII.

Date	A. Theology, Doctrine, and Beliefs	B. People/Events	C. Wider Culture	D. Texts
1885	Documentary Hypothesis. The hypothesis that the books of the Pentateuch were compiled from several stylistically distinct, written "sources." The analysis of these sources is called Source Criticism. Key figure: Julius Wellhausen.	The Evangelical Covenant Church of America is founded. It is initially called the Swedish Evangelical Mission Covenant of America. Julius Wellhausen proposes J and E as sources for Genesis. James Hannington, Anglican bishop, is martyred in Uganda.	Grover Cleveland becomes President of the United States. Impressionism (music). It employs sound as a suggestive, structural element. It characterizes the latter part of the French Romantic period. Key figures: Claude Debussy and Maurice Ravel. (ca.–1935) The first skyscraper is built in Chicago.	American Roman Catholic bishops of the Third Plenary Council of Baltimore, Maryland. A Catechism of Christian Doctrine. For almost sixty years, it dominates American Catholic catechesis as the *Baltimore Catechism*. Revised Version of the Bible. A revision of the King James Version commissioned by the Convocation of Canterbury. Its purpose is to change the KJV as little as possible while bringing it into line with the uncial biblical texts discovered in the eighteenth century. (work on the revision begun 1870)
1886		Thirty-two Ugandan Christians, "the Martyrs of Uganda," are martyred. Karl Barth is born. American bishops of the Episcopal Church adopt the Statement of the Chicago-Lambeth Quadrilateral.	Geronimo, Apache leader, surrenders. Robert Louis Stevenson. *Dr. Jekyll and Mr. Hyde*. Auguste Rodin. *The Kiss*. The American Federation of Labor is founded. Franz Liszt dies. He revolutionized keyboard technique and invented the symphonic poem.	Statement of the Chicago-Lambeth Quadrilateral. It contains a statement of desire for church unity as well as the doctrinal foundation for such unity. It is based on William Reed Huntington's *The Church Idea*.
1887		The Moody Bible Institute is founded.	Arthur Conan Doyle publishes the first Sherlock Holmes story.	
1888		The Lambeth Conference of 1888 approves the Chicago-Lambeth Quadrilateral.		
1889	New Thought. A focus on practical, eclectic spirituality. It is mostly Christian in background, but embraces insights from numerous religions, incorporating constructive thinking and meditation with nondoctrinal theology. Key organizations: Science of Mind, Unity, Divine Science. Christian socialism. In the United States, it rose contemporaneously with political socialism between the Civil War and World War II. Key figures: Dwight Porter Bliss, Edward Ellis Carr. Key institutions: The Society of Christian Socialists, the magazine *The Christian Socialist*.	Frances Xavier Cabrini begins a mission to the United States At the request of Pope Leo XIII, she begins charitable and religious work among Italian immigrants. She founds schools, orphanages, convents, and hospitals. The Catholic University of America is founded as the only pontifical university in the United States. The order of deaconess receives canonical authorization in the Episcopal church largely due to the campaigning of William Reed Huntington. The United Brethren approve the ordination of women. The Society of Christian Socialists is formed. The Unity School of Christianity, also known simply as "Unity," is formed as a nondoctrinal, New Thought organization.	Benjamin Harrison becomes President of the United States. Martin Heidegger is born.	*Lux Mundi* (Latin: Light of the World). "A series in the religion of the Incarnation." It is Anglo-Catholicism in a modern context, put together by Oxford Scholars.

Date	A. Theology, Doctrine, and Beliefs	B. People/Events	C. Wider Culture	D. Texts
1890	Social Gospel Movement. It is an attempt to apply biblical and theological principles to the changing urban environment. Originally having conservative (Salvation Army, rescue missions) as well as liberal expressions, the term eventually comes to be applied almost exclusively to liberal social reform. Center: Oberlin College. (Arose after the American Civil War, faded after WWI.)	The Central American Mission is founded. The Evangelical Alliance Mission (TEAM), is founded. Initially it is called the Scandinavian Alliance Mission of North America John Henry Cardinal Newman dies. He was one of the most famous converts from High Church Anglicanism to the Roman Catholic Church. Nigerians and South Africans are among the first African Christians to reject Western missionary control. (1890s) The Salvation Army comes to the United States. The Hungarian Reformed Church is formed in the United States by Hungarian refugees.	Movies are invented. Battle of Wounded Knee. The last major battle between American Indians and U.S. troops. A global influenza epidemic begins. César Franck, French Romantic composer, dies.	
1891			Immigration to the United States is mainly from eastern and southern Europe. (–1920) Basketball is invented.	Pope Leo XIII. *Rerum Novarum* (Latin: Of New Things). A papal encyclical, it is written in response to urban poverty and the rise of labor unions and socialism. It upholds the right of private property, but commits the church to social justice and charity.
1892		The Gospel Missionary Union is founded originally under the name World's Gospel Union. Karl Paul Reinhold Niebuhr is born. The Episcopal Church in the U.S.A. participates in its first Lambeth Conference. The Presbyterian Church in the U.S.A. makes biblical inerrancy an official doctrine of the church. Within the next five years several renowned Presbyterian professors are fired or resign.	The American Psychological Association is founded.	*Book of Common Prayer* (second American revision). A conservative revision, its aim is to "enrich" and make more "flexible" the 1789 book.
1893		Charles Briggs is suspended from the Presbyterian ministry for denying the inerrancy of Scripture. His is one of the most famous heresy trials of the time. Phillips Brooks, preacher and Episcopal bishop of Massachusetts, dies. He was the author of the hymn "O Little Town of Bethlehem." The Trappists become an independent order.	The first automobile is manufactured. Grover Cleveland becomes President of the United States. Peter Ilich Tchaikovsky, Russian Romantic composer, dies.	

Date	A. Theology, Doctrine, and Beliefs	B. People/Events	C. Wider Culture	D. Texts
1893 con't.		Pope Leo XIII brings all the Benedictine monasteries into the Benedictine Confederation with an Abbot Primate in Rome.		
1894		Helmut Richard Niebuhr is born.		
1895	Bible Church Movement. The late-nineteenth and twentieth centuries see the founding of hundreds of independent churches that are conservative in doctrine, emphasize biblical preaching, and practice congregational autonomy.	The first congregation to use the name Church of the Nazarene begins to meet. The Anti-Saloon league is formed. Notre Dame of Maryland is founded as the first American Catholic women's college. The Lutheran General Synod organizes the ministry of deaconesses. They serve in parishes, do home nursing, and operate schools.	Stephen Crane. *The Red Badge of Courage.* Wilhelm Roentgen discovers x-rays.	"The Five Points of Fundamentalism" are drawn up during the Niagra Bible Conference. They are: verbal inerrancy of Scripture, divinity of Jesus, the Virgin Birth, Substitutionary Atonement, and the physical resurrection and bodily return of Jesus. They become the foundation for *The Fundamentals.*
1896	Zionism. It is a belief held by facets of both Christianity and Judaism. Zionists believe that rightful title to the land of Israel and the city of Jerusalem is an inseparable part of God's covenant with the Jewish people. Key Christian figures: William Black, Arno C. Gaebelein. Key organization: American Christian Palestine committee.	Billy Sunday conducts his first revival. Bernard Mizeki, catechist and martyr in Rhodesia, dies. Zionism begins.	*Plessy v. Ferguson* (Supreme Court decision). It upholds "separate but equal" accommodations on railways and thus provides a constitutional basis for segregation. Anton Bruckner dies. He was one of the greatest late-Romantic symphonists. Herbert Spencer. *System of Synthetic Philosophy.* One of the earliest examples of evolutionary theory, it influences Social Darwinism. The Nobel Prize is established. The Dewey School is established by the University of Chicago. It is a laboratory for John Dewey's educational principles: learning through doing rather than a traditional formal curricula, combined with a minimal authoritarianism to prepare children for life in a democratic society. Dewey's ideas become part of the basis for the educational reform of the early twentieth century.	Pope Leo XIII. *Satis Cognitum* (Latin: It Is Sufficiently Well Known; English title: "On the Unity of the Church"). A papal encyclical declaring that unity between the various branches of the church is only possible when all acknowledge the authority of the papacy.
1897		Saint Theresa of Lisieux, "the Little Flower of Jesus," dies. She was a French Carmelite nun. She becomes the patron saint of foreign missionaries, aviators, and of France. The various branches of the Franciscan order reunite. The first congregation of the Church of God in Christ meets. The Christian and Missionary Alliance is formed when the	Johannes Brahms, romantic composer, dies. John Philip Sousa. "The Stars and Stripes Forever."	The Oxyrhynchus Papyri are discovered. The collection includes a Greek variant of the *Gospel of Thomas,* fragments of the Old and New Testaments, and the oldest known example of church music.

Date	A. Theology, Doctrine, and Beliefs	B. People/Events	C. Wider Culture	D. Texts
1897 con't.		Christian Alliance and the Evangelical Missionary Alliance merge.		
1898		The youth organization, Luther League of America, is founded by the Lutheran General Synod.	Marie and Pierre Curie discover radium. The Spanish-American War. Initially fought to protect American interests in Cuba, it results in the United States gaining control of Guam, Puerto Rico, and the Philippines. (–1899)	Theresa of Lisieux. *The Story of a Soul*. Written at the request of her superiors, it becomes one of the most widely read spiritual autobiographies. Eberhard Nestle. *Greek New Testament*. It is a moderate text based on the current critical editions of the Greek New Testament. Throughout its next twenty-four editions, it gradually adds ever more critical apparatus.
1899		The Gideons International is founded, originally as the Christian Commercial Travelers Association of America. The organization does evangelism through the distribution of Scripture. D. L. Moody, American evangelist, dies. Pope Leo XIII canonizes the Venerable Bede and makes him a doctor of the church.	Scott Joplin. "Maple Leaf Rag." Kate O'Flaherty Chopin. *The Awakening*. One of the nineteenth-century realists Aspirin is first synthesized. Ernest Hemingway is born.	Percy Dearmer. *The Parson's Handbook*. Ancient ceremonial adapted to the *Book of Common Prayer*.
1900	Gospel of Wealth. The belief that wealth is the consequence of moral rectitude and hard work and that charity weakens society. Key figures: Andrew Carnegie, Henry Ward Beecher.	The Eucharistic fast begins to disappear in the Roman Catholic Church. (early twentieth century) Pope Leo XIII consecrates humanity to the Sacred Heart.	The Boxer uprising opposes foreigners in China. Friedrich Nietzsche, German philosopher, dies. Naturalism. The literary movement that evolves from realism. It sees human beings as creatures bound by the laws of nature, without free will. Most major writers between 1900 and 1930 are influenced by naturalism. Key figures: Émile Zola in France; Theodore Dreiser, Stephen Crane, and Frank Norris in the United States. Sigmund Freud. *Interpretation of Dreams*.	
1901	Form Criticism. An approach to biblical interpretation that analyzes the structure of biblical texts to determine their history. Pentecostal Movement. Largely an offspring of the Holiness Movement, the Pentecostal Movement focuses on "Spirit baptism," a post-conversion work of the Holy Spirit, marked by glossolalia (speaking in unknown tongues). Key figures: Charles F. Parham, William J. Seymour, Eudorus N. Bell. Key	The Pentecostal Movement emerges. Hermann Gunkel applies form criticism for the first time to the book of Genesis.	Theodore Roosevelt becomes President of the United States. Queen Victoria of England dies. King Edward VII becomes king. Giuseppi Verdi, Romantic composer, dies. Educational reform begins in the United States early in the twentieth century. The emphasis of education is shifted from schools to the student, from preparation for a job to preparation for a life in society, from rote learning	*The American Standard Version* of the Bible is released. It is an Americanized version of the Revised Version. It becomes a popular student Bible. William Wrede. *The Messianic Secret in the Gospels*. Wrede proposes that during Jesus' life, most of his followers were unaware that he was the Messiah.

Date	A. Theology, Doctrine, and Beliefs	B. People/Events	C. Wider Culture	D. Texts
1901 con't.	events/organizations: Apostolic Faith Movement, Azusa Street Revival, Assemblies of God.		to learning by doing, from strict authoritarianism to development of self-control through teacher guidance. It is based largely on the ideas of John Dewey.	
1903		Pius X becomes pope. Pope Pius X reforms church music, restores Gregorian chant to common practice, promotes frequent communion. His directives spur the new liturgical movement. (–1914)	Orville and Wilbur Wright fly the first motorized airplane. The first World Series of Baseball is held. Jack London. *Call of the Wild.*	A. A. Hodges and B. B. Warfield revise the Westminster Confession of Faith with more of an eye to its biblical base than its faithfulness to Calvinism.
1904			Pablo Picasso paints in the cubist style. (–1917) Antonin Dvorak, Czech composer, dies.	
1905		Pope Pius X issues a decree recommending daily Communion to the entire laity. The Baptist World Alliance, an international fellowship of Baptist churches, is formed.		Max Weber. *The Protestant Ethic and the Spirit of Capitalism.* The origin of the notion of the Protestant work ethic.
1906		Joseph Schereschewsky, translator of the Bible (into Mandarin) and Anglican bishop in Shanghai, dies. William J. Seymour leads the Azusa Street Revival, one of the earliest instances of Pentecostal style worship. The Cumberland Presbyterian Church rejoins the Presbyterian Church in the U.S.A. after almost a century of existing as an organizationally distinct body. The Churches of Christ (Noninstrumental) becomes distinct from the Disciples of Christ/Christian Church. Within the Disciples of Christ/Christian Church (which is still more an informal association than a denomination) some churches call themselves Christian Church/Churches of Christ. They tend to be more conservative and independent. The 1906 United States census recognizes them as a separate group.	Upton Beall Sinclair. *The Jungle* The San Francisco earthquake kills 500 people.	Albert Schweitzer. *Quest of the Historical Jesus.* An eschatology-centered interpretation of the Gospel stories. It maintains that Jesus' original mission was to preach the imminent end of the age and that he suffered to save his people from the tribulation of the Last Day.
1907		Pope Pius X condemns 65 modernist propositions and places several modernist works on the Index of Forbidden Books. He also establishes in every diocese a board of censors whose purpose is to report people		Walter Rauschenbusch. *Christianity and the Social Crisis.* Brings the social gospel into the public arena. Francis Brown, S. R. Driver, and Charles A. Briggs. *A Hebrew and English Lexicon of the Old Testament.*

Date	A. Theology, Doctrine, and Beliefs	B. People/Events	C. Wider Culture	D. Texts
1907 con't.		and writings suspected of the heresy of modernism. Construction of Washington Cathedral (Episcopal) is begun in Washington, D. C. Northern Baptist Churches and mission societies unite to form the Northern Baptist Convention, which will later become the American Baptist Churches in the U.S.A.		
1908		The Roman Catholic Church in the United States is no longer considered a missionary church. The Gideons begin distributing Bibles. The first Pan-Anglican Congress is held. Pentecostal and Holiness churches unite into the Church of the Nazarene, which organizes as a denomination.	E. M. Forster. *A Room with a View.* The first steel and glass building is built.	*Graduale Romanum.* The official Vatican collection of chant melodies is compiled from medieval manuscripts by scholars, most from the Benedictine Abbey of Solesmes in France.
1909		William Reed Huntington, priest and leader in the Episcopal church, dies.	The National Association for the Advancement of Colored People (NAACP) is formed as an American, voluntary, interracial organization to fight racism. Robert E. Peary and Matthew Henson travel to the North Pole. Tel Aviv is founded as a Hebrew-speaking, Jewish city.	C. I. (Cyrus Ingerson) Scofield. *Scofield Reference Bible.* It is a King James Bible with dispensationalist interpretation in its notes.
1910	Fundamentalism. Largely a reaction to the new biblical criticism and to evolution, its agenda is defined in the 1920s. The "five points of fundamentalism" are verbal inerrancy of Scripture, the Virgin Birth, and the divinity, physical resurrection, and bodily return of Jesus Christ.	World Missionary Conference (Edinburgh). The conference marks the beginning of modern ecumenism. It has three facets: evangelism, service, and doctrine. Channing Moore Williams, missionary to Japan and China, dies. Christian psychiatric services for the mentally ill become increasingly common. Roman Catholic priests must take an oath against modernism. Billy Sunday first uses the term "sawdust trail" as a metaphor for would-be converts walking down the aisle at evangelistic meetings. Mother Teresa of Calcutta is born in Albania as Agnes Gonxha Bojaxhiu. A group of Catholic social service providers establish the Catholic Charities U.S.A. network.	The Boy Scouts of America is formed.	*The Fundamentals* are published. They are a twelve-volume series of tracts/paperbacks. Largely apologetic in nature, they attack modern biblical criticism. Their publication marks the beginnings of fundamentalism. (–1915)

Date	A. Theology, Doctrine, and Beliefs	B. People/Events	C. Wider Culture	D. Texts
1911		The Catholic Foreign Mission Society of America, better known as the "Maryknoll Missioners," is formed as a group of American Catholic priests dedicated to foreign missions.	Gustav Mahler, Austrian composer and conductor, dies. His symphonies form the bridge between the Romanticism of the nineteenth century and emerging harmonics and orchestral effects of the twentieth. Roald Amundsen is the first known person to travel to the South Pole. Aircraft are first used in combat in the Turkish-Italian War.	
1912		The Maryknoll Sisters of St. Dominic begin work as the first Catholic women's missionary congregation in the United States.	The Balkan Wars begin. They are two consecutive wars between the countries of the Balkan Peninsula for possession of European territories held by the Ottoman Empire. (–1913) Carl Gustav Jung. *Psychology of the Unconscious.* He breaks with Freud in part by investigating the parallels between ancient myths and psychotic fantasies. Arizona joins the United States as the 48th state. The first Girl Scout troop is formed. The first successful radio broadcast of words (as opposed to morse code) is made.	
1913	Ultradispensationalism (Bullingerism). This doctrine/hermeneutic maintains that the New Testament contains at least three dispensations, during which God deals with humanity in three distinct ways. Key figure: Ethelbert W. Bullinger. (begins before)	The International Union of Gospel Missions is formed to support the large number of new urban missions ministering to the urban poor. George W. Hensley introduces the practice of snake handling to Pentecostals in Tennessee. The "oneness" or "Jesus only" Pentecostals begin to baptize in the name of Jesus rather than using the traditional Trinitarian formula. The innovation creates a permanent split among Pentecostals.	Henry Ford introduces standardized parts and assembly-line techniques to his automobile plant. Woodrow Wilson becomes President of the United States. Bertrand Russell and Alfred North Whitehead. *Principia Mathematica.* An attempt to reduce mathematics to its most basic logical principles. (1910–) Phenomenology. This school of philosophy sees the philosophical enterprise as description of the structures of experience as they enter consciousness. Key figure: Edmund Husserl. Edmund Husserl. *Ideas: A General Introduction to Pure Phenomenology.* The seminal work of phenomenology. Charlie Chaplain makes his first film.	

Date	A. Theology, Doctrine, and Beliefs	B. People/Events	C. Wider Culture	D. Texts
1914		Saint Pius X dies. As pope he opposed the modernist movement in Roman Catholicism. He instituted the recodification of canon law, restored Gregorian chant, and established a new breviary. Benedict XV becomes pope. The Assemblies of God is formed.	Henry Ford has a 40–60% labor turnover in his automobile plant due to the new assembly-line techniques. He doubles wages and stabilizes the problem. The Panama Canal is opened. World War I begins. A global conflict, it is fought between the "Central Powers" and "the Allies." It costs $211 billion and 8.5 million lives. (–1918)	
1915		Thomas Merton is born. Aimee Semple McPherson begins her ministry.	Albert Einstein proposes his theory of general relativity. Neohumanism. A movement in literature, it opposes naturalism and calls for a reaffirmation of human free will and moral choice. Key figures: Irving Babbitt, Stuart Pratt Sherman, and Paul Elmer More.	
1916			The first Pro Golfers Association (PGA) championship is held. The first birth-control clinics are founded.	
1917		The Interdenominational Foreign Missions Association of North America is founded as an accrediting agency for non-denominational faith missions. "Our Lady of Fatima," an apparition of Mary, appears in Fatima, Portugal. Saint Frances Xavier Cabrini, Italian-American Roman Catholic nun, dies. She was the founder of the Order of the Missionary Sisters of the Sacred Heart. Edward Joseph Flanagan sets up the Home for Homeless Boys, which is later moved to Nebraska and renamed Boys Town.	The Russian Revolution begins. (–1922) The Balfour Declaration, issued by British foreign secretary Arthur James Balfour, pronounces British Palestine a national Jewish homeland. The British House of Saxe-Coburg changes its name to the House of Windsor.	Rudolf Otto. *The Idea of the Holy*. It attempts to define "the Holy" and humanity's experience of it. Pope Benedict XV. *Codex Juris Canonici* (*Code of Canon Law*). The modern code of canon law used by the Roman Catholic Church. It is a collection, redaction, and condensation of prior canon law. Begun by a commission appointed by pope Pius X, it is later authorized by Vatican II.
1918		Recitation of the Divine Office becomes obligatory for all priests (and some nuns) in the Roman Catholic Church. William Porcher DuBose, American theologian, dies. Billy Graham is born. The Forty Hours' Devotion begins to be celebrated annually in all Roman Catholic churches that typically reserve the Blessed Sacrament. Germany separates church from state. The Lutheran church still, however, receives taxes.	Nicholas II, the last Russian Tsar, is murdered. Max Planck proposes quantum theory. World War I ends. A worldwide influenza epidemic kills nearly 20 million people. (–1920)	

Date	A. Theology, Doctrine, and Beliefs	B. People/Events	C. Wider Culture	D. Texts
1919	Empirical theology. A type of liberal theology that reinterprets traditional Christian symbols and ideas to mesh with modern scientific and industrial thought.	InterVarsity Christian Fellowship, a campus ministry, holds its first conference. The Anglican church is disestablished (is no longer the state church) in Wales.	The Eighteenth Amendment to the United States Constitution institutes Prohibition, which bans the sale and transport of alcohol in the United States. The first trans-Atlantic flight is made.	Douglas Clyde Macintosh. *Theology as an Empirical Science.* The classic statement of empirical theology. Karl Barth. *Commentary on Romans.* A radical questioning of current theological ideas in the light of the world war, it is called "a bomb on the playground of the theologians." It becomes an important influence on dialectical/crisis theology and Lutheran thought.
1920	Dialectical theology (also called crisis theology). It is theology built on the dialectic of humanity and divinity mediated by Christ. Key figures: Karl Barth and Emil Brunner.	The Mennonite Central Committee is formed as a social relief and peacemaking agency. Pope Benedict XV canonizes Joan of Arc and Margaret Mary Alacoque, and makes St. Ephraem a doctor of the church. The patriarch of Constantinople calls for ecumenical understanding and "mutual cooperation" among "all the churches of Christ." Ralph Vaughan Williams, English composer, prefaces his musical setting of a text from Revelation with a statement of "Christian agnosticism": art is the vehicle that allows human beings to transcend the material world to intuit that which lies "beyond sense and knowledge." Karol Wojtyla (Pope John Paul II) is born in Wadowice, Poland.	Behaviorism. American psychologists focus on behavior rather than mental processes. Key figure: John B. Watson. (–1960) The League of Nations is founded. Mohandas "Mahatma" Gandhi emerges in India. Neoclassicism in music. A return to the notion that clarity of form is important. It adds a modified sense of tonality to the formal structures of the Baroque and classical periods. Key figures: Igor Stravinsky, Paul Hindemith, Sergey Prokofiev, Dmitry Shostakovich, Aaron Copland, Virgil Thomson. The Nineteenth Amendment to the United States Constitution gives women the vote. The "jazz age" begins. (–mid 1940s) The population of the United States has tripled in the last fifty years.	
1921		Princeton Theological Seminary becomes liberal. One of the last mainline schools to espouse exclusively a conservative, Reformed doctrine, Princeton now adds liberal faculty members to its ranks. The conservatives leave to form Westminster Theological Seminary. (–1929) The Magyar Synod is formed. United States Hungarian Reformed churches unite with the Reformed Church in the United States. The Baptist Bible Union is formed as a reaction to modernism in the Southern Baptist Church.	Warren G. Harding becomes President of the United States. Logical positivism. Like positivism, it rejects the speculation of metaphysic. However, it also rejects the traditional positivist idea that personal experience is the basis of knowledge. It focuses rather on scientific verification. Key figures: Ludwig Wittgenstein (early writings), Bertrand Russell, and G. E. Moore. The first regular radio broadcasts are aired. Ludwig Wittgenstein. *Tractatus Logico-Philosophicus.* A key work in the development of logical positivism.	

Date	A. Theology, Doctrine, and Beliefs	B. People/Events	C. Wider Culture	D. Texts
1922	Mary, Mediatrix of All Graces. The belief that Mary participates in the mediatory work of Christ in a unique way. Not only was she the mother of Jesus, who was the redeemer; not only did she remain with Jesus throughout his crucifixion; her holiness and unique relationship to Christ make her a powerful intercessor in heaven for the needs of humanity.	Francis of Sales becomes the patron saint of Roman Catholic writers. Pope Benedict XV authorizes a Mass of the Blessed Virgin Mary, Mediatrix of All Graces. (before) Pius XI becomes pope. Lyman Abbott dies. He was a Congregationalist minister and editor of the liberal paper, *The Christian Union*.	James Joyce. *Ulysses.* Sinclair Lewis. *Babbitt.* T. S. Eliot. *The Waste Land.* One of the most famous poems of the early twentieth century. A portrait of the despair of modern life. Jerusalem becomes the capital of the British mandate of Palestine. (–1948) Turkey becomes a republic. The Ottoman Empire ends.	
1923	Separatism. A fundamentalist practice that dictates that Christians avoid all doctrinal and moral impurity, especially contact with liberalism. Second-order separatists also don't associate with those who associate with liberals/apostates. Third-order separatists (a practice which arises in the 1970s) avoid those who don't practice second order separation.	Don Falkenberg founds Bible Literature International to produce and distribute Bibles, tracts, and Bible study material worldwide.	Calvin Coolidge becomes President of the United States. The first proposed Equal Rights Amendment to the Constitution of the United States is introduced into Congress. It would lift economic, legal, and social restrictions on women.	J. Gresham Machen. *Christianity and Liberalism.* Argues that historic Christianity and liberalism are irreconcilable to the point of being distinct religions.
1924		Dallas Theological Seminary is founded.	Insecticide is first used. Vladimir Ilyich Lenin, Russian revolutionary, dies. Giacomo Puccini, Italian composer of Romantic opera, dies.	
1925		Clinical Pastoral Education begins. Theresa of Lisieux is canonized. Scopes trial. John Thomas Scopes, a high school instructor, is convicted of teaching evolution. The prosecutor is William Jennings Bryan, the defender Clarence Darrow. Pope Pius XI institutes Feast of Christ the King. Pope Pius XI canonizes Peter Canisius and makes him a doctor of the church. The 1920s see the zenith of liberalism.	F. Scott Fitzgerald. *The Great Gatsby.* Arnold Schoenberg develops the twelve-tone method of composition. The Austrian composer furthers the atonality of twentieth century composition. (ca.) Nellie Ross becomes the first American woman governor when she is elected to the office in Wyoming. Adolf Hitler publishes *Mein Kampf.*	
1926	Liturgical movement. A "movement" beginning in Europe that prompts reconsideration of liturgy first by Roman Catholics and then by all major denominations. Lay participation in liturgy increases. Interest in the historical, psychological, and pastoral dimensions of liturgy grows. (1920s–1950s in the U.S., earlier in Europe)	Pope Pius XI makes St. John of the Cross a doctor of the church. One in ten radio stations are licenced to a religious organization.	Ernest Hemingway. *The Sun Also Rises.* Langston Hughes. *The Weary Blues.* It chronicles in poetry the experiences of African Americans living in the urban ghetto. Robert Goddard launches the first successful liquid-propelled rocket.	The Benedictines of St. John's Abbey in Collegeville, Minnesota, begin to publish the periodical *Orate Fratres*, later titled *Worship*, marking the beginning of the liturgical movement in the United States. Rudolf Karl Bultmann. *Jesus and the Word.* In its original German version and in English translation (1934), it introduces his method, commonly known as demythologizing, to the United States.

Date	A. Theology, Doctrine, and Beliefs	B. People/Events	C. Wider Culture	D. Texts
1927		Conservative members of the Christian Church/Disciples of Christ of Christ hold their first annual convention, the North American Christian Convention. The convention becomes the focal point for the Christian Church/Churches of Christ (Independent) congregations, which join together (without organizing as a denomination) to send out missionaries and to give voice to their opposition to the liberalism of Disciples of Christ leaders. The first World Conference on Faith and Order is held in Lausanne as a part of the movement toward doctrinal ecumenism. It is the first in a series of meetings that lay the foundation for the World Council of Churches. Dorothy Day rejects the "bourgeois" Episcopal church and becomes a socialist and a Roman Catholic. Aimee Semple McPherson founds the International Church of the Foursquare Gospel. Francis Xavier is named patron saint of missionaries. The North American Christian Convention of the Disciples of Christ splits from the Disciples of Christ over modernism. The Cistercian order brings all its congregations under an Abbot General in Rome. The General Assembly of the Presbyterian Church in the U.S. adopts a statement that says that the assembly cannot authoritatively determine what the "essentials" of the Christian faith are.	Martin Heidegger. *Being and Time.* A phenomenological work that looks at how awareness of being is influenced by time, cultural and natural objects, and impending death. It influences existentialism, though Heidegger does not see himself as an existentialist. Sinclair Lewis. *Elmer Gantry.* Charles Lindbergh makes the first solo flight across the Atlantic. *The Jazz Singer* is made. It is the first talking motion picture.	The British House of Commons rejects proposals for revision of the *Book of Common Prayer.* (–1928)
1928		Opus Dei is formed as a Roman Catholic organization whose purpose is nurture of the laity. It emphasizes spiritual direction and daily practice of the spiritual life. John A. Ryan founds the first Roman Catholic peace organization, The Catholic Association for International Peace.	The first Mickey Mouse cartoon is made. The first regular television broadcasts air. Women aged 21 in Great Britain are given the vote by Act of Parliament.	*The Book of Common Prayer* (third American revision). Commonly known as "the '28 Prayerbook," it is a continuation of the revisions begun in 1892. Walter Bauer. *Greek-German Lexicon of the New Testament.* One of the first lexicons to use newly discovered papyri and newly invented types of criticism. Throughout its four revisions, it becomes the most exhaustive lexicon

Date	A. Theology, Doctrine, and Beliefs	B. People/Events	C. Wider Culture	D. Texts
1928 con't.				ever constructed. (first revision, fourth revision: 1952) James Moffatt. *The Bible: A New Translation.* A translation done solely by a Scottish New Testament scholar. (New Testament: 1913. Old Testament: 1924)
1929		The New England Fellowship, forerunner of the National Association of Evangelicals, is formed. Westminster Theological Seminary is founded. Vatican City becomes an independent state. Charles Henry Brent, Episcopal church missionary bishop to the Philippines, dies.	Herbert Clark Hoover becomes President of the United States. Ernest Hemingway. *A Farewell to Arms.* William Faulkner. *The Sound and the Fury.* Black Friday. The stock market crashes, beginning the Great Depression.	
1930	Kerygmatic Theology. A mid-twentieth century theological emphasis associated with demythologization, it focuses on the early church's proclamation of Jesus as the Christ (as opposed to the historical Jesus). Key figure: Rudolf Bultmann. In the 1920s and 1930s, liberal-fundamentalist disputes over doctrine and the teaching of evolution in the schools rock most major denominations. Neo-orthodoxy. A Protestant (mostly Reformed) theological movement that seeks a return from liberalism to the central themes of the Reformation. Key figures: Karl Barth, H. Emil Brunner, H. Richard Niebuhr	Neo-orthodoxy reaches its zenith. (–1950s) Fulton J. Sheen conducts the first religious service ever broadcast. His radio program *The Catholic Hour* is on the air for over twenty years. (–1952) Walter A. Maier and Charles E. Fuller, radio preachers, build national audiences in the millions. (1930s and 1940s) Isaac Jogues and the North American Martyrs are canonized. They were Jesuit missionaries killed by the Iroquois in the mid seventeenth century.	The Nazis become a major party in Germany. Sinclair Lewis becomes the first American writer to win a Nobel Prize in literature.	
1931		Pope Pius XI makes Robert Bellarmine and Albertus Magnus Doctors of the Church. Zondervan Publishing House is founded.	The Westminster Statute reorganizes the British Empire into the Commonwealth of Nations. Spain becomes a republic.	*The Bible: An American Translation.* Often called the "Chicago Bible," its New Testament is the work of Edgar J. Goodspeed, an American New Testament scholar. Its Old Testament is translated by several scholars working in concert. (New Testament: 1923. Old Testament: 1927)
1932		The General Association of Regular Baptists is formed. "Regular" in this usage denotes historic (fundamentalist) as opposed modernist Baptist doctrine.		(Karl Paul) Reinhold Niebuhr. *Moral Man and Immoral Society.*
1933	Radical Catholicism. It maintains that society functions at its best when it is based on ordinary Christians living out	Dorothy Day founds the Catholic Worker, a lay organization advocating nonviolence, voluntary poverty,	The earliest atomic energy research is done. Franklin Delano Roosevelt becomes President of the	

Date	A. Theology, Doctrine, and Beliefs	B. People/Events	C. Wider Culture	D. Texts
1933 con't.	Christ's commands to love one's neighbors. It is based on service, socially useful labor, and a renunciation of materialism and violence. Key figures: Dorothy Day, Peter Maurin, and Daniel and Philip Berrigan and the Catholic Worker Movement. (–present)	meaningful work, and aid for the poor. Bernadette is canonized. The Soviet government sells the Codex Sinaiticus to the British Museum.	United States. He immediately implements his "New Deal" programs (–1939). *Humanist Manifesto.* Advocates a nontheistic, human-centered view of society. Adolf Hitler comes to power. The Eighteenth Amendment to the United States Constitution (Prohibition) is repealed. The Dachau concentration camp is built. Jews are imprisoned. The Holocaust begins.	
1934		The Evangelical and Reformed Church is established in the merger of the German Reformed Church and the Evangelical Synod of North America, who shares a German-language heritage, a similar form of church organization, and evangelical enthusiasm. The first African American ecumenical organization, the Fraternal Council of Negro Churches, is formed. Cameron Townsend founds a linguistic training program for Bible translators, thus beginning the Wycliffe Bible Translators.	Refrigerated transport begins to be used to transport food. Cole Porter. "Anything Goes."	Herbert W. Armstrong begins publishing *The Plain Truth,* the communication vehicle of an organization that will become his Worldwide Church of God.
1935		The term "Judeo-Christian Tradition" is first used as a unifying slogan to rally Christians and Jews together for the aid of European Jewry. (mid 1930s)	George Gershwin. *Porgy and Bess* The Nuremberg laws rescind Jewish rights in Germany.	
1936	Westminster School of Presbyterianism. In the midst of the fundamentalist-modernist controversy, the Westminster School fashions themselves as the inheritors of traditional Calvinism. Intellectual centers: Westminster Theological Seminary and the Orthodox Presbyterian Church. Key figure: J. Gresham Machen.	J. Gresham Machen organizes the Orthodox Presbyterian Church, which distances itself from the modernism of the Presbyterian Church (U.S.A.).	The United States no longer conducts public executions.	
1937		The Catholic Biblical Association of America, an association of Catholic scholars, first meets. The Bible Presbyterian Church splits from the Presbyterian Church of America (Orthodox Presbyterian Church). Bible Presbyterians assert a literal premillennial return of Christ to rapture his church.		

Date	A. Theology, Doctrine, and Beliefs	B. People/Events	C. Wider Culture	D. Texts
1938		H. Emil Brunner brings neo-orthodoxy to the United States. The Federation of College Catholic Clubs becomes the National Newman Club Federation. The World Home Bible League is formed with the purpose of placing a Bible in every home.	New criticism. Built on the Kantian ontology, it maintains that the structure of the literary work itself—not the historical context nor the intent of the author—is the most important factor in interpretation. Key figures: John Crowe Ransom, T. S. Eliot. *Kristallnacht* (Night of the Broken Glass). Nazis kill nearly a hundred Jews, smash thousands of Jewish-owned store windows, and set fire to synagogues. Hundreds of thousands of Jews flea Germany in fear of their lives. (November 9)	
1939		Fifty-three United States clerics present a petition to the White House asking for legislation to provide sanctuary for German Holocaust refugee children. A bill is brought before Congress, but it fails. Pius XII becomes pope. The Methodist Episcopal Church, the Methodist Protestant Church and the Methodist Episcopal Church, South unite into The Methodist Church.	John Steinbeck. *The Grapes of Wrath.* Germany invades Poland, beginning World War II. (–1945) Franklin Delano Roosevelt's "New Deal" programs end. Radar is first used. *The Wizard of Oz.* Sigmund Freud dies.	Reinhold Niebuhr. *The Nature and Destiny of Man.* It details "Christian realism," which acknowledges the ambiguity of ethical decision making.
1940		The Grail, an international organization for Catholic women, is formed.	Penicillin begins to be used. Sir Winston Spencer Leonard Churchill becomes British Prime Minister. (–1945)	Most major denominations produce hymnals based on a common set of hymns, to which are added denominational favorites. (1940s)
1941			Japan bombs the United States fleet at Pearl Harbor, bringing the United States into World War II. Massacres of Jews begin in the Ukraine.	*Christianity and Crisis* begins circulation. It is founded by theologians opposing World War II Germany.
1942		The Martyrs of New Guinea die after being betrayed to Japanese invaders by non-Christians. Wycliffe Bible Translators/Summer Institute of Linguistics takes its current dual structure: Bible translation agency, and scientific and educational agency. Pope Pius XII consecrates humanity to the Immaculate Heart of Mary.	The jet airplane engine is invented. On the west coast of the United States, 120,000 Japanese Americans are confined to internment camps by presidential order. Nazi leaders attend the Wannsee Conference to plan a "final solution" to the Jewish question. Six million Jews are killed in the Nazi Holocaust. In addition, almost ten million others are killed on the basis of ethnicity, race, or sexual orientation. (–1945).	C. S. Lewis. *Screwtape Letters.* The best-known (and perhaps lightest-weight) of the over forty works by this scholar, literary critic, and Christian apologist.

Date	A. Theology, Doctrine, and Beliefs	B. People/Events	C. Wider Culture	D. Texts
1943	Relational Theology. A mostly American emphasis in theology, it focuses on the relationship between people in addition to the traditional focus on divine-human interaction. Key institution: Faith at Work. Key figures: Leslie Weatherhead, Harry Emerson Fosdick. Neo-evangelicalism (later shortened to simply evangelicalism). It arises when some conservative Christians begin to question fundamentalism's separatism and anti-intellectualism. Organizations: National Association of Evangelicals, *Christianity Today*. Key figures: Harold John Ockenga, Carl F. H. Henry, Bernard Ramm, Billy Graham.	National Religious Broadcasters is founded. The National Association of Evangelicals is formed. Dawson Trotman incorporates the Navigators, whose purpose is teaching and discipleship, especially of students and military personnel.	The first electronic computer is invented. Income tax withholding is introduced in the United States. Sergi Rachmaninov, Russian composer, pianist, and conductor, dies. He was the last of the Russian Romantics.	Pope Pius XII. *Divino Afflante Spiritu* (Latin: With the Holy Spirit Teaching; English title: "On Biblical Awareness") (encyclical). Sanctions modern principles of exegesis for interpreting the Bible. Harry Emerson Fosdick. *On Being a Real Person*. One of the seminal works of relational theology.
1944		Torrey Johnson and Billy Graham found Youth for Christ International, Inc., an evangelism organization focusing on young people.	Aaron Copland. *Appalachian Spring*.	
1945	Indigenization of Third World churches. Roman Catholic, Anglican, and mainline Protestant churches raise up their own national leaders. They face the challenge of harmonizing Christian doctrine and traditional beliefs and practices. (Since World War II) Process Theology. Claiming that the doctrines of the unchangablity and impassibility of God are based on an outdated metaphysic, it builds its theology on relationalism, radical empiricism, and an emphasis on history and change. Key figures: Alfred North Whitehead and Charles Hartschorne. (–present) Midtribulationism. The eschatological doctrine that the church will remain on earth through the first half of the Great Tribulation. Key figures: J. Ockenga, Robert Gundry, and Gleason L. Archer. (post World War II)	The Evangelical Foreign Missions Association is formed as an association of evangelical missions organizations. The United Pentecostal Church is formed through the merger of the Pentecostal Assemblies of Jesus Christ and the Pentecostal Church, Inc. They baptize in the name of Jesus and have a demanding code of behavior. The Swedish Baptist General conference drops the "Swedish" from its name. Dietrich Bonhoeffer, German Lutheran pastor and writer, is executed by the Nazis. Mission Aviation Fellowship is founded to provide air transportation for missionaries working in remote areas.	Harry S Truman becomes President of the United States. Germany surrenders to the Allies. The United States drops atomic bombs on Hiroshima and Nagasaki, Japan. Japan surrenders to the Allied forces. World War II ends. George Orwell. *Animal Farm*. Portrays the dangers of totalitarianism. The Arab League is formed.	Kenneth Scott Latourette. *History of the Expansion of Christianity*. An optimistic look at the working of God in human institutions written by one of the twentieth centuries most distinguish scholars of Asian history and missions history. It focus on the Christian faith rather than on the institutional church. The Nag Hammadi library, a collection of thirteen Coptic papyrus codices from the first and second centuries, is found near Nag Hammadi, Egypt. The collection contains a manuscript of *The Gospel of Truth* and other gnostic writings. It sheds new light on the diversity of early Christianity.
1946	Biblical Theology Movement. It focus on the canon and content of Scripture as opposed to the historical development of the text. Biblical theologians believe that theology should grow	The Evangelical Association and the Church of the United Brethren in Christ unite into the Evangelical United Brethren Church after twenty years of negotiation.	Benjamin Spock. *Baby and Child Care*. The United Nations General Assembly meets for the first time.	The Presbyterian *Book of Common Worship* reflects a new interest among Protestants in sacramental liturgy.

Date	A. Theology, Doctrine, and Beliefs	B. People/Events	C. Wider Culture	D. Texts
1946 con't.	organically from biblical text. (ca.–1962)	Francesca Xavier Cabrini is canonized, becoming the first American citizen to be declared a saint. The United Bible Society is founded when Bible societies of Europe join with the American Bible Society. Pope Pius XII makes St. Anthony of Padua a doctor of the church. The first Urbana Student Missions Convention is held to foster an interest in evangelical foreign missions among college and university students. Sponsored by InterVarsity Christian Fellowship, it has since been held every three years.	The League of Nations is dissolved. Winston Churchill gives his "Iron Curtain" speech.	
1947		Fuller Theological Seminary is founded. John Ockenga becomes its first president establishing himself as one of the leaders of the new evangelical movement. Oral Roberts begins a revival ministry founded on healing and Pentecostal enthusiasm. It becomes one of the most successful and lucrative independent ministries of the post WWII period. The German Evangelical Lutheran Synod of Missouri, Ohio, and Other States changes its name to the Lutheran Church—Missouri Synod. The "New Life" movement, an active Christian existentialism within the Presbyterian Church, brings in record numbers of new members. (–1949) The Nobel Peace Prize is awarded to the British and Irish Friends Service Council and the American Friends Service Committee.	Albert Camus. *The Plague.* The first supersonic flight is made. Transistors are invented. The Fourth Republic in France begins.	Carl F. H. Henry. *The Uneasy Conscience of Modern Fundamentalism.* Henry calls conservative Christianity to recognize the larger political and social world. The Dead Sea Scrolls are discovered by two Bedouin shepherd boys looking for a stray animal on the cliffs near Qumran and the Dead Sea.
1948		The Accrediting Association of Bible Institutes and Bible Colleges is founded. It later becomes known as the Accrediting Association of Bible Colleges. (ca.) World Council of Churches is formed after a delay of seven years caused by World War II. The First Assembly of the World Council of Church is held in Amsterdam. Its theme is "Man's Disorder and God's Design."	Mohandas "Mahatma" Gandhi is assassinated. The State of Israel is proclaimed as a Jewish republic. The Berlin Airlift begins. (–1949)	The last edition *of the Index of Forbidden Books* is issued. Thomas Merton. *The Seven Storey Mountain.* The spiritual autobiography of a Trappist monk. It's popularity brings monastic spirituality to a wide audience.

Date	A. Theology, Doctrine, and Beliefs	B. People/Events	C. Wider Culture	D. Texts
1949	Inerrancy Controversy. Inerrancy is the doctrine that the Bible, if interpreted correctly, is always truthful, not only in matters of faith, but also in matters of history, ethics, and description of the world. It is one of the most visible controversies in conservative Protestantism. (post World War II through the present)	The inerrancy of the Bible begins to become a debated issue.	Richard Strauss, the last of the great Romantic composers, dies. George Orwell. *Nineteen Eighty-Four.* The city of Jerusalem is divided. The Old City is a part of Jordan, and the New City is the capital of Israel. (–1967) The Peoples Republic of China is formed. The North Atlantic Treaty Organization (NATO) is formed.	
1950	The '50s, '60s, and '70s see an emphasis on individual, experiential Christianity. The renewal movement promotes personal spirituality; evangelists work for personal conversions; religious self-help books and personal study Bibles allow individuals to nurture their spiritual life at home. The Assumption of the Blessed Virgin Mary. The doctrine that Mary was taken, body and soul, into heaven at the end of her earthly life.	The Assumption of the Blessed Virgin Mary becomes dogmatic. The Billy Graham Evangelistic Center is formed. Evangelical Free Church of America is formed from the merger of the Evangelical Free Church of America (Swedish) and the Evangelical Free Church Association (Danish and Norwegian). The Baptist Bible Fellowship International, a fundamentalist and mildly Calvinist denomination, is founded. Alphonsus Liguori is declared patron saint of confessors and moralists. The National Council of Churches is formed. Mother Teresa founds the Missionaries of Charity. Originally under the auspices of the archdiocese of Calcutta, it is later recognized as a pontifical congregation under the jurisdiction of Rome. Members take a fourth vow, pledging service to the poor. Methodists become the largest denomination in the United States. (mid nineteenth through the mid twentieth century) Bob Pierce forms World Vision. Initially founded to provide aid for Korean War orphans, it later expands to provide child sponsorship and relief to poor people worldwide.	Aleatory music. Uses chance to determine all or part of the structure of the music. The choice of sounds or the order of parts in the music is based on a roll of dice or the discretion of the musicians playing the piece. Different (sometimes ad hoc) musical notation is occasionally used. Key figures: John Cage and Earle Brown. The Korean War begins. (–1953) Margaret Mead. *Social Anthropology.*	Pope Pius XII. *Humani Generis* (Latin: Human Race; English titles: "Concerning False Opinions" or "On Evolution"). A papal encyclical condemning Existentialism and several other modern intellectual movements within and outside the Roman Catholic Church. It is a warning against innovative theology.
1951		Campus Crusade for Christ International is formed. The World Evangelical Fellowship is formed to facilitate	James Jones. *From Here to Eternity.* J. D. Salinger. *The Catcher in the Rye.*	Paul Tillich. *Systematic Theology.* Philosophical analysis can give insights into the nature of human experience but only revelation can

Date	A. Theology, Doctrine, and Beliefs	B. People/Events	C. Wider Culture	D. Texts
1951 con't.		discipleship and evangelism and to foster unity among evangelicals. It traces its roots to the World Evangelical Alliance of Britain. The Roman Catholic Church returns the Easter vigil service to the late evening of Holy Saturday. An archeological dig at the ruins of Qumran uncover an ancient Essene monastery. The ruins date from three periods: the seventh and eight century B.C.E., 135–31 B.C.E., and 1 B.C.E. to 68 CE.	Over thirteen million television sets are purchased in the United States. (1948–) Julius and Ethel Rosenberg are sentenced to death for giving secret atomic information to the Russians.	provide answers to human problems. (three volumes –1963) Helmut Richard Niebuhr. *Christ and Culture*. The classic expression of Niebuhr's life-long examination of the church and modern culture.
1952		The Full Gospel Business Men's Fellowship International is formed as a nondenominational charismatic men's organization.	The hydrogen bomb is invented. The Immigration and Naturalization Act lifts racial and ethnic barriers to United States immigration. King George VI of Britain dies. His daughter becomes Queen Elizabeth II.	*Revised Standard Version* of the Bible. Commissioned by the International Council of Religious Education, it is most commonly used by Christians of mainline Protestant denominations. Norman Vincent Peale. *The Power of Positive Thinking*. The merger of self-help and Protestant pietism.
1953	Religionless Christianity. It rejects traditional religion's separation of the sacred and temporal worlds. Key figure: Dietrich Bonhoeffer.	L. Ron Hubbard founds the Church of Scientology. The "church" is not Christian but is based on "applied religious philosophy."	Jean Paul Sartre. *Being and Nothingness*. Sartre maintains that individuals create their own world, i.e. they are the sum of their personal experiences. They must, therefore, rely on their own creativity rather than on social or religious authority. An important voice in Existentialism. Joseph Stalin, Soviet ruler, dies. James Baldwin. *Go Tell It on the Mountain*. John Dewey, American philosopher and educator, dies. Sergey Prokofiev, Russian composer, dies. Dwight D. Eisenhower becomes President of the United States. Simone de Beauvoir. *The Second Sex*. Edmund Hillary and Tenzing Norkay become the first people to successfully scale Mount Everest.	
1954		The Methodist Church begins to ordain women. Billy Graham launches an evangelistic crusade in England, beginning his reputation as an international evangelist. The Second Assembly of the World Council of Church is	*Brown v. the Board of Education of Topeka* (United States Supreme Court decision). It declares that racially separate school facilities are inherently unequal. Segregation is declared unconstitutional. Disposal of radioactive waste begins to be a problem.	

Date	A. Theology, Doctrine, and Beliefs	B. People/Events	C. Wider Culture	D. Texts
1954 con't.		held in Evanston. Its theme is "Jesus Christ the Hope of the World." The Dead Sea Scrolls are purchased for the Hebrew University. The American "Pledge of Allegiance" is modified to include the phrase "under God."	A polio vaccine is invented. William Golding. *Lord of the Flies.* Sun Myung Moon founds the Unification Church. At its core is numerology, astrology, anticommunist rhetoric and Scientology.	
1955	*Tre Ore* (Italian for "three hours"). It is a traditional Good Friday afternoon devotion with prayers and meditations on the three-hour crucifixion of Christ.	Pierre Teilhard de Chardin, scientist and mystic, dies. "In God We Trust" is required by law to be on all United States coins and paper money. The law is a response to the feared incursion of communism. Pope Pius XII decrees that Good Friday's main service be held in the afternoon or evening. *Tre Ore* (Italian for "three hours") is almost entirely discontinued in the Roman Catholic Church. Robert Schuller holds the first meeting of the Garden Grove Community Church at the Orange Drive-in Theater in California. His congregation is seated in 50 cars. Francis August Schaeffer founds L'Abri, a study center in the Swiss Alps where he offers a Christian critique of modern culture.	Martin Luther King, Jr. organizes a boycott of the Montgomery, Alabama, transit system to force desegregation of the buses. The United States begins to send financial aid and advisors to the government of South Vietnam to help prevent the spread of communism throughout southeast Asia. Albert Einstein dies.	Pierre Teilhard de Chardin. *Phenomenon of Man.* A modern scientist's take on mystical theology, it states that the universe is evolving toward ever-greater levels of consciousness and toward union with God. Derrick Sherwin Bailey. *Homosexuality and the Western Tradition.* An Anglican priest argues against the traditional condemnation of homosexuality using a reinterpretation of biblical passages and evidence from new behavioral sciences. His work opens discussion of the topic in the U.S and Europe.
1956		Protestants denominations begin to see some merit in birth control. (late 1950s) The Presbyterian church begins to ordain women. The Methodist church grants women full clergy rights. Jim Elliot is martyred while serving as a missionary to the Aucas of Ecuador.	The first aerial hydrogen bomb is tested over the Bikini Atoll. The first nuclear power plant is built in the United States.	*Christianity Today* is first published. It helps unite evangelicals into a national movement.
1957		The first Cursillo in the United States is held Congregational Christian Churches merge with the Evangelical and Reformed Church to form the United Church of Christ. The Eucharistic fast in the Roman Catholic Church is declared to be three hours for food and alcohol and one hour for nonalcoholic drink. The Southern Christian Leadership Conference is organized as a vehicle of nonviolent protest of racial inequality.	Leonard Bernstein. *Westside Story.* Sputnik I and II, the first artificial satellites, are launched.	William F. Arndt and F. Wilbur Gingrich. *A Greek-English Lexicon of the New Testament and Other Early Christian Literature.* It is an English translation and adaptation of the fourth edition of Walter Bauer's ground-breaking lexicon.

Date	A. Theology, Doctrine, and Beliefs	B. People/Events	C. Wider Culture	D. Texts
1958		John XXIII becomes pope. Pope John XXIII removes the limit on the number of cardinals. The Lutheran Church founds the Congregation of the Servants of Christ, a distinctly Lutheran monastic order, in Michigan. Ralph Vaughan Williams, English composer and hymnodist, dies. The Lambeth Conference of the Anglican Communion maintains that both family planning and birth control using artificial means are acceptable under some circumstances.	Black students begin to attend all-white schools in the United States. The first laser is produced.	J. B. Phillips. *The New Testament in Modern English*. Produced by a vicar of the Church of England, it is a lively and idiomatic translation that at times approaches paraphrase. (1947–)
1959		Pope John XXIII makes St. Lawrence of Brindisi a doctor of the church.	The John Birch Society is founded as a far-right, cold-war organization named after a Baptist missionary killed by Chinese communists. The Fifth Republic begins in France.	The *Berkeley Bible* (*Berkeley Version in Modern English*) is published.
1960	Liberation theology. A movement with roots in ministry among Latin America's poorest class, it maintains that theology cannot be done without reference to socio-economic context. The Bible, the leading of the Spirit, and social analysis all inform the struggle for social liberation, which in turn informs the other three. It has a large influence on some feminist and African-American theologians. Key figures: Gustavo Gutierrez, Jose Miguez Bonino. (gains inertia in the early 1960s) The Charismatic movement (also known as Neo-Pentecostalism). It is characterized by an emphasis on spiritual gifts, especially those enumerated in 1 Cor. 12:8–11. It values glossolalia, but doesn't make Pentecostalism's connection between tongues and the baptism of the Spirit.	In the 1960s the charismatic movement spreads throughout most major American denominations, including the Roman Catholic Church. The archbishop of Canterbury, Geoffrey Francis Fisher, visits Pope John XXIII. He receives the first formal reception of any archbishop of Canterbury since the Reformation. The Commission on Brotherhood for the "Christians" and the "Disciples of Christ" begins to design a new and more formal organization uniting the two churches. David R. Wilkerson, a Pentecostal minister, founds Teen Challenge, a ministry to inner city young people, especially gang members. Over 150 centers are established in the United States and abroad. The Teen Challenge drug program becomes one of the most successful ever. Pat Robertson founds the Christian Broadcasting Network. Fundamentalists and evangelicals begin founding "Christian Day Schools" to teach basic education, Bible, and spiritual living. (1960s–present)	John F. Kennedy becomes President. He is the first Roman Catholic to occupy that office. The birth-control pill becomes available to women in the United States. (ca.)	Henry H. Halley. *Halley's Bible Handbook*. A "pocket handbook" supplying biblical and historical facts that enable to average reader to read and interpret the Bible.

Date	A. Theology, Doctrine, and Beliefs	B. People/Events	C. Wider Culture	D. Texts
1961	Christian reconstructionism. Believing that divinely revealed truth is not subject the hermeneutic constraint of historical context, reconstructionists follow all the details of Old Testament law. (early 1960s–present)	The Third Assembly of the World Council of Church is held in New Delhi. Its theme is "Jesus Christ the Light of the World." The first English-speaking Cursillo, a Roman Catholic spiritual growth movement, is held. The American Unitarian Association merges with Universalist Church of America to form the Unitarian Universalist Association. The International Missionary Council merges with the World Council of Churches.	Joseph Heller. *Catch-22*. Yuri A. Gagarin becomes the first person in space. American President John F. Kennedy commits the United States to landing a man on the moon and returning him safely to the earth "before the decade is out." NASA launches its *Mercury* program. (–1963) Bay of Pigs. The American CIA supervises Cuban expatriates' invasion of Castro's Cuba. The expedition is a failure. The Supreme Court of the United States refers to secular humanism as a nontheistic religion. Ernest Hemingway dies.	Gabriel Vahanian. *The Death of God*. It begins the death-of-God movement, which claims the traditional conception of God has lost relevance for modern society.
1962	The Roman Catholic Church begins a new focus on laity. Vatican II sanctions the vernacular liturgy and the laity receiving the cup. Groups of lay Catholic pentecostals and charismatics meet for worship, prayer, and mutual encouragement. Renewal movements such as Cursillo and Marriage Encounter seek to strengthen individual Christians and families. (–present)	The Consultation on Church Union is formed. Its purpose is ecumenical dialog between American churches that are "truly catholic, truly evangelical, and truly reformed." All Catholic cardinals must be bishops. (–present) After Vatican II, Rome downplays indulgences, partly in response to the Catholic-Protestant dialog. Pope John XXIII canonizes Martin de Porres. Twenty-first Ecumenical Council: Vatican II. It becomes the symbol of the Roman Catholic Church's willingness to live actively in the modern world. The council issues important documents on divine revelation, the role of the church in the world, liturgy, ecumenical relations, anti-Semitism, and religious freedom. (178 meetings, 1962–1965) • Officially restores the catechumenate. • Increases lay participation in the Mass. • Approves vernacular liturgy. Latin is no longer the sole language of liturgy in the Roman Catholic Church. • Revises the breviary and changes its name to Liturgy of the Hours.	Vladimir Nabokov. *Pale Fire*. Cuban missile crisis. Anthony Burgess. *A Clockwork Orange*. Rachel Carson. *Silent Spring*. One of the earliest works of the environmental movement. John Glenn orbits the earth in a Mercury space craft. He is the first human being to do so.	The Second Vatican Council. *Lumen Gentium*. One of several documents that refers to the Virgin Mary as Mediatrix. It declares that she "participates in the Mediation of Christ in a unique and singular manner. (ca.) The Reformed Church and Lutheran churches in the U.S.A. begin to hold official talks. They produce "Marburg Revisited," which concludes that there are ". . . no insuperable obstacles to pulpit and altar fellowship." (–1966) *Oxford Annotated Bible*. An ecumenical study Bible that annotates the *Revised Standard Version* with study notes composed by American and European scholars from most of the major ecumenical denominations. (revised: 1973)

Date	A. Theology, Doctrine, and Beliefs	B. People/Events	C. Wider Culture	D. Texts
1963		Paul VI becomes pope. The Roman Catholic Church allows concelebration at all services, not just ordinations. The Roman Catholic Church gives its approval to the practice of cremation. Atheist Madalyn Murray O'Hair sues the school board of her son's school. The case (*William J. Murray III v. John N. Curlett*) is brought before the United States Supreme Court, which dictates that Bible reading, prayer, and religious ceremony must be removed from public schools. Pat Robertson coins the term "700 Club" to refer to those people willing to make a financial commitment to his broadcast ministry. C. S. Lewis, author, Christian apologist, and literary scholar, dies.	John F. Kennedy is assassinated. Lyndon B. Johnson becomes President of the United States. The March on Washington. Over 250,000 people engage in a nonviolent protest. Martin Luther King delivers his "I Have a Dream" speech. The march is instrumental in bringing about the Civil Rights Act of 1964 and the Voting Rights Act two year later. Betty Friedan. *The Feminine Mystique*. Israeli archeologist Yigael Yadin conducts a full-scale archeological expedition at Masada. (–1965)	Pope John XXIII. *Pacem in Terris* (Latin: Peace on Earth). A papal encyclical condemning all war in the nuclear age.
1964		The Eucharistic fast in the Roman Catholic Church is declared to be one hour. The *700 Club* begins to air as a regular broadcast.	The United States Civil Rights Act of 1964 outlaws discrimination on the basis of race in public facilities. It also prohibits discrimination by unions and many employers. The Beatles tour the United States for the first time. Martin Luther King wins the Nobel Peace Prize.	
1965	Catholic traditionalists. A group of Roman Catholics who consider the changes of Vatican II to be heretical. Key figures: Marcel Lefebvre and the Priestly Fraternity of St. Pius X. Though Pope Paul VI suspends Lefebvre from priestly duty in 1976, the movement continues.	Paul Tillich, theologian, dies. The Roman Catholic Congregation of Rites permits the laity to receive the cup at communion. Communion by intinction is also permitted. Mutual excommunications between the Eastern and Western churches are canceled by Pope Paul VI and Ecumenical patriarch Athenagoras I. Oral Roberts University opens. Albert Schweitzer, German theologian and medical missionary, dies.	The U.S. Voting Rights Act of 1965 mandates that voting registrars may not apply different standards for white and black voting applicants. Ten *Gemini* space flights are made. (–1966) American troops begin to engage in combat in Vietnam. The International Society for Krishna Consciousness is founded in New York.	Pope Paul VI. *Nostra Aetate* (In Our Times). Section four of this Vatican II document acknowledges Judaism's place in Christianity's spiritual foundations and denounces anti-Semitism. It is an important document in easing the historical Jewish-Catholic mistrust. Pope Paul VI. *Mysterium Fidei* (Latin: Mystery of Faith) (papal encyclical). Pope Paul VI reasserts the doctrine of transubstantiation, which he perceives as being threatened by modern thought. Bill Bright. *Have You Heard of the Four Spiritual Laws?* Campus Crusade publishes this tract as an evangelism tool, especially for use among college students. Over a billion copies are eventually printed in every major language.

Date	A. Theology, Doctrine, and Beliefs	B. People/Events	C. Wider Culture	D. Texts
1966		The Roman Catholic Church announces that no new editions of the *Index of Prohibited Books* will be published. Existing editions are declared to be no longer binding. The penalty of excommunication for reading listed books is lifted. Emil Brunner, Swiss Protestant theologian, dies.	Kwanzaa is first celebrated. It is a seven-day winter festival observing African-American heritage. National Organization for Women (NOW) is founded by women attending the Third National Conference of the Commission on the Status of Women.	*The Jerusalem Bible.* This largely Catholic Bible is based on the scholarship of *La Bible de Jérusalem*, a French translation of the original Greek and Hebrew rendered with extensive notes. United Bible Societies. *Greek New Testament.* A largely Alexandrian text, compiled to meet the needs of Bible translators throughout the world.
1967		Pope Paul VI reaffirms that celibacy is a requirement for the Roman Catholic priesthood. The Catholic charismatic renewal movement begins. The Roman Catholic Church simplifies the indulgence system. Occasions for obtaining indulgences are limited, and time equivalents are dropped. Protestants becoming Roman Catholics are no longer required to abjure their prior Protestant beliefs. The Marriage Encounter program comes to the United States from Spain and South America. Pope Paul VI visits the Orthodox patriarch in Turkey. Fuller Theological Seminary removes the inerrancy clause from its doctrinal statement, creating a backlash in conservative Christianity. The good news movement, a Methodist renewal movement, draws together the evangelicals within the denomination.	Arab-Israeli War ("the Six-Day War"). Both sides mobilize. Egypt closes the Gulf of Aqaba to Israel. Israel strikes preemptively and in six days wins the West Bank, Golan Heights, Gaza Strip, the Sinai Peninsula, and the Old City of Jerusalem. Israel captures the Old City of Jerusalem and annexes it. (June 5–10) The first football Super Bowl is held. The *Apollo* space flights take people to the moon. (–1972) Benjamin Britten, one of the best known British composers from the post-World War II period, dies. The Supreme Court of the United States declares antimiscegenation laws (laws prohibiting interracial marriage or sexual relationship) unconstitutional.	*Confession of 1967.* The most recent doctrinal statement of the Presbyterian Church (U.S.A.), it is a compilation of the Nicene and Apostles Creeds, the Heidelberg Catechism, the Scottish Confession, the Second Helvetic Confession, the Westminster Confessions and Catechisms, and the Barmen Declaration. It stresses Christian reconciliation, but ends up causing dissention on the part of conservative Presbyterians who want stronger affirmations of the virgin birth and divinity of Christ. Conservatives also oppose the statement that the Bible is "the witness without parallel" but written in the "words of men."
1968	Jesus Movement. A youth-oriented Christian counterculture movement in the late 1960s and early 1970s.	The Christian Church (Disciples of Christ) approves the "Provisional Design" bringing the church to denominational maturity. Thomas Merton, Trappist monk and spiritual writer, dies. Karl Barth, Swiss neo-orthodox theologian, dies. The Wesleyan Methodist Church and the Pilgrim Holiness Church unite to form the Wesleyan Church, a Holiness denomination with Methodist roots. The United Methodist Church is created through the merger	Martin Luther King, Jr. is assassinated. Student unrest disrupts universities worldwide.	Pope Paul VI. *Humanae Vitae* (Latin: Of Human Life) (papal encyclical). It condemns all forms of birth control except the rhythm method. Three new Eucharistic prayers are developed by the Roman Catholic Congregation of Sacred Rites as alternatives to the traditional Canon of the Mass. They become available in the 1970 *Missale Romanum*.

Date	A. Theology, Doctrine, and Beliefs	B. People/Events	C. Wider Culture	D. Texts
1968 con't.		of the Evangelical United Brethren Church and the Methodist Church. The Fourth Assembly of the World Council of Church is held in Uppsala. Its theme is "Behold I Make All Things New." Liberation theology catches the attention of the Roman Catholic Church and the world at a conference of Latin American bishops in Columbia.		
1969		The Festival of Corpus Christi is transferred to the Sunday after Trinity Sunday in some countries, including the United States. The Roman Catholic Church replaces Ember days with days of prayer for specific causes. The Roman Catholic Church selects a group of saints for veneration throughout the church. Other groups are selected for local veneration. Women are admitted as lay readers in the Church of England. The Covenant Fellowship of Presbyterians is formed as a lay renewal movement supporting evangelism. The Lutheran-Episcopal Dialogue begins. The Association of Evangelical Lutheran Churches is formed. Leaders in the Christian Church/Churches of Christ (Independent) encourage conservative congregations to have their names removed from Christian Church (Disciples of Christ) rolls.	Richard M. Nixon becomes President of the United States. The voting age in Great Britain is lowered to 18. The crew of *Apollo 11* become the first human beings to walk on the moon. Kurt Vonnegut, Jr. *Slaughterhouse-Five.*	The *Missale Romanum* is revised.
1970	Shepherding movement. Mainly found in charismatic churches, this movement emphasizes spiritual guidance for every member of a congregation through a hierarchy of elders. Key organization: Christian Growth Ministries.	Pope Paul VI makes St. Teresa of Avila and St. Catherine of Siena Doctors of the Church. They are the first women to be so named. Edmund Campion is canonized by Pope Paul VI as one of the "Forty English Martyrs." Altar rails are no longer legally required in Roman Catholic Churches. The Episcopal Church declares the office of deaconess to be within the traditional diaconate.	Four students are killed by national guard troops during a student demonstration at Kent State University.	Hal Lindsey. *The Late Great Planet Earth.* A multi-million copy, best-selling eschatological work. It taps into the apocalyptic fervor of the Jesus Movement and also speaks to mainstream Christians. *The New English Bible.* A British translation instigated by the Church of Scotland, it is based on the Greek text and the most current scholarship without reference to the King James Version. It is one of the earliest to attempt

Date	A. Theology, Doctrine, and Beliefs	B. People/Events	C. Wider Culture	D. Texts
1970 con't.		Millions of United States Hispanics become Protestant. (–1990) The Billy Graham Center is founded on the Wheaton College Graduate School campus to collect and archive information about missions and evangelism. The Lutheran church begins to ordain women. The World Alliance of Reformed Churches is formed in Nairobi Kenya. Its purpose is to create harmony among Reformed, Presbyterian, and Congregationalist churches, to discuss theological issues, and to do relief work.		translation into a strictly modern idiom. The vernacular Mass is approved by American Catholic bishops. The *New American Bible*. The first Roman Catholic translation directly from Greek into modern English, its translators referred neither to previous translation nor to the Latin.
1971		The Vernacular Mass becomes obligatory in the Roman Catholic Church by direction of Pope Paul VI. (Karl Paul) Reinhold Niebuhr, American Protestant theologian, dies. Jerry Falwell founds the Liberty Baptist College.	Igor Stravinsky, modern neo-classical composer, dies. The Twenty-sixth Amendment of the United States Constitution lowers the voting age to 18. The term "bioethics" is coined to describe reflection on the moral issues surrounding modern medicine and biology.	*New American Standard Bible*. A revision of the *American Standard Version*, it is a reliable, though occasionally wooden, translation of the original languages. Kenneth N. Taylor. *The Living Bible*. Not intended to be an exact translation of the original texts, this colloquial English paraphrase of the American Standard Version has sold millions of copies. (First installment, *Living Letters*, is published: 1962. New Testament is completed: 1967) Jim Wallis begins publishing the *Post-American*, later renamed *Sojourners*, to question the "cultural conformity" of modern Christianity and to call Christians to a faith that is not afraid to speak for peace and social justice.
1972		Roman Catholic priests worldwide are no longer required to wear the tonsure. For some time, the custom has not been required in the United States, England, or other places where it is not a recognized symbol of priesthood. Lay readers, doorkeepers, and subdeacons are no longer considered ordained ministers in the Roman Catholic Church. They continue to perform their functions as regulated, unordained ministers. The Church of England allows members of other churches to receive communion in Anglican churches.	Burglars break in to the Watergate Hotel.	

Date	A. Theology, Doctrine, and Beliefs	B. People/Events	C. Wider Culture	D. Texts
1972 con't.		The Northern Baptist Convention is renamed the American Baptist Churches in the U.S.A.		
1973		Jews for Jesus is incorporated by Moishe Rosen as an evangelical mission to Jews. Billy Graham speaks to an audience of 1,100,000 people during his Korean crusade. The National Right to Life Committee, formerly a Catholic group, reorganizes as an autonomous, nonsectarian organization spurred by Roe vs. Wade. The Trinity Broadcasting Network is formed with the goal of building a worldwide television network. Jimmy Swaggart begins a weekly television show of music and preaching. The Conservative Presbyterian Church in America splits from the Presbyterian Church in the United States (Southern Presbyterians) over biblical authority, women's ordinations, and potential union with the Northern Presbyterians.	*Roe v. Wade.* The United States Supreme Court rules that the states may not interfere with a woman's right to an abortion. The last American troops leave Vietnam. *The Washington Post* first brings the Watergate scandal to the public's attention.	Gustavo Gutierrez. *A Theology of Liberation* (English edition). Liberation theology is introduced to America.
1974		Several retired bishops in the Protestant Episcopal Church in the U.S. ordain eleven women to the priesthood against Episcopal law. The International Congress on World Evangelism in Lausanne, Switzerland, is attended by 3,700 representatives of 150 countries. They plan for evangelism of the world by the year 2000. Worship and Doctrine Measure. The Church of England gains the right to make many decision regarding its worship practices without approval of the British government. Jim Bakker, a South Carolina evangelist, founds the PTL (Praise the Lord) television ministry. The first Vineyard church begins as a small Bible study in Los Angeles.	Gerald R. Ford becomes President of the United States. Alexander Solzhenitsyn. *Gulag Archipelago.* The American Psychiatric Association removes homosexuality from its list of mental disorders, saying "by itself [homosexuality] does not necessarily constitute a psychiatric disorder." The first woman reformed Jewish rabbi is ordained in the U.S.	The *Graduale Romanum,* the official Vatican collection of chant melodies, is revised in response to the changes mandated by Vatican II.

Date	A. Theology, Doctrine, and Beliefs	B. People/Events	C. Wider Culture	D. Texts
1975	Constructive Theology. It questions the authority of Scripture, traditional interpretive methods, and history. Constructive theology maintains the that process of constructing theology must be tailored to the given social context. (mid 1970s ca.)	The General Synod of the Anglican Church finds the ordination of women to be theologically unobjectionable. Four more women are ordained without official denominational sanction to the Episcopal priesthood. The previous eleven women's ordinations are officially invalidated. The first American-born saint, Elizabeth Ann Bayley Seton, is canonized. Speaking before a group of 10,000 charismatic Catholics in Rome, Pope Paul VI gives his blessing to the Catholic renewal (charismatic) movement. The Fifth Assembly of the World Council of Church is held in Nairobi. Its theme is "Jesus Christ Frees and Unites."	Dmitry Shostakovich, modern Russian composer, dies. Bill Gates co-founds Microsoft with Paul Allen. Together they develop a version of the BASIC computer programming language for the MITS Altair, the first personal computer.	
1976		Pope Paul VI suspends Marcel Lefebvre, leader of the Priestly Fraternity of St. Pius X, from priestly duty. His Catholic traditionalist movement continues. The Episcopal Church General Convention passes legislation allowing women's ordination. The previously ordained fifteen women priests are accepted. Rudolf Bultmann dies.	The first synthetic gene is developed. Martin Heidegger, German Existentialist philosopher, dies.	Harold Lindsell. *Battle for the Bible*. Lindsell looks at the issue of biblical inerrancy and how it has become less and less central to the doctrinal stance of evangelical colleges and seminaries. Karl Rahner. *Grundkurs des Glauben*. (*Foundations of Christian Faith*). The most systematic theological work of one of Roman Catholicism's most important twentieth century theologians. It is traditional Catholic/Thomistic theology reworked with an eye to Kant and Heidegger. (English translation 1978) *Good News Bible*. A translation of the Bible made by Robert G. Bratcher and the American Bible Society. It uses only common, modern English words and constructions. It is released with illustrations (line drawings) made by Annie Vallotton. (New Testament completed 1966)
1977		James Dobson founds Focus on the Family. The organization produces radio programs, magazines, books, films, and videos whose aim is the strengthening of Christian families.	The neutron bomb is tested. Jimmy Carter becomes President of the United States. *Star Wars* is released. *Roots* airs.	Hans Küng. *On Being a Christian*. Written by a Swiss Roman Catholic scholar and translated into English, it is widely read in the United States and Europe. Küng's writing continues to maintain influence even after he is censured by the Vatican over his beliefs on papal infallibility.

Date	A. Theology, Doctrine, and Beliefs	B. People/Events	C. Wider Culture	D. Texts
1978		John Paul I becomes pope. John Paul II becomes pope. The Congress of National Black Churches is formed as an African-American ecumenical organization run on a conciliar model. Jonestown, Guyana, is the site of a mass-suicide/murder of followers of Jim Jones, a former San Francisco minister.	The Camp David Agreement is forged between Israeli and Egyptian leaders	The International Council of Biblical Inerrancy develops "The Chicago Statement on Biblical Inerrancy," providing evangelicals with a clear statement of the doctrine. The Common Lectionary, a cycle of assigned Scripture readings adapted from the Roman Catholic lectionary, becomes common in mainline churches in the late '70s and early '80s. New York Bible Society. *New International Version* of the Bible. Its goal is to translate the Bible into idiomatic usage common to the entire English-speaking world. It is the version most commonly used in evangelical churches in the United States.
1979		Jerry Falwell founds the Moral Majority as a vehicle of conservative Christian political influence. (–1989) Most major denominations begin to discuss whether they will ordain either heterosexuals who have sex outside of marriage or homosexuals. (–1993) The Protestant Episcopal Church in the United States of America changes its name to the Episcopal Church in the United States of America. Mother Teresa is awarded the Nobel Peace Prize. Larry Jones founds Feed the Children, an international nonprofit Christian organization that provides food, clothes, and medical supplies to victims of disasters. The Evangelical Council for Financial Accountability is formed as a self-regulatory evangelical agency. Its member organizations are required to adhere to a strict code of financial disclosure and conduct.	Integrated circuit technology booms. (–1989) AIDS comes to the United States (first known case). The Iranian monarchy ends. The Shah of Iran is overthrown, and the Ayatollah Ruhollah Khomeini, a Shiite Muslim clergyman, assumes power.	Arthur Carl Piepkorn. *Profiles in Belief.* A standard reference work on denominations in America. *Book of Common Prayer.* The fourth American revision is released. The Church of England authorizes the use of the *Alternative Services Book* as a supplement to *The Book of Common Prayer.* It reflects modern study of historical liturgical development. Kurt Aland. *Novum Testamentum Graece* (Latin: Greek new Testament). Typically referred to as "Nestle-Aland," it employs essentially the same Greek text as the United Bible Societies edition but with Aland's extensive critical apparatus. Though based on Nestle's work, it is radically revised. (26th edition)
1980		Women make up twenty-one percent of all seminary students in the United States. Robert Schuller builds the Crystal Cathedral. Marjorie Matthews is the first woman elected to the Methodist Church's episcopacy. Oscar Arnulfo Romero, Roman Catholic archbishop of San	Jean Paul Sartre, French philosopher and playwright, dies.	Most major denominations update their hymnals to include inclusive language and to remove the archaic "King James" English. (1980s).

Date	A. Theology, Doctrine, and Beliefs	B. People/Events	C. Wider Culture	D. Texts
1980 con't.		Salvador, is assassinated while celebrating Mass. He was a leading proponent of liberation theology and opponent of El Salvador's dictator. Pope John Paul II proclaims Francis of Assisi patron saint of ecologists. The Lutheran Church–Missouri Synod urges its members to become organ donors. They are the first denomination to do so.		
1981			Ronald Reagan becomes President of the United States. John Updike. *Rabbit Is Rich.* Space Shuttle orbiter *Columbia*, the first of the shuttles, is launched.	
1982	Sanctuary movement. A network of mainline Protestant churches brings Central American refugees to the United States using both legal and illegal means. Their purpose is both to ensure the safety of the immigrants and to protest the injustice of American immigration laws. Key figures: John Fife, Jim Corbett.	Six churches in Tucson and San Francisco declare themselves sanctuary churches. The Sudan Interior Mission unites with the Andes Evangelical Mission to form SIM International, one of the largest evangelical foreign missions agencies.	Alice Walker. *The Color Purple.* Michael Jackson's *Thriller* becomes the best-selling album in history. The Equal Rights Amendment fails to be ratified by the required 38 states before the deadline. The Amendment does not become a part of the United States Constitution.	The World Council of Churches. *Baptism, Eucharist, and Ministry.* A statement of essential doctrine, which all member denominations can supposedly accept. *New King James Version* of the Bible. The Authorized Version is edited to increase readability for modern readers. *The Reader's Digest Bible.* The Bible condensed to sixty percent of its original length.
1983		Pope John Paul II makes the first-ever papal visit to a Lutheran church to celebrate the 500th anniversary of the birth of Martin Luther. The American Northern and Southern Presbyterian Churches are reunited. Imprimatur is mandated by Roman Catholic canon law. Translations of Scripture, theological textbooks, liturgical books, and catechisms must be approved by the bishop of the author or publisher's diocese. The imprimatur guarantees that the material does not conflict with official Catholic teaching. The Sixth Assembly of the World Council of Church is held in Vancouver. Its theme is "Jesus Christ the Life of the World." According to the *Codex Iuris Canonici,* excommunication in the Roman Catholic Church begins to be seen as a "medicinal" censure rather than a life-long penalty.	United States Marines and Army Rangers invade Grenada.	*Codex Iuris Canonici.* (Latin: Code of Canon Law) A complete revision of the 1917 code, taking into account the theological impact of Vatican II. (January 25) The National Council of Churches releases an "inclusive language lectionary." It is based on the *Revised Standard Version* of the Bible, but contains inclusive language and references to God as "Father and Mother" Elizabeth Schüssler Fiorenza. *In Memory of Her.* A reconstruction, based on New Testament texts, of the role women played in the life of the early Christian community.

Date	A. Theology, Doctrine, and Beliefs	B. People/Events	C. Wider Culture	D. Texts
1984			Jesse Jackson becomes the first African-American candidate for United States President.	
1985		The United States Supreme Court decides that providing government financial aid to parochial schools is a violation of the first amendment to the Constitution. Sixteen sanctuary workers are indicted on charges of giving aid to illegal immigrants. Eight are convicted and given suspended sentences.		
1986		Women may become deacons in the Church of England.	The space shuttle *Challenger* explodes shortly after launch, killing all aboard. One in two marriages in the United States ends in divorce.	
1987		Pat Robertson, host of the 700 Club and head of the Christian Broadcasting Network, begins an unsuccessful bid for the United States Republican Presidential nomination. The Presbyterian Church in the United States of America merges with the Presbyterian Church in the United States to form the Presbyterian Church (U.S.A.). (1983–) Joseph Campbell, authority on mythology, dies. Jim Bakker, head of the PTL Ministry, resigns in the midst of a sexual and financial scandal. Jerry Falwell takes over.	Toni Morrison. *Beloved.*	The Vatican releases "Instruction on Respect for Human Life in its Origin and on the Dignity of Procreation," one of the most comprehensive discussions issued by a church organization on bioethics.
1988		The Evangelical Lutheran Church in America (ELCA) is formed through the merger of the Lutheran Church in America, the American Lutheran Church, and the Association of Evangelical Lutheran Churches. Carbon-dating tests on the Shroud of Turin place its origins in the thirteenth or fourteenth century. Jimmy Swaggart is removed from the Assembly of God ministry after he admits to having sex with a prostitute. He loses 69 percent of his TV viewers and 72 percent of his college enrollment.		

Date	A. Theology, Doctrine, and Beliefs	B. People/Events	C. Wider Culture	D. Texts
1989		The Episcopal church's first woman bishop, Barbara C. Harris, is consecrated.	George Bush becomes President of the United States. The army of the People's Republic of China, acting at the behest of government leaders, kills thousands of pro-democracy protesters in Tiananmen Square, Beijing.	
1990		Bill McCartney and Dave Wardell found the Promise Keepers, which provides training and support for Christian men.	Iraq annexes Kuwait. The United States sends troops to participate in Operation Desert Shield. Leonard Bernstein, composer, conductor, pianist, dies.	*New Revised Standard Version.* A revision of the *Revised Standard Version of the Bible* by a multidenominational group of scholars. It employs inclusive language.
1991		The Seventh Assembly of the World Council of Church is held in Canberra. Its theme is "Come, Holy Spirit, Renew the Whole Creation."	The Commonwealth of Independent States is founded. It is composed of former Soviet republics. Operation Desert Storm. The United States leads a military operation to force Iraq to leave Kuwait.	A Brief Statement of Faith is added to the Presbyterian *Book of Confessions.*
1992		The Evangelical Lutheran Church in America, the Presbyterian Church (U.S.A.), the Reformed Church in America, and the United Church of Christ declare that they are in full communion with one another. April Ulring Larson becomes the first woman Lutheran bishop.	In *Lee v. Weisman,* the United States Supreme Court reaffirms that it is unconstitutional for public schools to sponsor prayer, even at special ceremonies such as graduations.	*The Catechism of the Catholic Church.* The first "universal catechism" in almost four centuries, it is a reference work for Catholic bishops seeking to include the teachings of Vatican II in their catechesis.
1993		Archeologists in Israel find a stone with the inscription "King of Israel" and "House of David" in Aramaic. Norman Vincent Peale, American religious leader and "positive thinker," dies. David Koresh's Branch Davidians commit suicide by setting fire to their compound in Waco, Texas, after a fifty-one-day standoff with federal law enforcement personnel.	Bill Clinton becomes President of the United States.	
1994		The Church of England begins to ordain women to the priesthood. The Vatican officially recognizes Israel. Randy Clark's revival meetings at a Toronto Vineyard church produce ecstatic experiences—crying, falling, uncontrollable laughing and shaking— that participants attribute to the Holy Spirit. The "Toronto Experience" draws over 1.2 million people for nightly meetings over the next four years.		

Date	A. Theology, Doctrine, and Beliefs	B. People/Events	C. Wider Culture	D. Texts
1995		Jehovah's Witnesses reexamine the Scriptures that prompted them to predict Armageddon within a generation of 1914. "Generation" is taken to mean a historical era of undetermined length. Thirty-two African-American churches in the southern United States are bombed or set afire in the worst outbreak of arson since the civil rights movement. (–1996) Retired Bishop of the Episcopal Church, Walter Righter, is brought before an ecclesiastical court on charges of heresy (specifically of teaching false doctrine and violating his ordination vows) for ordaining a noncelibate homosexual deacon. He is acquitted.		
1996		Archeologists at Masada unearth a wine jug inscribed with the name of King Herod. It is the first object ever found bearing the name of the Herod of the Gospels. Religious renewal grows out of increased religious liberty in Russia. In less than six years, 340 monasteries, 10,000 parish churches, and 14 seminaries open. (1990–)		
1997	Churches have been springing up across the United States over the last five to ten years that emphasize casualness, expressiveness, and independence from mainline denominations.	The Church of England begins placing television commercials to try to counteract falling membership. Mother Teresa dies. Roman Catholic sister, founder of the Missionaries of Charity, and Nobel laureate, she is best known for her work among "the poorest of the poor" in Calcutta, India.		
1998	Megachurches, typically non-denominational churches with large memberships, spring up across the U.S., especially in suburban neighborhoods. They see their role as not just meeting religious needs but providing a social and cultural center as well.	Richard Seed, a U.S. physicist, announces he will begin work on producing a cloned human being. Although Seed sees no conflict between his work and his Methodist beliefs, Methodist churches in both the U.S. and the United Kingdom, along with many other churches, condemn his proposals. Pope John Paul II visits Cuba. His visit includes a meeting with communist leader Fidel Castro.	William Jefferson Clinton becomes the second president in United States history to be impeached.	

Appendix *x*

Overview Charts
of Church History

Church history timeline

Era labels:
- 30–70 Primitive Church
- 70–135 Early Sub-Apostolic Church
- 135–325 Ante-Nicene Church
- 326–451 Post-Nicene Church
- 451–1054 Early Medieval Church
- 1054–1378 Medieval Church
- 1378–1517 Late Medieval Church
- 1517–1598 Reformation
- 1600–1800 Early Modern Church
- 1800–Present Modern Church

Events:
- 30 Jesus is crucified
- 47-57 Paul's missionary journeys
- 70 Jerusalem falls
- 280-337 Constantine
- 313 Edict of Milan
- 325–381 Nicene Creed
- 354–430 Augustine of Hippo
- 397 Latin Vulgate
- 476 Fall of the Roman Empire
- 480-547 Benedict of Nursia
- 500–1000 Christianity is established in W. Europe
- 540–604 Gregory the Great
- 570–632 Mohammed
- 600 Gregorian Sacramentary
- 742–814 Charlemangne
- 800 Alcuin's Missal
- 1033–1109 Anselm of Canterbury
- 1054 Great East–West Schism
- 1066 Norman Conquest of England
- 1095–1291 Crusades
- 1181–1226 Francis of Assisi
- 1225–1274 Thoma Aquinas
- 1232 Inquisition begins
- 1320–1384 John Wycliffe
- 1348–1350 Black Death
- 1378–1417 Rome–Avignon schism
- 1434 Movable type is invented
- 1483–1546 Martin Luther
- 1509–1564 John Calvin
- 1516 Erasmus' Greek New Testament
- 1611 King James Bible
- 1726 First Great Awakening begins
- 19–20th cent. Liberalism
- 1914–1918 WW I
- 1939–1945 WW II
- 1943–present Evangelicalism
- 1962–1965 Vatican II

Periods:
- 27 B.C.E–476 C.E. Roman Empire
- 476–1050 Early Middle Ages
- 1050–1350 High Middle Ages
- 1350–1500 Renaissance
- 1500–1650 High Renaissance
- 1650–1800 The Enlightenment

Timeline scale: 100 200 300 400 500 600 700 800 900 1000 1100 1200 1300 1400 1500 1600 1700 1800 1900

228

30–70 Primitive Church   135–325 Ante-Nicene Church
70–135 Early Sub-Apostolic Church

48–135 Jewish vs. Gentile Christianity

130–? Gnosticism

225–647 Christological controversies

?–100 Clement of Rome
69–155 Polycarp

100–165 Justin Martyr

251–356 Antony of Egypt

160–225 Tertullian

51–110 New Testament
120 Didache
100 Gospel of Thomas

150 Marcion's canon

200 Canon selection is complete
175 Apostolic succession lists

325–381 Nicene Creed

30 Jesus is crucified

47 Council of Jerusalem

47–57 Paul's missionary journeys

325 Council of Nicea

249–305 Persecutions

249–251 Decian
257–260 Valerianic

303–305 Diocletian

70 Jerusalem falls
70 Temple is destroyed

77 Josephus' Jewish War

64 Rome burns
79 Vesuvius erupts

220–269 Goths invade Europe

280–337 Constantine
312 Victory at the Milvian bridge

313 Edict of Milan

50   100   150   200   250   300

27 B.C.E.–476 C.E. Roman Empire

229

326–451 Post-Nicene Church

451–1054 Early Medieval Church

4th–5th century Donatism

358–394 Cappadocian fathers

400–529 Pelagianism

530 Monophysite

255–647 Christological controversies

296–373 Athanasius

354–430 Augustine of Hippo

330–379 Basil the Great

339–397 Ambrose of Milan

342–420 Jerome

347–407 John Chrysostom

325 Council of Nicea

325–381 Nicene Creed

?–460 Patrick

480–547 Benedict of Nursia

540–604 Gregory the Great

428 Athanasian Creed

384 *Egeria's Travels*

397 Latin Vulgate

423 Rule of St. Augustine

451 Definition of Chalcedon

520 Boethius' *Consolation of Philosophy*

529–540 Rule of St. Benedict

326 Church of the Holy Sepulchre is built

325 Council of Nicea

381 Council of Constantinople

431 Council of Ephesus

451 Council of Chalcedon

511 Catholic Christianity is established in Gaul

395 Empire is divided into East and West

410–711 Visigoths invade Europe

429–533 Vandals storm the Mediterranean

440 Angles and Saxons invade Britain

476 Fall of the Roman Empire

570–632 Mohammed

568–573 Lombards invade Italy

602 Persians invade Rome

| 350 | 400 | 450 | 500 | 550 | 600 |

27 B.C.E–476 C.E. Roman Empire

476–1050 Early Middle Ages

451–1054 Early Medieval Church

540–604 Gregory the Great

673–735 Bede

680–754 Boniface

725–842 Iconoclastic controversies

731 Bede's *Ecclesiastical History of England*

600 Gregorian Sacramentary

800 Alcuin's Missal

789 Roman Rite is compulsory in the West

1033–1109 Anselm of Canterbury

1025–1028 Norway is converted

988 Russia is Christianized

1054 Great East–West Schism

830 Christianity reaches Sweden

602 See of Canterbury is founded

754 Germany is Christianized

664 Synod of Whitby

570–632 Mohammed

742–814 Charlemagne

602 Persians invade Rome

637–732 Arabs storm the Mediterranean

793–1016 Vikings invade Europe

1000 Leif Ericsson discovers America

Late 8th through early 9th century
Carolingian Renaissance

850 Moldboard plow and harness are invented

1000–1140 Romanesque architecture

975 Arab arithmetic comes to Europe

800–1806 Holy Roman Empire

476–1050 Early Middle Ages

650	700	750	800	850	900	950	1000	1050

1054–1378 Medieval Church

1059–1109 Investiture Controversy

1078–1500 Scholasticism

1033–1109 Anselm of Canterbury

1170–1221 Dominic

1079–1142 Peter Abelard

1181–1226 Francis of Assisi 1347–1380 Catherine of Siena

1090–1153 Bernard of Clairvaux

1098–1179 Hildegard of Bingen

1225–1274 Thomas Aquinas

1260–1327 Meister Eckhart

1100–1160 Peter Lombard

1265–1308 Johannes Duns

1118–1170 Thomas à Becket

1320–1384 John Wycliffe

1320 Dante's *Divine Comedy*

1155 Peter Lombard's *Sentences*

1265 Thomas Aquinas' *Summa Theologica*   1386 Chaucer's *Canterbury Tales*

1098 Anselm's *Cur Deus Homo*

1150 *Glossa ordinaria*

14th cent. Conciliar theory

1342–1417 Juliana of Norwich

1309–1376 Avignon papacy

1378–1417 Rome–Avignon schism

1054 Great East-West Schism

1237 Sarum Rite

1095–1291 Crusades

1231 Inquisition begins

1210 Franciscan Order

1216 Dominican Order

1084 Carthusian Order

1245–1247 Council of Lyons I & II

1179 Lateran Council III

1123 Lateran Council

1215 Lateran Council IV

1311–1313 Council of Vienne

1139 Lateran Council II

12th–13th cent. Jewish Kabbala

1180 Maimonides' *Mishneh Torah*

Mid 14th cent. Ockham's razor

1275–1292 Marco Polo is in China

1348–1350 Black Death

1291 Fall of Acre

1337–1453 Hundred Years' War

1105 Rashi dies

1187 Saladin takes Jerusalem

1214–1223 Genghis Khan's invasions

1066 Norman Conquest of England

1000–1140 Romanesque architecture

1140–1600 Gothic architecture

1050   1100   1150   1200   1250   1300   1350   1400

1050–1350 High Middle Ages

1350–1500 Renaissance

1378–1517 Late Medieval Church   1517–1598 Reformation

14th cent. Conciliar theory

1347–1380 Catherine of Siena   1412–1431 Joan of Arc

1320–1384 John Wycliffe

1342–1417 Juliana of Norwich

     1372–1415 John Huss

1489–1556 Thomas Cranmer

1469–1536 Erasmus   1491–1556 Ignatius Loyola

1483–1546 Martin Luther

1484–1531 Ulrich Zwingli

1509–1564 John Calvin

1513–1572 John Knox

1517 Luther's "Ninety-five Theses"

1516 Erasmus' Greek New Testament

1478–1834 Spanish Inquisition

1519 Zurich Reformation begins

1520 Anabaptist movement begins

1534 Jesuit Society is founded

1534 English Act of Supremacy

1541 Calvin establishes Geneva theocracy

1564–1642 Galileo

1378–1417 Rome–Avignon schism

1475–1564 Michelangelo

1452–1519 Leonardo

1473–1543 Copernicus

1492 Columbus reaches America

1434 Movable type is invented

1337–1453 Hundred Years' War

Mid 14th cent. Ockham's razor

1350   1400   1450   1500   1550   1600

1350–1500 Renaissance   1500–1650 High Renaissance

1600–1800 Early Modern Church

1624–1850 Deism

17th cent.–present Pietism

1624–1691 George Fox

1635–1750 Phillipp Spener

1703–1791 John Wesley

1703–1758 Jonathan Edwards

1715–1770 George Whitefield

1761–1834 William Carey

1468–1834 F. Schleiermacher

1678 *Pilgrim's Progress*

1726 First Great Awakening begins

Mid 18th cent. major denominations establish American organizations

1772 Circuit riders begin their ministry

1611 King James Bible

1593 English separatists are called Puritans

1650 Quakers are founded

1620 Pilgrims land on Plymouth Rock

1600   **1650**   **1700**   **1750**   **1800**

1596–1650 Descartes

1606–1669 Rembrandt

1642–1726 Newton

1658–1750 Bach

1632–1704 Locke

1640–1658 English (Puritan) Revolution

1618–1648 Thirty Years' War

1618 Kepler's laws

1564–1642 Galileo

1711–1776 Hume

1770–1827 Beethoven

1742–1804 Kant

1756–1791 Mozart

1712 Steam engine

1775–1783 American Revolution

1789–1799 French Revolution

Mid 18th–early 20th cent. Industrial Revolution

1650–1800 The Enlightenment

1800–present Modern Church

19th cent. Restoration Movement

19th–20th cent. Liberalism/Modernism

1895–present Fundamentalism

1901–present Pentecostalism

1860s–ca. 1900 Holiness Movement

1943–present Evangelicalism

1761–1834 William Carey

1768–1834 F. Schleiermacher

1801–1890 John Henry

1813–1883 Søren Kierkegaard

1886–1968 Karl Barth

1918– Billy Graham

1800–1830s Second Great Awakening

1800 Society of Biblical Literature

1825 American Unitarian Association

1826 Temperance movement begins

1830 Mormonism

1865 First faith mission is formed

1865 Salvation Army

1869–1870 Vatican I

1938 Neo-orthodoxy comes to the U.S.

1947 Dead Sea Scrolls are discovered

1948 WCC is formed

1962–1965 Vatican II

1770–1831 Hegel

1809–1882 Darwin

1818–1883 Marx

1856–1939 Freud

1879–1955 Einstein

1889–1976 Heidegger

1802 Atomic theory

1869 U.S. transcontinental railway

1876 Telephone

1893 Automobile

1903 Airplane

1914–1918 WWI

1939–1945 WWII

1950–1953 Korean War

1961–1973 Vietnam War (American involvement)

1800   **1850**   **1900**   **1950**

Appendix y

Genealogy Charts

Chart #1: Genealogy of the Creeds

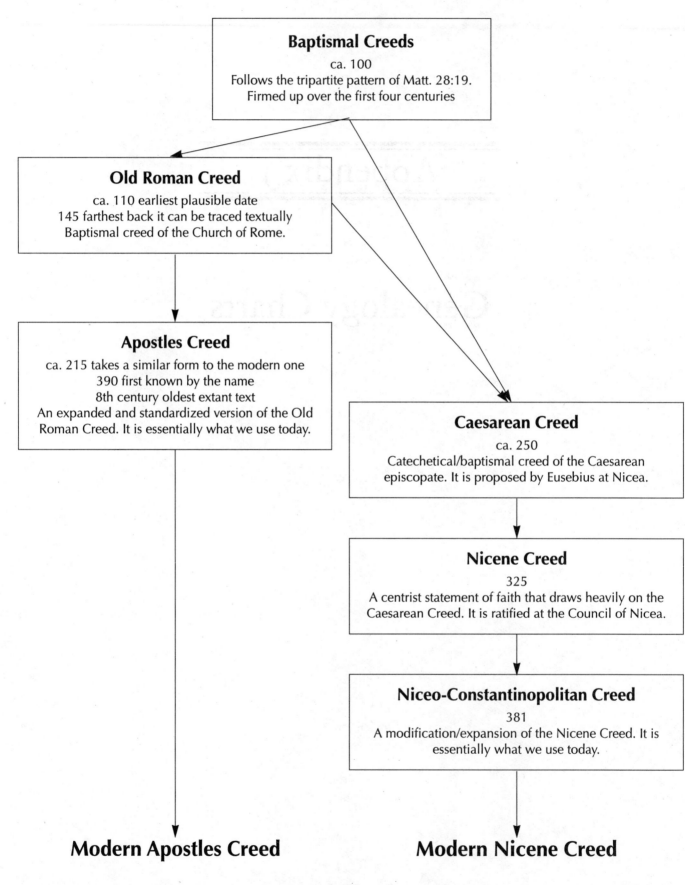

Baptismal Creeds

ca. 100
Follows the tripartite pattern of Matt. 28:19.
Firmed up over the first four centuries

Old Roman Creed

ca. 110 earliest plausible date
145 farthest back it can be traced textually
Baptismal creed of the Church of Rome.

Apostles Creed

ca. 215 takes a similar form to the modern one
390 first known by the name
8th century oldest extant text
An expanded and standardized version of the Old
Roman Creed. It is essentially what we use today.

Caesarean Creed

ca. 250
Catechetical/baptismal creed of the Caesarean
episcopate. It is proposed by Eusebius at Nicea.

Nicene Creed

325
A centrist statement of faith that draws heavily on the
Caesarean Creed. It is ratified at the Council of Nicea.

Niceo-Constantinopolitan Creed

381
A modification/expansion of the Nicene Creed. It is
essentially what we use today.

Modern Apostles Creed

Modern Nicene Creed

Chart #2: Genealogy of the King James Version

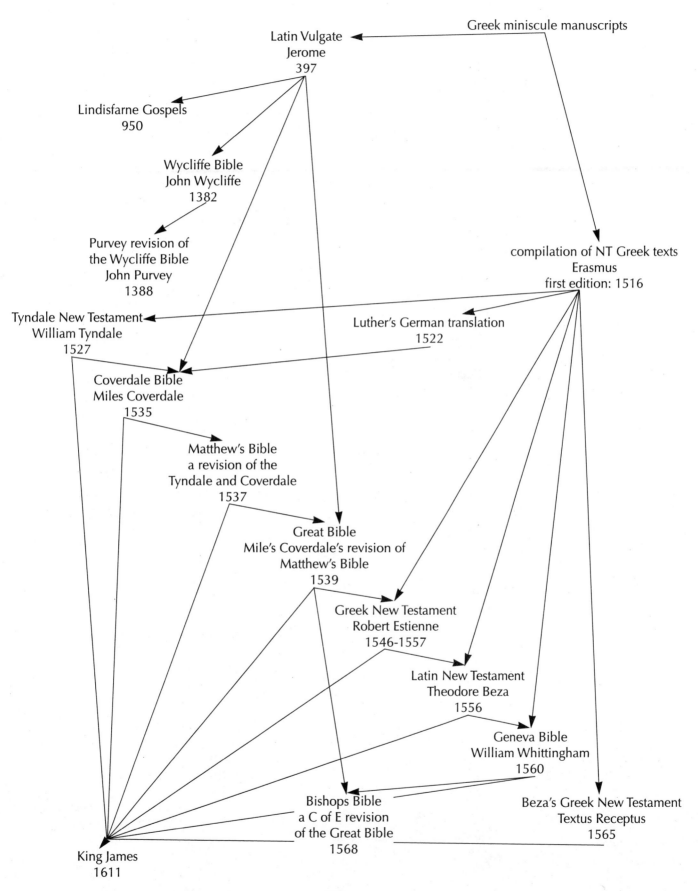

Greek miniscule manuscripts

Latin Vulgate
Jerome
397

Lindisfarne Gospels
950

Wycliffe Bible
John Wycliffe
1382

Purvey revision of
the Wycliffe Bible
John Purvey
1388

compilation of NT Greek texts
Erasmus
first edition: 1516

Tyndale New Testament
William Tyndale
1527

Luther's German translation
1522

Coverdale Bible
Miles Coverdale
1535

Matthew's Bible
a revision of the
Tyndale and Coverdale
1537

Great Bible
Mile's Coverdale's revision of
Matthew's Bible
1539

Greek New Testament
Robert Estienne
1546-1557

Latin New Testament
Theodore Beza
1556

Geneva Bible
William Whittingham
1560

Bishops Bible
a C of E revision
of the Great Bible
1568

Beza's Greek New Testament
Textus Receptus
1565

King James
1611

Chart #3: Genealogy of Modern Bible Versions

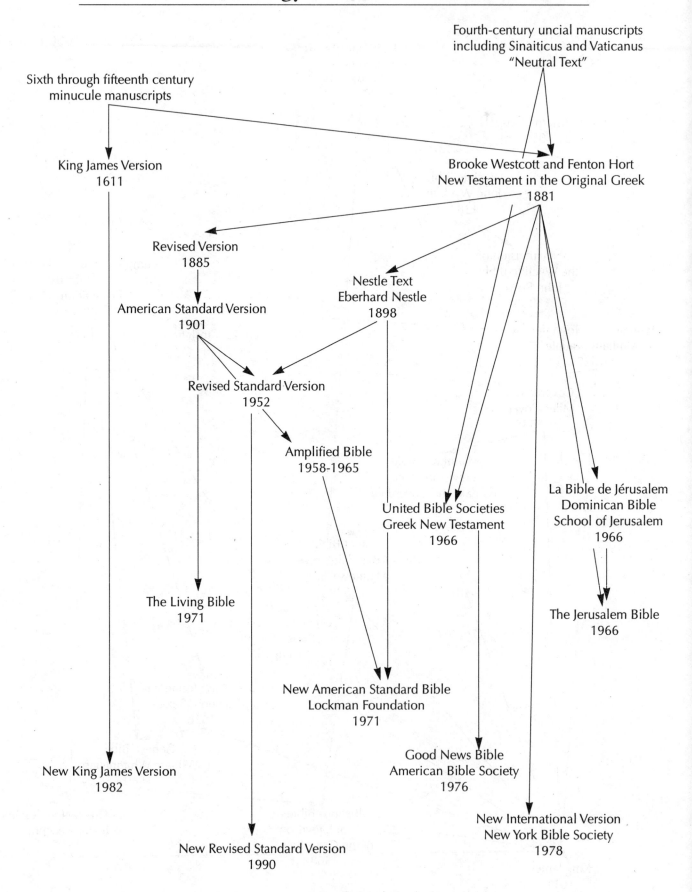

Fourth-century uncial manuscripts
including Sinaiticus and Vaticanus
"Neutral Text"

Sixth through fifteenth century
minucule manuscripts

King James Version
1611

Brooke Westcott and Fenton Hort
New Testament in the Original Greek
1881

Revised Version
1885

Nestle Text
Eberhard Nestle
1898

American Standard Version
1901

Revised Standard Version
1952

Amplified Bible
1958-1965

United Bible Societies
Greek New Testament
1966

La Bible de Jérusalem
Dominican Bible
School of Jerusalem
1966

The Living Bible
1971

The Jerusalem Bible
1966

New American Standard Bible
Lockman Foundation
1971

New King James Version
1982

Good News Bible
American Bible Society
1976

New International Version
New York Bible Society
1978

New Revised Standard Version
1990

Chart #4: Genealogy of the Western Liturgical Rite

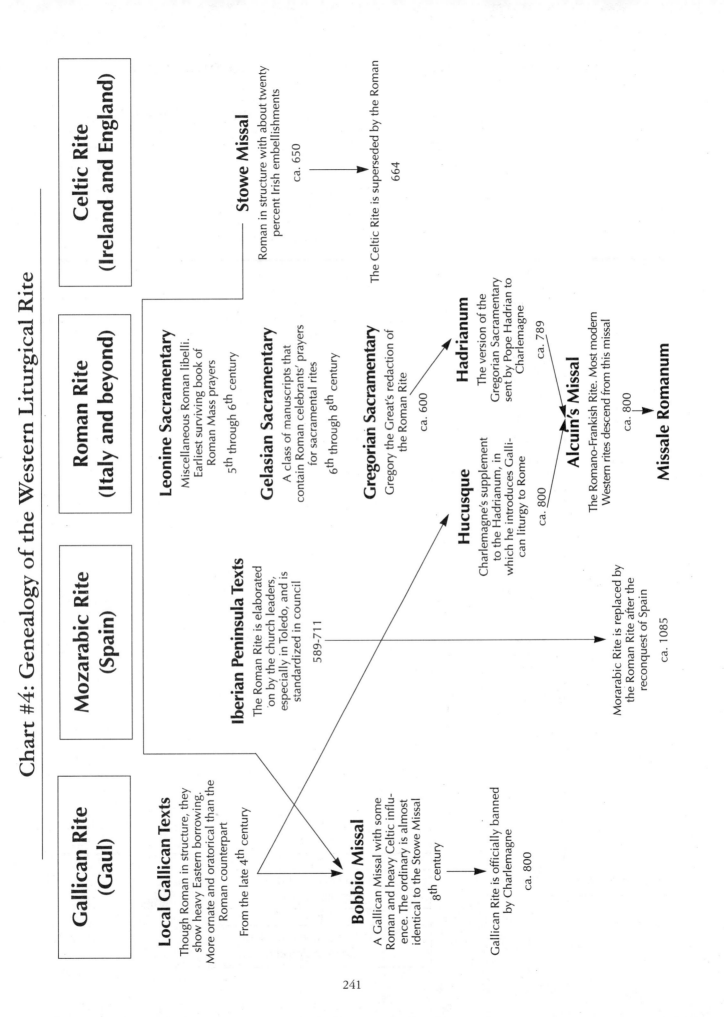

Gallican Rite (Gaul)

Mozarabic Rite (Spain)

Roman Rite (Italy and beyond)

Celtic Rite (Ireland and England)

Local Gallican Texts

Though Roman in structure, they show heavy Eastern borrowing. More ornate and oratorical than the Roman counterpart

From the late 4th century

Iberian Peninsula Texts

The Roman Rite is elaborated on by the church leaders, especially in Toledo, and is standardized in council

589-711

Leonine Sacramentary

Miscellaneous Roman libelli. Earliest surviving book of Roman Mass prayers

5th through 6th century

Gelasian Sacramentary

A class of manuscripts that contain Roman celebrants' prayers for sacramental rites

6th through 8th century

Gregorian Sacramentary

Gregory the Great's redaction of the Roman Rite

ca. 600

Stowe Missal

Roman in structure with about twenty percent Irish embellishments

ca. 650

The Celtic Rite is superseded by the Roman

664

Hadrianum

The version of the Gregorian Sacramentary sent by Pope Hadrian to Charlemagne

ca. 789

Hucusque

Charlemagne's supplement to the Hadrianum, in which he introduces Gallican liturgy to Rome

ca. 800

Alcuin's Missal

The Romano-Frankish Rite. Most modern Western rites descend from this missal

ca. 800

Missale Romanum

Mozarabic Rite is replaced by the Roman Rite after the reconquest of Spain

ca. 1085

Bobbio Missal

A Gallican Missal with some Roman and heavy Celtic influence. The ordinary is almost identical to the Stowe Missal

8th century

Gallican Rite is officially banned by Charlemagne

ca. 800

Chart #5: Genealogy of the Book of Common Prayer

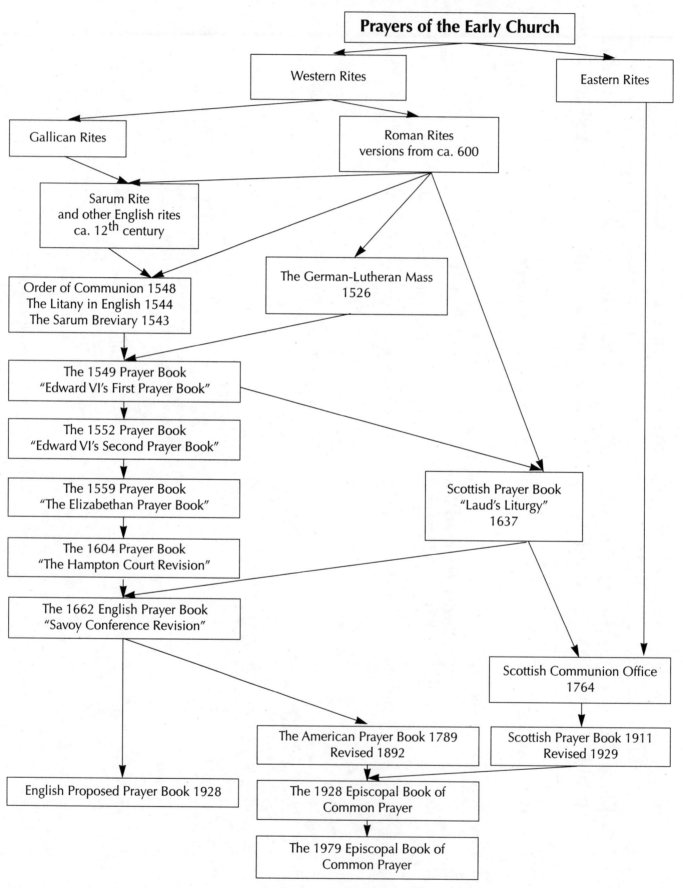

Prayers of the Early Church

Western Rites

Eastern Rites

Gallican Rites

Roman Rites
versions from ca. 600

Sarum Rite
and other English rites
ca. 12th century

Order of Communion 1548
The Litany in English 1544
The Sarum Breviary 1543

The German-Lutheran Mass
1526

The 1549 Prayer Book
"Edward VI's First Prayer Book"

The 1552 Prayer Book
"Edward VI's Second Prayer Book"

The 1559 Prayer Book
"The Elizabethan Prayer Book"

Scottish Prayer Book
"Laud's Liturgy"
1637

The 1604 Prayer Book
"The Hampton Court Revision"

The 1662 English Prayer Book
"Savoy Conference Revision"

Scottish Communion Office
1764

The American Prayer Book 1789
Revised 1892

Scottish Prayer Book 1911
Revised 1929

English Proposed Prayer Book 1928

The 1928 Episcopal Book of
Common Prayer

The 1979 Episcopal Book of
Common Prayer

Appendix z

Denominational Charts

Chart #1: Reformation Churches

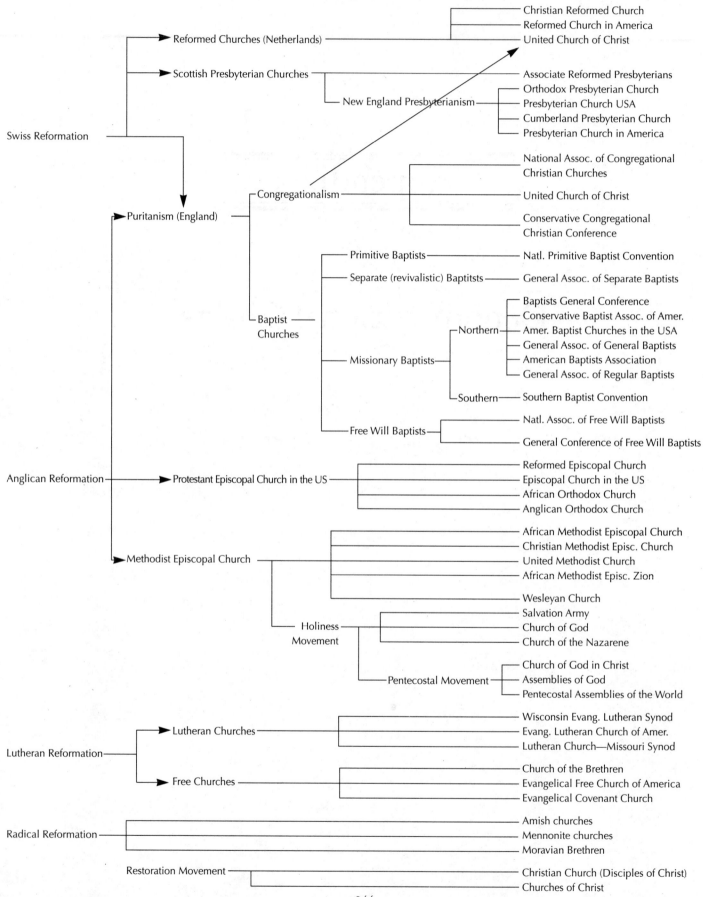

Swiss Reformation

Reformed Churches (Netherlands) —— Christian Reformed Church
—— Reformed Church in America
—— United Church of Christ

Scottish Presbyterian Churches —— Associate Reformed Presbyterians

New England Presbyterianism —— Orthodox Presbyterian Church
—— Presbyterian Church USA
—— Cumberland Presbyterian Church
—— Presbyterian Church in America

Puritanism (England)

Congregationalism —— National Assoc. of Congregational Christian Churches
—— United Church of Christ
—— Conservative Congregational Christian Conference

Baptist Churches

Primitive Baptists —— Natl. Primitive Baptist Convention

Separate (revivalistic) Baptitsts —— General Assoc. of Separate Baptists

Missionary Baptists —— Northern —— Baptists General Conference
—— Conservative Baptist Assoc. of Amer.
—— Amer. Baptist Churches in the USA
—— General Assoc. of General Baptists
—— American Baptists Association
—— General Assoc. of Regular Baptists

—— Southern —— Southern Baptist Convention

Free Will Baptists —— Natl. Assoc. of Free Will Baptists
—— General Conference of Free Will Baptists

Anglican Reformation

Protestant Episcopal Church in the US —— Reformed Episcopal Church
—— Episcopal Church in the US
—— African Orthodox Church
—— Anglican Orthodox Church

Methodist Episcopal Church —— African Methodist Episcopal Church
—— Christian Methodist Episc. Church
—— United Methodist Church
—— African Methodist Episc. Zion
—— Wesleyan Church

Holiness Movement —— Salvation Army
—— Church of God
—— Church of the Nazarene

Pentecostal Movement —— Church of God in Christ
—— Assemblies of God
—— Pentecostal Assemblies of the World

Lutheran Reformation

Lutheran Churches —— Wisconsin Evang. Lutheran Synod
—— Evang. Lutheran Church of Amer.
—— Lutheran Church—Missouri Synod

Free Churches —— Church of the Brethren
—— Evangelical Free Church of America
—— Evangelical Covenant Church

Radical Reformation —— Amish churches
—— Mennonite churches
—— Moravian Brethren

Restoration Movement —— Christian Church (Disciples of Christ)
—— Churches of Christ

244

Chart #2: Lutheranism

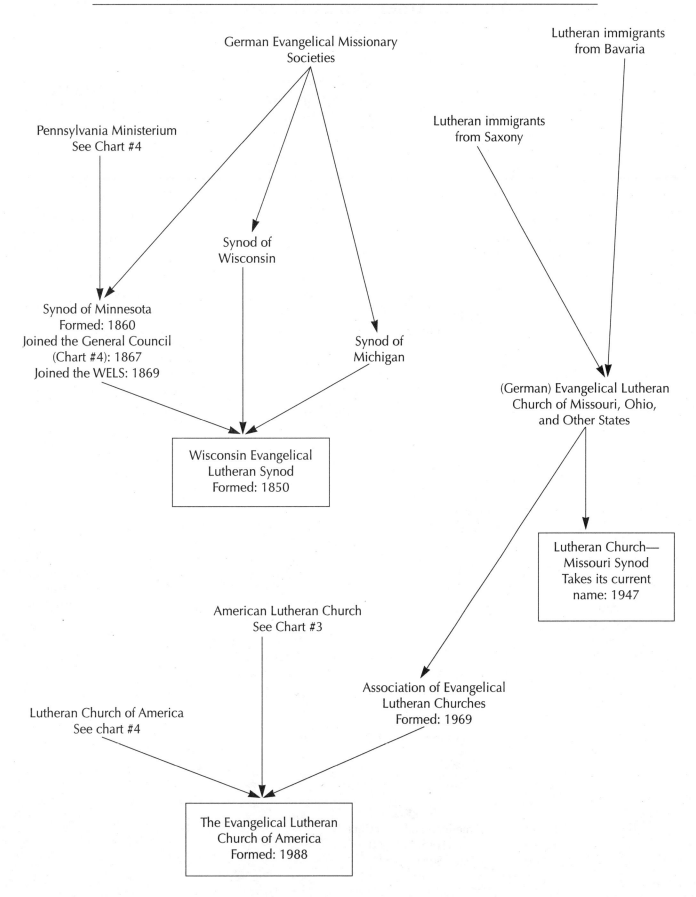

German Evangelical Missionary
Societies

Lutheran immigrants
from Bavaria

Pennsylvania Ministerium
See Chart #4

Lutheran immigrants
from Saxony

Synod of
Wisconsin

Synod of Minnesota
Formed: 1860
Joined the General Council
(Chart #4): 1867
Joined the WELS: 1869

Synod of
Michigan

(German) Evangelical Lutheran
Church of Missouri, Ohio,
and Other States

Wisconsin Evangelical
Lutheran Synod
Formed: 1850

Lutheran Church—
Missouri Synod
Takes its current
name: 1947

American Lutheran Church
See Chart #3

Association of Evangelical
Lutheran Churches
Formed: 1969

Lutheran Church of America
See chart #4

The Evangelical Lutheran
Church of America
Formed: 1988

Chart #3: American Lutheran Church

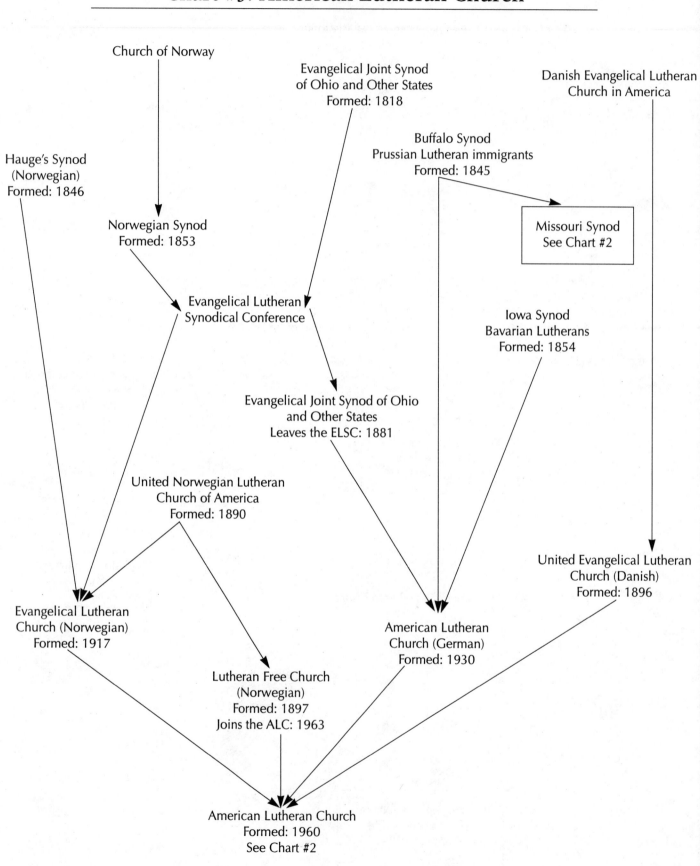

Church of Norway

Evangelical Joint Synod
of Ohio and Other States
Formed: 1818

Danish Evangelical Lutheran
Church in America

Hauge's Synod
(Norwegian)
Formed: 1846

Buffalo Synod
Prussian Lutheran immigrants
Formed: 1845

Norwegian Synod
Formed: 1853

Missouri Synod
See Chart #2

Evangelical Lutheran
Synodical Conference

Iowa Synod
Bavarian Lutherans
Formed: 1854

Evangelical Joint Synod of Ohio
and Other States
Leaves the ELSC: 1881

United Norwegian Lutheran
Church of America
Formed: 1890

United Evangelical Lutheran
Church (Danish)
Formed: 1896

Evangelical Lutheran
Church (Norwegian)
Formed: 1917

American Lutheran
Church (German)
Formed: 1930

Lutheran Free Church
(Norwegian)
Formed: 1897
Joins the ALC: 1963

American Lutheran Church
Formed: 1960
See Chart #2

Chart #4: Lutheran Church in America

Evangelical Lutheran Ministerium in
North America. 1748
Renamed: Pennsylvania Ministerium

Pennsylvania Ministerium
Withdraws: 1823

The General Synod of the Evangelical
Lutheran Church in the United States
Formed: 1820

Missouri Synod
See Chart #5

The General Council of the Evangelical
Lutheran Church in North America
Formed: 1820

The southern synods separate: 1863
Named: The United Synod of the
Evangelical Lutheran Church in the
South. 1886

Augustana Lutheran Church
An organization of
Swedish immigrants. Formed: 1860
Becomes independent: 1918

Evangelical Lutheran
Synodical Conference
Formed: 1872

Finnish Evangelical
Lutheran Church
(Suomi Synod)
Formed: 1890

American Lutheran Church
An organization of Danish immigrants.
Formed: 1872

United Lutheran
Church in America
Formed: 1918

Lutheran Church in America
Formed: 1962
See Chart #2

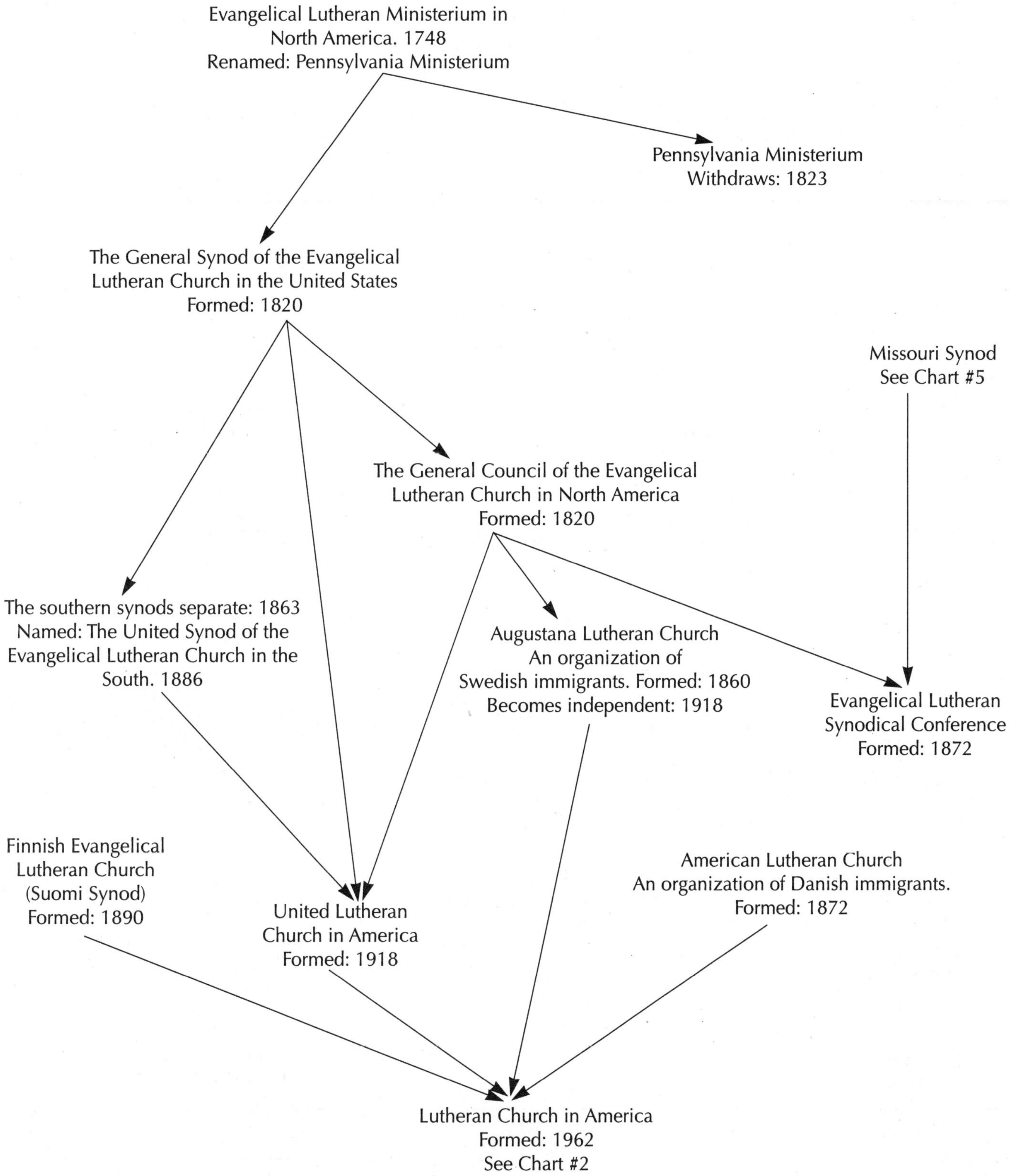

Chart #5: Presbyterianism

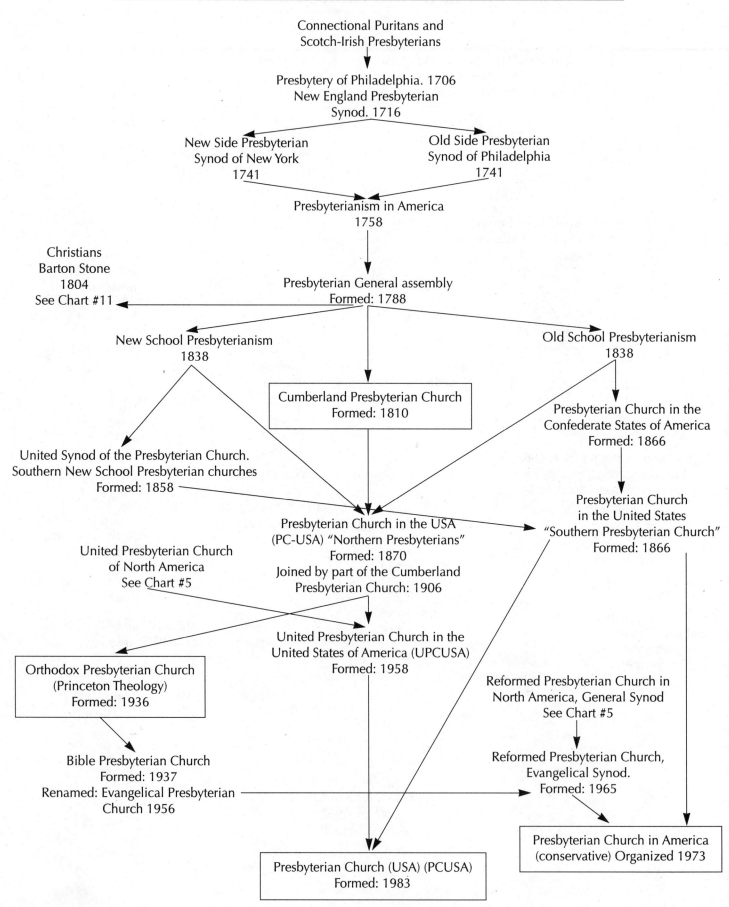

Connectional Puritans and
Scotch-Irish Presbyterians

Presbytery of Philadelphia. 1706
New England Presbyterian
Synod. 1716

New Side Presbyterian
Synod of New York
1741

Old Side Presbyterian
Synod of Philadelphia
1741

Presbyterianism in America
1758

Christians
Barton Stone
1804
See Chart #11

Presbyterian General assembly
Formed: 1788

New School Presbyterianism
1838

Old School Presbyterianism
1838

Cumberland Presbyterian Church
Formed: 1810

Presbyterian Church in the
Confederate States of America
Formed: 1866

United Synod of the Presbyterian Church.
Southern New School Presbyterian churches
Formed: 1858

Presbyterian Church
in the United States
"Southern Presbyterian Church"
Formed: 1866

Presbyterian Church in the USA
(PC-USA) "Northern Presbyterians"
Formed: 1870
Joined by part of the Cumberland
Presbyterian Church: 1906

United Presbyterian Church
of North America
See Chart #5

United Presbyterian Church in the
United States of America (UPCUSA)
Formed: 1958

Orthodox Presbyterian Church
(Princeton Theology)
Formed: 1936

Reformed Presbyterian Church in
North America, General Synod
See Chart #5

Bible Presbyterian Church
Formed: 1937
Renamed: Evangelical Presbyterian
Church 1956

Reformed Presbyterian Church,
Evangelical Synod.
Formed: 1965

Presbyterian Church in America
(conservative) Organized 1973

Presbyterian Church (USA) (PCUSA)
Formed: 1983

248

Chart #6: Scottish Presbyterianism

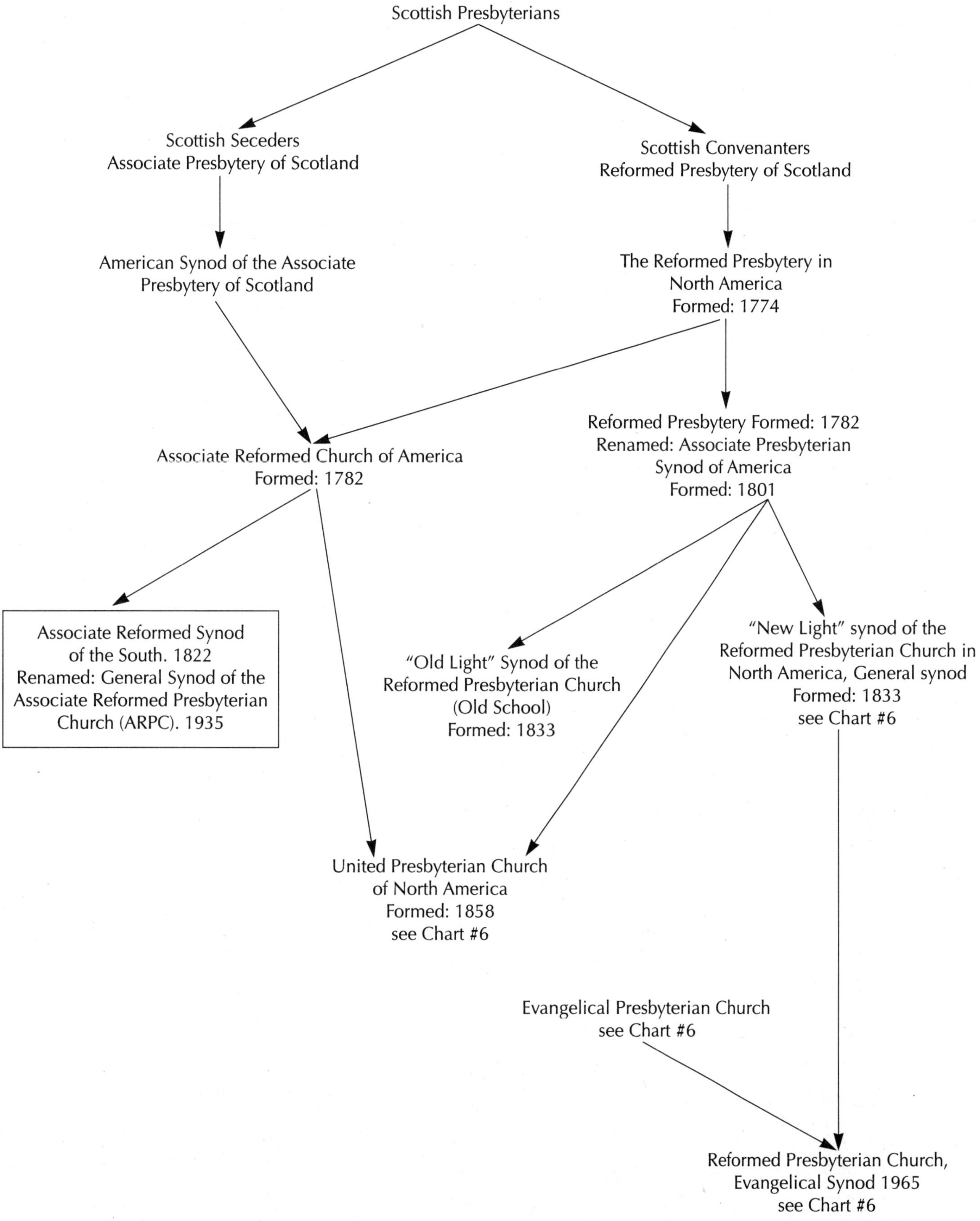

Scottish Presbyterians

Scottish Seceders
Associate Presbytery of Scotland

Scottish Convenanters
Reformed Presbytery of Scotland

American Synod of the Associate
Presbytery of Scotland

The Reformed Presbytery in
North America
Formed: 1774

Associate Reformed Church of America
Formed: 1782

Reformed Presbytery Formed: 1782
Renamed: Associate Presbyterian
Synod of America
Formed: 1801

Associate Reformed Synod
of the South. 1822
Renamed: General Synod of the
Associate Reformed Presbyterian
Church (ARPC). 1935

"Old Light" Synod of the
Reformed Presbyterian Church
(Old School)
Formed: 1833

"New Light" synod of the
Reformed Presbyterian Church in
North America, General synod
Formed: 1833
see Chart #6

United Presbyterian Church
of North America
Formed: 1858
see Chart #6

Evangelical Presbyterian Church
see Chart #6

Reformed Presbyterian Church,
Evangelical Synod 1965
see Chart #6

Chart #7: Reformed Churches

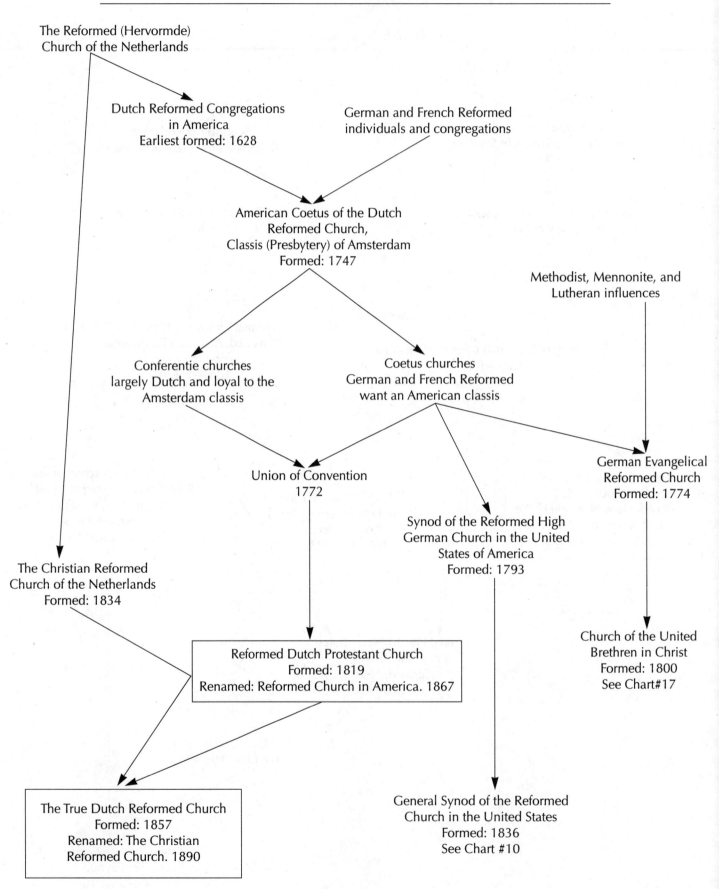

The Reformed (Hervormde)
Church of the Netherlands

Dutch Reformed Congregations
in America
Earliest formed: 1628

German and French Reformed
individuals and congregations

American Coetus of the Dutch
Reformed Church,
Classis (Presbytery) of Amsterdam
Formed: 1747

Methodist, Mennonite, and
Lutheran influences

Conferentie churches
largely Dutch and loyal to the
Amsterdam classis

Coetus churches
German and French Reformed
want an American classis

German Evangelical
Reformed Church
Formed: 1774

Union of Convention
1772

Synod of the Reformed High
German Church in the United
States of America
Formed: 1793

The Christian Reformed
Church of the Netherlands
Formed: 1834

Church of the United
Brethren in Christ
Formed: 1800
See Chart#17

Reformed Dutch Protestant Church
Formed: 1819
Renamed: Reformed Church in America. 1867

The True Dutch Reformed Church
Formed: 1857
Renamed: The Christian
Reformed Church. 1890

General Synod of the Reformed
Church in the United States
Formed: 1836
See Chart #10

Chart #8: Anglican Churches in the United States

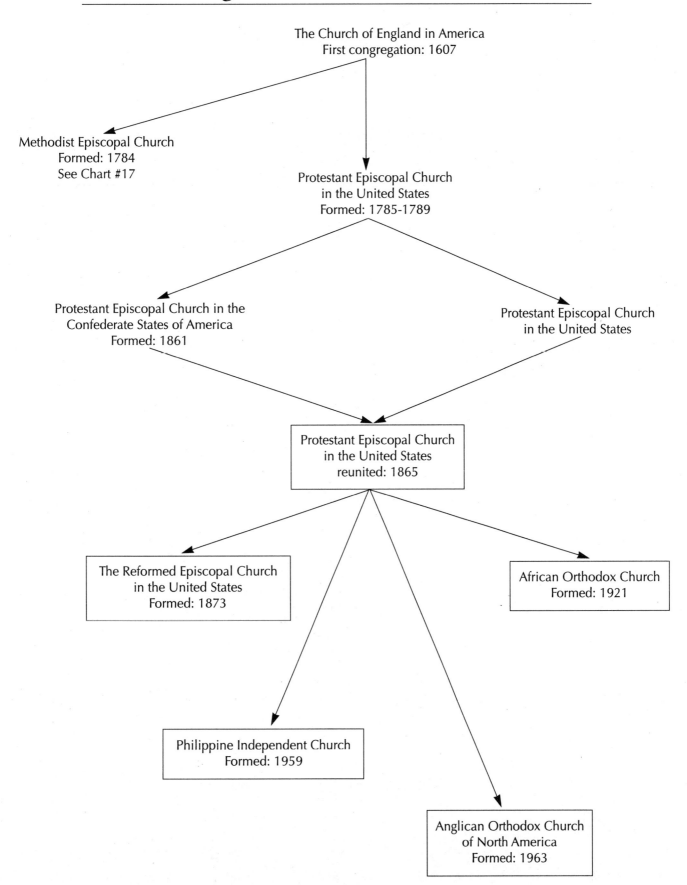

The Church of England in America
First congregation: 1607

Methodist Episcopal Church
Formed: 1784
See Chart #17

Protestant Episcopal Church
in the United States
Formed: 1785-1789

Protestant Episcopal Church in the
Confederate States of America
Formed: 1861

Protestant Episcopal Church
in the United States

Protestant Episcopal Church
in the United States
reunited: 1865

The Reformed Episcopal Church
in the United States
Formed: 1873

African Orthodox Church
Formed: 1921

Philippine Independent Church
Formed: 1959

Anglican Orthodox Church
of North America
Formed: 1963

Chart #9: Congregationalism

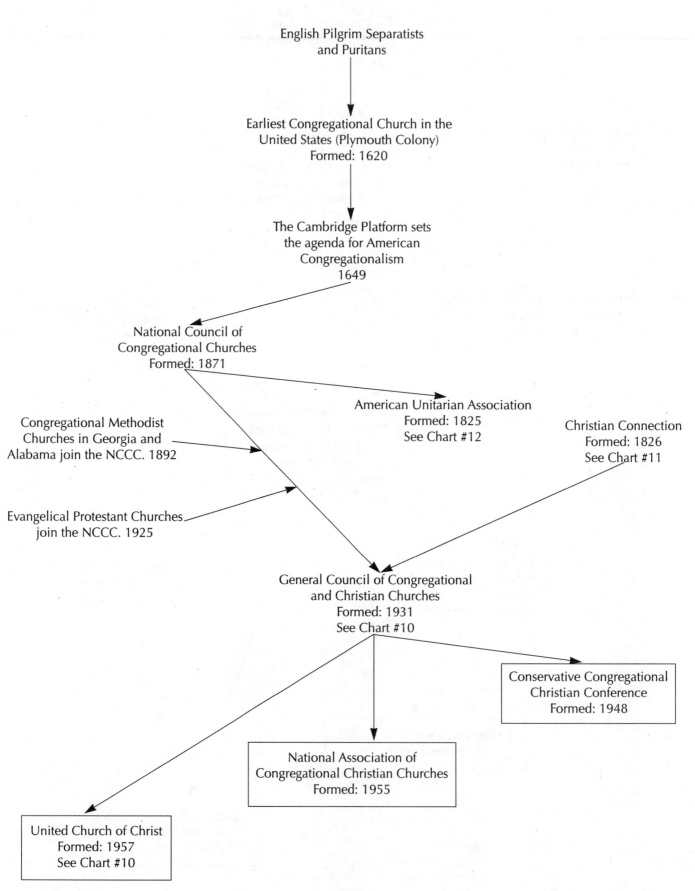

English Pilgrim Separatists
and Puritans

Earliest Congregational Church in the
United States (Plymouth Colony)
Formed: 1620

The Cambridge Platform sets
the agenda for American
Congregationalism
1649

National Council of
Congregational Churches
Formed: 1871

American Unitarian Association
Formed: 1825
See Chart #12

Christian Connection
Formed: 1826
See Chart #11

Congregational Methodist
Churches in Georgia and
Alabama join the NCCC. 1892

Evangelical Protestant Churches
join the NCCC. 1925

General Council of Congregational
and Christian Churches
Formed: 1931
See Chart #10

Conservative Congregational
Christian Conference
Formed: 1948

National Association of
Congregational Christian Churches
Formed: 1955

United Church of Christ
Formed: 1957
See Chart #10

Chart #10: United Church of Christ

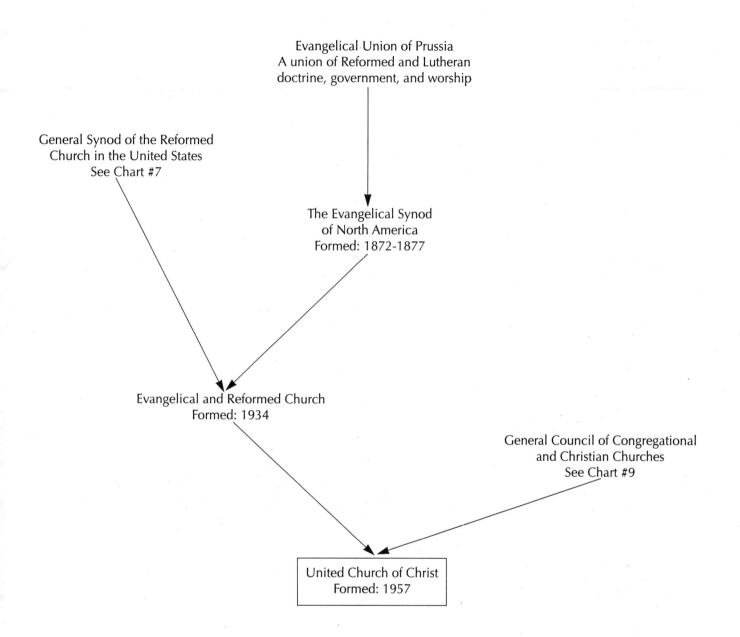

Evangelical Union of Prussia
A union of Reformed and Lutheran
doctrine, government, and worship

General Synod of the Reformed
Church in the United States
See Chart #7

The Evangelical Synod
of North America
Formed: 1872-1877

Evangelical and Reformed Church
Formed: 1934

General Council of Congregational
and Christian Churches
See Chart #9

United Church of Christ
Formed: 1957

Chart #11: Churches of the Restoration Movement

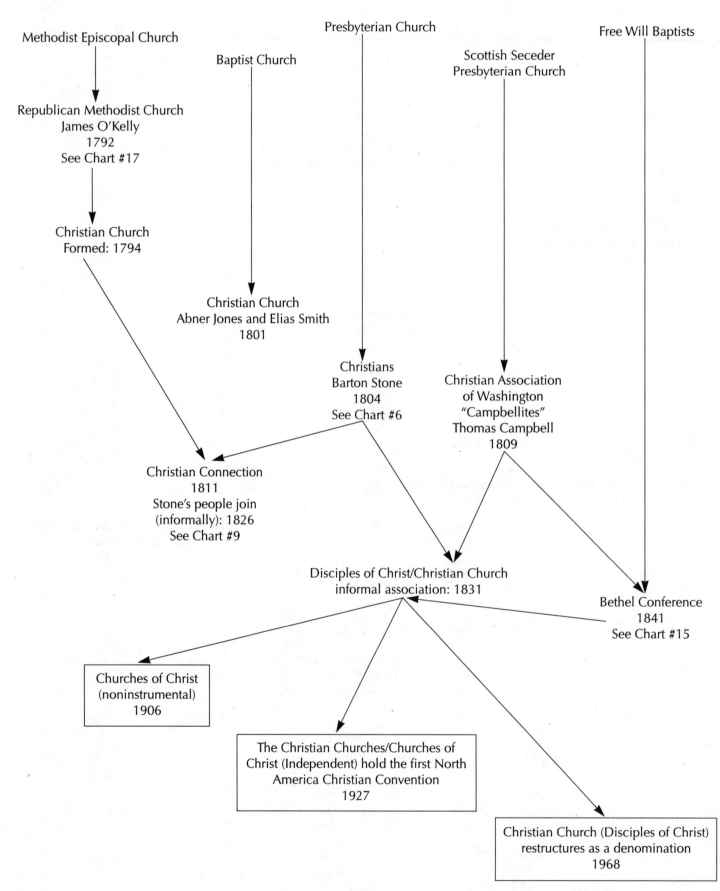

Methodist Episcopal Church

Baptist Church

Presbyterian Church

Scottish Seceder
Presbyterian Church

Free Will Baptists

Republican Methodist Church
James O'Kelly
1792
See Chart #17

Christian Church
Formed: 1794

Christian Church
Abner Jones and Elias Smith
1801

Christians
Barton Stone
1804
See Chart #6

Christian Association
of Washington
"Campbellites"
Thomas Campbell
1809

Christian Connection
1811
Stone's people join
(informally): 1826
See Chart #9

Disciples of Christ/Christian Church
informal association: 1831

Bethel Conference
1841
See Chart #15

Churches of Christ
(noninstrumental)
1906

The Christian Churches/Churches of
Christ (Independent) hold the first North
America Christian Convention
1927

Christian Church (Disciples of Christ)
restructures as a denomination
1968

Chart #12: Free Churches

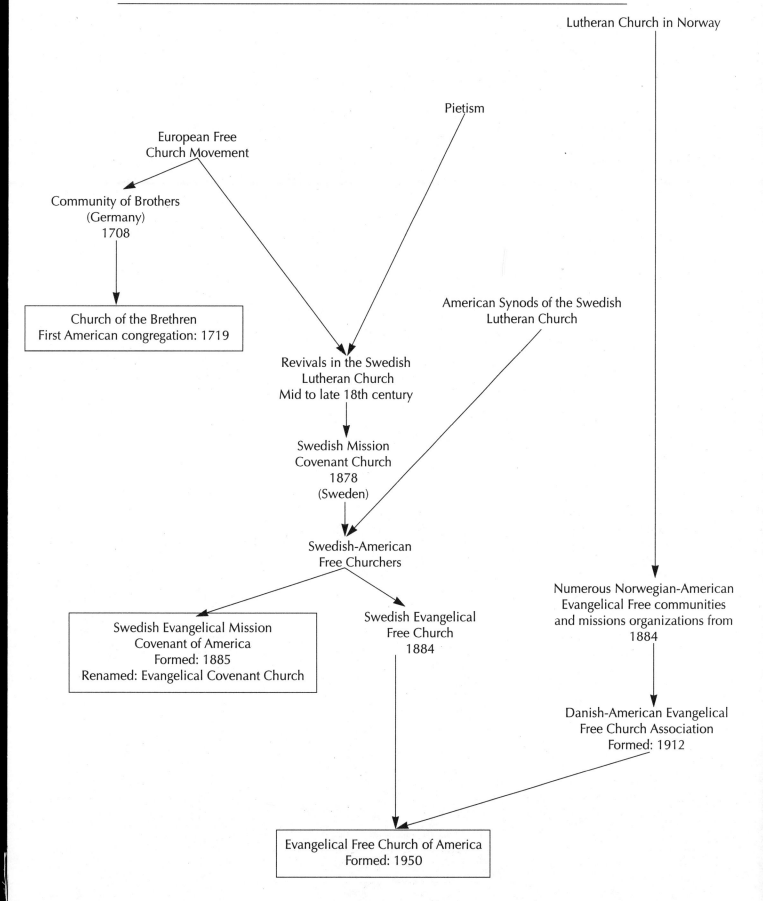

Lutheran Church in Norway

Pietism

European Free
Church Movement

Community of Brothers
(Germany)
1708

Church of the Brethren
First American congregation: 1719

American Synods of the Swedish
Lutheran Church

Revivals in the Swedish
Lutheran Church
Mid to late 18th century

Swedish Mission
Covenant Church
1878
(Sweden)

Swedish-American
Free Churchers

Numerous Norwegian-American
Evangelical Free communities
and missions organizations from
1884

Swedish Evangelical Mission
Covenant of America
Formed: 1885
Renamed: Evangelical Covenant Church

Swedish Evangelical
Free Church
1884

Danish-American Evangelical
Free Church Association
Formed: 1912

Evangelical Free Church of America
Formed: 1950

Chart #13 Baptist Churches

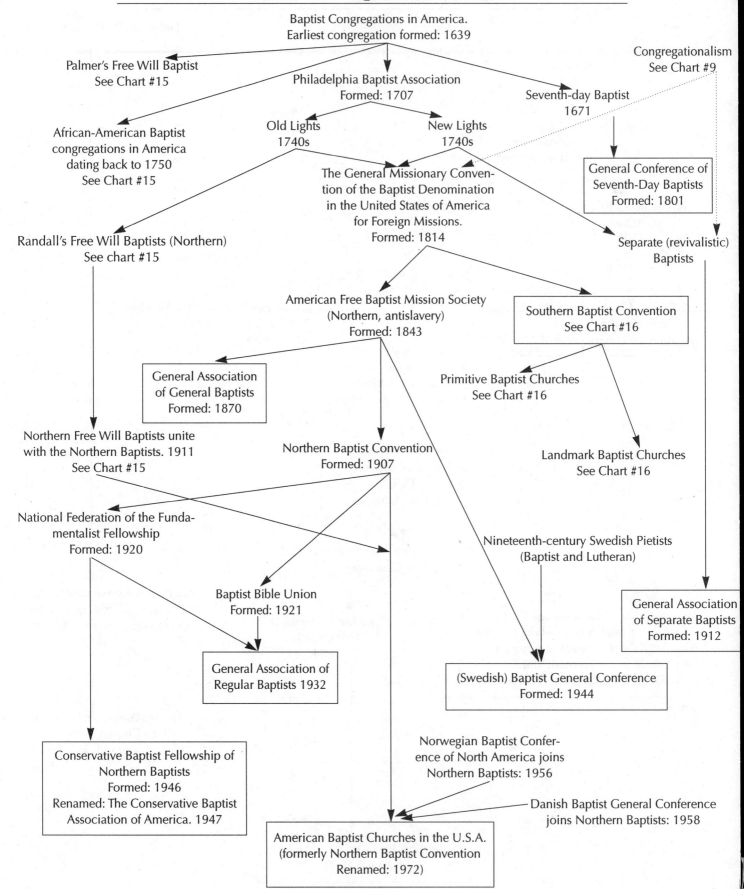

Baptist Congregations in America.
Earliest congregation formed: 1639

Congregationalism
See Chart #9

Palmer's Free Will Baptist
See Chart #15

Philadelphia Baptist Association
Formed: 1707

Seventh-day Baptist
1671

African-American Baptist
congregations in America
dating back to 1750
See Chart #15

Old Lights
1740s

New Lights
1740s

General Conference of
Seventh-Day Baptists
Formed: 1801

The General Missionary Convention of the Baptist Denomination
in the United States of America
for Foreign Missions.
Formed: 1814

Randall's Free Will Baptists (Northern)
See chart #15

Separate (revivalistic)
Baptists

American Free Baptist Mission Society
(Northern, antislavery)
Formed: 1843

Southern Baptist Convention
See Chart #16

General Association
of General Baptists
Formed: 1870

Primitive Baptist Churches
See Chart #16

Northern Free Will Baptists unite
with the Northern Baptists. 1911
See Chart #15

Northern Baptist Convention
Formed: 1907

Landmark Baptist Churches
See Chart #16

National Federation of the Funda-
mentalist Fellowship
Formed: 1920

Nineteenth-century Swedish Pietists
(Baptist and Lutheran)

General Association
of Separate Baptists
Formed: 1912

Baptist Bible Union
Formed: 1921

General Association of
Regular Baptists 1932

(Swedish) Baptist General Conference
Formed: 1944

Conservative Baptist Fellowship of
Northern Baptists
Formed: 1946
Renamed: The Conservative Baptist
Association of America. 1947

Norwegian Baptist Confer-
ence of North America joins
Northern Baptists: 1956

Danish Baptist General Conference
joins Northern Baptists: 1958

American Baptist Churches in the U.S.A.
(formerly Northern Baptist Convention
Renamed: 1972)

Chart #14: Predominantly African-American Baptists

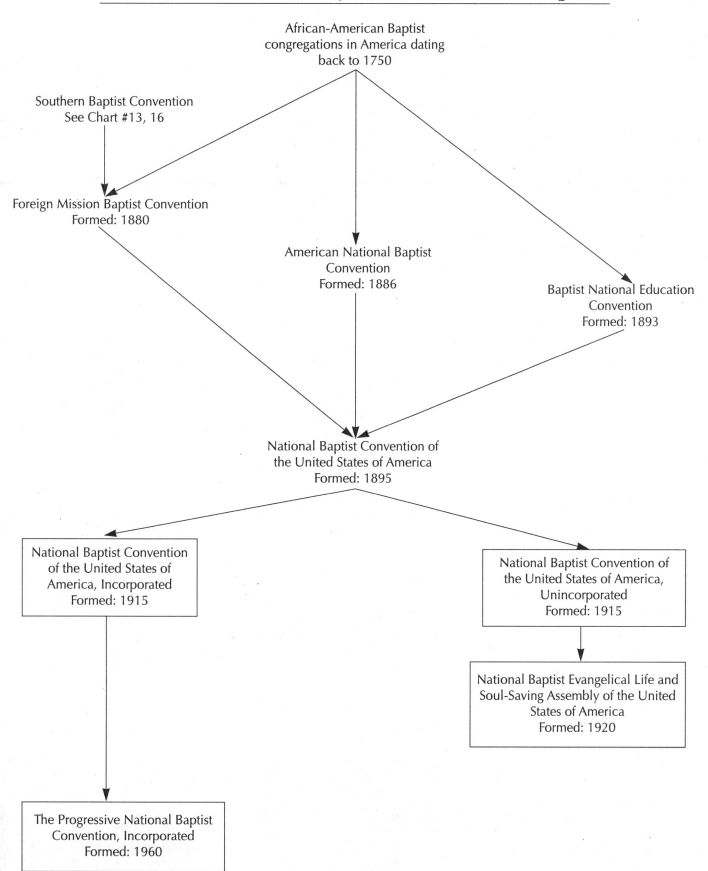

African-American Baptist congregations in America dating back to 1750

Southern Baptist Convention
See Chart #13, 16

Foreign Mission Baptist Convention
Formed: 1880

American National Baptist Convention
Formed: 1886

Baptist National Education Convention
Formed: 1893

National Baptist Convention of the United States of America
Formed: 1895

National Baptist Convention of the United States of America, Incorporated
Formed: 1915

National Baptist Convention of the United States of America, Unincorporated
Formed: 1915

National Baptist Evangelical Life and Soul-Saving Assembly of the United States of America
Formed: 1920

The Progressive National Baptist Convention, Incorporated
Formed: 1960

Chart #15: Free Will Baptists

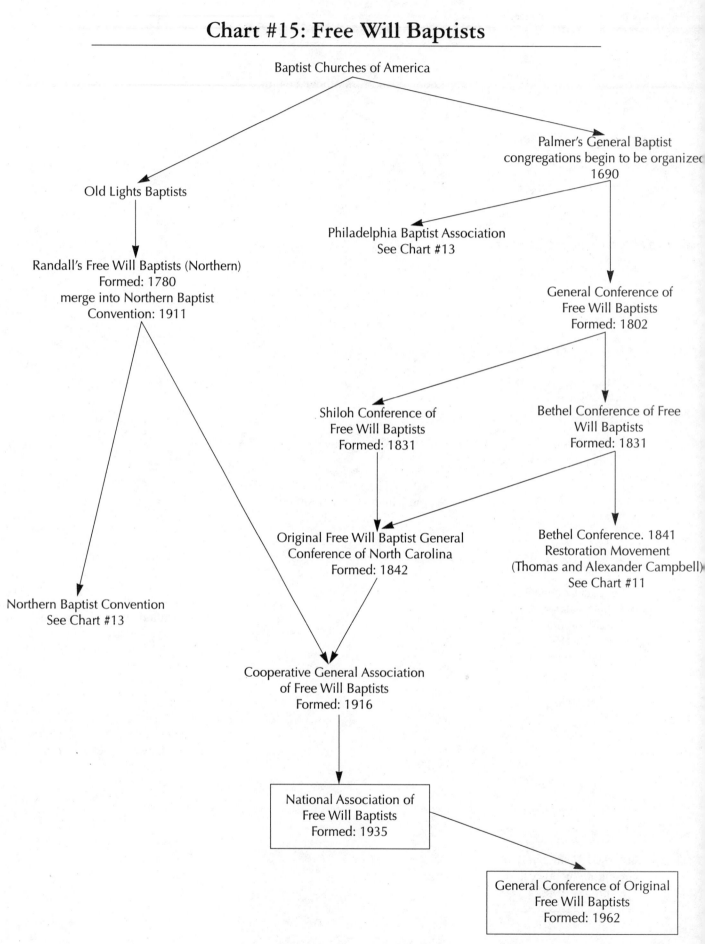

Baptist Churches of America

Old Lights Baptists

Palmer's General Baptist congregations begin to be organized 1690

Philadelphia Baptist Association
See Chart #13

Randall's Free Will Baptists (Northern)
Formed: 1780
merge into Northern Baptist
Convention: 1911

General Conference of
Free Will Baptists
Formed: 1802

Shiloh Conference of
Free Will Baptists
Formed: 1831

Bethel Conference of Free
Will Baptists
Formed: 1831

Northern Baptist Convention
See Chart #13

Original Free Will Baptist General
Conference of North Carolina
Formed: 1842

Bethel Conference. 1841
Restoration Movement
(Thomas and Alexander Campbell)
See Chart #11

Cooperative General Association
of Free Will Baptists
Formed: 1916

National Association of
Free Will Baptists
Formed: 1935

General Conference of Original
Free Will Baptists
Formed: 1962

Chart #16: Southern Baptists

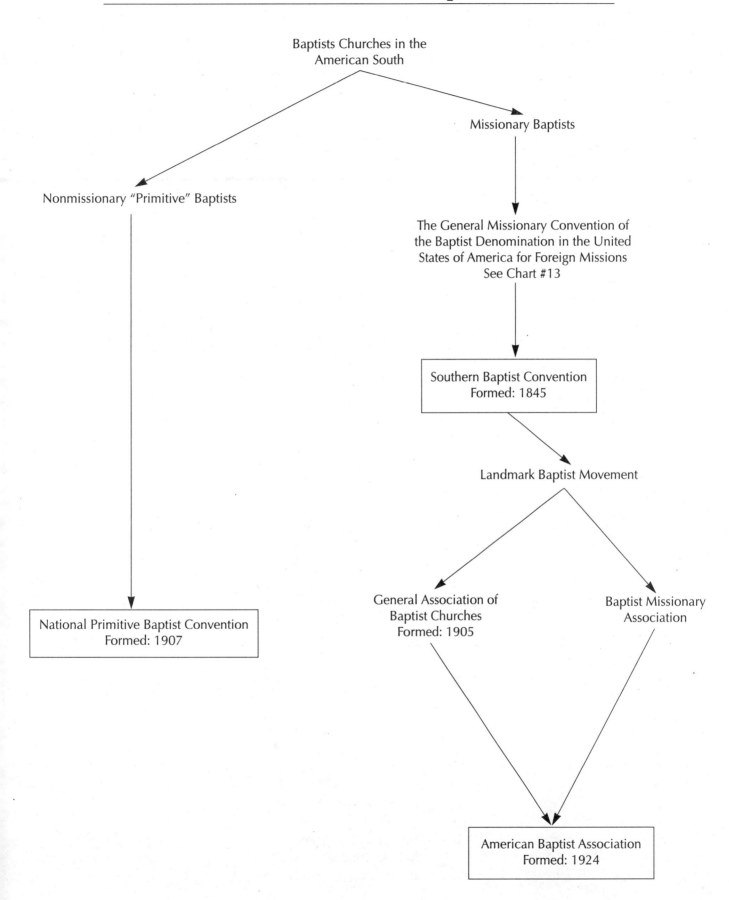

Baptists Churches in the
American South

Missionary Baptists

Nonmissionary "Primitive" Baptists

The General Missionary Convention of
the Baptist Denomination in the United
States of America for Foreign Missions
See Chart #13

Southern Baptist Convention
Formed: 1845

Landmark Baptist Movement

National Primitive Baptist Convention
Formed: 1907

General Association of
Baptist Churches
Formed: 1905

Baptist Missionary
Association

American Baptist Association
Formed: 1924

Chart #17: Methodism

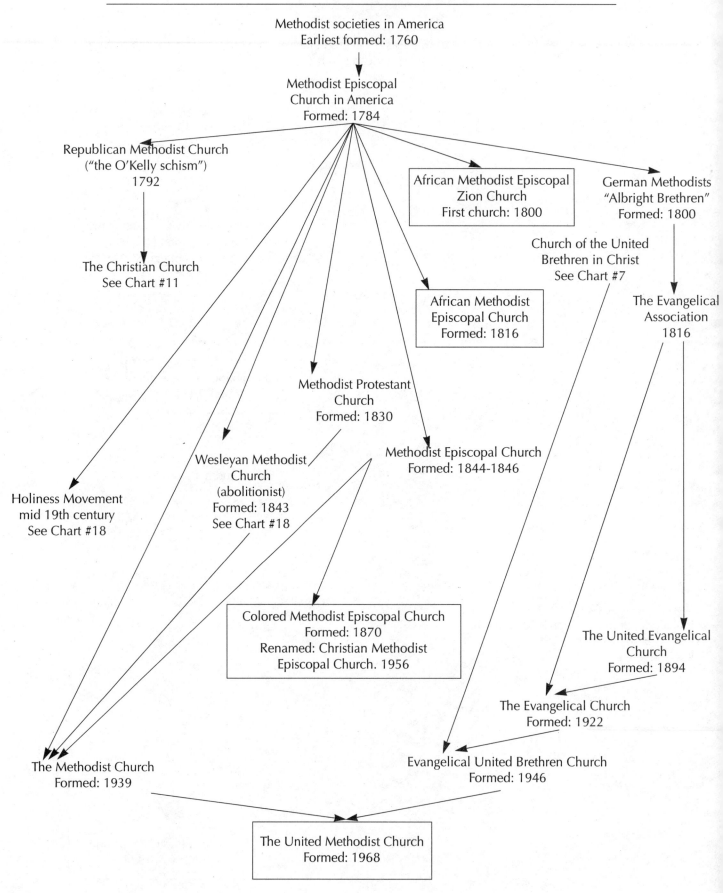

Methodist societies in America
Earliest formed: 1760

Methodist Episcopal
Church in America
Formed: 1784

Republican Methodist Church
("the O'Kelly schism")
1792

African Methodist Episcopal
Zion Church
First church: 1800

German Methodists
"Albright Brethren"
Formed: 1800

Church of the United
Brethren in Christ
See Chart #7

The Christian Church
See Chart #11

African Methodist
Episcopal Church
Formed: 1816

The Evangelical
Association
1816

Methodist Protestant
Church
Formed: 1830

Holiness Movement
mid 19th century
See Chart #18

Wesleyan Methodist
Church
(abolitionist)
Formed: 1843
See Chart #18

Methodist Episcopal Church
Formed: 1844-1846

Colored Methodist Episcopal Church
Formed: 1870
Renamed: Christian Methodist
Episcopal Church. 1956

The United Evangelical
Church
Formed: 1894

The Evangelical Church
Formed: 1922

The Methodist Church
Formed: 1939

Evangelical United Brethren Church
Formed: 1946

The United Methodist Church
Formed: 1968

Chart #18: Holiness and Pentecostal Churches

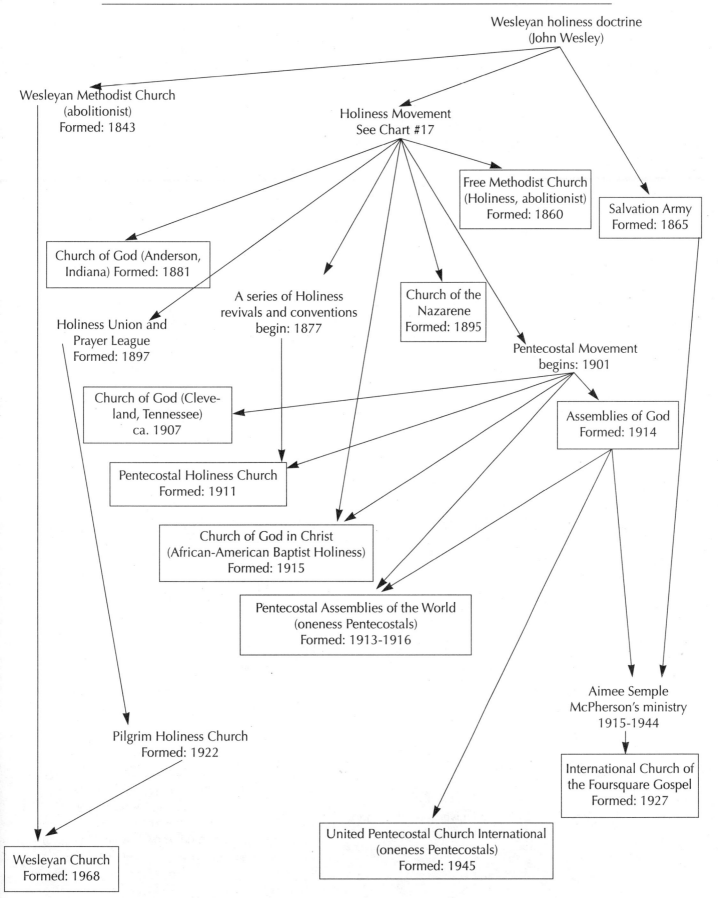

Wesleyan holiness doctrine
(John Wesley)

Wesleyan Methodist Church
(abolitionist)
Formed: 1843

Holiness Movement
See Chart #17

Free Methodist Church
(Holiness, abolitionist)
Formed: 1860

Salvation Army
Formed: 1865

Church of God (Anderson,
Indiana) Formed: 1881

A series of Holiness
revivals and conventions
begin: 1877

Church of the
Nazarene
Formed: 1895

Holiness Union and
Prayer League
Formed: 1897

Pentecostal Movement
begins: 1901

Church of God (Cleve-
land, Tennessee)
ca. 1907

Assemblies of God
Formed: 1914

Pentecostal Holiness Church
Formed: 1911

Church of God in Christ
(African-American Baptist Holiness)
Formed: 1915

Pentecostal Assemblies of the World
(oneness Pentecostals)
Formed: 1913-1916

Aimee Semple
McPherson's ministry
1915-1944

Pilgrim Holiness Church
Formed: 1922

International Church of
the Foursquare Gospel
Formed: 1927

Wesleyan Church
Formed: 1968

United Pentecostal Church International
(oneness Pentecostals)
Formed: 1945

Chart #19: Unitarian Universalist Association

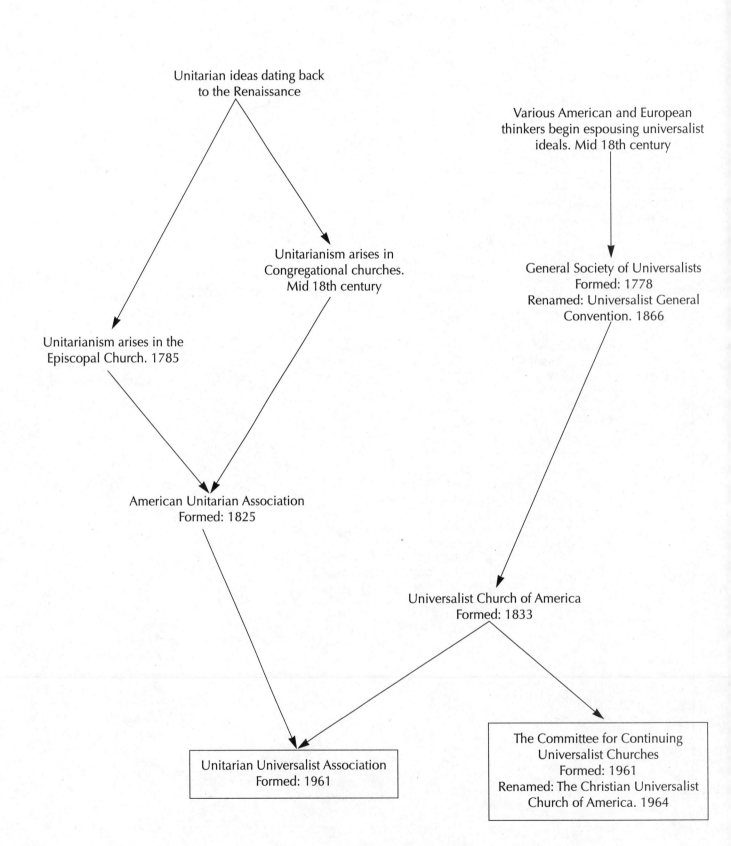

Unitarian ideas dating back
to the Renaissance

Various American and European
thinkers begin espousing universalist
ideals. Mid 18th century

Unitarianism arises in
Congregational churches.
Mid 18th century

General Society of Universalists
Formed: 1778
Renamed: Universalist General
Convention. 1866

Unitarianism arises in the
Episcopal Church. 1785

American Unitarian Association
Formed: 1825

Universalist Church of America
Formed: 1833

Unitarian Universalist Association
Formed: 1961

The Committee for Continuing
Universalist Churches
Formed: 1961
Renamed: The Christian Universalist
Church of America. 1964

Index

The following is a partial list of abbreviations that occur frequently in the Index:

BCP	*Book of Common Prayer*
BVM	Blessed Virgin Mary
C of E	Church of England
NCC	National Council of Churches
RCC	Roman Catholic Church
U.S.	United States
WCC	World Council of Churches

1816-z #17 African Methodist Episcopal Church formed
1820-c Missouri Compromise
1831-b Garrison wanted by Georgia officials for his anti-slavery work
1831-c Nat Turner rebellion
1831-b *The Liberator* released as abolitionist paper
1832-b New England Anti-Slavery Society organized
1834-c American Anti-Slavery Society formed
1837-b Presbyterians split over slavery
1840-c blackface minstrel shows
1843-b Sojourner Truth begins lecturing on abolition
1843-b Methodists split over slavery
1843-z #17 Wesleyan Methodist Church formed
1843-z #13 American Free Baptist Mission Society formed
1844-z #17 Methodist Episcopal Church, South formed
1844-b Methodist Episcopal Church clashes over
1845-b Baptist churches split over slavery
1855-c Frederick Douglass' *My Bondage and My Freedom*
1857-c Dred Scott decision
1860-z #18 Free Methodist Church formed
1860-b Methodists split over slavery
1861-b North and South Presbyterian Churches split
1863-c Emancipation Proclamation
1865-c Thirteenth Amendment abolishes slavery
1870-b voted out of Methodist Episcopal Church, South
1870-c admitted to colleges and universities
1870-z #17 Colored Methodist Episcopal Church
1880-z #14 Foreign Mission Baptist Convention
1886-z #14 American National Baptist Convention
1893-z #14 Baptist National Education Convention
1895-z #14 National Baptist Convention of the U.S.A.
1896-c *Plessy v. Ferguson*
1909-c Matthew Henson travels to North Pole
1915-z #14 National Baptist Convention of the U.S.A., Unincorporated
1915-z #18 Church of God in Christ formed
1915-z #14 National Baptist Convention of the U.S.A., Inc.
1920-z #14 National Baptist Evangelical Life and Soul-Saving Assembly, U.S.A.
1921-z #8 African Orthodox Church formed
1926-c Langston Hughes' *Weary Blues*
1934-b first African-American ecumenical organization
1954-c Supreme Court calls school segregation unconstitutional
1954-c *Brown v. the Board of Education*
1955-c Montgomery bus boycott
1956-z #17 Christian Methodist Episcopal Church takes current name

1958-c school desegregation begins
1960-z #14 Progressive National Baptist Convention, Inc.
1960-a African-American theology in liberation theology
1963-c March on Washington
1964-c Civil Rights Act passed
1965-c Voting Rights Act
1966-c Kwanzaa first celebrated
1982-c Alice Walker's *The Color Purple*
1984-c Jesse Jackson runs for U.S. President
1987-c Toni Morrison's *Beloved*
1995-b 32 African-American churches bombed or set afire
African Methodist Episcopal Church
1766-a Wesleyan Tradition
1787-b first congregation founded
1816-z #17 formed
1816-b chartered
African Methodist Episcopal Zion Church
1800-z #17
African Orthodox Church 1921-z #8 formed
African-American theology
1960-a liberation theology
Africanus, Julius Sextus. *See* Julius Africanus, Sextus
afterlife
553-a hell decreed to be eternal punishment
593-b Gregory the Great teaches purgatory
848-b Gottschalk: God predestines for hell/blessedness
998-b All Souls' Day instituted
1265-b Thomas devises classic doctrine of purgatory
1274-b doctrine of purgatory defined
1295-d *Harrowing of Hell*
1320-d Dante Alighieri's *Divine Comedy*
1439-b doctrine of purgatory defined
1520-b Ulrich Zwingli preaches against purgatory
1563-b existence of purgatory affirmed by Council of Trent
Against Heresies 185-d Irenaeus'
Against Jovinian 393-d Jerome's
Against Julian
440-d Cyril, patriarch of Alexandria's
Against the Iconoclasts 730-d John of Damascus'
Agapetus, pope. *See* Agapitus, pope
Agapitus, pope 535-b becomes bishop of Rome
Agapitus II, pope
946-b becomes bishop of Rome
Agatho, pope 678-b becomes bishop of Rome
Age of Reason 1750-c Enlightenment
Age of Reason 1794-d Thomas Paine's
Agincourt, battle of 1415-c
Agnes, Saint 304-b martyred at Rome
agnosticism
1869-b term *agnostic* coined by Thomas Huxley
1920-b Christian agnosticism
Agnus Dei 514-d
514-b introduced to Rome
701-b begins to be sung during the fraction
1000-d takes its modern form
1300-d in first complete Mass ordinary
Agrippa, Herod
41-c becomes last king of Judea
Aidan, Saint (bishop of Lindisfarne)
627-b founds Lindisfarne
651-b dies

AIDS 1979-c first case
airplanes
1783-c hot air balloon invented
1903-c first motorized flight made
1911-c first used in combat
1927-c Charles Lindbergh flies the Atlantic
1942-c jets invented
1945-b Mission Aviation Fellowship founded
Alacoque, Saint Margaret Mary
1670-a Devotion to the Sacred Heart of Jesus
1671-b enters convent at Paray-le-Monial
1673-b has "great apparition" of the Sacred Heart of Jesus
1690-b dies
1920-b canonized
Alamo 1836-c attacked by Mexican troops
Aland, Kurt 1979-d *Novum Testamentum Graece*
Alaric 410-c sacks Rome
Alaric II, King (of Visigoths)
507-c defeated by Clovis
Alaska 1741-c Vitus Bering discovers
alb
818-b an essential Eucharistic vestment
850-d mandated for those who say Mass
Alban of Britain, Saint 304-b martyred
Albert of Vercelli
1154-a Carmelite order
1209-d Carmelite Rule
Albert the Great. *See* Albertus Magnus, Saint
Albertus Magnus, Saint
1241-d begins to interpret Aristotle
1245-b teaches Thomas Aquinas
1280-b dies
1931-b made a doctor of the church by Pope Pius XI
Albigenses. *See also* Cathari
1179-b problem of addressed by Lateran Council III
1208-b Crusade launched against
1215-b condemned by Lateran Council IV
Albright Brethren 1800-z #17 formed
Albright, Jacob 1803-b officially organizes Evangelical Association
alchemy 425-c beginnings of
alcohol
1826-b American Temperance Society formed
1919-c prohibition bans sale and transport of alcohol in U.S.
1933-c prohibition repealed
Alcuin
735-b is born
766-b makes York a learning center
770-d compiles first formal catechism manual
780-a Carolingian Renaissance and Reforms
781-c becomes Charlemagne's royal tutor
793-b encourages manuscript production
793-b becomes abbot of St. Martin of Tours
798-a opposes adoptianism
800-a Allegorical interpretation of the Mass
804-b dies
Alcuin's Missal. *See also Appendix Y, chart #4*
800-d compiled
1570-d *Missale Romanum* based on
aleatory music 1950-c
ℵ. See *Codex Sinaiticus*

American Indians. *See* Indians, American
American Lutheran Church (German) 1930-z #3
American Lutheran Church. *See also Chart Z* #3
 1960-z #3 formed
 1988-b merges into the ELCA
American National Baptist Convention
 1886-z #14
American Psychiatric Association
 1974-c removes homosexuality from list of
  mental disorders
American Psychological Association
 1892-c formed
American Revolutionary War
 1773-c Boston Tea Party
 1775-c begins
 1778-c France intervenes in
 1779-c Spain enters
American Sisters of Charity
 1821-b founder dies
American Standard Version of the Bible
 1901-d
 1901-y #3
American Sunday School Union
 1824-b founded
American Temperance Society 1826-b formed
American Tract Society 1825-b formed
American Unitarian Association
 1825-z #19 formed
 1825-z #9 formed
 1825-b formed
 1961-b merges with Universalist Church
  of America
Amiatinus. See Codex Amiatinus
amice
 800-b first referred to
 850-d mandated for those who say Mass
Amish 1700-b split from the Swiss Brethren
Ammon 340-b one of first monks to visit
 Rome
Ampere, Andre Marie 1826-c *Electrodynamics*
Amplified Bible 1965-y #3
Amsterdam
 1609-b first modern Baptist church formed in
 1609-c Bank of Amsterdam founded
Amundsen, Roald 1911-c travels to South Pole
Anabaptists 1520-a
 1520-b movement begins in Germany
 1525-b expelled from Zurich
 1525-b Grebel rebaptizes a former Roman
  Catholic priest
 1526-b Moravian brothers settle in Moravia
 1527-d Schleitheim Confession
 1528-b killed by other Christians
 1536-b Menno Simons joins
 1536-b led by Simons
 1540-b begin to be called Mennonites in
  Holland
 1609-a influence early Baptists
Anacletus, pope 79-b becomes bishop of Rome
Analogy of Religion, Natural and Revealed, an
 1736-d
Analytical Concordance to the Bible
 1879-d Young's
Anastasius I, pope
 399-b becomes bishop of Rome
Anastasius II, pope
 496-b becomes bishop of Rome
Anastasius III, pope
 911-b becomes bishop of Rome

Anastasius IV, pope 1153-b becomes pope
anathemas
 428-d Athanasian Creed
 482-d *Henoticon* asserts Cyril's *Twelve
  Anathemas*
Anatomy of the Human Body
 1858-c Henry Gray's
Ancyra, Council of 314-b
Andes Evangelical Mission
 1982-b unites with Sudan Interior Mission
Andover Seminary 1808-b founded
Andrew, apostle 60-b dies
Andrew, James O.
 1844-b suspended for keeping slaves
Andrewes, Lancelot
 1556-b is born
 1626-b dies
 1648-d *Preces Privatae*
angel pope 1285-b dreams spread
Angelic Doctor. *See* Thomas Aquinas
angels
 120-b *Shepherd of Hermas* says everyone has
  guardian angel
 315-b appropriate devotion for detailed
 329-b begin to appear in Christian art
 400-b become prevalent in Christian art
 705-a Annunciation of the Blessed Virgin
  Mary
 1265-b Thomas Aquinas speaks of guardian
  angels
 1521-b Feast of Guardian Angels first
  recorded
 1521-a Feast of Guardian angels
 1670-b Feast of Guardian angels becomes
  universal
Angevine house
 1154-c begins reign in England
Angles. *See also* Germanic tribes
 440-c storm England
Anglican chant. *See also* Chant
 1597-d begins to be developed
Anglican church in colonial America
 1607-b first permanent Anglican church in
  America
 1701-b SPG fosters spread of Anglicanism
  in colonial America
 1730-b Bray oversees Anglican church in
  colonial America
 1775-b Americans no longer pray publicly
  for British monarchs
Anglican church. *See also* Church of England;
  England, Pre-Reformation church in
 1548-d *Order of the Communion*
 1549-d laity receives communion three
  times a year
 1729-a Methodism
 1754-c founds Columbia University
 1773-b Methodists receive sacraments at
 1787-b first colonial bishop consecrated
 1836-b first bishop in Australia consecrated
 1865-b first official Anglican monastic order
  formed
 1869-b disestablished in Ireland
 1919-b disestablished in Wales
 1945-a indigenization of third world
  churches
 1975-b finds women's ordination theologi-
  cally unobjectionable
 1994-b ordains women

Anglican Communion. *See also* Church of
 England
 1867-b first Lambeth Conference held
 1958-b Lambeth Conference finds birth
  control acceptable
 1960-b archbishop of Canterbury visits Pope
  John XXIII
Anglican divines
 1615-a Divine right of kings
 1625-a Caroline divines
 1630-a Receptionism
Anglican Orthodox Church of North America
 1963-z #8
Anglican Reformation
 1521-d King Henry VIII's *Defense of the Seven
  Sacraments*
 1521-d King Henry VIII declared
  "Defender of the Faith"
 1522-d support for Luther declines in
  England
 1532-b King Henry VIII orders submission
  of clergy
 1533-b King Henry VIII excommunicated
 1535-b Fisher and More executed
 1536-b dissolution of monasteries in England (stage one)
 1536-d Ten Articles
 1538-b King Henry VIII excommunicated a
  second time
 1538-b all churches must have a Bible
 1539-b Dissolution of monasteries in England (stage two)
 1544-d earliest English liturgy
 1547-c King Henry VIII dies
 1547-c King Edward VI becomes king
 1548-d *Order of the Communion*
 1548-b Edward VI removes saints' images
  from churches
 1549-b Court of High Commission established
 1549-d mixture of water with wine no
  longer ordered
 1549-d laity receives communion three
  times a year
 1550-b altars replaced by tables
 1551-b John Knox becomes chaplain to
  King Edward VI
 1552-b church services must begin with
  ringing of bells
 1552-b surplice the only prescribed vestment in C of E
 1552-b chasuble no longer used
 1553-d Forty-two Articles
 1553-d Edward VI orders *Reform of the
  Ecclesiastical Laws*
 1553-c Queen Mary Tudor becomes queen
 1553-d Mary Tudor abolishes *Book of
  Common Prayer*
 1555-b Queen Mary Tudor burns Ridley
  and Latimer for heresy
 1558-d Queen Elizabeth I becomes queen
 1559-b chasuble reimposed
 1559-a Puritanism
 1559-a Elizabethan Settlement
 1560-c Elizabeth I sends military aid to
  Scottish Protestants
 1562-b Elizabeth I sends military aid to
  Protestants in France
 1562-d John Jewel's *Apologia Ecclesiae
  Anglicanae*

1812-a Princeton theology claims to be
    keeper of
1818-a New Haven theology
1836-a opposed by transcendentalism
1837-d Auburn Declaration
1903-d *Westminster Confession of Faith* revised
1936-a Westminster School of Presbyterian-
    ism holds to
Calvinists
    1560-b the term "Huguenot" first applied
        in France
    1594-b Francis of Sales begins his mission to
    1633-b Particular Baptists are
    1633-a Particular Baptists
    1644-b forbid Christmas by Act of Parlia-
        ment in England
Calvin's *Institutes. See Institutes of the Christian
    Religion*
Cambridge
    1443-c King's College Chapel begun
Cambridge Platform
    1649-d is developed
    1649-z #9 is developed
Cambridge Platonists 1633-a
    1624-b influenced by Jakob Boehme
    1705-a latitudinarians are descendants of
Cambridge University
    1209-c is founded
    1581-b Beza presents the *Codex Bezae* to
Camisards
    1705-b begin guerilla revolt against
        French crown
Camp David Agreement 1978-c forged
camp meetings. *See also* revivals; Second Great
        Awakening; evangelistic meetings and
        crusades
    1800-b the first is held
    1801-b Cane Ridge Revival begins
Campbell, Alexander
    1788-b is born
    1809-b founds first Disciples of Christ
        church
Campbell, Joseph 1987-b dies
Campbell, Thomas
    1809-b founds first Disciples of Christ church
Campbellites. *See* Christian Association of
        Washington
Campion, Saint Edmund
    1581-d *Decem Rationes* (ten reasons)
    1581-b executed for treason
    1970-b canonized
Campus Crusade for Christ International
    1951-b
campus ministry
    1883-b Newman movement begins
    1919-b InterVarsity Christian Fellowship
        holds first conference
    1938-b Federation of College Cath. Clubs
        becomes National Newman Club
        Federation
    1946-b Urbana Student Missions Conven-
        tion first held
    1951-b Campus Crusade for Christ Interna-
        tional
Camus, Albert 1947-c *The Plague*
Canada
    1625-b Jean de Brébeuf arrives in Canada
    1625-b Samuel de Champlain arrives in
        Canada
    1867-c British North America Act
    1867-c Dominion of Canada created

Candide 1759-c Voltaire's
Candlemas. *See* Purification of the Blessed
        Virgin Mary
candles
    384-b paschal candle first referred to
    1175-b first noted use of on altars
Cane Ridge Revival 1801-b
    1827-a precursor to New Measures
Canisius, Saint Peter
    1597-b dies
    1925-b canonized
    1925-b named a doctor of the church
Canon of the Mass 390-d takes modern form
canon law
    314-b originates
    375-d *Apostolic Constitutions*
    530-d Dionysius Exiguus' collection
    550-d Johannes Scholasticus' *Synagoge
        canonum*
    1140-d Gratian's harmonization of
    1145-d Gratian's *Decretum* begins modern
        era
    1210-d first officially promulgated
        collection
    1234-d Raymond of Peñafort's *Extravagantes*
    1503-d Jean Chappuis' *Corpus Iuris Canonici*
    1553-d *Reform of the Ecclesiastical Laws*
    1604-d *Code of Canons* comes into effect in
        England
    1917-d *Codex Iuris Canonici*
    1983-d revised after Vatican II
canon of Scripture
    100-c Hebrew Canon firmed up
    150-d Marcion's
    194-d Muratorian
    200-a selection process nearly complete
    367-d Athanasius of Alexandria's New Tes-
        tament canon
    393-b Synod of Hippo publishes first com-
        plete list
canonical hours
    540-b term is first seen
    590-b term comes into popular usage
canonization of saints
    1163-b Anselm of Canterbury canonized
    1173-b Thomas Becket canonized
    1174-b Bernard of Clairvaux canonized
    1199-b Malachy canonized
    1220-b Hugh of Lincoln canonized
    1220-b first Carthusian
    1234-b Dominic canonized
    1391-b Bridget of Sweden canonized
    1461-b Catherine of Siena canonized
    1610-b Borromeo, Charles canonized
    1622-b Philip Neri canonized
    1622-b Francis Xavier canonized
    1622-b Teresa of Ávila canonized
    1665-b Francis of Sales canonized
    1671-b first South American canonized
    1671-b Rose of Lima canonized
    1712-b Pius V canonized
    1726-b John of the Cross canonized
    1726-b Aloysius Gonzaga canonized
    1729-b John of Nepomuk canonized
    1839-b Alphonsus Liguori canonized
    1881-b Cyril and Methodius canonized
    1920-b Joan of Arc canonized
    1920-b Margaret Mary Alacoque canonized
    1925-b Peter Canisius canonized

    1925-b Theresa of Lisieux canonized
    1946-b Cabrini, Francesca Xavier canonized
    1954-b Pius X canonized
    1962-b Martin de Porres canonized
    1975-b first American-born saint canonized
canonization process
    993-b earliest official
    1171-a canonization of saints
    1171-b right to canonize is reserved for the
        papacy
    1513-b first uses the Devil's Advocate
    1587-b the Sacred Congregation of Rites
        established
    1631-b Devil's Advocate becomes a essential
        part
    1634-b process is formalized
    1634-b reserved to the papacy
    1634-b modern requirements instituted
Canons 306-d Peter, bishop of Alexandria's
Canons of the cathedral
    755-d rule for is developed
Canons of the Synod of Dort 1619-d approved
cantatas
    1738-c Johann Sebastian Bach's Mass in
        B Minor
    1704-c Bach writes his first cantata
Canterbury Cathedral
    851-b sacked by Danes
    1067-b destroyed by fire
    1130-b rebuilding is consecrated
    1220-b shrine dedicated to Thomas à Becket
Canterbury. *See also* archbishop of Canterbury
    597-b monastery created at
    602-b see founded
    851-b Canterbury Cathedral sacked by
        Danes
    1067-b Canterbury Cathedral destroyed by
        fire
    1130-b Canterbury Cathedral rebuilding
        consecrated
    1220-b shrine at Cathedral dedicated to
        Thomas à Becket
    1386-d Geoffrey Chaucer's *Canterbury Tales*
Canterbury Tales 1386-d Geoffrey Chaucer's
canticles 375-a
    375-b Nunc Dimittis a part of daily prayers
    375-b Gloria in Excelsis used as canticle of
        morning prayer
    406-b Benedicite common throughout the
        world
    406-d earliest extant Greek text of the
        Gloria in Excelsis Deo
    414-d Te Deum composed
    550-b Magnificat becomes canticle most
        used during vespers
    680-d Te Deum
    680-d earliest extant Latin text of the Gloria
        in Excelsis Deo
    1150-b Gloria in Excelsis becomes regular
        part of Eucharist
    1512-b Benedictus qui venit sung after both
        elevations
cantors
    358-b chant responsorial psalmody
    365-b recommended by Council of Laodicea
Canute II, Viking leader
    1013-c completes Danish conquest of
        England
    1016-c becomes king of England

607-b St. Paul's Cathedral built
632-c pagans gain foothold in
664-b Roman calculation of Easter used
670-b dioceses set up in
673-b Council of Hertford firms up church organization
680-d earliest vernacular hymns in English
731-d Bede's *Ecclesiastical History of England*
747-b English churches must conform to Roman liturgy
768-b last church conforms to Roman practices
793-c Vikings invade
816-b uses dating from the Incarnation
878-b Alfred the Great keeps England Christian
940-b Dunstan expands school and abbey at Glastonbury
948-b Dunstan supervises post-Viking rebuilding
955-b Dunstan banished from England
959-b churches rebuilt in England
959-b organs begin to be used in churches
959-b Benedictine Rule introduced
959-b Dunstan becomes archbishop of Canterbury
984-b Saint Ethelwold, bishop of Winchester, dies
988-b coronation rite compiled
1013-c Canute II completes the Danish conquest of England
1016-c Canute II becomes king of England
1066-c Norman conquest of England
1066-c Middle English (language) period begins
1066-c House of Normandy begins its reign
1077-b first Cluniac house in England formed
1100-b Anselm clashes with King Henry I over investiture
1135-c House of Blois begins its reign
1154-c Angevine house (House of Plantagenet) begins its reign
1164-d Constitutions of Clarendon
1167-c earliest records of Oxford University
1174-c Henry II forces William of Scotland to recognize him as overlord
1175-b first Carthusian monasteries are established
1189-c Richard the Lionhearted becomes king
1189-b Ely cathedral finished
1208-b under papal interdict
1209-b King John excommunicated
1209-c Cambridge University founded
1213-b becomes papal fief
1213-b King John submits to the pope
1224-b Franciscans settle in Oxford
1225-b animosity for Rome grows
1290-c Jews expelled from
1380-b John Wycliffe sends out the Poor Preachers
1399-c House of Lancaster begins its reign
1443-c King's College Chapel begun at Cambridge
1461-c House of York begins its reign
1485-c House of Tudor begins its reign
1499-c England has seven capital offenses
1508-c King Henry VIII marries Catherine of Aragon

1508-c King Henry VIII becomes king
1521-d King Henry VIII declared "Defender of the Faith"
1521-d King Henry VIII's *Defense of the Seven Sacraments*
1522-d support for Luther declines
1532-b King Henry VIII orders submission of clergy
1533-b King Henry VIII excommunicated
1533-c King Henry VIII marries Anne Boleyn
1535-b John Fisher and Thomas More executed
1536-b Dissolution of monasteries in England (stage one)
1536-c Wales incorporated with
1536-c King Henry VIII's marriage to Anne Boleyn annulled
1538-b King Henry VIII excommunicated a second time
1539-b Dissolution of monasteries in England (stage two)
1540-c Henry VIII executes his chief advisor Thomas Cromwell
1540-b King Henry VIII marries Anne of Cleves
1540-c King Henry VIII marries Catherine Howard
1547-c King Henry VIII dies
1547-c King Edward VI becomes king
1549-b Court of High Commission established
1549-d laity receives communion three times a year
1550-c the modern English (language) period begins
1550-b altars replaced by tables
1551-b John Knox becomes chaplain to King Edward VI
1552-b chasuble no longer used
1552-b surplice the only prescribed vestment in the C of E
1552-b bells rung at the beginning of all church services
1553-d Forty-two Articles
1553-d *The Reform of the Ecclesiastical Laws*
1553-c Queen Mary Tudor becomes queen
1553-d Mary Tudor abolishes the *Book of Common Prayer*
1555-b Queen Mary Tudor burns Ridley and Latimer for heresy
1558-d Queen Elizabeth I becomes queen
1559-a Puritanism
1559-b chasuble reimposed
1560-c Elizabeth I sends military aid to Protestants in Scotland
1562-c Elizabeth I makes witchcraft a serious crime in England
1562-d John Jewel's *Apologia Ecclesiae Anglicanae*
1562-b Elizabeth I sends military aid to Protestants in France
1570-b Queen Elizabeth I excommunicated by Rome
1580-b Jesuits found a mission in England
1581-d Campion's *Decem Rationes* distributed at Oxford
1581-b Queen Elizabeth I executes the Forty English Martyrs

1582-b Separatists argue against the C of E
1585-b Elizabeth I sends aid to Protestants in the Netherlands
1585-b Jesuits expelled
1585-b Catholics persecuted
1586-b imprimatur mandated
1587-c Queen Elizabeth I executes Mary Queen of Scots
1593-b acts passed against Puritans
1593-b acts passed against Roman Catholics
1594-d Hooker's *Laws of Ecclesiastical Polity*
1595-d Lambeth Articles
1595-d supralapsarian doctrine common among Puritans
1597-d Anglican chant begins to be developed
1600-c English East India Company founded
1600-c charter granted to English East India Company
1603-c Elizabeth I, queen of England dies
1603-c witchcraft a capital crime
1603-c King James I becomes king
1603-c House of Stuart begins its reign
1603-c King James I unites Scottish and English crowns
1603-b King James I receives Millenary Petition
1604-d *Code of Canons* becomes C of E canon law
1604-b excommunication becomes more overt
1611-d King James I commissions a Bible translation
1612-b first Baptist church established
1612-b burning of heretics last recorded
1622-c King James I dissolves Parliament
1623-c patent law developed in England
1625-b King Charles I becomes king
1629-c King Charles I dissolves Parliament
1633-a Cambridge Platonists
1634-b altar rails restored
1634-b altars moved to the east wall
1637-b King Charles I imposes Anglican liturgy on Scotland
1638-c torture abolished in England
1640-c Long Parliament convenes
1640-b William Laud proposes "Etcetera Oath"
1640-c Long Parliament convenes
1640-c English Revolution begins
1641-b altar rails removed
1641-b Court of High Commission abolished
1642-c civil war breaks out: Royalist vs. Parliamentarians
1643-b Solemn League and Covenant accepted
1644-b Calvinists forbid Christmas by Act of Parliament
1645-d *Directory of Public Worship* replaces BCP
1648-b makes denial of the Trinity punishable by death
1649-b Presbyterian church becomes state church
1649-c King Charles I beheaded by the Parliamentarians
1650-c tea comes to England

1651-c Navigation Act enacted
1651-b the Quakers spread through England
1653-c Oliver Cromwell becomes Lord Protector
1655-c Oliver Cromwell readmits Jews
1655-c Oliver Cromwell dissolves Parliament
1658-c Puritan government of England ends
1660-c King Charles II returns to England
1660-b altar rails again installed
1660-c feudalism abolished in England
1661-b Savoy Conference held
1661-c Charles II crowned king
1662-b John Biddle founds first Unitarian congregation in
1662-b Act of Uniformity requires 1662 BCP
1662-b Feast of the Visitation of Our Lady becomes black-letter day
1662-b Licensing of Press Act prohibits anti-Christian books
1664-b Conventicle Act forbids non-C of E worship meetings
1665-b Five-Mile Act enacted
1665-c Great Plague in London kills 75,000 people
1666-b St. Paul's Cathedral destroyed in Great Fire
1672-b Nonconformity legalized
1674-c England claims America after Anglo-Dutch war
1675-b Sir Christopher Wren begins Saint Paul's Cathedral
1677-b Ecclesiastical Jurisdiction Act abolishes death penalty
1685-c King James II becomes king
1687-b James II calls for freedom of religious conscience
1688-c King James II dethroned
1688-c Glorious Revolution begins
1688-c William and Mary ascend
1689-c bands with Holland in war against Louis XIV's France
1689-b Toleration Act grants conditional freedom of religion
1695-b imprimatur no longer mandated
1702-c Queen Anne becomes queen
1713-c Peace of Utrecht
1713-c England may trade in Spanish America
1714-c House of Hanover begins its reign
1717-c first modern Masonic Grand Lodge
1718-b Schism Act repealed
1718-c British teachers need not be members of the C of E
1736-c witchcraft laws repealed
1736-c rubber comes to England from India
1744-c "God Save the Queen" published
1752-b Gregorian calendar adopted
1753-c Jews naturalized in England
1757-c India comes under British power
1765-b Robert Raikes founds Sunday schools
1765-b Sunday School Movement arises
1776-c the American colonies declare independence
1783-c signs peace treaty with America
1787-b first colonial bishop consecrated
1798-b foreign missionary arm of the C of E formed

1800-c England has more than 200 capital crimes
1800-c united with Ireland
1807-c slave trade banned
1813-b excommunicated persons aren't under civil disabilities
1828-b Catholics may hold public office in England
1828-b Corporation Act repealed in England
1830-c first railroad built between Liverpool and Manchester
1832-c British middle class men gain the vote
1833-c British Empire abolishes slavery
1836-c civil marriages established in England
1837-c House of Saxe-Coburg (later "Windsor") begins its reign
1837-c Queen Victoria ascends to throne
1840-b Christmas trees introduced to
1847-a Christian socialism
1853-c Crimean War begins
1854-b courts prosecute Denison for teaching the Real Presence
1865-d Pusey's *Church of England as a Portion of Christ's One Holy Catholic Church*
1865-b first official Anglican monastic order formed
1866-b lay readers conduct non-sacramental C of E services
1873-b D. L. Moody conducts evangelistic meetings
1884-c workingmen given the vote by Act of Parliament
1901-c King Edward VII becomes king
1901-c Queen Victoria of England dies
1914-c World War I begins
1917-c Saxe-Coburg changes its name to the House of Windsor
1918-c World War I ends
1918-c women aged thirty-plus given the vote
1927-d House of Commons rejects proposals for BCP revision
1928-c women aged twenty-one-plus given the vote
1939-c World War II begins
1940-c Churchill becomes British Prime Minister
1945-c World War II ends
1952-c Queen Elizabeth II becomes queen
1952-c King George VI dies
1954-b Billy Graham holds an evangelistic crusade
1969-c voting age reduced to 18
1969-b women may become lay readers in the C of E
1979-d *Alternative Services Book*
1994-b C of E ordains women
1997-b C of E places TV commercials

English (language)
440-c Old English period begins
880-b Works of Bede, Boethius, Gregory, etc., translated into
998-d Aelfric's *Lives of the Saints* written in
1000-c *Beowulf*
1038-b "Cristes Maesse" first referred to
1066-c Middle English period begins

1315-d Richard Rolle's poetry
1350-c Great Vowel Shift begins
1470-c Arthur legends
1544-d earliest English liturgy
1550-c modern English period begins
English East India Company 1600-c chartered
English Revised Version. *See* Revised Version of the Bible
English Revolution
1640-c begins
1640-c Long Parliament convenes
1642-c civil war breaks out: Royalist vs. Parliamentarians
1643-b Solemn League and Covenant accepted
1645-d *Directory of Public Worship* replaces BCP
1649-c King Charles I beheaded by the Parliamentarians
1649-b Presbyterian church becomes state church
1653-c Oliver Cromwell becomes Lord Protector
1655-c Oliver Cromwell dissolves Parliament
1658-c ends
1660-c King Charles II returns to England
English Society of St. John the Evangelist
1872-b community formed in U.S.
Enlightenment, the 1750-c
1604-c Galileo delineates law of gravity
1624-d empiricism attacked by Herbert
1624-d earliest rumblings of deism
1633-c Galileo confronted by the Inquisition
1638-c Galileo's *Discourses Concerning Two New Sciences*
1641-c rationalism
1683-c Isaac Newton explains tides
1684-c Isaac Newton discovers calculus
1687-c Newton's *Principia Mathematica*
1690-c John Locke's Essay *Concerning Human Understanding*
1690-c empiricism
1695-d Locke's *Reasonableness of Christianity*
1695-a deism
1695-d Toland's *Christianity Not Mysterious*
1730-d Tindal's *Christianity as Old as Creation*
1736-d Butler writes against deism
1740-c Hume's *Treatise of Human Nature*
1748-c Hume's *An Enquiry Concerning Human Understanding*
1762-c Jean Jacques Rousseau's *The Social Contract*
1771-c Denis Diderot's *Encyclopédie*
1776-c Declaration of Independence written
1776-c Adam Smith's *Wealth of Nations*
1780-b Emperor Joseph II reforms both church and state
1781-c Immanuel Kant's *Critique of Pure Reason*
1788-c Immanuel Kant's *Critique of Practical Reason*
1794-d Thomas Paine's *Age of Reason*
Enoch, I 50-d
Enquiry Concerning Human Understanding, an 1748-c Hume's
enthusiasm, religious
1738-a opposed by Old Side Presbyterianism
1831-a opposed by Old School Presbyterianism

439-c the West has been completely overrun by invaders
500-c many large landlords have their own armies and prisons
550-c literacy in decline after invasions
700-c waterwheel technology spreads through Europe
751-b Gregorian chant spreads throughout
800-c develops a distinct Western society
851-c crossbow invented
975-c arithmetic brought to Europe
1000-c abacus introduced to
1000-c literacy begins to reemerge
1050-c Astrolabes arrive in
1050-c European obsession with witchcraft begins
1085-c navigational equipment comes to Christian Europe
1100-c paper introduced
1230-c Crusades bring leprosy
1245-c Aristotle becomes prominent in Western Europe
1313-c first gunpowder weapons used
1348-c Black Death sweeps Europe
1379-b European countries split between pope and antipope
1520-c 20% of art nonreligious
1556-c influenza epidemic strikes
1640-b Jesuits have more than 500 colleges throughout
1700-c literacy 30-40%

Eusebius Hieronymus. See Jerome, Saint
Eusebius of Caesarea
315-b distinguishes between worship and devotion given to angels
323-d *Ecclesiastical History*
323-b says the fast before Easter two or three days
338-d *Life of Constantine*
340-b dies

Eusebius, pope 310-b becomes bishop of Rome
Eutyches
451-b condemned at Council of Chalcedon
Eutychian 275-b becomes bishop of Rome
Eutychianism
451-b condemned at Council of Chalcedon
527-b Justinian, emperor, promulgates laws against

Evangelical Alliance 1846-b formed to oppose Roman Catholicism
Evangelical Alliance Mission, the 1890-b
Evangelical and Reformed Church
1934-z #10 formed
1934-b established by merger
1957-b merges with Congregational Christian Churches

Evangelical Association
1803-b officially organized
1816-z #17 takes the name
1946-b merges with Church of the United Brethren in Christ

Evangelical Church
1922-z #17 formed
1946-b unites with the United Brethren Church

Evangelical Council for Financial Accountability 1979-b
Evangelical Covenant Church of America
1885-z #12 formed as Swedish Evangelical Mission Covenant of America

1885-b founded as Swedish Evangelical Mission Covenant of America
Evangelical Episcopalianism
1840-b vs. High Church Episcopalianism
Evangelical Foreign Missions Association
1945-b formed
Evangelical Free Church of America
1884-b earliest American roots
1950-z #12 formed
1950-b formed
Evangelical Joint Synod of Ohio and Other States 1818-z #3
Evangelical Lutheran Church 1917-z #3
Evangelical Lutheran Church in America. *See also Chart Z #2*; Lutheran church
1988-b formed
1992-b in full communion with Presbyterians, Reformed, and UCC
Evangelical Lutheran Ministerium in North America 1748-z #4
Evangelical Lutheran Synod and Ministerium of North Carolina 1803-b
Evangelical Lutheran Synodical Conference 1872-z #4
Evangelical Presbyterian Church
1937-b Bible Presbyterian Church splits from Presbyterians
1937-z #5 precursor formed
Evangelical Synod of North America
1872-z #10 formed
1934-b merges with German Reformed Church
Evangelical United Brethren
1946-b formed through merger
1946-z #17 formed
1968-b merges with the Methodist Church
evangelical liberalism 1880-a
evangelicalism
1848-b Wheaton College founded
1870-b Holiness Movement has significant impact on
1929-b forerunner of National Association of Evangelicals formed
1943-a neo-evangelicalism
1943-b National Association of Evangelicals formed
1947-b Fuller Theological Seminary founded
1947-b Ockenga becomes a leader of the movement
1947-d Carl Henry calls Christianity to the political world
1951-b World Evangelical Fellowship formed
1956-d *Christianity Today* first published
1960-b evangelicals begin founding "Christian day schools"
1967-b Good News movement, a Methodist renewal movement
1976-d Lindsell's *Battle for the Bible*
1978-d "The Chicago Statement on Biblical Inerrancy"
1979-b Evangelical Council for Financial Accountability
Evangelicals, Anglican
1782-a Clapham Sect
1807-d John Henry Hobart's *An Apology for Apostolic Order*
1836-b Charles Simeon dies

evangelism. *See also* missions
1612-b Congregation of the Oratory dedicated to
1801-b Congregationalists, Presbyterians evangelize frontier
1827-b revival etiquette discussed
1840-a evangelistic crusades emphasized by revivalism
1858-b Paulists founded to provide a reasonable evangelism
1861-b Women's Union Missionary Society evangelizes women
1865-b Salvation Army founded
1873-b D. L. Moody conducts meetings in U.S. and England
1899-b the Gideons distribute Scripture
1910-b Billy Sunday first uses the term "sawdust trail"
1923-b Bible Literature International formed
1944-b Youth for Christ International formed
1950-b Billy Graham Evangelistic Association founded
1951-b World Evangelism Fellowship formed
1954-b Billy Graham launches a crusade in England
1965-d *Have You Heard of the Four Spiritual Laws?*
1970-b Billy Graham Center founded
1974-b International Congress on World Evangelism in Lausanne
evangelistic meetings and crusades
1840-a emphasized by revivalism
1873-b D. L. Moody conducts meetings in U.S. and England
1910-b Billy Sunday uses the term "sawdust trail"
1954-b Billy Graham's to England
Evangelium veritatis. See Gospel of Truth
Evaristus 100-b becomes bishop of Rome
Eve
627-a Mary seen as new Eve
1667-d portrayed in *Paradise Lost*
evening prayer. *See also* evensong; vespers; Daily Office
215-b earliest evidence
379-b Phos Hilaron sung at
550-b Magnificat becomes the canticle used during vespers
1549-d BCP omits the confession of sin during
1552-b BCP reinserts the confession of sin during
evensong. *See also* vespers; Daily Office
1552-b Prayer of General Confession added in BCP
Everest, Mount
1953-c Edmund Hillary and Tenzing Norkay scale
Everyman 1475-d written
evil
188-a problem of
421-a Pelagianism vs. Augustinianism
850-a confirmation give grace to resist
evolution
1801-c first fossil remains of an extinct animal are discovered

Kierkegaard, Søren
  1813-b is born
  1846-c existentialism
  1846-a Christian existentialism
  1846-d *Fear and Trembling*
  1855-b dies
Kiev
  989-b Vladimir begins to spread
    Christianity in
King George's War 1740-c begins
King James Version of the Bible. *See also*
    Appendix Y, chart #2
  1604-b translation begins
  1611-d completed
  1611-y #3 completed
  1982-d *New King James Version* published
King, Martin Luther, Jr.
  1955-c organizes Montgomery bus boycott
  1963-c March on Washington
  1964-c wins Nobel Peace Prize
  1968-c assassinated
King Philip's War 1675-c begins
Kingsley, Charles 1847-a Christian socialism
King's College
  1443-c chapel begun at Cambridge
Kino, Eusebio Francisco, Jesuit missionary
  1681-b
kisses 725-a icons
kiss of peace 155-b part of worship in Rome
kithera 188-b allowed in the liturgy
kneeling 1552-a Black Rubric
Knights Hospitallers 1190-a Hospitallers
Knights of Columbus 1882-b founded
Knights of Labor
  1869-c first national labor union
Knights of St. John (Hospitallers)
  1113-b founded
Knights Templars, Order of
  1118-b founded
  1128-b obtains recognition from the church
knights. *See* chivalry; Crusades
knitting machine 1589-c invented
Knock, Ireland
  1879-b "Our Lady of Knock" appears
Knox, John
  1513-b is born
  1536-b enters priesthood
  1544-b leaves Roman Catholic priesthood
  1551-b becomes chaplain to King Edward
    VI of England
  1553-b flees Scotland for Geneva
  1555-b returns to Scotland
  1560-d Scots Confession
  1560-d *First Book of Discipline*
  1562-d *Book of Common Order*
  1572-b dies
  1587-d *History of the Reformation in Scotland*
    (posthumously)
Knox's Liturgy. See Book of Common Order
Kolb, F. 1528-d Theses of Berne
Konkordienbuch. See Book of Concord
Koran
  651-c canon formalized
  1143-c translated into Latin
Korean War
  1950-c begins
  1950-b Bob Pierce forms World Vision
Koresh, David 1993-b Branch Davidians com-
    mit suicide
kosher 49-b Peter and Paul disagree about

Kristallnacht 1938-c
Ku Klux Klan 1866-c formed
Küng, Hans 1977-d *On Being a Christian*
Kuwait 1990-c Iraq annexes
Kwanzaa 1966-c first celebrated
Kyrie Eleison 375-d
  375-b begins to be used
  529-b mandated during matins, vespers, and
    Mass
  598-b *Christe Eleison* first sung as a part of
  1300-d in the first complete Mass ordinary
Labor, Knights of
  1869-c founded as first national labor union
labor, manual
  1089-a Cistercian order
  1200-b Cistercians do less than other orders
  1700-b begins to be practiced by Trappists
labor unions
  1869-c first one founded
  1891-d Pope Leo XIII responds to
  1964-c racial discrimination prohibited
Lachmann, Karl
  1831-d *Greek New Testament*
  1835-b defends Marcan Hypothesis
Lactantius 314-d *On the Deaths of the Persecutors*
Lady Chatterley's Lover 1928-c D. H. Lawrence's
Lady Day. *See* Annunciation of the BVM
Lady, Our. *See* Mary, the Mother of Jesus; Mary,
    apparitions of
laity
  700-b communion in both kinds begins to
    disappear
  1032-b lay person is elected pope
  1177-b Beguines/Beghards founded as lay
    religious orders
  1229-b forbidden to read Scripture
  1520-d Luther opposes denial of cup to
  1549-d Anglican laity receives communion
    three times a year
  1792-b Pennsylvania Ministerium grants
    voting rights to
  1926-a liturgical movement increases partic-
    ipation of
  1928-b *Opus Dei* founded
  1962-b participation in the Mass is
    increased
  1962-a RCC begins new focus on the laity
  1965-b RC laity permitted to receive the
    cup at communion
Lalor, Teresa
  1799-b founds Catholic women's school
Lamb of God. *See also* Agnus Dei
  514-d Agnus Dei
Lambeth Articles 1595-d
Lambeth Conference
  1867-b first one held
  1888-b approves Chicago-Lambeth Quadri-
    lateral
  1892-b Episcopal church participates in
Lambeth Quadrilateral. *See* Chicago-Lambeth
    Quadrilateral
Lambeth, Synod of 1281-b
Lancaster, House of
  1399-c begins reign in England
Land Grant Act 1862-c
land reform 210-c fails
Landmark Baptist Movement
  1811-a baptismal exclusivism
  1848-a

1905-z #16 General Association of Baptist
    Churches formed
Lando, pope 913-b becomes bishop of Rome
language 1874-a speaking in tongues
Laodicea 365-b Council of
Large and Small Catechism
  1529-d Martin Luther's
  1580-d in the Book of Concord
Larger and Shorter Catechisms
  1647-d compiled
  1788-b General Assembly adopts *Larger
    Catechism*
Larson, April Ulring
  1992-b first woman Lutheran bishop
laser 1958-c first one produced
Last Supper 1498-c Leonardo finishes painting
last days. *See also* eschatology
  1906-d in *Quest of the Historical Jesus*
Late Great Planet Earth, The 1970-d Lindsey's
late Middle Ages 1350-c begin
later sub-apostolic period 100–135
Lateran Councils
  1123-b First
  1139-b Second
  1179-b Third
  1215-b Fourth
  1512-b Fifth
Lateran Synod 649-b
Latimer, Hugh
  1485-b is born
  1539-b opposes the Six Articles
  1555-b criticizes the Ave Maria
  1555-b burned as a heretic by Mary Tudor
Latin (language)
  189-b first Latin-speaking pope
  253-b Rome shifts to
  355-c used in Rome almost exclusively
  365-d Greek patristics translated into
  383-d *Vesta Itala* revised
  384-b becomes primary liturgical language
    in Rome
  392-d Jerome's *Gallican Psalter*
  397-d Latin Vulgate
  800-c is a distinct language from Romance
    vernaculars
  800-c has become language of scholarship
    and the church
  1135-c Arabic manuscripts translated into
  1143-c Koran translated into
  1543-b not used in Calvinist music
  1548-d English supplement to Latin Mass
  1700-c used only in church and interna-
    tional scholarship
  1962-b no longer the sole language of
    Roman liturgy
  1970-b vernacular Mass approved by Ameri-
    can RC bishops
  1971-b vernacular Mass becomes obligatory
Latin America 1823-c Monroe Doctrine
Latin Empire of Constantinople
  1204-c instituted
Latin fathers. *See also* church fathers
  225-a Ransom theory of the atonement
  1155-d central in Peter Lombard
Latin patriarchate
  1847-b no longer a
    titular role
Latins 1182-c killed in Constantinople
latitudinarianism 1705-a
Latourette, Kenneth Scott
  1945-d *History of the Expansion of Christianity*

liturgical movement
- 1903-b Pope Pius X spurs
- 1908-d *Graduale Romanum* published
- 1926-a
- 1926-d *Orate Fratres* marks U.S. beginning of liturgical uniformity
- 1662-b Act of Uniformity

liturgical year. *See* church year

liturgy 375-d Kyrie Eleison

Liturgy of St. Chrysostom 400-d

Liturgy of the Hours. *See also* breviary; Daily Office
- 1962-b breviary called

liturgy. *See also Appendix Y, chart #4; ritual*
- 120-b Sixtus I introduces Sanctus into the Mass
- 170-a distinctly Christian develops
- 215-d Hippolytus' *Apostolic Tradition*
- 251-b Lord's Prayer used during Eucharist
- 350-b Sanctus a part of the Eucharistic liturgy
- 374-d Gallican liturgy begins to be used in northwestern Europe
- 375-b Gloria in Excelsis used as a canticle of morning prayer
- 375-d *Apostolic Constitutions* a source of
- 375-b Kyrie Eleison begins to be used
- 379-b Phos Hilaron sung at evening prayer
- 383-b brings antiphonal singing and the Alleluia to Rome
- 384-b first reference to the nine hours of the Divine Office
- 384-d *Egeria's Travels*
- 385-b Ambrose introduces the Te Deum to Milan
- 390-d Canon of the Mass takes modern form
- 416-b must be approved by council or ecclesiastical authority
- 440-b Sanctus introduced into the Western liturgy
- 461-b "Mass" (the term) begins to be used
- 492-d Western petition-response style litany begins
- 492-b faithful recite same church-prayer as catechumens
- 500-d Trisagion first referred to
- 500-d Gelasian Sacramentary
- 514-b Agnus Dei introduced to Rome
- 529-b use of the Sanctus mandated
- 590-d Isidore's *De ecclesiasticus officiis*
- 598-b Christe eleison first sung as part of Kyrie Eleison
- 599-b Te Deum has become part of Roman liturgy
- 600-b Gregory the Great standardizes use of "Alleluia"
- 600-d Gregorian Sacramentary
- 628-d Leonine Sacramentary
- 650-d Stowe Missal
- 664-b Celtic superseded by Roman
- 692-b Mass of the Presanctified first recorded
- 700-b Communion in both kinds begins to disappear
- 700-b private Mass begins in northern Europe
- 701-b Agnus Dei begins to be sung during the fraction
- 745-d Bobbio Missal
- 747-b English churches must conform to Roman liturgy
- 789-d Gregorian Sacramentary given to Charlemagne
- 789-b fairly standardized
- 789-b Roman Rite used throughout Carolingian empire
- 800-b multiplicity of Masses begins
- 800-d Alcuin's Missal
- 800-d *Hucusque*
- 800-d Charlemagne introduces Gallo-Frankish liturgy to Rome
- 800-b Charlemagne suppresses Gallican Rite
- 867-b Slavonic liturgy approved
- 900-b sung polyphonically
- 1000-d *Benedicamus Domino* begins to be used
- 1000-d Agnus Dei takes modern form
- 1050-b Trisagion introduced to Good Friday liturgy
- 1085-b Mozarabic Rite supplanted by Roman
- 1090-b Gloria in Excelsis omitted during Lent and Advent
- 1099-b Priests may say Gloria in Excelsis Deo
- 1100-b private daily Mass is common
- 1150-b Gloria in Excelsis becomes regular part of Eucharist
- 1215-b Eucharist mandated at Easter
- 1237-d Sarum Rite in use at Salisbury cathedral
- 1240-d Franciscan Breviary is developed
- 1300-d first complete Mass ordinary
- 1528-d first French vernacular liturgy
- 1544-d earliest English (language) liturgy
- 1549-d *Book of Common Prayer*
- 1552-b General Confession added to BCP matins, evensong
- 1562-d *Book of Common Order*
- 1570-d *Missale Romanum*
- 1637-b Anglican imposed upon Scotland
- 1640-d *Bay Psalm Book* printed
- 1662-d *Book of Common Prayer* revised
- 1873-a Ritualism
- 1884-d the *Missale Romanum* revised
- 1892-d *Book of Common Prayer* revised
- 1926-a liturgical movement begins
- 1946-d Protestants become interested in sacramental liturgy
- 1955-b Good Friday is held in afternoon or evening
- 1955-b *Tre Ore* discontinued
- 1962-b discussed by Vatican II
- 1962-b vernacular liturgy approved in Vatican Council II
- 1962-b Vatican II revises the breviary
- 1968-d three alternative RC Eucharistic prayers developed
- 1969-d *Missale Romanum* revised
- 1970-b vernacular Mass approved by American RC bishops
- 1971-b vernacular Mass becomes obligatory
- 1979-d fourth American *Book of Common Prayer*
- 1983-d NCC releases "inclusive language lectionary"

Lives of the Saints
- 998-d Aelfric's

Living Bible
- 1971-d published
- 1971-y #3

Loci Communes 1521-d Melanchthon's

Locke, John
- 1632-c is born
- 1690-c empiricism
- 1690-c *Essay Concerning Human Understanding*
- 1695-d *Reasonableness of Christianity as Delivered in the Scriptures*
- 1704-c dies

Lockman Foundation
- 1971-y #3 publishes *New American Standard Bible*

locomotive 1784-c is patented

Loehe, Wilhelm
- 1939-b followers make up Lutheran Church—Missouri Synod

Log College
- 1735-b founded
- 1738-a opposed by Old Side Presbyterianism
- 1738-a a center of New Side Presbyterianism

logarithms 1614-c John Napier discovers

logic 1335-c Ockham's razor

logical positivism 1921-c
- 1921-c Ludwig Wittgenstein's *Tractatus Logico-Philosophicus* 1830-c logical empiricism and positivism

Logos
- 320-a Christological controversies
- 381-a Apollinarianism
- 451-a monophysitism vs. dyophysitism

Lollardry 1380-a
- 1382-b persecution of Lollards begins
- 1413-b Sir J. Oldcastle's rising begins
- 1431-b Lollards go underground

Lombard, Peter. *See* Peter Lombard

Lombards
- 568-c invade Italy
- 573-c advance on Rome
- 580-b destroy the Monte Cassino monastery
- 593-b Gregory establishes peace with
- 733-c capture Ravenna
- 1805-c Napoleon crowns himself with Lombard crown

Lombardy, Italy 612-b Bobbio is founded

London Confession
- 1633-a Particular Baptists
- 1644-d

London, England
- 43-c founded
- 597-b episcopal see created at
- 607-b St. Paul's Cathedral built
- 1009-c Danes attack
- 1065-b Westminster Abbey consecrated
- 1561-c St. Paul's Cathedral badly damaged by fire
- 1592-c plague strikes
- 1665-c Great Plague in London kills 75,000 people
- 1666-b St. Paul's Cathedral completely destroyed
- 1666-c Great Fire sweeps
- 1709-b German Reformed Church members leave for London
- 1710-b St. Paul's Cathedral completed
- 1795-c Joseph Haydn completes *London Symphonies*
- 1827-c public water supply purified in

1895-b Lutheran General Synod organizes the ministry of deaconesses
1896-z #3 United Evangelical Lutheran Church formed
1897-z #3 Lutheran Free Church formed by Norwegian-Americans
1898-b Luther League of America is founded by the Lutheran General Synod
1917-z #3 Evangelical Lutheran Church formed
1918-z #4 United Lutheran Church in America formed
1918-b Germany separates church and state
1930-z #3 American Lutheran Church (German) formed
1947-b Lutheran Church–Missouri Synod adopts current name
1958-b founds the Congregation of the Servants of Christ
1960-z #3 American Lutheran Church formed
1962-d holds talks with Reform Church in the U.S.A.
1962-z #4 Lutheran Church in America formed
1963-z #3 Lutheran Free Church joins American Lutheran Church
1969-b Association of Evangelical Lutheran Churches formed
1969-b begins dialogue with Episcopal church
1970-b Lutheran church ordains women
1983-b first papal visit to Lutheran church
1988-b ELCA formed
1992-b Larson becomes first woman Lutheran bishop
Lutheran Church–Missouri Synod
1839-b formed
1947-b adopts current name
1980-b urges members to become organ donors
Lutheran Free Church
1897-z #3 formed by Norwegian-Americans
1963-z #3 joins American Lutheran Church
Lutheran Observer, The 1831-d founded
Lutheran, The 1831-d predecessor founded
Lux Mundi 1889-d
LXX. *See* Septuagint
Lyon
177-b martyrs die in
1245-b First Council of
1274-b Second Council of
Lyra 188-b allowed in the liturgy
L'Abri 1955-b Francis Schaeffer founds
M.M. *See* Maryknoll Missioners
Macaulay, Zachary 1782-a Clapham Sect
Macbeth 1040-c murders Duncan
Machaut, Guillaume de
1300-c Ars Nova
1364-b composes first polyphonic Mass Ordinary
Machen, J. Gresham
1812-a Princeton theology
1923-d *Christianity and Liberalism*
1936-a Westminster School of Presbyterianism
1936-b organizes Orthodox Presbyterian Church
Machiavelli, Niccolo 1513-c writes *The Prince*
machine gun 1862-c invented

Macintosh, Douglas Clyde
1919-d *Theology as an Empirical Science*
Madame Bovary 1857-c Gustave Flaubert's
Madison, James 1809-c President of the U.S.
magazines
1743-d first religious in U.S. is published
1857-c *Atlantic Monthly* founded
1884-d *Christian Century* founded
1941-d *Christianity and Crisis* founded
1956-d *Christianity Today* founded
Magellan, Ferdinand 1522-c sails around world
Magna Carta 1215-c developed
Magnificat
550-b becomes canticle most used in vespers
Magnus, Albertus. *See* Albertus Magnus, Saint
Magnus liber organi 1175-d Leonin's
Magyar Synod 1921-b
Mahler, Gustav
1810-c Romantic period of music
1911-c dies
Maier, Walter A.
1930-b builds radio audience in the millions
Maimonides (Moses ben Maimon, Rambam)
1180-c Mishneh Torah
1190-c *Guide for the Perplexed*
1204-b dies
mainline denominations
1960-b charismatic movement spreads through
1978-d *Common Lectionary*
1979-b discuss sexuality and ordination
1980-d update hymnals
Mainz, Synod of
813-b mandates that priests wear stoles
848-b Gottschalk condemned by
major orders. *See* orders
majuscule script. *See* Uncial manuscripts
Makemie, Francis
1683-b comes to the American colonies
1706-b organizes first American presbytery
Malacca
1545-b Francis Xavier begins his mission to
Malachy, Saint
1148-b dies
1199-b canonized
Malay Archipelago
1545-b Francis Xavier begins mission to
Malik-el-Mu'azzam, Sultan
1219-c destroys the walls of Jerusalem
Malory, Sir Thomas 1485-c *Morte d'Arthur*
Manchus 1644-c come to power in China
Manhattan Island
1623-c Minuit buys Manhattan from the Algonquins
Mani. *See also* Manichaeism
373-a Manichaeism
Manichaeism 373-a
250-b begins
373-b Augustine of Hippo converts to
527-b Justinian, emperor, promulgates laws against
600-b has faded into obscurity
Maniere et Fasson, La 1528-d Guillaume Farel's
Manifest Destiny 1845-a
maniple
800-b almost universal in Western Europe
850-d mandated for those who say Mass
950-b becomes increasingly ornate
Manresa 1521-b Ignatius Loyola is at

"Man's Disorder and God's Design"
1948-b council of WCC
manual labor
1089-a Cistercian order
1200-b Cistercians do less than other orders
1700-b begins to be practiced by Trappists
manuscript copying
300-c papyrus replaced by parchment for the making of books
350-c Caesarean papyrus volumes replaced by vellum
350-c papyrus volumes replaced by vellum
420-b first done in Western monasteries
500-b most Western monasteries have copying rooms
766-c characterizes Carolingian Renaissance
793-b Carolingian minuscule begins to be used
1000-b central to monastic life
1109 oldest extant paper manuscript in Europe is copied
1275-c becomes a secular profession
1775-a necessitates textual criticism
manuscript transmission
741-b Fulda Abbey founded
manuscripts
100-d Chester Beatty Papyrus copied
325-d *Codex Vaticanus* copied
350-d *Codex Sinaiticus* copied
406-d *Codex Alexandrinus* copied
420-b first copied in Western monasteries
500-b most Western monasteries have copying rooms
500-d *Codex Bezae* copied
692-d *Codex Amiatinus* copied
793-b Carolingian minuscule begins to be used
1000-b copying central to monastic life
1581-b Beza presents *Codex Bezae* to Cambridge University
1626-d *Codex Alexandrinus* comes to England
1778-b first papyrus manuscript discovered in modern times
1844-d Tischendorf discovers *Codex Sinaiticus*
1859-b *Codex Sinaiticus* given to Tsar of Russia
1890-b Gregory devises cataloging system for uncial manuscripts
1933-b Soviets sell *Codex Sinaiticus* to British Museum
1945-d *Gospel of Truth* discovered
1947-d Dead Sea Scrolls discovered
1954-b Dead Sea Scrolls purchased for Hebrew University
Map, Walter
1176-b compiles legends of King Arthur
"Maple Leaf Rag" 1899-c Scott Joplin's
maps
170-c Ptolemy draws maps of 26 countries
1568-c Mercator projection developed
1570-c Abraham Ortelius' *Orbis Terrarum*
Marburg Colloquy 1529-b
Marburg Revisited 1962-d
Marcan Hypothesis 1835-b Lachmann defends
Marcellinus, pope
296-b becomes bishop of Rome
Marcellus II, pope 1555-b becomes pope
Marcellus, pope
306-b becomes bishop of Rome

1175-b first English Carthusian monastery founded
1177-b Beguines/Beghards founded
1190-a Hospitallers
1190-b Order of German Hospitallers founded
1198-b Order of German Hospitallers adopts Templar Rule
1200-b Cluniac order becomes distinct from Cistercian monasticism
1206-b Dominic founds first Dominican convent for women
1209-d Carmelite Rule drawn up
1210-b Franciscan order founded
1215-b Poor Clares founded
1215-b monasticism regulated by council
1216-a Dominican order
1216-b Order of Friars Preachers (Dominicans) founded
1223-d Franciscan Rule receives approval
1226-b St. Francis of Assisi dies
1233-b Servite order founded
1245-a implications of poverty for monastic vows discussed
1247-a mendicant friars
1253-b Clare of Assisi dies
1256-b Hermits of St. Augustine founded
1300-a monastic life begins to break down
1304-b Pope Benedict XI sanctions Servite order
1307-b French Knights Templar stripped of property
1311-b Council of Vienne examines Knights Templar's errors
1349-b RC Order of Bridgettine Sisters founded
1370-b RC Order of Bridgettine Sisters receives papal confirmation
1424-b Servites become mendicant friars
1513-b dissolution of monasteries in Norway
1517-b Observant Franciscans split from the Conventuals
1520-b Ulrich Zwingli preaches against
1529-d Capuchin order formed
1534-b Jesuits founded
1535-b Angela Merici founds the Order of St. Ursula
1539-b dissolution of monasteries in England
1562-b Teresa of Ávila founds Convent of St. Joseph
1563-b novitiate made obligatory by Council of Trent
1564-b Congregation of the Oratory founded
1568-a discalced
1568-b first Discalced Carmelite monastery founded
1578-b Oblates of Saint Ambrose founded
1579-b Discalced Carmelites founded
1579-b Calced Carmelites founded
1582-d Teresa of Ávila's *The Foundations*
1610-b first order for the disabled founded
1625-b Congregation of the Mission founded
1626-b Little Gidding founded
1664-b Pope recognizes two separate "observances" within Cistercian order

1700-b Trappists begin their strict practice
1727-b first convent in U.S. founded
1780-b many monasteries closed in Austria
1814-b Jesuits restored
1821-b American Sisters of Charity follow Rule of Vincent de Paul
1833-b Society of St. Vincent de Paul formed
1833-a Oxford Movement
1842-b Nashota begun
1858-b Paulist order founded
1865-b the Community of St. Mary begun
1872-b U.S. branch of Society of St. John the Evangelist formed
1880-b Order of the Missionary Sisters of the Sacred Heart founded
1893-b Trappists become an independent order
1893-b Benedictine Confederation formed
1897-b branches of the Franciscan order reunite
1927-b Cistercian bring congregations under an Abbot General
1948-d Merton's *Seven Storey Mountain*
1950-b Mother Theresa founds the Missionaries of Charity
1950-b Missionaries of Charity take a fourth vow
1958-b Lutheran church founds Congregation of the Servants of Christ
1997-b Mother Teresa dies
Monet, Claude 1860-c Impressionism
Mongols
   1245-b Crusade against called by Council of Lyons I
Monica, Saint 387-b dies (mother of Augustine)
Monologion 1078-d Anselm's
monophysitism 451-a
   451-b Copts split from Melchites over
   451-b condemned at Council of Chalcedon
   482-b Acacian schism begins
   530-b monophysites split from Chalcedonian church
   542-b spreads throughout Byzantine empire
   550-a Alexandria, Jerusalem, and Antioch largely monophysite
   575-a dominates in Alexandria
monotheism 325-a Christological controversy
monothelitism
   647-b forbidden by the *Typos*
   647-a vs. dyothelitism
   649-b Lateran Synod in Rome condemns
   680-b condemned in council
Monroe Doctrine 1823-c
Monroe, James 1817-c President of the U.S.
monstrances. *See also* reliquaries
   1475-b take the modern shape
Montanist Movement
   172-b begins
   200-b officially condemned
   206-b Tertullian joins
Montanus 172-a Montanist Movement
Monte Cassino
   529-b monastery founded
   580-b monastery destroyed by the Lombards
Montesquieu, Baron de la Brede et
   1748-c *The Spirit of Laws*
Monteverdi, Claudio 1643-c dies
Montgolfier, Jacques Étienne
   1783-c invents hot air balloon

Montgomery, Alabama
   1955-c desegregates buses
Moody Bible Institute 1887-b founded
Moody, D. L. (Dwight Lyman)
   1860-b becomes full-time Christian worker
   1873-b conducts evangelistic meetings in eastern U.S. and England
   1899-b dies
Moon, Sun Myung
   1954-c founds Unification Church
moon 1969-c human beings walk on
Moore G. E. 1921-c logical positivism
Moors
   533-c conquer the Vandals
   711-c invade Spain
   732-c Charles Martel stops their advance
   900-c Spain begins to drive out
   1492-c conquered in Spain
Moral Majority 1979-b founded
Moral Man and Immoral Society
   1932-d Reinhold Niebuhr's
moral law
   1730-d Tindal: it derives from natural law
morality plays. *See also* miracle plays
   1210-b develop
   1275-b gain formalized structure
   1475-d *Everyman*
   1500-b reach the height of their popularity
Moravia 1618-b Jesuits expelled from
Moravian Brethren. *See also* Moravian Church
   1526-b Moravian Brethren settle in Moravia
   1722-b Moravian Brethren adopt pietism
   1722-b Zinzendorf forms groups of
Moravian Church. *See also* Unitas Fratrum; Huss, John
   1526-b Moravian Brethren settle in Moravia
   1722-b Zinzendorf forms groups of Moravian Brethren
   1732-b Renewed Moravian Church begins missionary work
   1738-b influence John Wesley's conversion
   1794-b Friedrich Daniel Ernst Schleiermacher leaves
More, Henry 1633-a Cambridge Platonists
More, Paul Elmer 1915-c Neohumanists
More, Saint Thomas (Lord Chancellor of England)
   1516-d *Utopia*
   1535-b executed for not signing Oath of Succession
Morley, Thomas
   1597-d *A Plaine and Easie Introduction*
Mormonism 1830-a
   1830-d *Book of Mormon* published
   1830-b founded
   1838-b Joseph Smith flees to Missouri
   1844-b Joseph Smith murdered
   1847-b Brigham Young leads Mormons to Salt Lake
morning prayer. *See also* Daily Office
   375-b Gloria in Excelsis used as canticle of
   1150-b Gloria in Excelsis no longer used as canticle of
   1549-d *Book of Common Prayer* omits confession of sin
   1552-b *Book of Common Prayer* reinserts confession of sin
Morrison, Toni 1987-c *Beloved*
Morse code 1837-c Samuel F. B. Morse invents

Morse, Samuel F. B.
  1837-c invents telegraph and Morse code
Morte d'Arthur 1485-c Sir Thomas Malory's
Moses ben Maimon (Maimonides, Rambam)
  1180-c Mishneh Torah
  1190-c *Guide for the Perplexed*
  1204-b dies
Moslems. *See* Islam
Most Pure Heart of Mary, Office and Mass of
  1855-b approved
Most Precious Blood. *See* Blood of Christ
Mother Ann. *See* Lee, Ann "mother"
Mother of God. See *Theotokos*
Mother Teresa. *See* Teresa, mother, of Calcutta
movable type 1434-c invented
movies
  1890-c invented
  1927-c first talking, *the Jazz Singer,* made
  1939-c *Wizard of Oz*
  1977-c *Roots* airs
  1977-c *Star Wars* released
Mozarabic Rite. *See also Appendix Y, chart #4*
  590-d Isidore's *De ecclesiasticus officiis*
  1085-b supplanted by Roman Rite
  1500-d missal printed
  1502-d breviary printed
Mozart, Wolfgang Amadeus
  1756-c is born
  1768-c first opera
  1787-c *Don Giovanni*
  1791-c dies
Muhammad
  570-c is born
  622-c flees from Mecca
  630-c conquers Mecca
  632-c dies
Mühlberg, Battle of
  1547-c Charles V defeats Schmalkaldic
    League
Muhlenberg, Henry Melchior
  1742-b comes to America
  1748-b founds first Lutheran synod in
    North America
Muhlenberg, William Augustus
  1796-b is born
  1877-b dies
multiculturalism
  1800-a distinctly American Christianity
multiplicity of Masses 800-b begins
Münzer, Thomas
  1520-b Anabaptist Movement in Germany
Muratorian Canon 194-d
Murray, John 1778-a universalism
Murray O'Hair, Madalyn
  1963-b sues her son's school
Murray, William J. III v. John N. Curlett 1963-b
music
  96-b Clement I mentions psalm singing
  120-b Sixtus I introduces the Sanctus into
    the Mass
  188-b chant allowed in church music
  188-b Church fathers warn against instru-
    ments, polyphony, and dance
  199-d *Odes of Solomon*
  264-b Council of Antioch suppresses non-
    biblical hymns
  340-b Ephrem Syrus takes over melodies of
    Bardaisan's docetic hymns
  350-b Sanctus a part of the Eucharistic
    liturgy

  358-b Ambrose of Milan introduces simpler
    hymns
  358-b responsorial and antiphonal psalmody
    begin to be used
  358-b church music undergoes radical
    changes
  360-b Hilary models hymns after Ephrem
    Syrus of Edessa
  360-b first Latin hymns sung
  365-b Schola Cantorum established by
    Council of Laodicea
  365-b Council of Laodicea disapproves of
    metrical hymnody
  373-b hymnodist Saint Ephrem Syrus of
    Edessa dies
  373-b Ephrem Syrus of Edessa adapts hereti-
    cal chants
  374-b antiphonal and responsorial singing
    of psalms
  375-b Gloria in Excelsis Deo used as canti-
    cle of morning prayer
  375-b Nunc Dimittis a part of daily prayers
  375-b Kyrie Eleison begins to be used
  379-b Phos Hilaron sung at start of evening
    prayer
  383-b antiphonal singing and the Alleluia
    come to Rome
  385-b Ambrose introduces Te Deum to
    Milan
  400-b Gloria Patri used as a closing verse for
    antiphonal psalms
  406-b Benedicite common throughout the
    world
  450-b rhyme used in hymns
  461-b Schola Cantorum founded in Rome
  461-d Pope Leo the Great's *Sacramentarium*
  524-d Boethius' *De institutione musica*
  550-b bells first used in churches in France
  550-b Magnificat becomes canticle most
    used in vespers
  563-b hymns must take their texts from
    Scripture
  599-b Te Deum has become part of Roman
    liturgy
  599-b Gregorian chant begins to take form
  604-b bells first used in churches in Rome
  633-b hymns may take their text from
    poetry
  633-b Council of Toledo allows poetic text
    to be used in hymns
  672-b Gregorian chant developed
  680-d earliest vernacular hymns in English
  701-b Agnus Dei begins to be sung during
    the fraction
  731-b first known church organ
  751-b Gregorian chant spreads through
    Europe
  751-b Gregorian chant introduced to France
  753-b monastery at Metz becomes center for
    Gregorian chant
  789-b church music fairly standardized
  800-b Exultet takes modern form
  850-b polyphony develops in liturgical
    chant
  900-b organum begins to develop
  935-c notation using letters developed
  950-b Winchester Cathedral installs organ
  959-b organs begin to appear in England's
    churches

  1000-d Salve Regina written
  1025-b four-line notation developed
  1105-c some of the first vernacular, secular
    musical poetry
  1108-d Bernard's *Contempt of the World*
  1110-c Cotton's *Musica*
  1175-d Leonin's *Magnus liber organi*
  1175-d "Jesus the Very Thought of Thee"
  1190-b begins to be written in three and
    four parts
  1199-b bells rung at the elevation of the ele-
    ments
  1260-c modern notation developed
  1300-c ars nova developed
  1300-d *Messe de Tournai*
  1310-c time signatures first used
  1325-b complex harmony banned
  1350-c composers write secular and sacred
  1350-c two- and three-part harmony written
  1364-b first known polyphonic setting of
    Mass Ordinary
  1400-b organs used during Plainsong
  1400-b organs used during the Mass
  1430-c develops during the Renaissance
  1465-c first printed
  1474-c Guillaume Dufay dies
  1497-b earliest known polyphonic Requiem
    Mass composed
  1524-d first Protestant hymnal
  1543-b Calvin limits congregational singing
    to monophony
  1552-b bells must be rung at beginning of
    all C of E church services
  1562-b Council of Trent declares music
    must be uplifting
  1570-b bells required to be rung at eleva-
    tion and Sanctus
  1597-d Morley's *A Plaine and Easie Introduc-
    tion*
  1597-d Anglican chant begins to be devel-
    oped
  1600-c baroque period
  1604-c Seconda Prattica
  1608-b Philipp Nicolai, German hymn
    writer, dies
  1623-c William Byrd dies
  1640-d *Bay Psalm Book* printed
  1643-c Claudio Monteverdi dies
  1674-b Isaac Watts, English hymn writer,
    dies
  1675-c four-part singing becomes common
  1695-c Henry Purcell dies
  1700-d Ken's "the Doxology"
  1704-c Bach writes his first cantata
  1707-d Watts' *Hymns and Spiritual Songs*
  1709-c the pianoforte invented
  1720-c classical period
  1729-b Bach's *St. Matthew's Passion*
  1738-c Bach's Mass in B Minor
  1739-d Charles Wesley's *Hymns and Sacred
    Poems*
  1741-c Antonio Vivaldi dies
  1756-c Wolfgang Amadeus Mozart born
  1770-d Billings' *The New England Psalm
    Singer*
  1780-b liturgy simplified
  1780-c first modern piano invented
  1791-c Wolfgang Amadeus Mozart dies
  1795-c Haydn completes *London Symphonies*

1799-c Haydn's *Creation* (oratorio)
1800-b William Billings dies
1808-c Beethoven's Symphony No. 5
1809-c Joseph Haydn dies
1810-c Romantic period
1822-d *Boston Handel and Haydn Society Collection of Church Music*
1824-c Beethoven's *Missa Solemnis*
1826-c Weber's *Oberon* (opera)
1827-c Ludwig van Beethoven dies
1828-c Franz Schubert dies
1840-c Nicolò Paganini dies
1840-c blackface minstrel shows
1842-c New York Philharmonic Society founded
1847-c Felix Mendelssohn dies
1854-c Foster's "I Dream of Jeanie with the Light Brown Hair"
1858-d *Psalms and Hymns*
1859-c Decatur's "Dixie"
1861-d *Hymns Ancient and Modern*
1869-c Hector Berlioz dies
1882-c Chromaticism
1883-c Richard Wagner dies
1886-c Franz Liszt dies
1886-c Symphonic poem
1890-c César Franck dies
1893-c Peter Ilich Tchaikovsky dies
1896-c Anton Bruckner dies
1897-d Oxyrhynchus Papyri discovered
1897-c Johannes Brahms dies
1899-c Joplin's "Maple Leaf Rag"
1901-c Giuseppe Verdi dies
1903-b Pius X restores Gregorian chant
1904-c Antonin Dvořák dies
1908-d *Graduale Romanum* published
1911-c Gustav Mahler dies
1920-b Christian agnosticism
1920-c the jazz age begins
1924-c Giacomo Puccini dies
1925-c twelve-tone method invented
1925-c atonality furthered
1934-c Porter's "Anything Goes"
1935-c Gershwin's *Porgy and Bess*
1940-d a common set of hymns forms basis for hymnals
1943-c Sergi Rachmaninov dies
1944-c Copland's *Appalachian Spring*
1950-c Aleatory
1953-c Sergey Prokofiev dies
1957-c Bernstein's *West Side Story*
1958-b Ralph Vaughan Williams dies
1964-c the Beatles first tour U.S.
1967-c Benjamin Britten dies
1971-c Igor Stravinsky dies
1974-d *Graduale Romanum* is revised
1980-d hymnals updated
1990-c Leonard Bernstein dies

music, church
96-b Clement I mentions psalm singing
120-b Sixtus I introduces Sanctus into the Mass
188-b church fathers warn against instruments, polyphony, and dance
188-b chant allowed in church music
199-d *Odes of Solomon*
264-b Council of Antioch suppresses non-biblical hymns
340-b Ephrem Syrus takes over melodies of Bardaisan's docetic hymns

350-b Sanctus a part of the Eucharistic liturgy
358-b Ambrose's contribution
358-b undergoes radical changes
358-b responsorial and antiphonal psalmody begin to be used
358-b Ambrose of Milan introduces simpler hymns
360-b first Latin hymns sung
360-b Hilary models hymns after Ephrem Syrus of Edessa
365-b Council of Laodicea disapproves of metrical hymnody
365-b Schola Cantorum established by Council of Laodicea
373-b Ephrem Syrus of Edessa adapts heretical chants
373-b Hymnodist Saint Ephrem Syrus of Edessa dies
374-b antiphonal and responsorial singing of psalms
375-a canticle
375-b Nunc Dimittis a part of daily prayers
375-b Kyrie Eleison begins to be used
375-b Gloria in Excelsis Deo used as canticle of morning prayer
379-b Phos Hilaron sung at start of evening prayer
383-b antiphonal singing and the Alleluia come to Rome
384-d Exultet
385-b Ambrose introduces Te Deum to Milan
400-b Gloria Patri used as a closing verse for antiphonal psalms
406-b Benedicite common throughout the world
450-b rhyme used in hymns
461-b Schola Cantorum founded in Rome
461-d Pope Leo the Great's *Sacramentarium*
524-d Boethius' *De institutione musica*
550-b Magnificat becomes canticle most used during vespers
550-b bells first used in churches in France
563-b hymns must take their texts from Scripture
599-b Te Deum has become part of the Roman liturgy
599-b Gregorian chant begins to take form
604-b bells first used in churches in Rome
633-b hymns may take their text from poetry
633-b Council of Toledo allows poetic text in hymns
672-b Gregorian chant developed
680-d earliest vernacular hymns in English
701-b Agnus Dei begins to be sung during the fraction
731-b first known church organ
751-b Gregorian chant introduced to France
751-b Gregorian chant spreads through Europe
753-b monastery at Metz becomes center for Gregorian chant
789-b fairly standardized
800-b Exultet takes modern form
850-b polyphony develops in liturgical chant
900-b Organum begins to develop

950-b Winchester Cathedral installs large organ
959-b organs begin to appear in England's churches
1000-d Salve Regina written
1025-b Guido D'Arezzo introduces musical notation system
1108-d Bernard's *Contempt of the World* a source for
1175-d "Jesus the Very Thought of Thee"
1175-d Leonin's *Magnus liber organi*
1190-b begins to be written in three and four parts
1199-b bells rung at the elevation of the elements
1300-d *Messe de Tournai*
1325-b complex harmony banned
1364-b first known polyphonic setting of the Mass Ordinary
1400-b organs used during the mass
1400-b organs used during Plainsong
1497-b earliest known polyphonic Requiem Mass composed
1524-d first Protestant hymnal
1543-b Calvin limits congregational singing to monophony
1552-b bells must be rung at beginning of all C of E church services
1562-b Council of Trent declares music must be uplifting
1570-b bells required to be rung at the elevation and Sanctus
1597-d Morley's *A Plaine and Easie Introduction*
1597-d Anglican chant begins to be developed
1608-b Philipp Nicolai, German hymn writer, dies
1640-d *Bay Psalm Book* printed
1674-b Isaac Watts, English hymn writer, dies
1700-d Ken's "The Doxology"
1707-d Watts' *Hymns and Spiritual Songs*
1738-c Bach's Mass in B Minor
1739-d Charles Wesley's *Hymns and Sacred Poems*
1770-d Billings' *New England Psalm Singer*
1780-b liturgy simplified
1800-b William Billings dies
1822-d *Boston Handel and Haydn Society Collection of Church Music*
1824-c Beethoven's *Missa Solemnis*
1858-d *Psalms and Hymns*
1861-d *Hymns Ancient and Modern*
1897-d Oxyrhynchus Papyri discovered
1903-b Pius X restores Gregorian chant
1903-b Pope Pius X reforms
1908-d *Graduale romanum* published
1920-b Christian agnosticism
1940-d a common set of hymns forms basis for hymnals
1958-b Ralph Vaughan Williams dies
1974-d *Graduale romanum* revised
1980-d hymnals updated
music conservatories 1537-c first
Musica 1110-c Cotton's
Muslims. *See also* Islam
711-c invade Spain
1244-b recapture Jerusalem

Newman, John Henry, Cardinal
  1801-b is born
  1833-d *Tracts for the Time*
  1833-a Oxford Movement
  1845-b becomes a Roman Catholic
  1864-d *Apologia Pro Vita Sua* (Apology for
    His Life)
  1890-b dies
Newman movement 1883-b
Newton, Sir Isaac
  1642-c is born
  1683-c explains tides
  1684-c discovers calculus
  1687-c *Philosophiae Naturalis Principia
    Mathematica*
  1726-c dies
Newtonian physics 1750-c Enlightenment
Niagra Bible Conference
  1895-d "The Five Points of Fundamentalism"
Nicene Councils
  325-b first council, first session
  327-b first council, second session
  787-a second council
  1582-c Gregorian calendar calibrated to first
    council
Nicene Creed. *See also* chart Y#1
  250-d Caesarean Creed basis for
  325-b drawn up
  341-b considered by smaller councils
  381-d takes a nearly modern form
  381-b amended and confirmed
  589-b Filioque clause added
  589-b put into final form
  796-b Filioque clause defended
  800-b begins to be said as part of Romano-
    Frankish Mass
  825-d Filioque clause becomes common in
  1014-b begins to be recited during Roman
    Mass
  1274-b Filioque clause officially added
  1580-d in the Book of Concord
Niceo-Constantinopolitan Creed. *See* Nicene
  Creed
Niceta, bishop of Remesiana in Dacia
  414-d composes Te Deum
Nicholas I, Saint (pope) ("Nicholas the Great")
  858-b becomes bishop of Rome
  867-b dies
Nicholas II, pope
  1058-b becomes bishop of Rome
  1059-b condemns lay investiture
Nicholas II, Russian tsar 1918-c murdered
Nicholas III, pope 1277-b becomes pope
Nicholas IV, pope 1288-b becomes pope
Nicholas of Cusa 1440-d *De Docta Ignorantia*
Nicholas, Saint (bishop of Myra)
    ("Santa Claus")
  342-b dies
  1740-b Santa Claus becomes part of Christ-
    mas in America
Nicholas the Great. *See* Nicholas I, Saint (pope)
Nicholas V, pope
  1447-b becomes pope
  1450-b founds Vatican Library
Nicolai, Philipp 1608-b dies
Nicomedia 303-b cathedral built in
Niebuhr, (Karl Paul) Reinhold
  1846-c existentialism
  1892-b is born

  1932-d *Moral Man and Immoral Society*
  1939-d *Nature and Destiny of Man*
  1971-b dies
Niebuhr, Helmut Richard
  1894-b is born
  1930-a Neo-orthodoxy
  1951-d *Christ and Culture*
Nietzsche, Friedrich
  1846-c existentialism
  1883-d *Thus Spake Zarathustra*
  1900-c dies
Nigeria
  1890-b Africa Christians begin to reject
    missionary control
Night of the Broken Glass. *See* Kristallnacht
Nineteen Eighty-four 1949-c George Orwell's
Ninety-five Theses 1517-b Martin Luther's
Ninian, Saint (bishop in Galloway)
  394-b begins mission to Scotland
  430-b dies
Nixon, Richard M. 1969-c President of U.S.
No Cross, No Crown 1682-d William Penn's
Nobel Peace Prize
  1947-b granted to Quaker organizations
  1964-c Martin Luther King awarded
  1979-b Mother Teresa awarded
Nobel Prize
  1896-c is established
  1930-c Sinclair Lewis first American to win
    Nobel Prize in literature
  1947-b Nobel Peace Prize granted to
    Quaker organizations
  1964-c Martin Luther King awarded Nobel
    Peace Prize
  1979-b Mother Teresa awarded Nobel Peace
    Prize
Noche Obscura del Alma. See *Dark Night
  of the Soul*
Nominalism
  1078-a Realism
  1080-a
  1106-a Conceptualism
  1290-a Scotism
  1502-b Martin Luther educated in
Nonconformity 1672-b legalized in England
none 200-b recognized as a private prayer hour
nonviolence
  1933-b Catholic worker advocates
  1963-c March on Washington
Norbertines. *See* Premonstratensian Canons
Norkay, Tenzing 1953-c scales Mount Everest
Norman conquest
  1066-c of England
  1066-c begins Middle English Period
  1066-c Battle of Hastings
  1171-c of Ireland
Normandy, House of
  1066-c begins reign in England
Norris, Frank 1900-c naturalism
Norse
  698-d Viking art in the Lindisfarne Gospels
  793-c Vikings raid island of Lindisfarne
  793-c Vikings invade England
  806-b Norse sack Iona monastery
  845-c Norse invaders take Paris
  869-b Edmund, king of East Anglia,
    martyred by Vikings
  1014-c Brian Boru retakes Ireland from
    Vikings

  1025-b Norway converted
  1028-b King Olaf II establishes Christianity
    in Norway
  1513-b dissolution of the monasteries in
    Norway
  1537-c Norway conquered by Denmark
  1537-b Norway becomes officially Lutheran
North Africa
  245-b has ninety bishops
  306-b religious toleration extended to
  431-b Christianity suppressed in
  533-c Moors conquer the Vandals
  535-b Catholicism restored in
  647-c Arabs conquer
  698-b Arabs destroy Carthage
North America
  1000-c discovered by Leif Ericson
  1492-c discovered by Columbus
  1497-c John Cabot voyages to
North American Christian Convention/Inde-
  pendent Christian Churches
  1927-z #11 formed
North American Christian Convention of the
  Disciples of Christ
  1927-b splits from the Disciples of Christ
North American Martyrs
  1642-b killed while working as missionaries
  1930-b canonized
North Atlantic Treaty Organization
  1949-c formed
North, Dudley
  1692-c proposes law of supply and demand
North Pole 1909-c Peary and Henson travel to
Northern Baptist Convention. *See also* American Baptist Churches in the U.S.A.
  1907-z #13 formed
  1907-b formed
  1956-z #13 Norwegian Baptist Conference
    of North America joins
  1958-z #13 Danish Baptist General Confer-
    ence joins
Northern Baptists. *See* American Baptist
  Churches in the U.S.A.; American Free
  Baptist Mission Society; Northern Free
  Will Baptists; Northern Baptist Convention
Northern Free Will Baptists
  1911-z #13 unite with the Northern
    Baptists
Northumberland, England
  698-d Lindisfarne Gospels
Northwest Ordinance 1789-c
Norway
  1025-b converted
  1028-b King Olaf II establishes Christianity in
  1513-b dissolution of the monasteries in
  1537-b becomes officially Lutheran
  1537-c conquered by Denmark
Norwegian Baptist Conference of North America
  1956-z #13 joins the American Baptist
    Churches
Norwegian Synod 1853-z #3 formed
Nostra Aetate 1965-d Pope Paul VI's
nothingness
  1953-c Sartre's *Being and Nothingness*
Notre Dame Cathedral, Paris
  1163-c construction begins
  1182-c consecrated
  1190-c University of Paris springs up around

Notre Dame of Maryland
  1895-b founded as first Catholic women's
    college
Notre Dame, University of 1842-b founded
Novalaise 906-b monks flee to Turin
Novatian 250-d *On the Trinity*
Novatianist schism 251-a
  251-b begins
novitiate
  1563-b made obligatory by Council of Trent
Novum Instrumentum
  1516-d Desiderius Erasmus'
  1546-d Estienne' *Greek New Testament* a
    revision of
Novum Testamentum Graece 1979-d Aland's
  1979-d Kurt Aland's
Noyes, John Humphrey
  1848-b founds Oneida Community
nuclear energy
  1956-c first nuclear power plant built in U.S.
nuclear weapons
  1945-c atomic bomb dropped
  1952-c hydrogen bomb invented
  1954-c radioactive waste disposal problems
    begin
  1956-c first aerial hydrogen bomb tested
  1977-c neutron bomb tested
nuclei 1830-c in plant cells discovered
numerology
  1954-c Moon founds Unification Church
Nunc Dimittis
  375-b a part of daily prayers
  375-d
Nuremberg laws
  1935-c rescind Jewish rights in Germany
Nuremberg, Religious Peace of
  1532-b grants Protestants free exercise of
    religion
Oath of Allegiance
  1673-a required of English civil servants
Oath of Succession
  1534-b King Henry VIII requires all
    subjects to sign
  1535-b John Houghton executed for refus-
    ing
  1535-b Fisher and More executed for not
    signing
Oath of Supremacy
  1673-a required of English civil servants
oaths 1179-a Waldenses reject
Oberammergau Passion Play 1634-b first per-
    formed
Oberlin College
  1833-b founded
  1833-b becomes first coeducational college
    in U.S.
  1865-a Holiness Movement
Oblates of Saint Ambrose 1578-b founded
Observant Franciscans
  1517-b split from the Conventuals
O.Carm. *See* Carmelite order
O.Cart. *See* Carthusian order
O.C.D. *See* Discalced Carmelites
O.C.S.O. *See* Trappists
Ockeghem, Johannes
  1497-b composes earliest known polyphonic
    Requiem Mass
Ockenga, Harold John
  1943-a neo-evangelicalism
  1945-a midtribulationism

1947-b becomes first president of Fuller
    Seminary
1947-d becomes a leader of new evangelical
    movement
Ockham's razor 1335-c first postulated
Odd Fellows, Independent Order of
  1819-c introduced to U.S.
Odes of Solomon 199-d
Odo of Cluny 935-c *Enchiridion musices*
Oecolampadius, John (Johannes Hussgen)
  1522-b wins Basel over to Reformation doc-
    trine
  1525-a sacramentarianism
  1528-b secures Canton of Berne's support
    for Reformation
  1529-b defends sacramentarianism at
    Colloquy of Margurg
  1531-b dies
Oecumenical Councils. *See* Ecumenical
    Councils
Oecumenical patriarch. *See* patriarchs
Office and Mass of the Most Pure Heart of Mary
  1855-b approved
Office, Divine. *See* Divine Office
O.F.M. *See* Franciscan order
O.F.M.Cap. *See* Capuchin order
O.F.M.Conv. *See* Conventual Franciscans
"O God, our Help in Ages Past"
  1707-d included in *Hymns and Spiritual
    Songs*
O Gracious Light. *See* Phos Hilaron
oil 390-a Chrism
Olaf II, Saint, King (of Norway)
  1028-b establishes Christianity in Norway
O Lamb of God. *See* Agnus Dei
Old Catholic Church 1870-b founded
Old English
  440-c is brought into England
  998-d Aelfric's *Lives of the Saints*
  1000-c *Beowulf*
  1038-b first known references to "Cristes
    Maesse," i.e., Christmas
  1066-c Middle English period begins
Old Latin Bible. See *Vetus Itala*
Old Light Synod of the Reformed Presbyterian
    Church (Old School)
  1833-z #6 formed
Old Lights 1740-a Great Awakening
Old Roman Creed. *See* chart Y#1
  110-d earliest possible date
  145-d oldest text
Old School Presbyterianism 1831-a
  1831-b tries Barnes, Duffield, and Beecher
    for heresy
  1838-z #5 Old School Presbyterianism
Old Side Presbyterianism
  1738-a
  1758-b is reconciled to New Side
Old Testament
  96-b Clement I mentions psalm singing
  110-a
  155-b reading is a part of worship in Rome
  245-d Origen's Hexapla
  358-b responsorial and antiphonal psalmody
    begin to be used
  392-d Jerome's *Gallican Psalter*
  1545-a Council of Trent declares it to be
    authoritative

1682-d Simon's *Critical History of the Old
    Testament*
1907-d Brown, Driver, and Briggs' *Hebrew
    and English Lexicon of the Old Testament*
1961-a Christian Reconstructionism
Olga of Russia 950-b converts to Christianity
Omar I, Caliph
  638-a creates new Muslim calendar
On Baptism 206-b Tertullian's
On Being a Christian 1977-d Küng's
On Being a Real Person 1943-b Fosdick's
On Christian Doctrine
  430-d Augustine of Hippo's
On Christian Life and Manners
  188-d Clement of Alexandria's
On Crimes and Punishments 1764-c Beccaria's
On First Principles 225-d Origen's
On Free Will (De Libero Arbitrio)
  1524-d Erasmus'
On Miracles 1230-d Caesarius of Heisterbach's
On Preserving Widowhood 450-d Fastidius'
On Religion: Speeches to Its Cultured Despisers
  1799-d Schleiermacher's
On the Body and Blood of our Lord
  831-d Radbertus'
On the Church 1377-d Wycliffe's
On the Deaths of the Persecutors 314-d Lactantius'
On the Trinity 250-d Novatian's
Oneida Community 1848-b
Oneness Pentecostals 1913-b
ontological argument for the existence of God
  1078-a
  1078-d used by Anselm
ontology
  1938-c New criticism
  1690-c Locke's *Essay Concerning Human
    Understanding*
open Communion 1814-a
opera 1924-c Giacomo Puccini dies
Opium Wars 1839-c break out
Opus Dei 1928-b is formed
Opus maius 1268-c Roger Bacon's
Oral Roberts University 1965-b
oral tradition 1545-a Council of Trent
Orange, Council of 529-b
Orate Fratres 1926-d
Oratory, Congregation of
  1564-b formed
  1612-b approved
Oratory of Divine Love 1517-b
Oratory of St. Philip Neri. *See* Congregation of
    the Oratory
Orbis Terrarum 1570-c Abraham Ortelius'
orchestra 1842-c first American founded
Order of Cistercians of the Strict Observance
    (Trappists)
  1664-b pope recognizes two separate "obser-
    vances" within Cistercian order
  1700-b begun
  1893-b becomes an independent order
  1948-d Merton's *The Seven Storey Mountain*
  1968-b Thomas Merton dies
Order of Communion (English) 1548-y #5
Order of Friars Minor (Franciscan order)
  1210-b founded
  1210-d *Regula primitiva* (Franciscan rule)
  1223-d rule receives papal approval
  1224-b settle in Oxford
  1226-b founder dies

468-b Simplicius
483-b Felix III
492-b Gelasius
496-b Anastasius II
498-b Symmachus
514-b Hormisdas
523-b John I
526-b Felix IV
530-b Boniface II
533-b John II
535-b Agapitus
536-b Silverius
537-b Vigilius
556-b Pelagius I
561-b John III
575-b Benedict I
579-b Pelagius II
590-b Gregory I
604-b Sabinian
607-b Boniface III
608-b Boniface IV
615-b Deusdedit
619-b Boniface V
625-b Honorius I
640-b Severinus
640-b John IV
642-b Theodore I
649-b Martin I
654-b Eugene I
657-b Vitalian
672-b Adeodatus II
676-b Donus
678-b Agatho
682-b Leo II
684-b Benedict II
685-b John V
686-b Conon
687-b Sergius I
701-b John VI
705-b John VII
708-b Sisinnius
708-b Constantine
715-b Gregory II
731-b Gregory III
741-b Zacharias
752-b Stephen III (II)
757-b Paul I
768-b Stephen IV (III)
772-b Hadrian I
795-b Leo III
816-b Stephen V (IV)
817-b Paschal I
824-b Eugene II
827-b Gregory IV
827-b Valentine
844-b Sergius II
847-b Leo IV
855-b Benedict III
855-b Joan (legendary)
858-b Nicholas I
867-b Hadrian II
872-b John VIII
882-b Marinus I
884-b Hadrian III
885-b Stephen VI (V)
891-b Formosus
896-b Boniface VI
896-b Stephen VII (VI)
897-b Romanus

897-b Theodore II
898-b John IX
900-b Benedict IV
903-b Leo V
904-b Sergius III
911-b Anastasius III
913-b Lando
914-b John X
928-b Leo VI
928-b Stephen VIII (VII)
931-b John XI
936-b Leo VII
939-b Stephen IX (VIII)
942-b Marinus II
946-b Agapitus II
955-b John XII
963-b Leo VIII
964-b Benedict V
965-b John XIII
973-b Benedict VI
974-b Benedict VII
983-b John XIV
985-b John XV
996-b Gregory V
999-b Silvester II
1003-b John XVII
1003-b John XVIII
1009-b Sergius IV
1012-b Benedict VIII
1024-b John XIX
1032-b Benedict IX
1045-b Silvester III
1045-b Gregory VI
1046-b Clement II
1048-b Damasus II
1049-b Leo IX
1055-b Victor II
1057-b Stephen X (IX)
1058-b Nicholas II
1061-b Alexander II
1073-b Gregory VII
1086-b Victor III
1088-b Urban II
1099-b Paschal II
1118-b Gelasius II
1119-b Callistus II
1124-b Honorius II
1130-b Innocent II
1143-b Celestine II
1144-b Lucius II
1145-b Eugene III
1153-b Anastasius IV
1154-b Hadrian IV
1159-b Alexander III
1181-b Lucius III
1185-b Urban III
1187-b Gregory VIII
1187-b Clement III
1191-b Celestine III
1198-b Innocent III
1216-b Honorius III
1227-b Gregory IX
1241-b Celestine IV
1243-b Innocent IV
1254-b Alexander IV
1261-b Urban IV
1265-b Clement IV
1271-b Gregory X
1276-b Innocent V

1276-b Hadrian V
1276-b John XXI
1277-b Nicholas III
1281-b Martin IV
1285-b Honorius IV
1288-b Nicholas IV
1294-b Celestine V
1294-b Boniface VIII
1303-b Benedict XI
1305-b Clement V
1316-b John XXII
1334-b Benedict XII
1342-b Clement VI
1352-b Innocent VI
1362-b Urban V
1370-b Gregory XI
1378-b Urban VI
1389-b Boniface IX
1404-b Innocent VII
1406-b Gregory XII
1417-b Martin V
1431-b Eugene IV
1447-b Nicholas V
1455-b Callistus III
1458-b Pius II
1464-b Paul II
1471-b Sixtus IV
1484-b Innocent VIII
1492-b Alexander VI
1503-b Julius II
1503-b Pius III
1513-b Leo X
1522-b Hadrian VI
1523-b Clement VII
1555-b Paul IV
1559-b Pius IV
1566-b Pius V
1572-b Gregory XIII
1585-b Sixtus V
1590-b Urban VII
1590-b Gregory XIV
1591-b Innocent IX
1592-b Clement
1534-b Paul III
1550-b Julius III
1555-b Marcellus II
1605-c Leo XI
1605-c Paul V
1621-c Gregory XV
1623-c Urban VIII
1644-c Innocent X
1655-c Alexander VII
1667-c Clement IX
1670-c Clement X
1676-c Innocent XI
1689-c Alexander VIII
1691-c Innocent XII
1700-b Clement XI
1721-c Innocent XIII
1724-b Benedict XIII
1730-b Clement XII
1740-b Benedict XIV
1758-b Clement XIII
1769-b Clement XIV
1775-b Pius VI
1800-b Pius VII
1823-b Leo XII
1829-b Pius VIII
1831-b Gregory XVI

1967-b Protestants joining RCC no longer abjure Protestant beliefs
1970-b millions of U.S. Hispanics become Protestant
Protrepticus 188-d Clement of Alexandria's
Provincial Council (Roman Catholic)
  1829-b first in U.S.
"Provisional Design"
  1968-b Christian Church (Disciples of Christ) approves
Provoost, Samuel
  1787-b consecrated bishop of New York
Psalms and Hymns 1858-d
psalms
  96-b Clement I mentions psalm singing
  358-b responsorial and antiphonal begin to be used
  374-b Basil the Great speaks of antiphonal and responsorial singing
  392-d Jerome's *Gallican Psalter*
  400-b Gloria Patri used as a closing verse for
  400-d Gloria Patri
  1640-d *Bay Psalm Book*
  1858-d *Psalms and Hymns*
Pseudepigrapha 50-d Jewish
Pseudo-Clementine literature 130-d
psychiatric care
  1910-b Christian services become increasingly available
Psychology of the Unconscious 1912-c Jung's
psychology
  1879-c first experimental laboratory founded
  1892-c American Psychological Association founded
  1900-c Freud's *Interpretation of Dreams*
  1910-b Christian psychiatric care becomes increasingly available
  1912-c Jung's *Psychology of the Unconscious*
  1920-c behaviorism
  1974-c APA removes homosexuality from list of mental disorders
PTL (Praise the Lord) ministry
  1974-b Jim Bakker founds television ministry
  1987-b Jim Bakker, head of PTL ministry, resigns
  1987-b Jerry Falwell takes over
Ptolemy 170-c draws maps of 26 countries
public health. *See also* medicine
  1827-c public water supply purified in London
  1854-c cholera linked to polluted water
  1864-c pasteurization invented
  1899-c aspirin first synthesized
  1936-c refrigerated transport first used
  1940-c penicillin first used
  1979-c first known AIDS case in U.S recorded
publishing. *See also* printing
  1640-d first American book printed
  1724-c Longman's Publishing House founded
  1732-c *Poor Richard's Almanack*
  1743-d first religious magazine in U.S. published
  1789-b first church publishing house formed
  1857-c *Atlantic Monthly* founded
  1884-d precursor to *The Christian Century* published

1931-b Zondervan Publishing House founded
1941-d *Christianity and Crisis* founded
1956-d *Christianity Today* founded
Puccini, Giacomo
  1810-c Romantic period of music
  1924-c dies
Puerto Rico
  1898-c Spanish-American War begins
pulpits
  1547-b installed in all English churches
punishment
  553-a hell decreed to be eternal punishment
  1265-b Aquinas teaches it is purged in purgatory
  1393-a Indulgences
Purcell, Henry 1695-c dies
purgatory. *See also* prayer for the dead; indulgences
  593-b Gregory the Great teaches
  998-b All Souls' Day instituted
  1179-a Waldenses
  1265-b Thomas Aquinas devises the classic doctrine
  1274-b doctrine defined at Council of Lyons II
  1320-d Dante's *Divine Comedy*
  1439-b doctrine defined at Council of Florence
  1520-b Ulrich Zwingli preaches against
  1563-b existence affirmed by Council of Trent
Purification of the BVM (Presentation of Christ in the Temple; Candlemas) 350-a
  350-b feast begins to be celebrated
  541-b instituted by the Byzantine Emperor Justinian I
purificators
  1295-b first mentioned
  1550-b become common
Puritan Revolution. *See* English Revolution
Puritans and Puritanism
  1555-b English Protestants flee to Geneva
  1559-a Puritanism
  1559-b arise in England
  1559-d Elizabethan prayer book
  1563-b Separatists first called
  1563-d *Foxe's Book of Martyrs*
  1593-b acts passed against Puritans in England
  1595-d Lambeth Articles
  1595-a Sabbatarianism
  1603-b present the Millenary Petition
  1604-b attend Hampton Court Conference
  1620-b Plymouth colony founded
  1630-b Puritans establish Massachusetts Bay Colony
  1633-a Particular Baptists
  1634-b oppose William Laud
  1640-d *Bay Psalm Book* printed
  1647-d Westminster Confession
  1658-c Puritan government of England ends
  1661-b Savoy Conference convened
  1675-c settlers wage King Philip's War
Pusey, Edward Bouverie
  1800-b is born
  1833-a Oxford Movement
  1865-d "The Church of England a Portion of Christ's one Holy Catholic Church . . ."
  1882-b dies

Quadragesima. *See* Lent

Quakers (Religious Society of Friends)
  1647-b Fox's preaching lays foundation for
  1651-b spread through England
  1652-b the society founded
  1660-b begin to immigrate to American colonies
  1675-b purchase land and settle in New Jersey
  1678-d Robert Barclay's *Apology for the True Christian Divinity*
  1681-b Pennsylvania colony granted to William Penn
  1682-d William Penn's *No Cross, No Crown*
  1684-b approximately 7000 have settled in Pennsylvania
  1688-b protest slavery in the American colonies
  1691-b George Fox dies
  1697-a Quietism
  1718-b William Penn dies
  1776-b may no longer hold slaves
  1787-b have no member who is slave owner
  1828-b liberals split from Orthodox
  1947-b Nobel Peace Prize given to
quantum theory 1918-c Max Planck proposes
quartodecimanism 154-b Polycarp asserts
Quebec, Canada
  1608-c becomes first permanent French outpost in Americas
  1609-c French colony established
  1625-b Jean de Brébeuf arrives in Canada
Queen Anne's War 1702-c begins
Quest of the Historical Jesus 1906-d Schweitzer's
Quicunque vult. See Athanasian Creed
Quietism
  1311-b errors examined by Council of Vienne
  1647-b Fox's preaching lays foundation for Quakers
  1697-a
  1697-b Miguel de Molinos known for
Quinisext Council. *See* Trullan Synod
Quintus Septimius Florens. *See* Tertullian, Quintus Septimius Florens
Quirinius, P. Sulpicius, Syrian legate
  6-c conducts census
Qumran
  68-c destroyed
  1947-d Dead Sea Scrolls discovered
  1951-b Essene monastery discovered at
rabbis. *See also* Judaism
  200-c Judah the Priest codifies Mishnah
  1141-c Judah Ha-Levi dies
Rabbit Is Rich 1981-c John Updike's
race
  1896-c Supreme Court upholds separate accommodations based on
  1952-c Supreme Court declares segregated schools unconstitutional
  1964-c discrimination prohibited
  1965-c voting discrimination forbidden
  1967-c Supreme Court declares laws prohibiting interracial marriage unconstitutional
Rachmaninov, Sergi 1943-c dies
racism
  1909-c NAACP founded to fight
  1957-b Southern Christian Leadership Conference is organized
radar 1939-c first used

814-d collection of is compiled
959-b Rule of St. Basil introduced to
England
970-d *Regularis Concordia*
1119-d Charter of Charity
1198-b German Hospitallers adopt Templar
Rule
1209-d Carmelite Rule developed
1223-d Rule of Franciscan Order receives
papal approval
1226-d Carmelite Rule approved
1233-b Order of Servites follows Rule of St.
Augustine of Hippo
1256-b Hermits of St. Augustine founded
under Rule of St. Augustine of Hippo
1517-b Franciscan split over strict observance of Rule
1529-d Capuchin Rule developed
1821-b American Sisters of Charity follow
Rule of Vincent de Paul
rural areas 275-b Christianity in
Russell, Bertrand
1913-c *Principia Mathematica*
1921-c logical positivism
Russia
950-b Olga converts
988-b Christianity becomes state religion of
989-b Vladimir begins to spread Christianity throughout
1214-c Genghis Khan invades
1462-c Ivan the Great becomes first tsar
1581-b Russian Orthodox church attempts
unity with RCC
1581-b Pope Gregory XIII tries to reconcile
Catholicism and Russian Orthodoxy
1584-c Ivan "the Terrible," tsar of Russia, dies
1689-c Peter the Great becomes Tsar
1773-b harbors the suppressed Jesuit order
1820-b Jesuits expelled from
1853-c Crimean War begins
1859-b *Codex Sinaiticus* given to tsar of Russia
1917-c Russian Revolution begins
1918-c Nicholas II, the last tsar, murdered
1933-b Soviet government sells *Codex
Sinaiticus* to British Museum
1951-c Rosenbergs give atomic secrets to
1991-c USSR succeeded by Commonwealth
of Independent States
1996-b religious renewal grows
Russian Orthodox church
1581-b unity attempted with Roman
Catholicism
1589-b gains independence from Constantinople
1870-b establishes first diocese in U.S.
Russian Revolution 1917-c begins
Rutgers University 1766-c founded
Ruusbroec, Jan van. *See* Ruysbroeck, Jan van
Ruysbroeck, Jan van
1293-b is born
1326-a mysticism
1350-d *Adornment of the Spiritual Marriage*
1728-d *A Serious Call to a Devout and Holy
Life* based on
RV. *See* Revised Version of the Bible
Ryan, John A.
1928-b founds first Roman Catholic peace
organization
S. *See Codex Sinaiticus*

S.J. *See* Jesuits
Saadia ben Joseph, Babylonian Jewish scholar
942-c dies
Sabbatarianism. *See also* Sunday
1595-a
1618-b King James I allows recreation on
Sunday
1624-b blue laws first passed in America
1781-b Lord's Day Observance Act revives
Sabbath. *See* Sunday; Sabbatarianism; Seventh-
day Adventists; Seventh-day Baptists
1863-a Seventh-day Adventists
Sabellianism. *See* Monarchian controversy
Sabinian 604-b becomes bishop of Rome
Sacculum
1502-b chalice and paten brought to altar in
sack of Rome
410-c Alaric I, King of the Visigoths, sacks
Rome
422-d inspires *City of God*
1527-c Holy Roman Emperor Charles V
sacks Rome
sacramentals 1155-a
sacramentarianism
1525-a propounded
1529-b Oecolampadius defends at Colloquy
of Marburg
sacramentaries. *See* missals and sacramentaries
Sacramentarium 461-d Pope Leo the Great's
sacraments. *See also* baptism; Eucharist;
penance; marriage; confirmation; ordination; unction
206-b baptism, unction, and laying on of
hands distinguished in initiation rites
312-a Donatist controversy
386-d Ambrose on
460-b confirmation emerges as separate rite
from baptism
882-b marriage considered by some to be
one
1142-d thirty listed by Hugh of St.-Victor
1155-d first reference to seven
1155-a distinguished from sacramentals
1265-b Aquinas maintains confirmation
instituted by Christ
1438-b list of seven formally affirmed
1520-d Luther asserts two, not seven
1520-b Zwingli preaches two, not seven
1521-d King Henry VIII's *Defense of the Seven
Sacraments*
1545-a Council of Trent and
1547-b Council of Trent declares seven
instituted by Christ
1773-b early Methodists receive from Anglican church
Sacred College. *See* cardinals
Sacred Congregation of Rites
1587-b established
Sacred Heart of Jesus
1670-a Devotion to Sacred Heart of Jesus
1670-b Feast of the Sacred Heart celebrated
for first time
1673-b Margaret Mary Alacoque's "great
apparition" of
1765-b Feast of the Sacred Heart becomes
liturgical feast
1856-b Feast of the Sacred Heart becomes
universal
1900-b humanity consecrated to

Sacred Heart of Mary. *See* Immaculate Heart
of Mary
Sacred Rites, Congregation of
1965-b permits laity to receive the cup at
communion
1968-d develop three alternative Eucharistic
prayers
sacrifice
249-c pagan required of Christians
303-b mandated by Diocletian
1551-a propitiatory sacrifice
sacring bells. *See* bells
sacristies 400-b earliest built
Saint Sabina, Roman martyr 126-b dies
saints, cult of
1841-a Roman Catholic romanticism
focuses on
saints. *See also* hagiography; canonization of
saints; canonization process; relics
373-a All Saints' Day
357-a hagiography
725-a icons
730-d *Martyrology of Bede*
787-a relics
787-a veneration vs. worship
993-b earliest canonization of
1548-b Edward VI orders saints' images
removed from English churches
1833-a Oxford Movement elevates place of
1841-a Roman Catholic romanticism focuses
on cult of saints
1946-b Cabrini is first American citizen
declared a saint
1969-b RCC selects a group for veneration
Saladin
1187-b takes Jerusalem
1191-c fortifies walls of Jerusalem
Salem, Massachusetts 1692-c witchcraft trials
Salian house 1024-c begins reign in Germany
Salinger, J. D. 1951-c *The Catcher in the Rye*
Salisbury cathedral 1258 finished
Salisbury Rite. *See* Sarum Rite
Salome
28-b Herod beheads John the Baptist at her
request
Salonica 50-b Paul's second missionary journey
Salvation Army
1865-z #18 formed
1865-b founded
1865-a Holiness Movement
1890-b comes to U.S.
1890-a Social Gospel
salvation. *See also* justification; sanctification
435-a semipelagianism
610-a double predestination
1302-d declared impossible outside the
church
1612-a Calvinism vs. Arminianism
Salvator Noster 1476-b
Salve Regina
1000-d written
1135-b sung processionally at some feasts
1220-b monks of Cluny recite it daily
1221-b Dominicans use at compline
1568-b recited after compline
1884-b recited at all low masses
Samaria
6-c Herod Archelaus deposed as ruler of
San Francisco earthquake 1906-c kills 500

stigmata
  1224-b first known case
  1224-b Francis of Assisi manifests stigmata
"Stille Nacht Heilige Nacht" 1818-d Mohr
    and Gruber's
stirrups 708-c introduced to Europe
Stock, Simon. See Simon Stock, Saint
stock market 1929-c crashes
stole
  700-b first mentioned
  813-b priests in Frankish Empire wear
  850-d mandated for those who say Mass
Stone, Barton W. See Christians (Barton Stone)
  1804-b leads a group calling themselves
    merely "Christians"
Story of a Soul, The 1898-d Theresa of Lisieux's
Stowe, Harriet Elizabeth Beecher
  1852-c Uncle Tom's Cabin
Stowe Missal. See also Appendix Y, chart #4
  650-d
Strasbourg cathedral
  1354-c mechanical clock installed
Strasburg
  1605-b Christmas trees first mentioned
Strauss, David Friedrich 1835-d Life of Jesus
Strauss, Richard
  1810-c Romantic period of music
  1949-c dies
Stravinsky, Igor
  1920-c Neoclassicism in music
  1971-c dies
Strict Baptists 1814-a open communion
striking of the breast 420-b recommended
Stuart, House of (England)
  1603-c begins reign
students. See also colleges and universities;
    campus ministry
  1968-c student unrest disrupts universities
    worldwide
  1970-c Kent State demonstrations
stylites
  459-b Simeon Stylite dies
  493-b Daniel the Stylite dies
subdeacons
  251-b first mentioned
  600-b no longer wear tunics
  1000-b tunics universal among
  1972-b RCC no longer recognizes it as
    major order
subjective idealism 1710-c
submission of clergy 1532-b
Subscription Controversy
  1720-a
  1729-d Adopting Act
substitutionary atonement
  1895-d "The Five Points of Fundamentalism"
Sudan Interior Mission 1982-b unites with
    Andes Evangelical Mission to form SIM
    International
Suez Canal 1869-c opened
suffering
  451-a Docetism
  519-b Theopaschites say God suffered
  519-a Theopaschites
sufficient grace 1598-a
suicide
  68-c Emperor Claudius Nero commits sui-
    cide
  561-b condemned by Council of Braga

  1978-b Jonestown, Guyana, site of mass-sui-
    cide/murder
  1993-b Koresh's Branch Davidians commit
    suicide
Suleiman I ("Suleiman the Magnificent")
  1520-c becomes Sultan of Turkey
Sulpice, Society of St.
  1790-b arrives in America
Summa theologica 1245-d Alexander of Hales'
Summa theologica 1265-d Thomas Aquinas'
Summer Institute of Linguistics/Wycliffe Bible
    Translators
  1934-b Townsend founds training program
    for Bible translators
  1942-b takes its current dual structure
Summis Desiderantes 1484-d Pope Innocent
    VIII's
Sun Also Rises, The 1926-c Hemingway's
Sunday
  95-b Eucharist celebrated on
  321-b becomes day of rest
  780-a legislated as day of rest
  1027-b battle prohibited on
  1595-a Sabbatarianism
  1618-b King James I allows recreation on
  1624-b first American "blue laws"
    instituted
  1781-b recreation prohibited by Lord's Day
    Observance Act
Sunday, Billy
  1896-b conducts first revival
  1910-b first uses the term "sawdust trail"
Sunday schools
  1765-b Sunday School Movement rises in
    England
  1811-b Robert Raikes founds Sunday
    schools
  1824-b American Sunday School Union
    founded
  1835-a Sunday School Movement in
    America
Suomi Synod. See Finnish Evangelical Lutheran
    Church
Super Cathedram 1300-d Boniface VIII's
superman 1883-d Nietzsche's
supersonic flight 1947-c first
Supplication of Pope Gelasius 492-d
supralapsarianism. See also predestination
  1595-d in England
Supremacy, Act of. See Act of Supremacy
Supreme Court of the United States
  1830-c Worcester sues State of Georgia over
    Cherokee sovereignty
  1896-c Plessy v. Ferguson upholds segregation
  1954-c Brown v. the Board of Education
  1961-c refers to secular humanism as a non-
    theistic religion
  1963-b William J. Murray III v. John N.
    Curlett
  1967-c declares antimiscegenation laws
    unconstitutional
  1973-c Roe v. Wade
  1985-b disallows government financial aid
    to parochial schools
  1992-c reaffirms school prayer as unconsti-
    tutional
surplice
  1100-b becomes vestment of lower clerical
    orders
  1552-b becomes only prescribed C of E
    vestment

Suso, Henry
  1295-b is born
  1326-a mysticism
  1328-d Little Book of Eternal Wisdom
  1366-b dies
Swaggart, Jimmy
  1973-b begins weekly television show
  1988-b removed from ministry by Assem-
    blies of God
Sweden
  830-b Anskar founds first Christian church
    in
  1104-b receives metropolitical rank
  1349-b Saint Bridget founds Order of Brid-
    gettine Sisters
  1373-b patron saint dies
  1593-b adopts Augsburg Confession
  1600-b persecutes Roman Catholics
  1638-b Swedes found Lutheran settlement
    in Delaware
Swedish Baptist Church
  1852-b first congregation formed in U.S.
Swedish Baptist General Conference
  1879-b national body formed
  1944-z #13 formed
  1945-b drops "Swedish" from its name
Swedish Evangelical Free Church
  1884-z #12 formed
Swedish Evangelical Mission Covenant of
    America. See Evangelical Covenant
    Church of America
Swedish Mission Covenant Church
  1878-z #12 formed
Swift, Jonathan 1726-c Gulliver's Travels
Swiss Brethren
  1525-b begin a fellowship
  1700-b Amish split from
Swithun, Saint 862-b dies
Switzerland
  350-b Christianity reaches Geneva
  1350-b mystics in
  1519-b Reformation begins in Zurich
  1522-b biblical customs mandated in
    Zurich
  1523-b religious ornamentation banned in
    Zurich
  1525-b Zurich abolishes Catholic Mass
  1528-d Theses of Berne
  1528-b Berne agrees to support Reformation
  1529-c civil war erupts between Protestants
    and Catholics
  1531-b Bullinger succeeds Zwingli as Chief
    Pastor of Zurich
  1531-b reformation halted in
  1536-d First Helvetic Confession
  1536-b Calvin becomes coadjutor of Geneva
  1538-b Calvin expelled from Geneva
  1541-b theocratic regime begins in Geneva
  1552-b Geneva lauds Calvin's Institutes
  1553-b Michael Servetus executed in
    Geneva
  1553-b Knox flees to Geneva
  1559-a Geneva a model for Puritanism
  1559-b Calvin founds Genevan Academy
  1560-d Geneva Bible translated
  1564-b Beza becomes head of Calvinism in
    Geneva
  1974-b International Congress on World
    Evangelism in Lausanne

440-c Germanic tribes invade England
452-c Pope Leo I persuades Attila not to
    invade Rome
455-c Vandals attack Rome
455-c Pope Leo I persuades Gaiseric not to
    sack Rome
473-c Visigoths take southern Gaul
507-c Clovis defeats Alaric II
530-c Persian War begins
533-c Moors conquer the Vandals
568-c Lombards invade Italy
573-c Lombards advance on Rome
579-c Persian War renews
602-c Persia invades Rome
614-c Persia takes Jerusalem
711-c Moors invade Spain
793-c Vikings raid England
806-b Norse sack Iona monastery
845-c Norse invaders take Paris
851-c crossbow begins to be used in France
1009-c Danes attack London
1050-c chain mail begins to be used in
    Europe
1139-c use of crossbow against Christians
    banned
1214-c Genghis Khan invades China, Persia,
    and Russia
1313-c first gunpowder weapons used in
    Europe
1337-c Hundred Years' War begins
1338-c cannons first used
1438-c mobile artillery first used
1453-c Hundred Years' War ends
1455-c Wars of the Roses begins
1525-c shotgun invented
1529-c Swiss Civil War begins
1572-c Peace of Constantinople ends Turk-
    ish attacks on Europe
1618-c Thirty Years' War begins
1667-c hand grenades invented
1675-c King Philip's War begins
1689-c French and Indian Wars begin
1701-c War of Spanish Succession begins
1702-c Queen Anne's War begins
1740-c King George's War begins
1746-c Battle of Culloden Moor
1754-c French and Indian War begins
1789-c French Revolution begins
1799-c Napoleonic Wars begins
1812-c War of 1812 begins
1836-c Alamo attacked by Mexican troops
1839-c Opium Wars begin
1853-c Crimean War begins
1862-c machine gun invented
1898-c Spanish-American War begins
1911-c airplanes first used in combat
1912-c Balkan Wars begin
1914-c World War I begins
1918-c World War I ends
1939-c Germany invades Poland
1939-c World War II begins
1939-c radar first used
1941-c Japan bombs Pearl Harbor
1941-c U.S. enters World War II
1942-b Japanese invade New Guinea
1945-c atomic bomb dropped
1945-c World War II ends
1950-c Korean War begins
1952-c hydrogen bomb invented

1956-c first aerial hydrogen bomb tested
1961-c Bay of Pigs
1963-d Pope John XXIII's *Pacem in Terris*
    condemns
1965-c U.S. troops engage in combat in
    Vietnam
1967-c Arab-Israeli War begins
1973-c last American troops leave Vietnam
1977-c neutron bomb tested
1983-c U.S. invades Grenada
1990-c Operation Desert Shield begins
1991-c Operation Desert Storm begins
Warfield, Benjamin B.
    1812-a Princeton theology
    1903-d revises Westminster Confession
        of Faith
War of 1812 1812-c begins
War of Spanish Succession 1701-c begins
Wars of Religion
    1562-b begin
    1598-b end
Wars of the Roses 1455-c begin
washing of the feet
    393-a Maundy Thursday
    425-b common on Holy Thursday
washing of the head
    425-b common on Palm Sunday
Washington Cathedral (Episcopal)
    1907-b begun in Washington, D.C.
Washington, D.C.
    1963-c March on Washington
Washington, George
    1789-c first U.S. President
Washington Post
    1973-c brings Watergate to public's attention
Waste Land, The 1922-c T. S. Eliot's
Watch Tower Bible and Tract Society of Penn-
        sylvania. *See* Jehovah's Witnesses
watchmaker argument for the existence of God
    1794-d Paley's *A View of the Evidences of
        Christianity*
Watchmen of the East
    1827-a oppose "New Measures"
Water Street Mission 1872-b formed
water. *See also* holy water, baptistery
    700-c waterwheel technology spreads in
        Europe
    1549-d no longer ordered mixed with wine
        in C of E
    1827-c purified in London
Watergate scandal
    1972-c break-in
    1973-c becomes public
Waterloo, Battle of
    1815-c Napoleon Bonaparte abdicates after
waterwheel technology
    700-c spreads in Europe
Watson, John B. 1920-c behaviorism
Watt, James
    1775-c manufactures steam engines
Watts, Isaac
    1674-b dies
    1707-d *Hymns and Spiritual Songs*
Way of Holiness, The 1845-d Phoebe Palmer's
Way of Perfection, The 1565-d Teresa of Ávila's
way of the cross
    1400-b stations developed in Cordova
    1458-b the term "stations" first used
    1500-b walked from Pilate's house to Calvary

Wealth of Nations 1776-c Adam Smith's
wealth. *See also* poverty; poverty, voluntary
    321-b possible for the ordained
    1900-a Gospel of Wealth
weapons. *See also* warfare
    851-c crossbow begins to be used in France
    1050-c chain mail begins to be used in
        Europe
    1139-c use of crossbow against Christians
        banned
    1313-c first gunpowder weapons used in
        Europe
    1338-c cannons first used
    1438-c mobile artillery first used
    1525-c shotgun invented
    1667-c hand grenades invented
    1862-c machine gun invented
    1911-c airplanes first used in combat
    1939-c radar first used
    1945-c atomic bomb dropped
    1952-c hydrogen bomb invented
    1956-c first aerial hydrogen bomb tested
    1977-c neutron bomb tested
Weary Blues, The 1926-c Langston Hughes'
weather forecasting
    1337-c first scientific attempt
Weatherhead, Leslie 1943-a relational theology
Weber, Carl Maria von
    1810-c Romantic period of music
    1826-c *Oberon*
Weber, Max
    1905-d *Protestant Ethic and the Spirit of
        Capitalism*
Webster's Dictionary 1828-c is published
Wednesday 590-a Ash Wednesday
Wellhausen, Julius
    1885-a Documentary Hypothesis
    1885-b proposes J and E as sources for Genesis
Wenceslas, Holy Roman Emperor
    1393-b has John of Nepomuk killed
Wenceslas, Saint (duke of Bohemia)
    929-b killed by family
Wesley, Charles
    1707-b is born
    1729-a Methodism
    1736-b arrives as missionary in Georgia
    1739-d *Hymns and Sacred Poems*
    1788-b dies
Wesley, John
    1703-b is born
    1729-a Methodism
    1729-b begins to attend Oxford
    1729-b joins the Holy Club
    1736-b arrives as missionary in Georgia
    1738-b converted
    1739-b begins to form Methodist societies
    1755-d issues first "paragraph Bible"
    1766-a Wesleyan Tradition
    1769-b sends first Methodist missionaries to
        America
    1773-b Methodist preachers agree to follow
    1784-b *Deed of Declaration*
    1791-b dies
Wesleyan Church
    1766-a Wesleyan tradition
    1968-z #18 formed
    1968-b formed through merger
Wesleyan Methodist Church
    1843-z #18 formed
    1843-z #17 formed

Bibliography

African Methodist Episcopal Church. "Historical Perspective." http://www.ame-church.org/amehist.htm

Ahlstrom, Sydney E. *A Religious History of the American People.* 2 vols. Garden City, NY: Doubleday/Image Books, 1975.

Aland, Kurt, et al., eds. *The Greek New Testament.* 3d ed. New York: United Bible Societies, 1975.

Alexander, David, and Pat Alexander, eds. *Eerdmans' Handbook to the Bible.* Grand Rapids: Wm. B. Eerdmans, 1973.

Anselm of Canterbury. *Why God Became Man and the Virgin Conception and Original Sin.* Translated by Joseph M. Colleran. Albany: Magi Books, 1969.

Armstrong, Karen. *A History of God: The 4000-Year Quest of Judaism, Christianity and Islam.* New York: Alfred A. Knopf, 1993.

Augustine of Hippo. *Confessions.* Translated by R. S. Pine-Coffin. New York: Penguin Books, 1961.

Bahat, Dan. *Carta's Historical Atlas of Jerusalem: An Illustrated Survey.* Jerusalem: Carta, 1983.

Barnstone, Willis, ed. *The Other Bible.* San Francisco: HarperSanFrancisco, 1984.

Bede. *A History of the English Church and People.* Translated by Leo Sherley-Price. Revised by R. E. Latham. New York: Dorset Press, 1968.

Booty, John E. *The Church in History.* New York: Seabury Press, 1979.

Burke, James. *The Day the Universe Changed.* Boston: Little, Brown, 1985.

Cairns, Earle E. *Christianity Through the Centuries.* 3d ed. Grand Rapids: Zondervan, 1996.

Cantor, Norman F., and Michael S. Werthman, eds. *Early Modern Europe: 1450–1650.* New York: Thomas Y. Crowell, 1967.

Catholic Encyclopedia. http://www.knight.org/advent/cathen.

Chadwick, Henry, and G. R. Evans. *Atlas of the Christian Church.* New York: Facts on File. 1987.

Christian and Missionary Alliance. "An Extended Outline of the History of the C&MA." http:www.gospelcom.net/cmalliance/message/history.htm

Christian Science Monitor archives. http://www.csmonitor.com/archive/archive.html

Christie-Murray, David. *A History of Heresy.* New York: Oxford University Press, 1976.

Church of God in Christ. "The Story of Our Church." http://www.cogic.org/hist.htm

Church Hymnal Corporation. *The Proper for the Lesser Feasts and Fasts: Together with the Fixed Holy Days.* 3d ed. New York: Church Hymnal Corporation, 1980.

Comfort, Philip W. *Complete Guide to Bible Versions.* Wheaton, IL: Tyndale House/Living Books, 1996.

Cross, F. L., and E. A. Livingstone. *The Oxford Dictionary of the Christian Church.* 3d ed. New York: Oxford University Press, 1997.

Dearmer, Percy. *The Parson's Handbook.* London: Oxford University Press, 1949.

Dix, Dom Gregory. *The Shape of the Liturgy.* San Francisco: Harper and Row, 1945.

Dowley, Tim. *Eerdmans' Handbook to the History of Christianity.* Grand Rapids: Wm. B. Eerdmans, 1977.

Evangelical Lutheran Church in America. "ECLA Family History." http://www.ecla.org/co/timeline/index.html.

_____ "Roots of the Evangelical Lutheran Church in America." http:www.elca.org/co/roots.html (July 18, 1997).

Facione, Francis P. "An Historic Overview of the Old Roman Catholic Church." http:listserv.american.edu/catholic/other/history1.html

Farmer, David Hugh. *The Oxford Dictionary of Saints.* Oxford: Oxford University Press, 1987.

Ferguson, Everett. *Encyclopedia of Early Christianity.* New York: Garland Publishing, 1990.

Fiorenza, Elisabeth Schüssler. *In Memory of Her.* New York: Crossroad, 1983.

Franciscan Institute Outreach. "The Franciscan Experience ... Since 1182." http:198.62.75.1/www1/ofm/fra/FRAmain.html (March 15, 1998).

Frend, W. H. C. *The Rise of Christianity.* Philadelphia: Fortress Press, 1984.

Frontline. "From Jesus to Christ." PBS Online. http://www.pbs.org/wgbh/pages/frontline/shows/religion/

Garraty, John A., and Peter Gay, eds. *The Columbia History of the World.* New York: Harper and Row, 1972.

González, Justo L. *The Story of Christianity.* 2 vols. San Francisco: Harper and Row, 1984.

_____ *A History of Christian Thought.* 2 vols. 2nd ed. Nashville: Abingdon Press, 1971.

Bibliography

Greenlee, J. Harold. *Introduction to New Testament Textual Criticism.* Grand Rapids: Wm. B. Eerdmans, 1964.

Grun, Bernard. *The Timetables of History.* 3d ed. New York: Simon and Schuster/Touchstone, 1991.

Halley, Henry H. *Halley's Bible Handbook: An Abbreviated Bible Commentary.* Grand Rapids: Zondervan, 1962.

Happold, F. C. *Mysticism: A Study and an Anthology.* New York: Penguin Books, 1970.

Hatchett, Marion J. *Commentary on the American Prayer Book.* New York: Seabury Press, 1980.

Herrin, Judith. *The Formation of Christendom.* Princeton: Princeton University Press, 1987.

Hillerbrand, Hans J. *The Reformation: A Narrative History Related by Contemporary Observers and Participants.* Grand Rapids: Baker Book House, 1985.

Hodges, Miles. "The High Middle Ages." http://www2.cybernex.net/~mhodges/west/high-middle.html (February 26, 1998).

Ignatius of Loyola. *The Spiritual Exercises of St. Ignatius.* Translated by Anthony Mottola. New York: Doubleday/Image Books, 1964.

Jeremias, Joachim. *Jerusalem in the Time of Jesus: An Investigation into Economic and Social Conditions during the New Testament Period.* Philadelphia: Fortress Press, 1969.

John of the Cross. *Selected Writings.* Edited by Kieran Kavanaugh. Classics of Western Spirituality. New York: Paulist Press, 1987.

Johnston, William, ed. *The Cloud of Unknowing and the Book of Privy Counseling.* Garden City, NY: Doubleday/Image Books, 1973.

Jones, Cheslyn, Geoffrey Wainwright, and Edward Yarnold. *The Study of Liturgy.* New York: Oxford University Press, 1978.

Julian of Norwich. *Showings.* Translated by Edmund Colledge and James Walsh. The Classics of Western Spirituality. New York: Paulist Press, 1978.

Kalberer, Augustine. *Lives of the Saints: Daily Readings.* Chicago: Franciscan Herald Press, 1975.

KDG Wittenberg. Lutherstadt Wittenberg. http:www.wittenberg.de (January 1, 1998).

Keen, Maurice. *English Society in the Later Middle Ages: 1348–1500.* New York: Penguin Books, 1990.

Kelly, J. N. D. *The Oxford Dictionary of Popes.* Oxford: Oxford University Press, 1986.

Koester, Helmut. *Introduction to the New Testament.* 2 vols. Philadelphia: Fortress Press, 1982.

Latourette, Kenneth Scott. *A History of Christianity.* 2 vols. New York: Harper and Row, 1975.

Le Mée, Katharine. *Chant: The Origins, Form, Practice, and Healing Power of Gregorian Chant.* New York: Bell Tower, 1994

Leff, Gordon. *Medieval Thought: St. Augustine to Ockham.* London: Merlin Press. Reprint: Atlantic Highlands, NJ: Humanities Press, 1983.

Leith, John H., ed. *Creeds of the Churches: A Reader in Christian Doctrine from the Bible to the Present.* 3d ed. Atlanta: John Knox Press, 1982.

Mann, A. T. *Sacred Architecture.* Rockport, MA: Element, 1993.

Manschreck, Clyde L. *A History of Christianity: Readings in the History of the Church.* 2 vols. Grand Rapids: Baker Book House, 1981. First published by Prentice Hall, 1962–1964.

Marty, Martin E. *Pilgrims in Their Own Land: 500 Years of Religion in America.* New York: Penguin Books, 1984.

McManners, John, ed. *The Oxford Illustrated History of Christianity.* New York: Oxford University Press, 1990.

Microsoft Encarta. Redmond, WA: Microsoft Corporation/Funk & Wagnall's Corporation, 1994.

Moorman, John R. H. *A History of the Church in England.* 3d ed. London: A & C Black, 1986.

Murphy, Cullen. "Who Do Men Say That I Am?" *The Atlantic Monthly.* http://theAtlantic.com/atlantic/unbound/cullen/cmjesus.html (December 1986).

Nafzger, Samuel. "Lutheran Church— Missouri Synod: A Brief History." Lutheran Church—Missouri Synod. http://www.lcms.org/www/lcms/NAFZGER.HTM

New York Public Library Desk Reference. 2d ed. New York: Prentice Hall General Reference/Stonesong Press, 1993.

New American Desk Encyclopedia. New York: Penguin Books/a Signet Book, 1989.

Noss, John B. *Man's Religion.* 5th ed. New York: Macmillan, 1974.

Oberman, Heiko A. *Luther: Man between God and the Devil.* Translated by Eileen Walliser-Schwarzbart. New York: Doubleday/Image Books, 1982.

Order of Friars Minor. "Historical Sketch of the Order of Friars Minor." http://www.ofm.org/1/info/INFhist.html (January 5, 1997)

Palmer, R. R., and Joel Colton. *A History of the Modern World to 1815.* 5th ed. New York: Alfred A. Knopf, 1978.

Peerman, Dean G., and Martin Marty, eds. *A Handbook of Christian Theologians.* Enlarged ed. Nashville: Abingdon Press, 1984.

Pelikan, Jaroslav. *The Excellent Empire: The Fall of Rome and the Triumph of the Church.* San Francisco: Harper and Row, 1987.

_____ *The Christian Tradition: A History of the Development of Doctrine*. 5 vols. Chicago: University of Chicago Press, 1971–1989.

Perkins, Pheme. *Reading the New Testament: An Introduction*. New York: Paulist Press, 1978.

Perrin, Norman, and Dennis C. Duling. *The New Testament: An Introduction*. 2d ed. New York: Harcourt Brace Jovanovich, 1982.

Piepkorn, Arthur Carl. *Profiles in Belief*. Vols. 1–4. San Francisco: Harper and Row, 1977–1979.

Pierre Riché. *Education and Culture in the Barbarian West Six through Eighth Century*. Translated by John J. Contreni. Columbia, SC: 1976.

Presbyterian Church (USA). "Where did the Presbyterian Church Originate?" http://www.pcusa.org/pcusa/info/pcorigin.html (August 1997).

Prichard, Robert W., ed. *Readings from the History of the Episcopal Church*. Wilton, CT: Morehouse-Barlow, 1986.

Randall, Mike. "A Brief History of the BBFI." Baptist Bible Fellowship International. http://www.bbfi.org/history/

Reid, Daniel G., ed. *Dictionary of Christianity in America*. Downers Grove, IL: InterVarsity Press, 1990.

Sadie, Stanley, ed. *The New Grove Dictionary of Music and Musicians*. 20 vols. New York: Grove's Dictionary of Music, 1980.

Saint Benedict Center. "The Ecumenical Councils of the Roman Catholic Church." http://www.catholicism.org/pages/ecumenic.htm (May 1998).

Taylor, Jeremy. *The Rule of Holy Living and the Rule of Holy Dying*. Compiled by Roger L. Roberts. Treasures from the Spiritual Classics. Wilton, CT: Morehouse-Barlow, 1981.

Teilhard de Chardin, Pierre. *The Phenomenon of Man*. New York: Harper Colophon Books, 1959.

Thompson, Bard, comp. *Liturgies of the Western Church*. Philadelphia: Fortress Press, 1961.

Trager, James. *The People's Chronology: A Year-By-Year Record of Human Events from Prehistory to the Present*. Revised ed. New York: Henry Holt, 1994.

Turner, Alice K. *The History of Hell*. New York: Harcourt Brace, 1993.

United Methodist Church. "Historical Statement." http://www.umc.org/about/historic.html.

United Church of Christ. "History of the United Church of Christ." http://www.ucc.org/who/history.html (July 18, 1997).

Walton, Robert C. *Chronological and Background Charts of Church History*. Grand Rapids: Zondervan, 1986.

Waltz, Robert B. "The Textus Receptus." http://www.skypoint.com/~waltzmn/TR.html (February 17, 1998).

Woolverton, John Frederick. *Colonial Anglicanism in North America*. Detroit: Wayne State University Press, 1984.

World Almanac and Book of Facts 1998. Mahwah, NJ: World Almanacs Books, 1998.

Young, Serinity. *An Anthology of Sacred Texts by and about Women*. New York: Crossroad, 1984.

We want to hear from you. Please send your comments about this book
to us in care of the address below. Thank you.

ZondervanPublishingHouse
Grand Rapids, Michigan 49530
http://www.zondervan.com